Going to the Dogs

CultureAmerica
Erika Doss
Philip J. Deloria
Series Editors
Karal Ann Marling
Editor Emerita

Going to the Dogs

Greyhound Racing, Animal Activism,

and American Popular Culture

GWYNETH ANNE THAYER

UNIVERSITY PRESS OF KANSAS

For Tafi
and
for Z.

Published by the
University Press of
Kansas (Lawrence,
Kansas 66045), which
was organized by the
Kansas Board of Regents
and is operated and
funded by Emporia State
University, Fort Hays
State University, Kansas
State University, Pittsburg
State University, the
University of Kansas, and
Wichita State University

Library of Congress Cataloging-in-Publication Data

Thayer, Gwyneth Anne.
    Going to the dogs : greyhound racing, animal activism, and American popular culture / Gwyneth Anne Thayer.
        pages cm—(CultureAmerica)
    Includes bibliographical references and index.
    ISBN 978-0-7006-1913-9 (cloth : alk. paper)
 1. Greyhound racing—United States—History.
 2. United States—Popular culture. I. Title.
    SF440.T44 2013
    798.8'50973—dc23
                                                2012050036

British Library Cataloguing-in-Publication Data is
available.

Printed in the United States of America
10 9 8 7 6 5 4 3 2 1

The paper used in this publication is recycled and
contains 30 percent postconsumer waste. It is acid
free and meets the minimum requirements of the
American National Standard for Permanence of
Paper for Printed Library Materials Z39.48–1992.

CONTENTS

LIST OF ILLUSTRATIONS

PREFACE AND ACKNOWLEDGMENTS

I am often asked why I decided to write a book on the history of greyhound racing.

The answer is simple: I adopted an ex-racing greyhound in 2004 after the heartbreaking, premature loss of my beloved mutt, Tafi.

Guiding my search for the companionship of another dog was the thought that I should find one with a story of its own. I soon inquired within the greyhound adoption community about the history of greyhound racing in the United States, but I was troubled by the lack of historical information available. I wanted to know more about the men and women who worked in the industry: Who were they? What was their relationship to their greyhounds? When was the sport's heyday in this country? Why were so many tracks closing? I also wanted to know about the lives of the racing dogs. How were they raised? How were they treated at the tracks? Was greyhound racing cruel, as I had so often heard?

Everyone seemed to have a different opinion about the sport, and I was increasingly dissatisfied with the answers I was getting. Furthermore, I was looking for a book topic, and it looked like the perfect subject had just fallen into my lap.

Paired with my new greyhound, I set out on a path of discovery. It was no small irony that my greyhound's name from puppyhood was Zachary More Curious.

This book is the final product of the years of research that followed, which, much to my delight, took me to all corners of the United States. It represents my work and ideas alone, and accordingly, I am responsible for any errors. However, I could not have completed this monumental task without the help and support of others. Most important, this book would not have been possible without the cooperation of two groups of individuals: those in the business of greyhound racing and those who hope to end it. I have tried to be fair and honest during this entire process, and I have readily admitted and acknowledged (to both parties) that I must consult extensively with those who love greyhound racing as well as those who abhor it. It has admittedly been an uncomfortable tightrope to walk upon, but I have done my best to follow an ethic of integrity throughout the process.

For those in the business of greyhound racing, I am deeply indebted to Louise Weaver, assistant vice president, archivist, and historian at the

Derby Lane Kennel Club, who supported my research efforts and was helpful in countless ways. I would especially like to thank Gary Guccione, executive director of the National Greyhound Association in Abilene, Kansas. Gary answered hundreds of my questions, whether by phone call, e-mail, or personal interview. Kathy Lounsbury at the Greyhound Hall of Fame was a tremendous resource, and along with the resident greyhounds, helped me find countless archival treasures during my many visits to Abilene. This book would simply not have been possible to complete without the help and support of Louise, Gary, and Kathy.

Paul Hartwell, of the Hartwell family racing dynasty, was always enthusiastic and helpful when I challenged him to dig into the past and remember the early years of greyhound racing and to recount his father's stories. I am grateful to Mr. Hartwell and his family for allowing me to visit him in Carlsbad, California, in 2010 to conduct an oral history interview. Not long before his death, Keith Dillon graciously invited me into his home in Olathe, Kansas, for an oral history interview, now archived at the Kansas State Historical Society. Jim Frey also agreed to an oral history interview that is now housed at Baylor University. Both showed me great kindness as I asked questions about their many years of work in the industry. Mr. Frey even shared records with me from his personal files about the Florida strikes.

I must also thank all of the individuals involved in the greyhound racing business with whom I corresponded or spoke to personally, including Tim Leuschner, Wayne Strong, Janet Strong, John Hartwell, Edward Trow, Robert Trow, Craig Randle, Arden Hartman, Bill Lee, Bill Bell, Karen Keelan, Arthur Agganis, Francie Field, Chuck Marriott, Jack Sherck, Dennis Bicsak, Henry Cashen, Teddy Palmer, Becky Brannon, Leslie Wootten, Marsha Kelly, Jeff Prince, Hoye Perry, Vera Rasnake, Theresa J. Hume, Myra Sullivan, Jesse Sullivan, Dawn Stressman, Gary Temple, Ron Wohlen, Tracy Wildey, and the entire staff at the Flying Eagles Kennel in Abilene, Kansas. Some individuals asked not to be identified, but I'd like to extend my thanks to them as well. Veterinarians that I spoke with regarding various aspects of canine health or the greyhound racing industry include Dr. Scott Schwarting, Dr. Roberta Lillich, Dr. William Dugger, Dr. Jon F. Dee, Dr. Kent Law, Dr. Linda Blythe, Dr. Brad Fenwick, Dr. Jill Hopfenbeck, and Dr. Gail Golab.

During the course of my research I was able to visit the following dog tracks with live racing, although some have since closed: the Palm Beach Kennel Club; Derby Lane (St. Petersburg, Florida); Southland Park Gaming & Racing (West Memphis, Arkansas); Birmingham (Alabama) Race Course;

Wonderland Greyhound Park (Revere, Massachusetts); and Raynham-Taunton (Massachusetts) Greyhound Park.

Gaming industry analyst Will Cummings was extremely helpful and shared important industry data with me; he also reviewed the final chapter and offered insights that only a seasoned industry analyst could provide. Tim O'Brien, the great-grandson of Owen Patrick Smith, the inventor of the mechanical lure, was a delight to speak with as well. Late in my research I came upon the work of Brian Duggan, with whom it was a pleasure to correspond and discuss the history of sight hounds. Steven Crist, who began his career at the dog tracks in Boston before he turned to the horses, kindly granted me an interview; he is presently the editor of the *Daily Racing Form*. Geoff Pesek kindly shared information about his grandfather John Pesek, who was a champion wrestler and a Nebraska greyhound breeder. Others who were of great help include Bill Nack, Sir Mark Prescott, Douglas Reed, Dr. David Schwartz, Dr. Chris Wetzel, Wes Singletary, Eugene Martin Christiansen, Mike Huggins, Emma Griffin, Perky Beisel, Steven A. Riess, and Donald Hausler.

For those involved in the animal protection movement or in greyhound adoption, I would like to thank Susan Netboy, Joan Eidinger, Robert Baker, Gail Eisnitz, Wayne Pacelle, Dr. Bernard Unti, Christine Dorchak, Mrs. Frantz Dantzler, Louise Coleman, Mardy Fones, Ray Wong, and Ruth Hemphill. Susan Netboy shared her extensive video news archive with me as well as all issues of the *Greyhound Network News*. In addition to serving as a reviewer, Dr. Unti kindly consulted with me on a number of animal advocacy issues and shared some important documents pertaining to the history of greyhound racing. Robert Baker and Gail Eisnitz shared their personal files of their past investigations into greyhound racing. My gratitude is extended to numerous animal protection organizations that either opened their archival holdings to me or cooperated in my research efforts in some way, including the Humane Society of the United States, the San Francisco Society for the Prevention of Cruelty to Animals, the Animal Welfare Institute, GREY2K USA, and the Massachusetts Society for the Prevention of Cruelty to Animals. Dr. Dale Schwindaman, one of the architects of the Animal Welfare Act, kindly offered his recollections as well.

As an archivist I am also acutely aware of the critical role of archivists, librarians, and their assistants for all researchers and writers. I personally visited the following repositories during my research and benefited from the expertise of the staff: the Kansas State Historical Society; the National

Agricultural Library at the U.S. Department of Agriculture; the Kentucky State Archives; the California State Archives; the State Archives of Florida and the State Library of Florida; the Massachusetts Historical Society; the Boston Public Library; the University of Nevada, Las Vegas, Lied Library; the Huntington Library (California); the National Sporting Library (Virginia); the Library of Congress; the University of Memphis; the Spencer Research Library at the University of Kansas at Lawrence; the Texas State Library and Archives; the UCLA Film and Television Archive; the UCLA Library Department of Special Collections; the Fort Lauderdale History Center; the Wolfsonian-Florida International University; the Historical Museum of Southern Florida; the Hollywood Historical Society; the Vanderbilt University Law Library; the Barton County (Kansas) Historical Society; North Carolina State University Libraries; the National Library of Medicine at the National Institute of Health; Stanford University Special Collections; the University of Southern California Doheny Memorial Library; the Nashville Public Library; the Multnomah County Public Library (Oregon); the Los Angeles Public Library; the Walker Library at Middle Tennessee State University; the Keeneland Library (Kentucky); and the Miami-Dade County Public Library.

In addition, I utilized the unique resources of the following institutions, even though I did not visit them personally: the Oregon Historical Society Research Library; the Oregon State Archives; the University of Oregon libraries; the George Meany Memorial Archives at the National Labor College; the New York State Library; the Ohio Historical Society; the Salmon Brook Historical Society (Connecticut); the Boston University Libraries; the University of Maryland Libraries; the South Dakota State Archives/South Dakota State Historical Society; the San Joaquin County (California) Historical Society and Museum; the Southern California Library; the Emeryville (California) Historical Society; the Oakland History Room at the Oakland Library (California); the University of Montana K. Ross Toole Archives at the Mansfield Library; the Montana Historical Society; Washington State University Library Special Collections; University of California Santa Barbara; the Nevada State Museum in Las Vegas; the University of Nevada at Reno Special Collections Department at the Getchell Library; the Oklahoma Historical Society; the Wisconsin Center for Film and Theater Research at the Wisconsin Historical Society; the Writers Guild Foundation Shavelson-Webb Library; and the Arizona State University Libraries.

Closer to home, I must thank my dear friends who put up with my absences, both emotional and physical, as I worked on this project, which was several years in the making. They include Jami Awalt, Greg and Margaret Kyser, Ginger Tessier, and Dr. Anita Agarwal. All of these individuals have taken on the task of keeping me happy and in good health—and they deserve a huge amount of credit for standing by my side in good and in bad times.

Other friends and family helped in an equally important way: providing much-needed accommodations during my many research trips across the country. They include my brother, Dr. Alex Thayer; my cousin, Dr. Michael Weiss; and my friends, Marcea, Paul, Hugh, and Hope Barringer; Laura Merrill; and Felicia Anchor. I would also like to thank Dr. Lindsey Murray, Dr. Phil Chanin, and Becky Kantz for their support. Additionally, Eli J. Bortz helped me navigate the process of finding the best publisher for my book. I would also like to extend my thanks to my canine support team, especially Vickie Brown and the other staff members at The Farm at Natchez Trace. Without these individuals looking after my own greyhound, I would not dare to travel.

Within my former place of employment in Nashville, Tennessee, the Tennessee State Library and Archives, there were numerous colleagues who helped me locate hard-to-find materials, such as government documents and obscure databases. Others who offered much-needed support include Vince McGrath, Stephanie Sutton, Chaddra Moore, Greg Yates, Kathy Lauder, Felicia Lott, Anne Whitver, Charlotte Reichley, Cathi Carmack, Trent Hanner, Stewart Southard, Gibb Baxter, Kimberly Wires, Misty Bach, and the amazing Susan Gordon.

I would be remiss if I did not thank my special "advisory team" of friends with expertise in diverse disciplines. Carrie Daughtrey, from the U.S. Attorney's Office in Nashville, helped me decipher early case law and legal language. FBI Special Agent Clifford Scott Goodman, with his fiercely disciplined legal mind, forced me to rethink some of my assumptions about greyhound racing. Janet Goodman, an environmental scientist, eagerly read drafts of my book and offered insightful comments. Both Clifford and Janet were assisted in their efforts by the very special (and always adorable) Carl Goodman, who brought a smile to my face on countless occasions. Vanderbilt University economist Jacob Sagi also offered important insights for which I am grateful.

I would like to thank the MTSU history department for funding much of my travel research early on in this book project, as well as the College of Graduate Studies and the Association of Graduate Students in History. Above all, I would like to thank Dr. Jan Leone, Dr. Susan Myers-Shirk, Dr.

Wayne C. Moore, and Dr. Rebecca Conard. Rebecca has been tremendously supportive throughout my entire career as a historian; she is a fabulous mentor and deserves great credit for helping me see this book to its completion.

I must especially thank my parents. My mother always had a common-sense approach to my book, and as a historian in her own right, knows when my writing is at its best. My father, a master editor and retired university professor, took time to read the final manuscript with a careful eye. I am lucky to have such a supportive family who can also engage with my work on a critical level.

In addition to my reviewers and the entire staff of the University Press of Kansas, especially Fred Woodward, Erika Doss, Susan Schott, and Kelly Chrisman Jacques, and freelance copyeditor Lori Rider, a very special thank you goes to my former editor, Ranjit Arab. I could not have asked for a better editor; this book would simply not have been possible without his help. I am tremendously lucky that he expressed interest in my work and remained supportive to the end.

I want to thank one very special dog: my very own ex-racing greyhound, the appropriately named Zachary More Curious, for inspiring me to write this book, a history of his people.

And last in this long list, but always first in my heart, I dedicate this book to the memory of my beloved mutt, Tafi.

LIST OF ABBREVIATIONS

Organizations, Industry Terminology, and Legislation
AFL: American Federation of Labor
AGC: American Greyhound Council
AGTOA: American Greyhound Track Operators Association
AKC: American Kennel Club
APPMA: American Pet Products Manufacturers Association
ARCI: Association of Racing Commissioners International
ASPCA: American Society for the Prevention of Cruelty to Animals
AVMA: American Veterinary Medical Association
AWA: Animal Welfare Act
AWI: Animal Welfare Institute
GHF: Greyhound Hall of Fame
GOBA: Greyhound Owners Benevolent Association
GPA: Greyhound Pets of America
GPL: Greyhound Protection League
HSUS: Humane Society of the United States
IGRA: Indian Gaming Regulatory Act
IHRA: Interstate Horse Racing Act
INGRA: International Greyhound Racing Association
MBKC: Miami Beach Kennel Club
MSPCA: Massachusetts Society for the Prevention of Cruelty to Animals
NCA: National Coursing Association
NGA: National Greyhound Association
OTB: offtrack betting
PETA: People for the Ethical Treatment of Animals
REGAP: Retired Greyhounds as Pets
SFSPCA: San Francisco Society for the Prevention of Cruelty to Animals
SPCA: Society for the Prevention of Cruelty to Animals
USDA: United States Department of Agriculture
WCTU: Women's Christian Temperance Union
YMCA: Young Men's Christian Association

ROVER OR RACER?

Americans simply cannot agree on the role of the dog. The greyhound is no exception. Perhaps no breed has sparked greater controversy in the United States than the racing greyhound. Its unique and complex position in present-day American society as a dog specifically bred for racing continues to spark bitter controversy.

The hue and cry is certainly not new. The greyhound racing industry found itself under intense media scrutiny during the last several decades of the twentieth century, but the nature and image of the sport has in fact long been debated in various forums within American popular culture. The main characters in an ABC television sitcom derived from the Neil Simon Broadway play *The Odd Couple* grappled with the question of dog racing in a 1971 episode. The show stars Tony Randall as Felix Unger and Jack Klugman as Oscar Madison, two men forced by circumstance to live together in a New York apartment. This unlikely pair features a fussy, protohomosexual character (Felix) in perpetual domestic (but comedic) conflict with his fellow divorcé, the curmudgeonly Oscar. The latter acquires a racing greyhound after winning a bet, but the two men's attitudes toward the dog in question reflect the growing divide in perceptions regarding the institution of greyhound racing. The men in fact hold widely divergent views on the subject. The show presents pro- and anti-greyhound racing ideologies, anticipating a vigorous public debate by several decades.

Although Felix's views change once he enjoys the fruits of a gambling windfall, he is initially horrified that Golden Earrings, Oscar's greyhound, is, in his view, being exploited for profit. Oscar, on the other hand, believes that the greyhound is a racing animal, not a pet. Their dialogue perfectly captures the central disagreement that soon faced American greyhound racing fans and animal lovers:

Oscar: Felix, racing dogs aren't like regular dogs. You put 'em in a
   kennel and you race them.
Felix: It's inhuman.
Oscar: We're not dealing with humans.

When Oscar continues to insist that greyhounds are treated well and given good food, plenty of exercise, and a comfortable kennel, Felix protests, "What about somebody to love them?" Oscar retorts bitterly, "How many people have that?"

When the conversation later resumes, Felix is still bemoaning the fate of the love-starved animal, declaring the sport "barbaric" and Golden Earrings's past as exploitative. Oscar declares that greyhounds are "professional" dogs, different from other canines in that "they love to do it [race]; that's what they were born to do."

Felix tartly responds, "How do you know? Were you there in a box seat of creation in the beginning of greyhounds?"[1]

Felix's statement is meant to be comical, but it encapsulates the central disagreement driving the debate over dog racing. Broadly speaking, traditionalists viewed the role of dogs both as predetermined and as limited to duties beneficial to humans. In contrast, some Americans were beginning to embrace a modified perspective toward all dogs, one that characterized animals as deserving lives free of toil. Proponents espousing this view believed that certain animals, including dogs, should even be given an opportunity to attain something close to "personhood," or at least the right to have their physical and emotional needs met.

Even long before Felix and Oscar's fictional debate was broadcast on ABC, American popular culture had already captured a broad range of perspectives on dog racing. When greyhound racing first emerged in the United States, its public image was defined by a mix of positive and negative views. The sport was occasionally linked with organized crime and other social ills, but also with modernity, tourism, and glamour. Al Capone's involvement in dog racing was long suspected, but the absence of proof that he and his cohorts had their hands specifically in greyhound racing operations did not keep various journalists and Hollywood writers from linking the sport to organized crime. *Dark Hazard,* a film released in 1934 based on W. R. Burnett's 1933 novel of the same name, chronicles the downfall of a Midwestern family man who turns to gambling on the dogs. In the 1942 film *Johnny Eager,* starring Robert Taylor and Lana Turner, the back rooms of the (fictional) Algonquin Park dog track in Chicago serve as the center of operations for Eager's organized crime network. Frank Capra's 1959 film *Hole in the Head,* starring Frank Sinatra, portrays the dog tracks as not only a meeting place of glamour and excitement but also a venue where shady moneymakers like to congregate.[2]

Still, a more positive portrayal managed to secure a hold on American airwaves. Hearst Metrotone news clips from the early 1930s and various Warner Brothers Vitaphone broadcasts from the 1930s and 1940s (such as Sport Slants or Tropical Sportland features) played up the sport's dramatic, modern feel. The skill of the canine athletes was often highlighted through slow-motion footage of leaping greyhound racers and exuberant commentary about their racing prowess. The programs championed the sport's draw for tourists and emphasized the frequency with which vacationers from the north traveled to Florida so that they could enjoy the "southern novelty of canine competition."[3] Comparisons to horse racing were common, with announcers breathlessly promoting "hot puppies instead of ponies"—dogs that rivaled Kentucky's best thoroughbred horses in their appeal.[4] The unbridled enthusiasm for the sport conveyed on the screen lasted for decades. In 1956 racing greyhounds from the West Flagler Kennel Club in Miami provided 45 million television viewers of the *Steve Allen Show* with a special treat: the novelty of a pack of muzzled greyhounds leaping out of a Greyhound bus in the opening shot of the October 7 broadcast.[5]

Only in subsequent years did some television programs begin to examine, albeit tentatively, the possibility that greyhound racing might have a darker side for the dogs that were integral to the industry. "Greta, the Misfit Greyhound," released in 1963 as a part of Walt Disney's Wonderful World of Color series, features a perky, fawn greyhound bitch burdened by her knowledge that there is more to life than chasing an artificial bunny on a racetrack. Coldly abandoned by her owner—referred to by the narrator as a "fringe operator"—as if she were a "beer can," Greta strikes out on her own. This dog clearly differs from her fellow racers, however. The story emphasizes that even though most greyhounds love to run and compete, Greta is through with feeling like a "mindless automatic number" who lives day to day without love or affection.[6]

By the closing decades of the twentieth century American television audiences were encountering an altogether more negative view of the sport. In the premiere broadcast of *The Simpsons* in December 1989, even Homer Simpson, a caricature of the working-class family man, looks down on greyhound racing. When he finds himself unexpectedly short of money for Christmas gifts after his son Bart has wasted the family savings on a tattoo, Homer is desperate for options, but he declares, "I may be a total washout as a father, but I'm not going to take my kid to a sleazy dog track on Christmas Eve." Although he initially resists the idea of gambling at (the fictional) Springfield Downs, he ends up "winning" a racing dog that jumps into his arms after being abandoned by his cruel owner. The new pet, subsequently named Santa's Little Helper, becomes a part of the family and is featured in a later episode, "Two Dozen and One Greyhounds."[7]

The debate continues into the twenty-first century. During the 2012 Super Bowl broadcast on NBC, an advertisement filmed at the Tucson dog track reached an estimated one hundred million American viewers. Equipped with his bright red Skechers shoes, Mr. Quiggly—a pudgy bulldog and unlikely racing star—is able to outrun a pack of racing greyhounds. Curiously, even though the Arizona desert is visible in the background, the announcer and thus ostensibly the venue are British. Evidently company executives felt that the best way to present the sport—and use it to sell shoes—was to give the track an air of European sophistication. The commercial was a hit with most viewers, but it sparked outrage among anti-racing activists who felt that the advertisement painted a false picture of the dog-racing industry and glorified the conditions at the Tucson track, a facility that they claimed was one of the worst in the business.[8] One critic (and greyhound adopter) stated that the commercial "makes racing look like an acceptable thing—that it's a good thing, that it's fun, when these dogs are literally running for their lives."[9] Such a claim was built upon America's contradictory feelings toward greyhound racing, a tangled history with roots that began in the nineteenth century, and in some ways even long before that.

Taken together, the varied portrayals of greyhound racing reviewed above, combined with countless published and televised exposés on the cruelty of the sport, likely helped shift the American consciousness in an altogether new direction: a growing sense that greyhound racing was unequivocally wrong and needed to be eliminated entirely. This book explores this gradual transition in American culture and offers an explanation of the diverse factors that fueled it.

Modern greyhound racing in the United States evolved from the ancient sport of coursing, which was popular in the late eighteenth and nineteenth centuries in England. Coursing was eventually introduced in the United States during the late nineteenth century, likely by recreational hunting groups (many of which were led by military officers stationed in the American West), greyhound fanciers, and various European immigrants. The English tradition of coursing carried elite associations but gradually lost this connection as it was absorbed into American culture. Although oral traditions attribute the importation of greyhounds to the need to control jackrabbit infestations in the western United States, organized coursing largely emerged as a sport practiced for pleasure, apart from agricultural purposes.

COURSING JACK-RABBITS AT GREAT BEND, KANSAS.—Drawn by J. M. Tracy from a Sketch by Hough & Ricker.

"Coursing Jack-Rabbits at Great Bend, Kansas," from *Harper's Weekly*, drawn by J. M. Tracy from a sketch by Hough & Ricker, December 18, 1886. (Nashville Public Library, Special Collections)

Coursing contests were popular in pockets of the American West (especially California) well past the turn of the nineteenth century.

Broadly defined, coursing involves a competition between two greyhounds as they chase the same prey, usually jackrabbits or other small but fleet-footed quarry. The contest begins when a "slipper" releases the two dogs simultaneously. A judge, following a set of standard rules, determines which greyhound displays superior agility and speed. Traditionally, the demonstration of the dogs' athletic skills rather than the death of the quarry was the chief aim of the competition. Objections to the large-scale killing of rabbits in coursing meets were raised occasionally, but Victorian sentimentalism had very little currency in western regions where the ethos of "the survival of the fittest" dominated human-animal relations. The sport was largely subsumed by organized greyhound racing after the first decades of the twentieth century.[10]

Greyhound racing on an oval track emerged in the United States as a consequence of Owen Patrick Smith's development of the mechanical lure in the decade before World War I. Smith, a savvy small-town promoter from

South Dakota, was uncomfortable with the act of killing and perhaps suspected that he could profit from a modified version of coursing that eliminated it. His gradual refinement of the "electric rabbit" ended up laying the groundwork for commercialized dog racing. He designed a mechanical lure to replace live quarry, the lure now fashioned as an artificial rabbit mounted on a moveable, electric device positioned on the exterior rail of the racetrack. The lure operator could send the mechanism around the track at high speed with the push of a button. Because they are sight hounds, greyhounds instinctively chase anything that moves; the fact that a live rabbit is no longer part of the equation is of little consequence to the greyhound. The mechanical lure has been modified to some degree over the past century, but its creation was the critical milestone in the development and evolution of greyhound racing.

Through the promotional efforts of Smith and his associates, the "Sport of Queens" was gradually transformed into a spectator sport featuring eight greyhounds simultaneously chasing a mechanical lure around an oval track.[11] Smith and other promoters were thus able to showcase dog racing in a manner that was perfectly suited for large and diverse audiences. Of equal note, racing enthusiasts and gamblers could wager a little money on a dog at a track as they watched a race. Greyhound racing began to take root in parts of the United States during the late 1920s and early 1930s. Crowds of eager followers emerged in places such as St. Louis, Missouri; Cincinnati, Ohio; New Orleans, Louisiana; and Butte, Montana. After a period of fits and starts in which tracks would open one day and be closed down by the local sheriff the next—known as racing "on the fix"—dog racing slowly gained a grassroots fan base. Even though coursing had flourished mostly in the Great Plains and California, greyhound racing achieved its first broad popularity in Florida and Massachusetts, as well as in a few western states such as Arizona and Oregon.

Many communities were decidedly unenthusiastic about the local introduction of greyhound racing and fought each incursion of the dogmen (those who bred, trained, and raced the greyhounds) and their hounds with vigor.[12] During the 1920s, dog racing alienated many Americans simply because of the sport's perceived association with illegal gambling and vice. One detractor, a local police chief, declared that he would rather have smallpox strike his little town of Hanson, Massachusetts, than see the "bums and gangsters" that would be drawn to town by the dog tracks.[13] Largely because of this attitude, tracks often remained open only as long as it took for the local authorities to locate them and shut them down, sometimes by force.

Owen Patrick Smith, inventor of the mechanical lure. (Image courtesy of the Special Collections and University Archives, University of Oregon Libraries)

The Blue Star Amusement Company in Emeryville, California, established in 1919, is widely acknowledged to have been the country's first greyhound track, but the facility did not enjoy lasting success. Even though most early tracks were short-lived, they still left their mark upon the American consciousness. The track in Cicero, Illinois, allegedly controlled by Al Capone during the Prohibition era, is a prime example of how underworld associations tarnished the reputation of dog racing. Nonetheless, in spite of the rather haphazard process of track openings and closings according to the vagaries of local law enforcement, promoters were eventually able to target fertile ground (i.e., specific states) for establishing legalized gambling on greyhound racing. In 1926, through Owen Patrick Smith's creation of the International Greyhound Racing Association (INGRA), the sport could begin to become more organized and regulated, although not without its fair share of squabbles and controversies.

Gambling on greyhound racing emerged as a legalized activity in a few states beginning in the 1930s.[14] A track's success or failure was based upon a complicated interplay of factors, including, but not limited to, local and state politics, the strength of the thoroughbred horse-racing lobby, the

New Orleans Kennel Club track on opening night, October 24, 1926. This photograph shows the use of electric lighting, which brought in larger crowds to the greyhound races. (Greyhound Hall of Fame)

degree and effectiveness of animal protectionism in the community, the strength of churches and/or other antigambling forces, and, by the end of the twentieth century, the existence of a state lottery and/or other competing gambling operations such as untaxed Indian gaming establishments or commercial casinos. After taking these factors into account, a savvy, effective promoter could himself often make the critical difference in ensuring that racing could be successfully legalized in a virgin state. States such as Kentucky where thoroughbred horse racing was popular usually found ways to harness political forces that were eager to overpower greyhound racing interests. Dog track operators in Erlanger, Kentucky, for example, fought a losing battle against their opponents, although not before bringing their grievances all the way to the U.S. Supreme Court.[15] In essence, depending upon a state's unique social, cultural, and political dynamics, greyhound racing either flourished or foundered.

Florida has always dominated the landscape of dog racing in the United States. Early promoters lured visitors to the Florida greyhound tracks with images of glamour and sophistication as well as a "sun and fun" aesthetic

80-249

Derby Night

*New Kensington
Kennel Club*

IN.G.R.A.

SATURDAY NIGHT, OCTOBER 26, 1935

New Kensington Derby Night, Saturday Night, October 26, 1935. This greyhound track operated near Pittsburgh, Pennsylvania, during the early 1930s. The International Greyhound Racing Association (INGRA) banner can be seen on the upper left. (Greyhound Hall of Fame) characterized by voluptuous bathing beauties. An expanding market for tourism in the early 1920s nurtured the rise of dog racing in the Miami area, a pattern that was repeated in other regions of the Sunshine State throughout the following decades. Advertisements in the 1930s made a concerted effort to associate greyhound racing with an exclusive clientele. Through its connection to English coursing, dog racing already boasted a link, albeit a tenuous one, with a vaguely aristocratic past. This remote association with wealth and the upper class was aggressively exploited by Florida promoters. Advertisements led Floridians and tourists to believe that the Miami tracks were a "mecca for the elite of sportdom."[16] In fact, despite this claim, dog races were often frequented by a broad array of fans, including large numbers from the middle and working classes.

After World War II the sport was legalized in various other states, including Arkansas, Colorado, Rhode Island, New Hampshire, and Vermont, to name just a few examples. Armed with more disposable income after the war than before, Americans were eager to participate in a growing consumer culture that emphasized pleasure over production, and the tourist industry expanded tremendously. In Florida in the 1950s the number of visitors doubled, which proved to be a direct boon to the greyhound-racing industry. Elsewhere some tracks, such as Wonderland in Revere, Massachusetts, would reach million-dollar handles well into the 1980s.[17]

Early on, institutionalized greyhound racing in the United States acquired a structure that in many ways changed very little throughout the twentieth century. In contrast to thoroughbred horse racing, racing greyhounds are not assigned racing appointments as individual competitors (with the possible exception of special stakes races). Rather, entire racing kennels acquire a booking, that is, a racing contract, with a racetrack.[18] In the early years, when racing was seasonal, dogmen would travel the racing circuit, securing, for example, a booking at a Florida track in the winter and one at a New England track in the summer. There were a number of such racing circuits in existence, but all of them required seasonal travel from track to track, often over long distances.[19]

The causes of greyhound racing's eventual decline are, like the reasons for its growth, multifaceted and complicated. The sport's popularity among the American public began to wane in the last decades of the twentieth century. A more competitive and diversified entertainment market rendered it increasingly difficult for greyhound promoters to attract fans to the tracks. State lotteries, Native American gaming venues, riverboat casinos, and slot machine parlors—and more recently the Internet—all emerged as competitors for the gambling dollar. Even though the industry successfully legalized the sport in new states during the 1970s and 1980s, there were failures that eventually negated these successes. The industry's inability to legalize pari-mutuel wagering on greyhound racing in California during the 1970s was a grave disappointment. Although a hotbed of coursing at the turn of the previous century, the state resisted the development of dog racing. Instead, it was thoroughbred horse racing that managed to secure a monopoly over the state's pari-mutuel market. The industry's failure to thrive in Kansas, a state with deep-rooted ties to greyhound breeding and coursing traditions, was another especially deep blow. A flurry of track closures from 1990 to 2010 was for many observers a harbinger of the industry's inevitable demise.

Internal disagreements also compromised the sport's ability to thrive. Long-standing tensions between the dogmen and track owners concerning racing contracts were tremendously damaging. On a number of occasions, most notably in 1935, 1948, 1957, and 1975, the dogmen struck at a number of tracks, demanding better purses. They had long felt that track operators wielded too much control during the booking process, arguing that they awarded racing contracts on a "take it or leave it" basis. The American public evinced little sympathy for the dogmen's financial woes and difficulties with track management, since dogmen were increasingly viewed as guilty of exploiting animals for profit. Increasing kennel sizes led to new problems, namely, an excessive number of greyhounds produced for the industry, which in turn resulted in rising rates of greyhound euthanasia. State subsidies designed to buttress the weakening pari-mutuel industry did little to win the public over to the dogmen's point of view.

Before these troubles surfaced, however, greyhound racing in the United States had emerged as a sporting pastime in an era of cheaper and simpler amusements. The sport found comfortable space to grow and flourish through its associations with rural culture, gambling, popular leisure, and a burgeoning tourism industry. On the other hand, its development was complicated in the mid-twentieth century by the evolving welter of attitudes and values concerning the treatment of animals, the powerful competition from other sporting and gambling activities, and the stigma of being less than a proper pursuit. Success in drawing gamblers and other spectators to new tracks remained largely dependent on a variable calculus of local socioeconomic conditions, cultural preferences, and consumer habits. As the greyhound racing industry expanded, promoters continuously battled an array of negative, often class-based perceptions about the sport.[20] At one point or another, dog racing has been associated with organized crime, political corruption, moral debasement, animal cruelty, and other social problems. Its troubled image is partially a consequence of its apparently unbreakable link to the working class and "lowbrow" culture, this even when "respectable" middle- and upper-class Americans continued to patronize the tracks.[21] Somehow, thoroughbred horse racing largely managed to escape a similar stigma, even though the working and middle classes also attended these races. More recently, however, thoroughbred horse racing has also come under fire for its treatment of racehorses, especially lower-value claiming horses.[22]

The issue of class is perhaps the most challenging element of the American institution of dog racing to decipher, especially in a country that admits to its existence only reluctantly. Who actually attended the dog races? Historical attendance reports are sometimes available, but they speak to how many—rather than who—attended the races. A few scattered sociological studies exist, most of which were conducted in the last few decades of the twentieth century.[23] Aside from tantalizing bits of information to be gleaned from these queries, the sources offer little more than circumstantial evidence for firm conclusions. Other means of pinpointing early greyhound-racing audiences must be used. Where were tracks opened? What do contemporary photographs show us? What newspapers and magazines covered the sport, and how was it presented? Can the accounts be taken at face value? Historians have tackled this tricky interpretative task when studying greyhound racing in the United Kingdom, but a similar effort has not been attempted within the realm of American greyhound racing.[24]

In addition to the question of class, the rise of animal advocacy in the United States is another central theme in this book. The ethos of kindness toward animals was first conceptualized in the ancient world, but for centuries their welfare was most widely accepted as entirely subordinate to the will of humankind. Early modern thinkers began to challenge man's position of authority over animals and explored the possibility that animals were worthy of moral consideration.[25] Animal protection as a social and political force began to emerge in the late nineteenth century.[26] Americans were introduced to animal advocacy on a significant, national scale when Henry Bergh founded the American Society for the Prevention of Cruelty to Animals (ASPCA) in New York City in 1866.

The ASPCA was initially involved in children's causes as well as agitation for improved treatment of urban working horses and other animals. Eventually Bergh's society and like organizations focused specifically on animals, while other groups came forth to improve the lives of abused or neglected children. A hallmark of the Progressive era that followed soon thereafter was the creation, development, and systematization of social welfare agencies. Bureaucracies designed to address specific social concerns gradually emerged, and reform efforts became more professionalized. Initiatives designed to battle moral lapses in society were no longer issued solely from the domain of good Christian men and women. Such efforts became a part of the larger struggle of social reformers to improve society and protect the poor from vice. Their campaigns frequently involved educated, middle-class reformers targeting the working class, leading many historians to argue that their efforts were a form of social control.[27]

During the first few decades of the twentieth century, scattered references to the cruelty of coursing do surface, although such objections were few and far between. They were often cast aside as the actions of "do-gooders," social reformers who tried to deprive Americans of their "rightful" pleasures, particularly alcohol but also gambling. Coursing was always a relatively minor presence in American culture and rarely caught the attention of the national press before the 1970s. A 1947 feature in *Life* did not even entertain the possibility that the sport was cruel to animals in general, or even rabbits in particular.[28]

Coursing's close cousin—greyhound racing—did eventually attract the national eye, however. The sport's growing visibility in American popular culture (and the gambling that inevitably accompanied it) proved to be a double-edged sword. Critics who noticed dog racing's widening appeal were quick to point out the more controversial aspects of the sport. Animal protectionists, who had long believed that greyhound racing was marred by cruel practices, launched an aggressive assault against dog racing in the late 1970s. Although there had always been some complaints about its treatment of animals, early objections to coursing and dog racing had usually centered on the welfare of the rabbit (or other live quarry used in training or competition) rather than the dog. Animal advocates had questioned the acceptability of using greyhounds to kill live prey, especially when presented as sport and entertainment. But the nature of the criticism gradually shifted to concerns over the care of the dogs themselves. With the rise of the animal rights movement in the 1970s, the industry was increasingly subject to damaging exposés about its cruel treatment of greyhounds, especially the mass destruction of dogs once they were no longer viable for racing. Appalled by this practice, some volunteers took action by establishing greyhound adoption groups throughout the country. Moreover, even with the introduction of organized greyhound adoption in the early 1980s, which created a formal means of securing permanent, loving homes for ex-racers, many reformers advocated the total abolition of dog racing. Nevertheless, the growing popularity of adopted greyhounds did little to quash the acrimonious debate over greyhound racing itself.

Much to their distress, those in the greyhound racing business also continued to see the reputation of the sport tarnished by the media. A number of documented cases of abuse surfaced in the 1980s and 1990s, causing a public-relations nightmare for racing insiders. The industry blamed "bad apples" and labeled the abuses as isolated incidents, whereas critics claimed that the problem was systemic. However Americans chose to interpret the events, the news was hard to miss. CNN, HBO, and other broadcast media operations aired graphic exposés on the cruelty of greyhound racing, reaching millions of viewers who previously might have had little or no objection to the sport. Phrases such as a "Dachau for dogs" and an "Auschwitz of dog racing" were tossed about to describe egregious cases of abuse in the greyhound industry, with one woman interviewed in 2006 saying, "If you don't speak out, you have . . . a Holocaust of greyhounds."[29]

Given these circumstances, the greyhound racing industry found itself under increasing pressure to institute reforms. In response, it took steps to improve the care of racing dogs in all phases of their careers. Many animal protectionists argued that these actions were rarely sufficient and little more than empty political gestures. Even if the industry were to institute dramatic reforms (it did, in fact, create its own greyhound welfare organization, the American Greyhound Council [AGC], in 1987) and effectively eliminate all possibility of abuse, it is unlikely to recover from its tarnished reputation. This phenomenon could fairly be described as a "sins of the fathers" syndrome; in the eyes of many critics, some of the past wrongs were so egregious as to preclude forgiveness. It explains why those men and women in the business who are well intentioned often feel so frustrated by and alienated from animal protectionists, and it reveals why the quality of public dialogue over the sport is so poor.

Key cultural developments in the United States have thrown these communities into conflict. The twentieth century brought about changing views of work and play, which in turn directly affected the lives of animals. Most critically, Americans have witnessed a tremendous shift in the perceived role of dogs. While for most of human history canines were assigned various utilitarian duties, ranging from herding, hunting, guarding, and fighting, they are now chiefly embraced as domestic companions. The dramatic rise of pet keeping can be attributed to a number of societal changes. Harriet Ritvo observes that pet keeping in England was strongly influenced by both status and capitalism, as pets became reflections of their owners' class.[30] Pets were popular during the Victorian age, when a "domestic ethic of kindness" was embraced by middle-class Protestant families. A similar pattern emerged in the United States. Katherine C. Grier, the author of *Pets in America,* proposes that keeping and nurturing pets was a means of achieving self-cultivation. As the country became increasingly urbanized, pet keeping was a way to explore one's conflicting feelings toward civilized domesticity and the natural animal (i.e., animality).[31]

The commercial structure of the modern pet-keeping industry emerged from 1840 to 1930, but affection for companion animals in the United States became "fully integrated into mass consumer culture" only in the twentieth century, according to Susan Jones, author of *Valuing Animals.*[32] Americans incorporated the "companionship and affection implicit in pet keeping" into the consumer realm as the primary value of dogs shifted from utilitarian to emotional.[33] The acquisition of a purebred dog could even serve as a sign of growing income and status in American homes. After World War II pet keeping became even more deeply embedded in consumer culture. To cite but one example, American Kennel Club (AKC) registrations, which track the purchase of purebred dogs, grew from 442,875 in 1960 to 1,129,200 in 1970.[34]

Today, the prominent position of dogs as consumer objects cannot be underestimated. Pet keeping in the United States is a $36 to $43 billion industry, outselling even baby-care products. Given this statistic, it is perhaps not surprising that dogs are often referred to by their doting caretakers as "fur babies." Now more than ever, dogs are a part of the family: in 1998, 24 percent of dogs lived outdoors, outside of the house, whereas in 2006 the number was down to 13 percent. Whereas in 1995, 55 percent of dog owners referred to themselves as their pet's "mommy" or "daddy," the number had risen to 83 percent in 2001. Surveys have shown that somewhere between 50 and 70 percent of Americans now regard their pets as family members. The possibilities for consumption that result from these shifting attitudes are endless. Not surprisingly, our habits are carefully tracked by organizations such as the American Veterinary Medical Association (AVMA) and the American Pet Products Manufacturers Association (APPMA).[35]

The evolving relationship between consumerism and dogs has had an adverse effect on the greyhound racing industry. People once drawn to racetracks for entertainment eventually began to question the ethics of betting

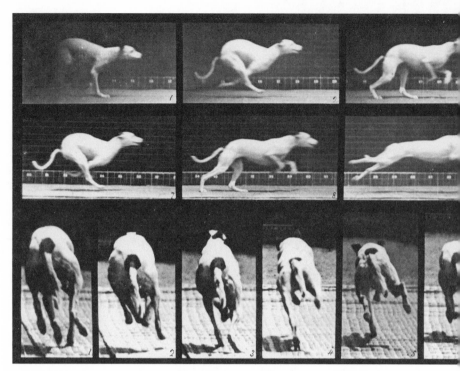

Eadweard Muybridge Collection, Plate #710 of animal locomotion series, study collotypes of white racing greyhound Maggie, 1887. (University of Pennsylvania Archives)

on animals. Dogs once expected to earn their keep were now coddled, free of duties or obligations. Pets had an emotional rather than economic value, a shift seen nowhere more clearly than in the racing greyhound. Once a commodity, greyhounds were gradually transformed into pets in the public eye, emotional assets with the additional cachet for their adopters as being "rescues." When pets, including greyhounds, became a new kind of consumer product—one that could be loved and cuddled rather than bet on—the racing industry began to realize that the growing greyhound adoption movement might be a mixed blessing. Few denied the importance of finding good, permanent homes for ex-racers, but the obvious need to do so exposed a gaping hole in the system of dog racing: the overbreeding of greyhounds and the overwhelming need to care for them or destroy them once their careers were over.

In contrast to previous years, when greyhounds were almost exclusively viewed on the racetrack, greyhounds are now seen more frequently in public dog parks, at adoption events, and, for some, on our sofas and in our

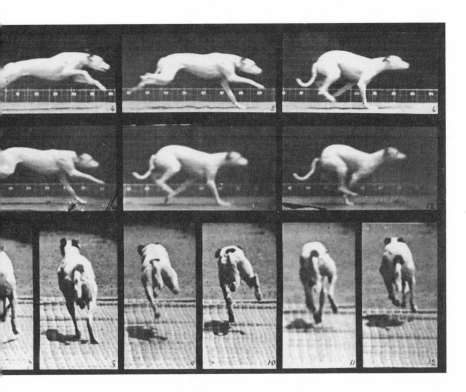

beds. Just what is a greyhound, and how have they been used throughout history? Greyhounds are sight hounds, long thought to be one of the oldest dog breeds (perhaps having originated in the Middle East), but recent DNA evidence throws some of these long-held theories into question.[36] Greyhound-like dogs can be seen in a variety of early artistic representations, ranging from ancient Egyptian and Greek paintings to medieval tapestries. They are undoubtedly the fastest of all canines, capable of reaching speeds of 45 miles per hour. When not in motion, however, they tend to be relaxed, even lazy, thus resulting in the nickname "the 45-mile-an-hour couch potato." American racing greyhounds are presently registered with the National Greyhound Association (NGA; formerly the National Coursing Association [NCA]) and are bred specifically for racing competitions, whereas AKC greyhounds, of which there are far fewer, are bred for conformation to the AKC breed standard and do not race. The greyhound, with its short and smooth coat, comes in a variety of colors, including brindle, fawn, white, black, and a number of variations in between. They tend to be about 27 to 30 inches tall, weighing anywhere from 55 to 80 pounds.[37] Greyhounds are naturally lean and muscular, leading those who are unfamiliar with the breed to sometimes conclude—erroneously—that they are malnourished or starved even when they are in perfect health. Their flexible spines, large hearts, and powerful lungs allow them to achieve tremendous speeds, even after only a few strides. Their innate running abilities naturally led humans to use them for hunting purposes, although their skills were later called upon for recreational sporting activities.

To date, few books have attempted to tackle the history of greyhound racing in the United States. Cynthia A. Branigan's book *The Reign of the Greyhound* provides a sweeping overview of the breed from prehistory to the present and does not focus exclusively on American greyhound racing. A few informal memoirs have been written by individuals with extensive personal experience in the industry. Of these, Paul C. Hartwell's *The Road from Emeryville: A History of Greyhound Racing*, published in 1980, is the most notable. His book is both a memoir and a general history of the sport and serves as the most reliable history of the sport currently available. Leslie A. Wootten, like Hartwell, the descendant of an industry pioneer, published a short history of a champion racing greyhound, *Keefer: The People's Choice*, in 2007. Three years later Ryan H. Reed came out with a book documenting his travels from racetrack to racetrack, *Born to Run: The Racing Greyhound from Competitor to Companion*. This work cannot be characterized as a history of the sport but is instead more of a travelogue or personal discovery narrative about greyhound racing. *The History of Greyhound Racing in New England*, published by Robert Temple, is a brief, journalistic account of some of the high points of racing in Massachusetts, Rhode Island, New Hampshire, Connecticut, and Vermont, with an emphasis on star greyhounds and regional highlights.[38]

A foray into the study of organized greyhound racing requires a familiarity with some basic industry terminology. The form of legalized gambling conducted at greyhound tracks in the United States since the 1930s is known as pari-mutuel wagering. This system of betting emerged in France in the 1860s, and its name roughly translates as "betting among ourselves" or "betting among each other." It involves the pooling of all wagers into one pot from which track management takes a commission and pays the winning bettors, namely, those who bet on dogs finishing in the first three or four places. The amount of money bet on a given greyhound determines the odds. When more money is wagered on a dog, the odds decrease; when less money is wagered, the odds increase.[39]

Chapter 1, "Chasing Rabbits," looks back to the origins of greyhound racing in the United Kingdom, namely, coursing. Coursing later found some devotees in the United States but was eventually transformed into

Racing greyhound in motion, 2008. (Ray Wong, photographer)

greyhound racing. Chapter 2, "Boom or Bust," charts the uneven but dynamic growth of the new sport of greyhound racing in the 1920s and introduces the dogmen who were integral to its development before legalization. Chapter 3, "Horses, Hounds, and Hustlers," samples locations where dog racing was suppressed or encouraged. Kentucky, New York, and California all serve as case studies that expose thoroughbred horse racing as a chief opponent to dog-racing interests. In Massachusetts and other states, even when gambling on greyhound racing was legalized, the sport was still not welcomed by all community members. Chapter 4, "Halcyon Days, Florida Nights," traces the phenomenal popularity of greyhound racing in Florida and the celebrity culture that began to accompany it. Chapter 5, "Doggone Mad," examines the damaging media reports and graphic exposés focused on the alleged cruelty of greyhound racing. The end of the twentieth century inaugurated a period of aggressive criticism of the dog-racing industry, an assault from which the sport has never recovered. Chapter 6, "The Fall," tracks the postwar growth of greyhound racing that was gradually undermined by a variety of sociocultural changes. The expansion and diversification of American mass culture pulled gamblers and fans away from the tracks to new and different venues.

Despite greyhound racing's visibility in communities across the United

States for almost a century, its presence in American culture has largely been overlooked by scholars. In contrast, the sport's close cousin, thoroughbred horse racing, has long attracted both popular and scholarly attention.[40] Until now, the socioeconomic, political, and ideological factors that fueled the rise and fall of dog racing in the United States have never been examined as a whole. *Going to the Dogs* provides a broad narrative of American greyhound racing in the twentieth century. The story is not limited to greyhounds in pursuit of the mechanical rabbit; it is the story of Americans at work, at play, and at odds. This book will interpret dog racing as a dynamic cultural phenomenon, a pastime that has long attracted passionate supporters and detractors. The subject remains a hotly debated one: Americans continue to struggle over their competing views about the role of dogs—and indeed, of all animals. For some, the sport belongs to a lifestyle. An attack against greyhound racing is interpreted as nothing less than a cultural assault. For others, the lives and livelihoods of animals are at stake. This past century has seen a colossal shift in how we perceive and understand greyhound racing. The purpose of *Going to the Dogs* is to elucidate how and why this cultural transformation took place.

CHAPTER ONE

CHASING RABBITS

This rabbit thing is going to haunt us no matter where we go.
Dogman F. B. "Happy" Stutz, "In California, Money Talked,"
Greyhound Hall of Fame

Once Owen Patrick Smith created the mechanical lure, he had effectively set the stage for organized greyhound racing in the United States. Beyond its raw utility, his invention was also, in a sense, a cultural metaphor. His new device represented the influence of the nascent animal protection movement, which, at this point, chiefly espoused the ideology of kindness to animals and had far less to say about their "rights." Substituting an electric rabbit for a live rabbit, if only on the racetrack, was a preliminary effort to lessen the element of "blood sport" in greyhound racing. Greyhounds still trained on live rabbits, but at least when in the public eye, a more respectable spectacle could take place. Certain blood sports were associated with the lower class, even though, paradoxically, coursing was rooted in an elite European practice, as were other field sports such as foxhunting. To the greyhound, however, the shift from live to electric lure was of no concern: anything in rapid movement was worth chasing. His instinct for hunting had long ago been cast into his DNA.

Well before greyhounds were employed as racers in the United States and later as common household companions, they had been valued for hundreds of years as hunters, often as sight hounds used to chase jackrabbits, although their prey included coyotes, antelopes, and other larger fleet-footed wildlife.[1] The greyhound was first introduced to the Americas when Spaniards seeking land, gold, and glory arrived with their greyhounds and mastiffs. These dogs sometimes accompanied the conquistadors and were used to intimidate and kill indigenous people during violent raids. When compared with present-day representations of racing greyhounds, which often picture them in varying positions of benign slumber, Theodor de Bry's early engraving of hounds attacking Indians (perhaps after a "chase") shows the startling distance the greyhound has come in American consciousness.[2]

From a vicious, killing beast to a gentle household pet, the greyhound has occupied positions of absolute polarity in American history.

Differing viewpoints exist about the origin of the greyhound, with new DNA evidence casting doubt on old theories. The breed was long believed to have been used for hunting activities in ancient Egypt and possibly Mesopotamia, and to have reached Italy and Greece via the Middle East between 400 BCE and 100 CE. Now, however, greyhounds are thought to have relatively modern origins and were likely bred from more northern stock than North African sight hounds such as the Saluki.[3] Early examples of coursing can be somewhat difficult to distinguish from hunting. The Greek historian Xenophon (431–349 BCE) penned the first known treatise on hunting, but he does not mention coursing with sight hounds. Arrian, however, an ethnic Greek writing more than 500 years later during the height of the Roman empire, wrote specifically about this practice.[4] For many centuries to come, purists who embraced coursing followed his advice: "The true Sportsman does not take out his dogs to destroy the Hares, but for the sake of the course, and the contest between the dogs and the Hares, and is glad if the hare escapes."[5] Coursing enthusiasts have long made it clear that the kill was not the purpose of the competition.

Queen Elizabeth I (1533–1603) was a fan of coursing, as were other members of the aristocracy throughout England in her time. One chronicler noted that her endorsement and participation gave coursing "a degree of fashion and celebrity previously unknown," with many following her lead and practicing the sport with "undiminished zeal."[6] The queen called upon her earl marshal, Thomas, Duke of Norfolk, to institute rules of coursing, most of which were then followed for centuries. During her reign, greyhound breeders "jealously preserved the secret of how their dogs were bred, and rarely, if ever, allowed a stranger to mix the blood of his kennel with theirs."[7] The link between the aristocracy and greyhound ownership continued for centuries in England. In his 1908 essay on coursing, British sportsman Ainsty noted that the possession of a greyhound was "considered as the mark of a gentleman" in England well into the nineteenth century.[8]

In fact, the sport had been popular among the upper classes in the British Isles (and beyond) long before the reign of Queen Elizabeth. Before coursing was codified, William the Conqueror (ca. 1028–1087) had enacted forest laws that restricted greyhound ownership. Such laws tightly regulated sport hunting by dictating that only certain classes could own and hunt with their dogs. As H. Edwards Clarke succinctly puts it, "Forest Laws were . . . born of this conflict between king and nobles hunting for pleasure and sport and

"Coursing with Grayhounds," from the *Gentleman's Recreation*, 1686, drawn by Richard Blome, and reprinted in 1911 in *British Sports and Sportsmen*. (UNLV Libraries, Special Collections)

the lower orders hunting for the pot."[9] Later, the Game Act of 1671 even limited who could kill a hare, firmly establishing hare coursing (and hare hunting) as an upper-class pastime.[10]

Public coursing in England began during the reign of Charles I (1625–1649).[11] The sport continued to develop and expand, with royal estates and baronial manors conducting coursing events in rural settings.[12] In 1858 the National Coursing Club was established in England along with codified "Rules of Coursing" largely based on the Duke of Norfolk's standards.[13] Following the example of the Jockey Club in England, coursers registered their greyhounds in a stud book in order to document the purity of their breeding.[14] The Waterloo Cup became the most famous prize awarded to coursers in Great Britain.[15]

By this time coursing had evolved from a hunting competition into a carefully regulated contest in which two greyhounds chased a hare in an open field. One dog was judged to be the superior courser according to a set of established rules. The greyhound that killed the hare was not necessarily adjudged the victor; in fact, the purpose of the match was to showcase superior agility and running prowess rather than the raw ability to kill. As one enthusiast succinctly explained, "The dogs' object is the death of the hare; the courser's object is to test the relative speed, working abilities, and endurance of the competitors, as shown in their endeavours to accomplish their object. . . . The possession of the hare is of little consequence, except to the pothunter . . . who is quite out of the pale of genuine coursing society."[16] Greyhounds hunt by sight rather than by smell, and their most distinguishing characteristic is their remarkable speed: they are without question the fastest canines, able to achieve speeds of up to 45 miles per hour. But hares frequently prove to be the more agile of the two, thus creating quite a competition and a spectacle.

The growing popularity of coursing inspired English sportsmen to write about training techniques and other aspects of the sport. One expert noted in 1825 that the "training of the greyhound may be reduced to the same scientific rules as that of the race-horse."[17] In fact, the greyhound athlete was sometimes provided with elegant quarters, although perhaps not quite as grand as those provided for the thoroughbred. A number of Englishmen published treatises on the care of the greyhound athlete, most notably John Henry Walsh, who used the nom de plume Stonehenge.[18] Stonehenge's writings were later exported to the United States and quoted by numerous greyhound enthusiasts who followed. He boasted impressive credentials as an expert in field sports. Not only was he one of the original founders of the

National Coursing Club in England, but he also served as chief editor of the London *Field,* a general sporting periodical, for more than thirty years. Some of his recommendations on training greyhounds, including the proper diet for the greyhound athlete, have proved to be long lasting. He ranked horse meat as the best option for feeding coursing hounds, a practice that continued well into the twentieth century in the United States.[19]

Early published discussions of coursing in England were infused with commentary about social class, especially as the sport began to attract wider popularity. Traditional open coursing had long been associated with the aristocracy. In 1886 the British greyhound enthusiast Hugh Dalziel argued in exclusive favor of this style of coursing, which did not permit fences or other barriers that could impede the chase. He was adamantly against closed coursing, which limited the competition to a fenced-in area, even though he noted with some surprise that there were, in fact, men of position who engaged in this form of the sport. He likened the hare in closed coursing to a creature coming out of a prison only to fall victim to men who sought "unearned increment."[20] Dismissing closed coursing as "effeminate Cockney coursing," he argued that breeding greyhounds for coursing in small enclosures would destroy the most valuable qualities of the breed.[21] He roundly dismissed the closed version as "a mere caricature of the ancient and noble sport, thus travestied for purposes of gate money and gambling."[22] Dalziel acknowledged that the ownership of greyhounds was slowly being diffused through all classes, attributing this change to the modification of game laws and the general increase of wealth and leisure time.[23] The growth of railways and the increased activity of the press also led to wider participation.[24] As coursing had continued to grow in England, the sport had gradually become more widely available to all classes in society.[25] In fact, the tide had already started to turn well before the sport even reached the United States.

Even though coursing had long been popular in the United Kingdom, it was relatively unknown in the United States before the Civil War.[26] Sportsman W. S. Harwood speculated in 1899 that private coursing started to gain popularity in the United States around 1850. Public events came later and were more strictly managed.[27] The earliest coursing club in the United States, the California Pioneer Coursing Club, was established in 1867 by Clem Dixon.[28] He preserved English rules but also adapted them to fit conditions unique to the state. Hares were abundant, and the prize of the competition was a trophy cup. There were no entrance costs for the contest; club members simply paid a monthly fee.[29] In 1874 fifty members of the California Pioneer Coursing Club met to plan a fall match in Merced; the

A DAY'S COURSING ON THE DOWNS AT PLUMPTON

"A Day's Coursing on the Downs at Plumpton," from *The Graphic*, December 14, 1878. (Author's Collection)

Merced Plains in the San Joaquin Valley, not far from Modesto, were said to be ideal for coursing.[30] In addition, organized coursing began to flourish in San Francisco and in areas well beyond the state, such as St. Louis. The Occidental Coursing Club of Newark, California, was established in the 1880s and remained active throughout the 1890s. Coursing in California was sometimes practiced on open plains, but eventually closed coursing (often in parks) became the norm.

The sport of coursing rapidly acquired class associations in the United States. According to Joseph A. Graham, an authority on sporting dogs, enclosed park coursing was the fashionable Sunday sport in California in 1898.[31] He praised coursing's "ancient and honorable character and its association with the early aristocracy of sport" but noted that in the United States it was practiced to a more limited degree than foxhunting or shooting. Significantly, he pointed to class-based differences in the execution of the sport based upon an assortment of factors. Depending on his social position a sportsman might prefer open to closed coursing and private to public coursing. Likewise, either greyhounds or whippets could be selected for the chase. Even though closed coursing was eventually favored in California, Graham affirmed that according to the English tradition open coursing was still the only legitimate form of the sport.[32]

Experts such as Graham also drew a clear distinction between coursing in a proper manner and whippet racing, which was followed chiefly by miners and colliers in England and only infrequently in the United States. He was firm in his disapproval of gambling during coursing events and asserted that without regulations against betting the competition could degenerate into little more than a "gambling affair."[33] Another chronicler of the sport, Harwood, was equally severe, stating that those who engage in this activity with the dogs are little more than gamesters.[34]

Launched in 1873, *Forest and Stream* magazine covered the rise of coursing in the United States. The periodical prided itself on attracting wealthy men who enjoyed simple rural pursuits and revealed coursers' aspirations to high class.[35] Most of the literature spotlighting the early years of American coursing was loaded with terms that reflected a desire to associate the sport—and the greyhounds—with the aristocracy. Harwood remarked that the greyhounds ran magnificently, with "the blood of a royal ancestry . . . in their veins."[36] American coursers sought to follow the tradition of thoroughbred horse breeders in securing the noblest blood from England in order to create a "fine and virile race" of American dogs.[37] One *Forest and Stream* article, "The Royal Sport of Coursing," described greyhounds flamboyantly,

National Coursing Meet, Wichita Greyhound Kennel Club, Spencer Tracks,
photograph by Virgil T. Brown, ca. 1929. (Greyhound Hall of Fame)

as "silken-coated blue bloods [*sic*]" with "great lustrous eyes" and speed that
was legendary, even mystical.[38] An 1887 *Forest and Stream* bulletin declared
the object of the Coursing Club of California to be to "promote, encourage and improve the breeding of a superior class of greyhounds . . . [and] to
elevate coursing to the position it occupies in other countries; namely, the
grandest field sport of the world."[39]

Class-based tensions persisted, however, as a number of sporting chroniclers documented a more complicated and nuanced picture, sometimes
even within the very articles that emphasized the royal origins of the sport.
For instance, Harwood described the crowd viewing a coursing event as "a
motley throng," with urban men from the Atlantic and Pacific coasts, some
of whom were British natives. There were people arriving in "lumbering
country-place hacks," "ramshackle livery rigs," and "country wains drawn
by big horses bespeaking their French or English origin." In essence, anyone who could "rent or borrow a conveyance of any shape, style, or age"
could join the crowd.[40] The American Coursing Club, established in 1886,
held its first annual competition in Cheyenne Bottoms, near Great Bend,
Kansas, and continued to meet for a number of years.[41] In 1888 the crowd

of 2,000 gathered there was described as mixed, both in terms of gender and class: "Larger numbers of ladies were present [than on the previous day], and much dressiness and style made itself apparent on every hand, uniquely commingling with the ruder garb of the humbler spectators."[42] In subsequent years major coursing competitions (such as the American Waterloo Cup) were held in Davenport, Iowa (1897); St. Louis, Missouri (1902); and Oklahoma City, Oklahoma (1903).

During the last several decades of the nineteenth century, coursing was attracting a mixed crowd, drawing in both respected community members (such as lawyers, doctors, etc.) and a humbler demographic. Women were occasionally present, although certainly not the predominant audience. While in the United States it might have been easier to portray coursing in old England as a classy event, this characterization clearly became muddied when applied to coursing as it was practiced in small communities in the Great Plains. Nor did coursing contests always take place without disputes or disorder, even when so-called gentlemen were involved. In 1888, during the American Coursing Club's meet in Great Bend, Kansas, an intoxicated participant displeased with the judge's decision called the judge a "d—d [damned] English fraud," causing a fracas and spoiling the afternoon "for 2,000 people, among whom it might well be supposed that ladies and gentlemen predominated."[43] One sportsman, Dr. Van Hummel, claimed that by reporting disturbances at the events the magazine had damaged the reputation of the American Coursing Club among his wealthy friends in the East. Van Hummel was informed in turn that his word alone was not enough to prove that distinguished men such as August Belmont wanted to come out west but were afraid to on account of the "hoodlums," as *Forest and Stream* had characterized the members and visitors.[44] The correspondent declared it was doubtful that another meet would take place the following year, perhaps due to the quarrelling.

Most accounts of coursing competitions in the Great Plains were less critical and more celebratory of the sport's elite heritage. One coursing event in 1889 included a grand parade along the main street in Hutchinson, Kansas.[45] A *Forest and Stream* correspondent remarked that this display was the finest ever seen at an American coursing meet, and as the greyhounds marched up the street with their owners, "one was reminded of the old days in England."[46] Over and over chroniclers attested to the sport's burgeoning popularity in the United States. One wrote in 1889 that the nation would soon host the best and fastest dogs in the world, predicting with great optimism that clubs would eventually exist across the entire country, where greyhounds would achieve names for themselves that would long be remembered.[47] This anticipated surge in popularity never in fact translated into the widespread establishment of the sport.

Organized coursing was also established on the East Coast for a time, a response to emerging interest in the sport locally and the availability of broad plains around New York, Long Island, and New Jersey.[48] In 1889 J. Herbert Watson organized the first meeting of the Eastern Coursing Club at the Hoffman House in New York. After electing its board of directors, the group decided to adopt the rules of the American Coursing Club and began a search for suitable property on Long Island.[49] The first meet took place on December 7, 1889, and soon drew fire from the Society for the Prevention of Cruelty to Animals (SPCA). The club countered the criticism, asserting that its coursing men were "not, as some of the hysterical editorial paragraphers of the press allege, dudes, nor dudlets, nor apers of British customs, nor idle young fellows with more money than brains. They are business and professional men, holding positions of trust, engaged in honorable pursuits. Taken one and another, they are fairly representative of the respectable right-thinking, intelligent class of society."[50]

This spirited rebuttal was issued after the "slipper" of the Eastern Coursing Club was arrested on charges of cruelty that had been instigated by the American Society for the Prevention of Cruelty to Animals (ASPCA).[51] The

Irish Cup coursing competition, Mick Horan, slipper, with Swanky Boy and Miss Ethel, 1949. Horan is releasing the two greyhounds simultaneously by use of a special collar and leash known as a slip. (Greyhound Hall of Fame)

slipper was responsible for releasing the two competing hounds at precisely the same time so that no unfair advantage arose in pursuit of the hare. The slip was used in traditional coursing contests in England and Ireland, and its purpose and design in the United States were fundamentally the same.[52] In response to this action against coursing by an animal advocacy organization, a bill was introduced into the New York state legislature to exempt the coursing of hares (when conducted by incorporated coursing clubs) from interference by anticruelty forces. The Eastern Coursing Club asked, rhetorically, if their sport was declared cruel, what could be made of similar sporting activities involving beagles or other dogs?[53] Likewise, they questioned, why was coursing different from killing hares with a gun? Jackrabbits usually died immediately after being caught by a greyhound, but a gunshot did not always cause instantaneous death.

Here, too, in assertions regarding supposedly proper and improper ways to conduct the sport, class overtones persist. Standards of play are assumed to vary according to one's socioeconomic background. Class-based variations were readily evident in the United States, with some coursers in 1888 rejecting the practices of certain Long Islanders as contrary to the rules of gentlemen's coursing. New York's Hempstead Coursing Club used fox terriers to run rabbits, a choice that according to one sportsman (and also a member of the SPCA) was only fit for the lower classes. This critic, C. J. Peshall, commented that the men of Long Island were not in fact adhering to the rules embraced by "gentlemen and sportsmen" in England. Rather, they were engaged in "rabbit baiting," which was favored by the lower classes in England, the "pit men and miners."[54] He specifically invoked Dalziel's description of this debased form of the sport as "poor man's coursing." Peshall emphasized that proper English rules must be followed at all times because coursing, when improperly practiced, was unmanly and cruel.

While the establishment of the first organized coursing clubs in the United States can be confirmed, the paths that first brought greyhounds to the United States are still largely undocumented and usually only mentioned in passing. In all, scarce written evidence exists chronicling the importation of the breed during the nineteenth century. In truth, a number of groups were likely responsible for the introduction of sporting with greyhounds, although American military officers stationed at isolated western forts stand out as an early key group of recreational hunters who clearly valued greyhounds. Coursing had gained a small but sure following by 1885, at which point its adherents may have sought more aggressive ways to import kennels of greyhounds. A number of sources document more concerted efforts to import greyhounds from British kennels in the mid–1890s, with one Californian and his fellow enthusiasts described as sparing "no expense or trouble in bringing over dogs [coursing greyhounds] from England."[55]

The majority of modern-day greyhound racing fans, however, point to the Irish (and sometimes also the British) as chiefly responsible for introducing coursing to the United States. Many of those who propagate this idea are simply passing on family lore that has long been accepted as truth. Oral traditions that credit Irishmen for importing greyhounds for the purpose of eradicating jackrabbits have obfuscated the more complex truth. In recent years a measure of romanticism has been attached to Irish customs, and it may better serve the imagination and interests of dog-racing aficionados to persist in linking themselves to this heritage. Coursing in the British Isles is still commonly and consciously linked with its aristocratic roots, and this association with the social elite has long been welcomed and emphasized by American greyhound industry leaders.

Although greyhounds were frequently exported from Ireland in later years, it was not likely the Irish who were primarily responsible for bringing them to the Great Plains.[56] In truth, most Irishmen coming to the United States in the nineteenth century were fleeing abysmal economic conditions and in most cases simply did not have the means to import valuable animals. Most of these immigrants settled in urban areas on the East Coast and were employed as laborers. The far smaller numbers of Irish immigrants who arrived in the western plains often settled in small cities or along the railroad lines. Some of these men became small-wage earners on railroads and roadways; for example, the Union Pacific Railway principally employed Irish men for its construction labor in the 1860s.[57] One greyhound owner, breeder, and racer, C. N. Lambert, later claimed that the Irish working on the railroads were responsible for bringing over many of the greyhounds, but this assertion cannot be proven.[58] Whatever the case, these early Irish settlers working on railroads could not have been significantly responsible for the large-scale introduction of greyhounds into the American West.

Furthermore, the period in which Irish immigrants supposedly did bring greyhounds to the region in large numbers was probably later than is commonly believed by those in the dog-racing industry. In fact, many of the Irishmen who were integral to the development of American greyhound racing were not deeply involved in it until after World War I. Greyhounds were not likely imported on a more substantial scale until the 1880s and 1890s and in still greater numbers only in the early twentieth century. Very many of those who were involved were not even Irish, as with the example of dogman Ollie Ostendorf. Born in Illinois in 1878, and of German heritage, his family traveled to Gothenburg, Nebraska, in a covered wagon when he was three years old. As a youngster he acquired unregistered greyhounds that competed against neighborhood dogs in coursing matches held on Sunday afternoons and holidays. Later, when he was about sixteen, the parish priest gave Ostendorf a pair of greyhounds imported from Ireland. He eventually entered them in a Watersville, Kansas, coursing meet and continued to race greyhounds for the remainder of his life. For Ostendorf, track racing eventually superseded coursing meets. He followed O. P. Smith as new tracks were opened, first in Tulsa and later in Miami.[59]

The greyhound racing community has also pointed to American farmers as responsible for the introduction of greyhounds in the West, noting that the breed proved useful as a means of eliminating jackrabbits. Critics of dog racing, such as anti-greyhound racing activist and greyhound adoption pioneer Hugh Geoghegan, have wholeheartedly rejected this point of view, arguing that the greyhound industry has "generated a ridiculous and false history to explain coursing in the United States" and in doing so has attempted to "excuse" the use of live rabbits in training racing greyhounds. He notes, correctly, that racing organizations have often claimed that wheat farmers brought greyhounds to the United States to control the overpopulation of jackrabbits. But Geoghegan asserts that it is "absurd, to say the least, to imagine a farmer paying the modern day equivalent of $1,000 to $2,000 for a dog to kill rabbits!"[60] He instead maintains that the first full-blooded greyhounds to come to the United States were show dogs owned by members of the Westminster Kennel Club and American Kennel Club. Although purebred greyhounds were in fact imported by fanciers during the late nineteenth century, many sportsmen tended to disfavor their use, instead preferring greyhounds bred specifically for coursing rather than for the bench. It is more than likely that fanciers were not, in fact, primarily responsible for the importation of greyhounds intended specifically for coursing.

Conflicting accounts persist of who brought greyhounds into the country —and even when this occurred—but there is little doubt about where in the United States coursing readily flourished. The heart of the American greyhound industry has long been Abilene, Kansas, and it is no coincidence that the lifeblood of the sport has long been nurtured in the trans-Mississippi West. Coursing is most easily conducted on the sort of wide, flat, open spaces that abound in the plains states, including the Dakotas, Nebraska, Kansas, and Oklahoma. Homesteaders who moved west traveled with horses and wagons in the years before railroads were in place. It is unlikely that many of these settlers took full-blooded greyhounds along with them on their journey west.[61]

Homesteaders and other adventurers arriving in Kansas encountered a culture that was in many ways raw, violent, and open to pursuits involving risk or gambling.[62] Abilene stood at the terminus of the famous Chisholm Trail, one of the numerous pathways by which Texas cowboys brought their livestock north for slaughter. The Texas cattle trade was especially active from 1867 to 1885. The Chisholm Trail, later called the Abilene Trail, was popular for cattle drives until about 1892. The Ellsworth Trail was used until 1875, and the Western Trail to Dodge City was popular after 1875; Dodge City was probably the longest-lived cattle town, but Abilene, Ellsworth, Caldwell, and Wichita, Kansas, were all important cattle headquarters as well. Stories of the Wild West are often shrouded in myth rather than based on fact, but there is little doubt that cash was plentiful as a result of profits derived from the cattle drives, and gambling was widely popular.[63] The likelihood that greyhounds were used for sport within these adventure-seeking populations is thus high. Sportsman Joseph A. Graham has supported this line of reasoning, arguing in 1904 that greyhounds were "early introduced on the plains by cattlemen who had a taste for sport."[64]

The burgeoning cattle industry attracted wealthy Easterners and other newcomers who were drawn to the lucrative nature of the business. A new ranching aristocracy emerged in the northern plains, and according to one historian, "their idea of pleasure reflected the growing sophistication of the East."[65] In Victoria, Kansas, wealthy Englishmen kept a racetrack for horses and a smaller one for dogs.[66] The ranching boom reached its high point in the 1880s, but for decades before that visitors came to the area seeking pleasure and sport.[67] Two well-known cattlemen involved in the business for years were described in 1887 in a sporting periodical as "ardent" greyhound men and "as fond of a big hunt as anybody well could be."[68]

Purebred greyhounds were always prized, but so-called cold-blooded greyhounds—hounds that resembled full-bloods but had no papers to document their lineage—and various other greyhound mixes with deerhounds, wolfhounds, and related breeds were all valued for their speed and ability to hunt. Historian John E. Baur notes that it was as a "working companion of the hunter . . . that the pioneer dog was of greatest value a century or more ago in the trans-Mississippi West."[69] But another scholar, Eugene D. Fleharty, found that purebred greyhounds (used for hunting deer, antelope, rabbit, raccoon, coyote, and wildcat) were in fact the "breed of choice" for many settlers arriving in the Great Plains during the 1870s.[70] Fleharty does not indicate how these expensive dogs were acquired, but he remarks that they often died of heat exhaustion after the chase. Both cattlemen and other denizens of the Old West hunted with greyhounds, but the region also attracted another breed of sports enthusiast: wealthy Europeans and Americans—many of whom were military officers—seeking diversion or adventure. These men often traveled long distances with their sporting dogs in order to hunt antelope, buffalo, wolves, coyotes, rabbits, and other animals.

Indeed, a significant number of military officers stationed in the American West after the Civil War owned and used greyhounds for hunting expeditions. General George Armstrong Custer, who actively cultivated an image of the gentleman-sportsman, was well known as a lover of hunting dogs. While stationed in remote forts, he liked to surround himself with a tight community of admirers; historians have likened his entourage to a "royal family."[71] Custer recorded some harrowing hunting adventures with his "fine English greyhounds," one of which resulted in the death of his horse and a perilously close call with an angry buffalo.[72] Custer's wife Elizabeth groused about her husband's "lordly" greyhound Byron, with whom she had shoving matches in order to secure adequate space to sleep.[73] Still, both the general and his wife were fond of the dogs, many of whom seemed to be treated more like family pets than working hunters. Elizabeth Custer notes that her husband often had a "droll fashion" of "putting words into their mouths" as a form of entertainment as they rode along together, greyhounds in tow.[74]

In addition to the prominent example of Custer, many lesser-known army officers on the frontier provided themselves with entertainment through sporting activities involving greyhounds.[75] Those who recounted their adventures hunting with greyhounds included Colonel Philippe Regis de Trobriand at Fort Stevenson, Dakota Territory; General Eugene A. Carr; and Lieutenant Fayette Roe (as well as his wife Frances M. A. Roe) at Fort Lyon, Colorado Territory.[76] One contemporary army surgeon noted that conversations with officers in Kansas often turned to "dogs and their different breeds and training."[77] The *Dodge City Times* reported on a race in 1877 between dogs belonging to Lieutenant Cornelius Gardener of Fort Dodge and those owned by James Kelly, who often paid $50 to $200 for a high-quality greyhound.[78] Although sporting activities were certainly not limited to the officer class, extended hunting trips, often furnished with fine accoutrements and multicourse meals, reinforced the officers' status as "paragons of leisure."[79]

The quarry of choice for hunters with greyhounds included both small and large game; there is occasional mention of using hounds in buffalo hunts, which peaked in the early 1870s. In 1878 Lieutenant Colonel Richard Irving Dodge detailed his hunting adventures in the "great west," observing that groups of greyhounds were ideal for "coursing" antelope, although he had "never yet seen a single greyhound pull down an unwounded antelope."[80] Dodge also commented on the qualities of the American jackrabbit, stating that it was almost identical to the English hare, and remarkably large and swift. He declared that "when the plains have become settled and civilised [sic], and the large game killed off, he [the jackrabbit] will furnish to the sportsman an unfailing source of pleasure, and I doubt not the time will come when coursing this animal will be as common here as coursing the hare in England."[81] One year later sportsman John Mortimer Murphy pointed specifically to the abundance of hares that could potentially afford much sport to army officers.[82]

Individual adventurers documented their experiences in great detail, such as Grantley F. Berkeley, who in 1861 published a book about English sportsmen on the western plains.[83] In 1859 he had left England via Liverpool and landed in New York eager to head west to the prairie. One of his travel mates brought along a greyhound intended for use in coursing hares or deer. In 1879, when Murphy published detailed accounts of his sporting adventures in the far West, he attested that the "greyhound can be employed in coursing hares and antelopes," whereas other breeds were better suited for different prey.[84]

Some of the adventurers employing greyhounds on sporting expeditions were upper class, in several cases led by European aristocrats or American military officers. In 1854 a hunting party led by Sir George Gore, an English baronet, brought along a pack of forty to fifty "magnificent dogs," including greyhounds, on a large buffalo hunt.[85] Another group, organized by Colonel W. C. McCarty, brought together a number of exceptionally wealthy English sportsmen to undertake a hunting expedition. Together with their greyhounds they took along horses, servants, and even musicians. A full brass and string band accompanied the group to provide the men with entertainment when they sought respite from their exertions.[86]

All of these examples point to a more varied use of greyhounds in hunting activities in the American West, one far from the rigid and exclusive rules of English coursing. The western plains continued to serve as a novel hunting ground for sportsmen as coursing variously emerged or grew in popularity in several locales. Such activities involving greyhounds were often similar to or even advertised as coursing events, but they sometimes more closely resembled hunting. For traditionalists a true coursing contest required the presence of a judge who followed a set of rules, preferably rules imported from England.

Organizations such as the Valley Hunt Club in the San Gabriel Valley in California were also devoted to outdoor sports and kept a kennel of foxhounds and greyhounds. Unlike the group outings in the Great Plains described above, some clubs elsewhere provided women with an active role in the hunt. Membership in the Valley Hunt Club included "some of the finest men and women cross-country riders in California" and attracted distinguished visitors as well.[87] Hunting in Southern California was described in detail in the 1892 issue of *The Californian*. Adventures of the day were recounted in glowing terms, as the riders, both men and women, departed with greyhounds to hunt jackrabbits. Hares were considered to be pests in California vineyards as well as on farms, so hunting was encouraged. The riding was described as "fast and furious," and the gentleman who was first able to seize the overtaken rabbit would cut its ears off and present them to the first lady who was "in at the death."[88] Later, the group would picnic together with the recipient female riders donning the rabbit ears in their riding hats as trophies of the hunt.[89]

The rabbit at the heart of the chase was rarely destined to become a decorative addition to a hat, but coursing contests usually did result in the death of the quarry. Even though the object of coursing was not to kill the jackrabbit, this was the frequent outcome of the competition. Early objections to coursing remained focused on the fate of the animal being chased, typically the hare, rather than on the greyhounds in pursuit. Greyhounds obviously loved to run, and their use in this sport was not yet criticized.[90] Coursers were confident that this emerging American pastime was healthy, enjoyable, and, not insignificantly, associated with an ancient aristocratic tradition. But early reformers, beginning with humane societies such as the ASPCA, were already questioning the practice of sending hares out to be chased, usually to the death, for sport.

Compassion for jackrabbits was far from widespread. Farmers had long believed the animal, which was abundant throughout the West, to be a pest.[91] Damages inflicted by jackrabbits were widely documented and labeled as a curse to western American farmers.[92] The infestation of jackrabbits on farms was severe enough to attract the attention of the federal government as early as the 1890s. The U.S. Department of Agriculture (USDA), established in the late nineteenth century to promote more effective management of agricultural lands in the expanding American West, soon began to disseminate science-based information on agricultural practices. From 1897 to 1912 the USDA office responsible for pest control was the Bureau of Biological Survey. Shortly before, in 1896, the assistant chief of the Division of Ornithology and Mammalogy at the USDA, T. S. Palmer, published a lengthy bulletin addressing the scourge of jackrabbits in the arid regions of the West. He had undertaken to study the animal in order to devise strategies to manage the problems they caused farmers. Palmer detailed how they could be combated and suggested several methods of control, including hunting with firearms, organized rabbit drives, the establishment of a bounty system, poisoning, and fencing.[93]

Rabbit hunts could even become popular social activities. A hunt in Garden City, Kansas, in 1894, was commemorated with a wide-angle photograph of a community group assembled at the northeast corner of Chestnut and Main Streets, across from the Warren Hotel. Men and boys stand in front of (and on top of) a harness shop and restaurant, brandishing rifles and surrounded by hundreds of dead hares.[94] With so many of this kind of early photograph having survived, their very purpose was likely to celebrate and memorialize the fruits of the kill. Typically, rows of dead animals—usually hares, but sometimes coyotes or other predators that threatened farms or livestock—are prominently displayed.

In addition to hunts, rabbit drives (conducted without firearms) were an extremely popular means of eliminating jackrabbits.[95] When a farming community organized a rabbit drive, it frequently turned into a festive social event. In 1892 the town of Traver, California, celebrated its "birthday" with a rabbit drive and barbecue.[96] Palmer detailed the standard course of the event: "A drive always means a gala day, and is a favorite way of celebrating some special occasion."[97] Individuals traveled from surrounding towns, sometimes attracted by special rates offered by the railroads. Once a large enough crowd was assembled, the participants, armed with sticks or clubs, drove the rabbits into a central corral, where they were beaten to death. Drives took place in the winter or spring and could result in the destruction of ten or even twenty thousand hares in one day. Men and boys were usually the only community members involved in the slaughter, although occasional references describe women and children taking part in the killing, such as at a San Joaquin Valley drive when schools were even closed for the occasion.[98]

Numerous photographs of rabbit drives have survived, including some from the late nineteenth century. These images can be chilling to the modern eye, which, as a result of many decades of aggressive campaigning against animal cruelty by the humane movement, is frequently more sensitized to the suffering of animals.[99] Some photographs capture men and boys in the midst of bludgeoning hares, their sticks silhouetted against the sky. Others present close-up views of the kill but still show large crowds in the distance. While in most cases contemporaries who describe rabbit drives sound confident of their utility and worth, there is occasionally an undertone of discomfort about their unrestrained violence and abundant bloodletting. In his official 1896 USDA publication, Palmer admits that the "decline of rabbit driving is hardly to be deplored" and that it "may be questioned whether such frequent scenes of butchery can have anything but an injurious effect on a community."[100]

A Chicago reporter, one perhaps unaccustomed to rural customs, observed a rabbit drive in California in 1893. He described the corral where both men and boys bludgeoned the rabbits to death as an "indescribably pitiful and distressing" scene. The reporter wrote that to "slash and beat the poor screaming animals to death is the work of but a short time, but it

"A Jackrabbit Drive in California," Charles C. Pierce, photographer, 1892. These events took place well into the 1930s and would have been in recent memory of some of the older dogmen who maintained that rabbits were pests. (Library of Congress)

brings tears to many an eye, and makes the heart sore to witness the finish." The writer breathed a sign a relief when the massacre ended, calculating that by the end of the day, around 20,000 rabbits had been killed.[101]

While Palmer acknowledges that jackrabbits are useful for the sport of coursing, he did not endorse coursing as an effective means of jackrabbit extermination. He, too, identifies the early 1860s as the sport's beginning in California, noting that organized clubs came a bit later.[102] The National Coursing Association (NCA), founded in 1888 and headquartered in Hutchinson, Kansas, used 320 acres for coursing and imported jackrabbits from California, New Mexico, and Wyoming.[103] The NCA's purpose was to develop this "national" sport throughout the United States, with the plan to breed rabbits on their native soil and then ship them to coursing events. Such meetings could thus also be held "at the very doors" of all of the large cities, where "people can enjoy the chase as well at home as they can on the Western plains."[104]

In his discussion of coursing Palmer introduces an intriguing point; he asserts that the "demand for rabbits for this sport seems to have been largely instrumental in bringing about the [nonlethal] rabbit drives in California, and as many as a thousand or more have been obtained in one of the large drives."[105] He notes that most of the rabbits used for coursing in California were caught in the San Joaquin Valley. As early as 1888 or 1889 they were shipped to various coursing events throughout the West. These events could require as many as 50 to 100 rabbits, with their price ranging from $5.50 to $9.00 per dozen.[106]

In fact, contrary to claims that coursing was employed as a means of ridding the West of jackrabbits, the sport was often supported by an interstate market for live jackrabbits. Even at this early date the demand for jackrabbits in coursing competitions artificially affected their value: they may have been virtually ubiquitous and were widely considered a nuisance, but coursers were still willing to pay hefty prices for hares in order to enjoy their sport. From 1894 to 1895, western suppliers furnished 200 to 300 jackrabbits to the St. Louis Coursing Association.[107] Some jackrabbits shipped to various points in the United States and Canada brought as much as $2 apiece at the time. Coursing's long-standing popularity among western farmers and others accustomed to an agricultural lifestyle explains why those who sought to eliminate jackrabbits by any means possible eventually came into conflict with animal advocates who decried their suffering. Dogmen raised in this environment were often perplexed, even angry, when animal protectionists questioned their use of rabbits for sport.[108] For them, jackrabbits were destructive pests, and greyhounds were doing what they were bred to do, regardless of how or where the jackrabbits were obtained.

Owen Patrick Smith's desire to eliminate the use of live rabbits in sporting activities reflects the slow shift that was taking place in American society toward greater acceptance of humane values and the decline of an agrarian mentality that embraced a utilitarian view of animals. To recall an earlier point, the meaning of "humane" as it pertained to coursing and early greyhound racing at this time was usually limited to the treatment of the rabbits rather than the dogs. Animal protection was still in its infancy as an organized movement, even though the ethos of kindness toward animals had emerged in European thought well before the eighteenth century.[109] As the movement started to gain currency in American culture, its leaders and supporters tended to come from urban rather than rural areas.

To that end, coursing continued to draw a rural audience well after the creation of the mechanical lure for organized greyhound racing. This is evidenced by a series of complaints sent to Kansas governor Henry J. Allen in 1921: some individuals—even those living in the West, where rabbits were widely labeled as pests—were condemning coursing and other blood sports as cruel.[110] The nature of the objections varied. In the eyes of one

Five unidentified coursers in Kansas with their winner's trophy and greyhounds
Cherry Flower, Fritzie Fay, and Une Meadows, ca. 1930. (Greyhound Hall of Fame)

contemporary female reformer from Kansas City, alcohol and animal cruelty were linked: "the reason for the deplorable condition in Kansas was
Prohibition—the class of citizens that plainly rule the state being deprived
of liquor must find some other outlet for the vileness in them and have chosen cruelty."[111] In fact, such Progressive-era reformers often combined their
advocacy for animals with their work for the Women's Christian Temperance Union (WCTU) and other reform agencies. Other critics focused primarily on animal suffering. John Ise, a representative of the local humane
society and a professor of economics at the University of Kansas, argued
that a recent coursing meet held by the Lawrence Coursing Club involved
weakened jackrabbits who had little chance for escape. He noted that the
promoters had advertised "wild jacks" but that they had been "cooped up in
boxes for days." He further charged that the event was "cheap, brutal, cow-
ardly amusement, without a single essential of sportsmanship in it." What
Ise objected to was thus not the killing of jackrabbits per se but the excessive
suffering that the coursing meet caused. He did also note, however, that
coursing was "not a gentleman's pastime," and he added, with some trepi-
dation, that Mexicans and "certain other classes" were showing a growing

interest in the sport.[112] In response to these and other objections against coursing, one state attorney concluded, "In the absence of any specific law defining what brutal sports are it seems to be a difficult question for the Attorney General's office to interpret."[113]

Despite these voices of dissent, coursing competitions were still held well into the 1970s, albeit for limited audiences. For this small rural community of fans, unperturbed by the killing of rabbits, coursing continued to be an enjoyable sport in and of itself.[114] Even though it had gradually declined in popularity, coursing still often served as a proving ground for track greyhounds. In fact, for many years the two enjoyed a "symbiotic" relationship.[115] If and when coursing did attract publicity, the sport, along with its greyhound athletes, was increasingly likely to be characterized as an objectionable rural custom that was cruel to rabbits. Coursing's visibility in the United States continued to diminish, and its erstwhile connection with the upper class had faded. Much to its detriment, the sport was linked primarily with an unsophisticated, rural crowd, and by the mid–1920s coursing had essentially been superseded by greyhound racing, a spectacle considerably more palatable to the modern eye.

CHAPTER TWO

BOOM OR BUST

The greyhound people are the ones who really had it tough in the old days, with tracks opening and closing sometimes overnight. They were like gypsies.
Murray Kemp, "Sixty Minutes, Murray Kemp," Multnomah Kennel Club founder and longtime president & AGTOA president, 1966–1968

The 1920s were the golden age of sports in the United States. Fans across the country worshipped their sports heroes, spending hours glued to their radios, waiting for Babe Ruth's next home run or Jack Dempsey's next knockout. Even a racehorse, Man o'War, became a celebrity in his own right. Sports broadcasting on the radio attracted millions of followers, but, as the decade progressed, more and more Americans yearned to experience the action and excitement in person. Larger incomes, increased leisure time, and loosening strictures against play allowed Americans to do just that. Economist Stuart Chase was prompted to declare that around one-quarter of the entire national income was now spent on recreation.[1] At the beginning of the decade greyhound racing was poised to capture its share of the nation's attention, but a major obstacle remained: how to transform a rural amusement into an urban phenomenon with a potential for profit. One man, Owen Patrick Smith, had the vision to put it all together. Fueled by his determination to promote the commercialized use of his mechanical lure, Smith laid the foundation for the new sport of greyhound racing in Emeryville, California, in 1919. Emeryville, located between Berkeley and Oakland, was a railroad hub and an industrial town populated by blue-collar workers, many of whom were single men passing in and out of the area.

California—as well as Emeryville—had long welcomed gamblers. Men of chance had been arriving in California in droves since the gold rush of 1849. The frontier culture of the far West was the "modern fountain of new gambling practices," according to John M. Findlay, and attracted those who were willing to take risks and seek change.[2] Californians were also likely to embrace new forms of gambling and other novelties that appeared to promise the rapid acquisition of wealth. The Bay Area had become a gambling hub in the mid-nineteenth century despite periodic attempts at reform. At the turn of the twentieth century one former gambler in San Francisco declared that locals would "bet on anything, from a dogfight in the street, to a presidential election."[3]

Emeryville itself was founded in 1896 to secure the profits of the California Jockey Club horse racetrack. Local tolerance for gambling dated back to the establishment of the Oakland Trotting Park in the early 1870s. Saloons, card clubs, and Chinese lotteries flourished as well as horse racing and boxing matches. Various forms of gambling continued well into the twentieth century even though California's 1909 Walker-Otis anti-racetrack gambling law temporarily quashed betting on the horses.[4] Prohibition simply encouraged more crime: speakeasies, houses of prostitution, and offtrack betting joints all found a comfortable niche in Emeryville. In spite of all legislative reform efforts, Emeryville had the reputation of being a "city of vice" by the 1920s.[5]

In addition to its notoriety as a gambling hub, Emeryville is often credited as the first to feature a public greyhound race with the newly designed electric lure. The creation and successful use of the mechanical lure was a breakthrough in the history of greyhound racing, although the "electric rabbit" was in truth developed only after a lengthy process of trial and error. Smith had been working on the device for more than a decade, most notably during experimental runs in Salt Lake City, Utah (1907), and Tucson, Arizona (1910), but California also looked like a promising venue in which to showcase his invention.[6]

Coursing had already been immensely popular in pockets of the state at the turn of the nineteenth century, and its devotees still sought to continue their sporting adventures despite periodic restrictions on gambling. Smith was able to parlay this enthusiasm for coursing into a new, larger-scale, and more commercialized theater. Built in 1919 at a cost of $67,000, the new dog-racing facility in Emeryville was christened the Blue Star Amusement Park. Measuring 25 feet wide and 990 feet long, the oval track encompassed the space of a football field. The racing distance around the track was $3/16$ of a mile. Several different types of dog races were held in this new venue, including a hurdle race and a one-quarter-mile championship. Smith's business partner, George Sawyer, had previously operated a boxing arena in Emeryville, but when it closed Sawyer simply relocated the bleachers to the new dog track. Races were scheduled for the weekends; daily attendance ranged from 200 to 300.[7]

Greyhound track in Emeryville, California, known as the Blue Star Amusement Park, 1919. This track is widely accepted as the first dog track in America to open to the public. (Emeryville Historical Society and Oaks Card Club)

Smith served on the board of directors of the Blue Star Amusement Park and Sawyer was appointed president. George W. Heintz, who broke with Smith in 1922 and opened his own tracks, was a Blue Star stockholder. Smith had envisioned using gate receipts for profits, at first resisting the notion that betting would inevitably accompany dog racing. This may seem surprising given Emeryville's reputation as a gambling haven, but those who knew Smith attest that he was a man of integrity. Nonetheless, despite his initial reservations, Smith eventually realized that gambling was necessary in order to pay the bills. He decided to operate under the motto, "Keep the cheap player out, he brings on the reform moves."[8] Efforts to eliminate bookies and legalize pari-mutuel wagering on dog and horse racing in California followed later, but at the time all gambling operations at the tracks were illegal.

Emeryville operated in 1919 and 1920 as well as for a few days the following year, but never again afterward.[9] The reasons for its failure are not entirely clear. Smith's allegedly autocratic leadership style may have been a factor, and his occasional disagreements with his business partners did not help matters. The track did attract a diverse audience, including men wearing everything from "bib overalls to black suits topped off with Derby hats,"[10] as well as a few adventuresome women. But in the end, Emeryville simply did not draw large enough crowds despite its proximity to the larger city of Oakland. The high cost of admission, 99 cents, might also have been a deterrent. Night racing, a key innovation that debuted several years later in Florida, had not yet been introduced.

After Emeryville's closure, Smith and Sawyer rallied their supporters and regrouped in Tulsa, Oklahoma.[11] This track closed temporarily after several

weeks, then another was opened in Chanute, Kansas. East St. Louis, Illinois, followed. This pattern of openings and closings became typical not only for Smith but for anyone who tried to promote the new sport of dog racing. Tracks would run for a day or even a week but would then be raided by the local police. Subsequent attempts to reopen a racing facility frequently succeeded, only to be thwarted by law enforcement because of the illegal presence of gambling. Dog owners might travel from Chicago to St. Louis and then on to Florida to race for a few days, only to move on again. Certain areas did show greater promise, however. By the late 1920s Arch De Geer felt that "St. Louis is the best town on the greyhound circuit, in attendance and in betting. Cincinnati comes next and Miami third."[12] The most impressive statistic of this era was reported by the *Washington Post:* attendance at a derby greyhound race in 1930—around 20,000 spectators—was higher than the number of fans at the baseball games in St. Louis.[13]

Other venues operated on the edge of the law, their existence far more tenuous and their survival far from assured. Oklahoman Jesse Ollie Payne recounted what it was like in the 1920s to run a track "on the fix" and come face to face with the law. After county law enforcement had been bribed, several races might take place at a track, but in many cases a raid still ensued. In Payne's experience, the ticket sellers were arrested rather than the dogmen because it was legal to race dogs but not to gamble. In his "gypsy days" Payne would wander from track to track, sometimes enjoying a three-week stay in a town before encountering trouble; at other times he witnessed the ticket sellers being arrested at least two or three times in one night. He describes one early raid in Charleston, West Virginia: "I was in the paddock with one of the dogs [and] was going out on the track and they raided it. . . . When the shooting started the fellow in the judge's stand had a white suit on and I saw him a'running across the infield and jump the back fence. . . . But so many of the tracks, that's how they usually wound up."[14]

Other dogmen, including Joel Hooper, recount similar scenarios of tracks opening and closing according to the "fix":

[They] would load 12 to 16 dogs in an old homemade trailer pulled by an old dilapidated car, and start out for a track that they were not sure would run. They would have to drive five to 1,500 miles along narrow twisting dirt roads made impassable by rain. There were no legalized tracks, everything was run under a FIX, and if the sheriff, judge and district attorney didn't get his PELONE [pay loan] the track didn't run. Sometimes the track would open, and there wasn't enough GRAVY to go around so the joint would close and the lights would go out. Then they would hear of a track that "might" open a little later, they would pull up stakes and head for that one. If they got there before the track opened each man would do his thing until the track opened. Some would work as a carpenter or helper, some as painters, some at anything that they could get to do. Some of the more affluent ones sent telegrams. Western Union had a stock telegram just for the dog boys. It read, "THE SPOT LOOKS GOOD. SEND FIFTY." Our old friend Bill Hass had an individual one, it read, "DARLING SELL ANOTHER COW."[15]

The peripatetic lifestyle and related challenges these men faced on the road were formidable. At the time many of the racing greyhounds were bred in the plains states, especially Oklahoma, Kansas, and Texas, so the dogmen were constantly on the road, far from home, seeking one available venue after another. The fate of a track, on the other hand, depended on the confluence of several factors: the availability of racing dogs together with their trainers, an audience ready and willing to gamble, and the cooperation of local law enforcement officials.[16] Alternatively, if the police attempted to shut down a track, in many cases all that was needed to counteract their efforts was a friendly judge willing to issue a temporary injunction that allowed racing to continue. But promoters could avoid trouble altogether in communities that embraced gambling. When Smith set up a track in Butte, Montana, his assistant, Murray Kemp, later described the mining town as "wide open," with some bars and gambling houses open around the clock.[17] At the same time, however, many tracks never got off the ground: an attempt to establish a dog track in Chanute, Kansas, failed almost immediately. One dogman quipped that "there weren't enough people around Chanute in those days to support a crap game, much less a racetrack."[18]

By the mid–1920s a core group of pioneer dogmen had accepted Smith's lure, and dog racing seemed to be well positioned for growth. But success was by no means certain. It became increasingly evident that the fundamental draw of the sport was gambling. Betting was still frowned upon by many Americans, and the environment associated with dog tracks often bore the stamp of working-class vice. Promoters and dogmen were thus blazing an uncertain trail as they traveled from state to state and track to track in order to popularize the sport. Greyhound historian Paul C. Hartwell emphasizes just how tenuous the sport's beginnings were, asserting that "if a core of thirty or forty dogmen had folded and gone back to the farm and one or two track operators had given up . . . there would be no such thing as a greyhound racing industry."[19] His father, Paul Hartwell, Sr., worked as a racing secretary and traveled to thirty-seven different race venues between July 1926 and the fall of 1931.[20]

It was clearly a challenge to promote a sport that was not in itself against the law but obviously functioned as an avenue for illegal gambling. Still, newspapers did print advertisements encouraging men and women to attend the races. In many cases dog racing was combined with other forms of entertainment, including live music, dancing, boxing, and even roping and riding contests (in Tulsa). Greyhound owner and trainer Arch De Geer recalled an early promotional effort in Oklahoma, noting that they had "entries for the Tulsa [greyhound] Derby and the Kentucky Derby posted side by side in a drugstore in downtown Tulsa."[21] A 1921 *Kansas City Star* editorial boasted of the Tulsa facility's resemblance to Churchill Downs and other horse tracks, conceding that it was not quite as large but certainly a "gem for its size." The same article described a banner affixed to the front of a local streetcar that advertised dog races.[22] A dog track advertisement printed in the *St. Louis Star* promoted a "Ladies' Night" and pledged to provide direct wire returns from the Jack Dempsey-Jack Sharkey boxing match.[23] Even though many of the early tracks ran illegally, their operations were widely known, and racing results were published in local newspapers. Programs were also readily available at corner stores, a practice that became increasingly common as dog racing gradually achieved greater prominence and stability within American culture.

Greyhound racing's successful expansion thus depended largely on its grassroots appeal. Dog racing's core audience in the 1920s was largely made up of regular working people who helped create the sport's identity "from the bottom up," even as promoters increasingly sought to characterize greyhound racing as the elite "Sport of Queens." Cultural historian Michael Kammen notes that popular culture operated in local and regional communities deeply divided by class. He also suggests that much of American "popular culture" was still regionally based at the time, with a national "mass culture" not yet clearly defined; other scholars, however, have contended that local and regional culture was in fact understood to constitute national identity. To that end, dog racing's local and regional popularity beginning in the 1920s—the "lure of the local"—can be explained and interpreted on broader national terms.[24]

Betting habits varied widely throughout the United States, but gambling had long been a popular activity with the urban working class.[25] Gambling operations at early racetracks were varied and sometimes complex, given the overriding need to hide betting activity from the authorities. A number of strategies were used to conceal the fact that gambling was actually taking place.[26] A 1927 newspaper article refers to the myriad techniques (including "oral betting") employed to circumvent the illegality of pari-mutuel wagering.[27] One method required the bettor to purchase a picture of his favorite greyhound (with the track redeeming those of the winners) instead of receiving a pari-mutuel ticket or receipt. To avoid losses bookies could selectively "run out" of pictures, forcing bettors to buy photographs of dogs that were less likely to win. Another subterfuge involved the purchase of a supposed ownership share of a greyhound. If the dog was successful, bettors would exchange their tickets for "dividends" calculated by the odds.[28] If a bettor naively demanded actual ownership of the dog after the race, he would likely be told to go find the other 200 shareholders and negotiate the sale with them. Few greyhounds were ever actually purchased by these means, in part because the listed price of the greyhound was far beyond its actual value.[29] Critics in the Atlanta area, where a track briefly operated in the late 1920s, referred to the "profit-sharing" plan as the "gaudy façade of a gambling hell."[30] In yet another system, gamblers could buy a particular seat or section at the stadium that represented a specific dog.[31] Such systems were not regulated, of course, so unexpected problems could arise.

Bookmakers at the tracks during the early years were often seen "waving their arms and calling the odds, while those wishing to wager could shop from one bookmaker to another to find the most favorable odds on the greyhound of their choice."[32] These bookmakers, called "bookies," frequented gambling venues and accepted bets from the public with mutually agreed-upon odds. Because this system of betting was entirely unregulated, fraud was rampant. When bookmakers began to target his dog track in Emeryville, Smith apparently orchestrated an arrangement with local law enforcement authorities by which he could continue operations. Hartwell explains that "this established a pattern for racing by one form of political payoff or another that persisted for the following ten or fifteen years."[33]

At some tracks bookmakers conveniently disappeared after the day's racing and wagering. In other cases it was difficult to find enough gamblers to participate. De Geer described the scene at a 1922 race in Hialeah, Florida: "One bookmaker handled all the betting, and if the book didn't win, we didn't get our purses. They'd hold up a race if just one car drove in. Somebody would holler, 'Wait a minute! Here comes a car! He might want to bet!' And they'd wait. There was so little money around in those days they weren't taking a chance missing any of it."[34] Purses eventually became more substantial, but until wagering was legalized and regulated, few if anyone really knew how much money had been exchanged through bookies.[35]

By the mid–1920s more tracks than ever before were in operation, likely somewhere around twenty-five, but exact numbers are difficult to verify.[36] While many racing facilities across the country opened to enthusiastic crowds but foundered soon thereafter, Florida showed early promise as a rich and fertile ground for an expanding customer base. Smith's track in Hialeah, which had opened in early 1922, was one of these charmed venues. Although the track initially ran at a loss, Smith and his associates were determined to make it work. The men, who had only recently arrived from East St. Louis, were forced to find creative solutions to basic operational problems. For instance, during the first year the power used to run the mechanical lure was supplied by a Fordson tractor. The following year, a World War I vintage Curtiss airplane motor was employed.[37]

Attractions besides racing were devised to draw in larger audiences. A grandstand was erected for a live band, with its members attired in white uniforms. Live music was thus introduced as an important complement to the spectacle of greyhound racing. Yet Hialeah's managers knew that they needed to find a way to draw in still larger crowds in order to survive in an environment that also offered horse racing. As a consequence of savvy publicity efforts, dog racing began to attract a few celebrities, such as boxing champion Jack Dempsey in 1924.[38] This effort to draw in nationally recognized athletes and other celebrities proved to be a highly effective means of promoting the sport in Florida as well as in other venues. Many of those attracted to the publicity storm were working-class athlete-heroes—boxers, wrestlers, and baseball players.

Most critically, it was during the early 1920s that night racing with electrical illumination was unveiled at Hialeah. Night racing proved to be an extraordinary boon to the sport, since it allowed working people to attend the

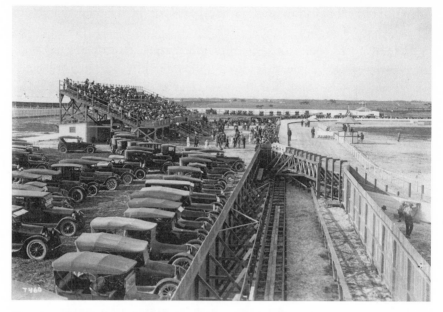

"People at the Greyhound Racing Track," in Hialeah, Florida, photographed by William A. Fishbaugh, 1922. (State Archives of Florida)

dog races after a day on the job. In Florida at least, dog racing at night also precluded direct competition with thoroughbred horse racing, which took place during the day, although some of the spectators at horse races were of a different ilk. Even beyond the realm of greyhound racing, electrical illumination at nighttime entertainment venues allowed Americans more time to devote to pleasurable pursuits.[39]

A distinguishing characteristic of 1920s American cultural life in general was the increased amount of recreational time available to middle-class families. The emerging consumer culture of the 1920s affected the middle class profoundly, contributing to a gradual shift in values, expectations, and recreational habits.[40] The Puritan ethic that had long equated play with sin was loosening its grip in the American consciousness. Both middle- and working-class Americans confronted a wide range of new, commercialized entertainment possibilities as well as the means to enjoy them.[41] Modern conveniences allowed Americans to devote more time to pleasurable activities. A dizzying array of choices was presented to the public in search of fun. Ready audiences were exposed to these options through advertising, which had also achieved greater prominence by the 1920s, a transition that had been in process for decades.[42] This gradual shift from a production- to a consumption-based society proved to be a boon specifically for greyhound racing in its early years.

Enthusiasm for sports was also growing, not only in direct participation but also in spectatorship.[43] Because of the increasing affordability of automobiles—Americans had only recently started to purchase cars in large numbers—families were now able to enjoy vacations as well as weekend recreational outings. Cars allowed Americans to travel to new destinations, giving rise to driving for pleasure, known as motoring. The 1920s were the first decade in which automobiles became a central factor in the everyday lives of average families in the United States. The introduction of credit financing made the acquisition of such expensive possessions more realistic for ordinary Americans.[44] By the end of the 1920s, almost 27 million automobiles were in use.[45] Cars served nicely as a comfortable, safe means of transporting spectators to dog tracks, a development that undoubtedly helped fuel the growth of the sport.

As greyhound racing continued to develop, Smith realized that he needed to establish an umbrella organization in order to oversee the new sport effectively. His desire to control the management of greyhound racing led to the creation of the International Greyhound Racing Association (INGRA), on March 3, 1926, in Miami.[46] Although the organization never in fact operated internationally, his decision to characterize it as such spoke to his ambition to expand the sport. Smith was elected high commissioner by the board of governors and opted to install his headquarters in St. Louis, but his term was brief. He died suddenly of pneumonia on January 15, 1927, leaving a power vacuum in the newly established organization. According to Hartwell, one of the very few to have chronicled INGRA's beginnings, new officials were elected on February 28, 1927, including George Sawyer as secretary and treasurer and P. J. Sullivan as president. But several months later, Sullivan resigned.

The events that followed are difficult to piece together given that virtually all of the organization's records have vanished. As early as July 11, newspaper reports made special note of the fact that Smith's widow, Hannah M. Smith, had assumed the helm and was the only woman overseeing a major sporting operation.[47] Two years later, on March 28, 1929, St. Louis attorney Edward Joseph "Eddie" O'Hare was elected president of INGRA.[48] O'Hare, also the president of the Hawthorne track in Chicago, was rumored to be an associate of Al Capone, a link that threatened to tarnish INGRA's reputation. There is still no doubt today that INGRA leadership struggled to present a clean public image given the considerable strength of underworld influences at gambling venues at the time.[49]

INGRA was created in the absence of any other board or agency authorized to oversee the evolving sport of dog racing. State racing commissions came into play only later, beginning in the 1930s, as pari-mutuel wagering was becoming legal state by state. The National Coursing Association (NCA), by contrast, distanced itself from dog track operations since it was far more concerned with coursing than track racing. The NCA's main purpose, in truth, was to serve as a registry for purebred greyhounds. Apart from a contentious battle with the American Kennel Club (AKC) over greyhound registration protocols in 1935, the NCA showed little interest in shaping the racetrack environment. In a telling comment, dogman Arch De Geer stated in 1932 during an NCA executive committee meeting that "the time is not ripe for the National Coursing Association to have anything to do with the tracks. The Association first, and the tracks come next."[50] He was referring to a dispute between breeders and dog tracks over purses, one of many to erupt in the following decades. His sentiments reflected the ever-widening divide between the management of coursing and the establishment of greyhound racing.[51]

As described in INGRA's 1928 constitution and by-laws, the organization was created to "improve and perpetuate" the emerging sport of greyhound racing and to work toward increasing public interest and confidence in the sport. Its leaders were to promulgate rules to govern racing, resolve disputes, and introduce additional safeguards intended to ensure the integrity of the sport. The INGRA president was charged with considerable responsibilities, which included the "strict supervision over all member tracks, to prevent unauthorized betting or liquor selling upon the grounds . . . and to investigate any rumor charging any Greyhound owner with offering, agreeing, conspiring or attempting to lose any race."[52] The intent behind INGRA's regulations, similar to the rules issued decades later by state racing commissions, was to ensure fair and appropriate behavior at gambling venues rather than to protect the welfare of the dogs.

INGRA also registered greyhounds and issued training licenses. In 1926, 3,837 greyhounds were registered, and in 1927, 247 trainers received licenses. A trainer's license required a $1 application fee, a listing of the applicant's three previous employers, and two endorsements from "reputable persons."[53] The applicant certified that he was over eighteen years old; he was also asked to list the name of the kennel that he trained for or owned. INGRA leaders thus had reason to expect the industry to blossom and predicted a growing demand for the greyhounds needed for racing—as many as 30,000 in 1928.[54] An additional goal was to improve the quality of racers, consciously terming them "thoroughbred greyhounds."[55] At the time the

THE COURSING NEWS

AUGUST, 1926

THE COURSING NEWS—Published Quarterly, $5.00 a year with Stud Book
Advertising Rates—Full page per issue, $5.00. Half page $3.00. Quarter
page $2.00. Ads running four times go in Stud Book free.

THE RIGHT IDEA. 'COLD BLOODS" ARE WORTHLESS. ONLY REGISTERED
GREYHOUNDS ARE WORTH KEEPING.

"The Right Idea. 'Cold Bloods' Are Worthless. Only Registered Greyhounds Are Worth Keeping." The 1926 cover of the *Coursing News* captured the seismic change that was taking place in the world of greyhound racing on the cusp of legalization. *Coursing News,* cover drawing, August 1926. (Greyhound Hall of Fame) most valuable greyhounds were worth up to $5,000, but pups with racing promise generally sold for several hundred dollars. In order to improve the quality of racers and further the sport in the United States, dogmen such as Otto R. Wohlauf took several trips abroad and imported a great many greyhounds from England. However, an article in the INGRA *Racing Greyhound Stud Book* reported that the very best greyhounds in England could not be bought: the lords and earls refused to part with their finest bloodstock.

Member tracks were required to display the green INGRA banner on the premises and to print the insignia on tickets or programs.[56] In its published review of the 1928 racing season, INGRA boasted of more than 700 nights of "clean sport" and the "very significant fact that no member track of this organization has ever been built on a 'fly by night' basis, that no meeting [dog racing competition] has ever been operated for the sole purpose of making quick profits with no intention of returning the next year."[57]

Although these declarations may have been made in earnest, they belied the reality of dog racing at the time. Hartwell observed that even though INGRA did "much to assure the public that the races were run honestly," such efforts were meant to draw the public's attention away from dishonest practices that were still in evidence, such as commissions taken in betting rooms before races were even run.[58] Although he himself had never been employed at an INGRA track, Hartwell believed that the dogmen themselves were, "to a man, quite critical of the organization."[59] The dogmen, so he reported, believed that INGRA's control over dog racing was often autocratic and self-serving. He pointed to "shadowy objectives" embedded in the organization's rules; specifically, he attests that O'Hare understood, once he became INGRA's president, that control of the dogmen would in itself bring absolute control over the industry.[60] While Smith had exercised his presidential authority most visibly by mandating the use of his own lure at INGRA tracks, O'Hare expressed less concern over which device was in use, intent instead on implementing rules that, according to Hartwell, had they been effective, would have kept all dogmen and all tracks under the "monolithic thumb" of INGRA in perpetuity.

It is clear from Hartwell's statements that the independent and feisty dogmen chafed under active management and restrictive control. Men drawn to greyhound racing in these years were the wandering and adventurous sort; they knew from the outset that the sport demanded frequent travel and humble accommodations. Their strong propensity for personal and professional independence, when coupled with INGRA's assertion of strong, hierarchical control, eventually led to serious difficulties. Additionally, and

ALL MEMBER TRACKS MAY BE IDENTIFIED BY THIS PENNANT
DIRECTLY ABOVE THE JUDGES STAND.

TRADE MARK REGISTERED

CABLE ADDRESS: INGRA

The Trade Mark will also be found on the stationery, tickets and passes of all Member
Tracks of the INTERNATIONAL GREYHOUND RACING ASSOCIATION

International Greyhound Racing Association (INGRA) green banner, ca. 1928.
(Greyhound Hall of Fame)

most critically, dogmen proved to be ineffective organizers who repeatedly failed to work together in order to negotiate better contracts with increasingly powerful track operators.

Yet firsthand accounts of track life in the mid- to late 1920s also reveal a dynamic if also edgy environment seemingly immune to the strictures of INGRA. The management model crafted by the association did succeed in imposing a measure of authority over the track operations, but the lives of dogmen remained unpredictable during these years. Nor, of course, were all facilities overseen by INGRA, and some tracks still proved to have greater staying power than others regardless of their affiliation. Many dogmen were undoubtedly unconcerned about whether racing facilities were accredited by INGRA or not. Dogman F. B. "Happy" Stutz commented that "most all of those [early] tracks were not licensed or supervised by any authority, but were a product of our permissive society which followed World War I."[61]

This pattern did begin to change when states started to legalize racing, but early dogmen themselves frequently commented on the variability of operations at the first tracks and the hard-scrabble lifestyle. Dogman Orville Barber reminisced, "It was a long way from what we have now. There was only an outside rabbit, and the audiences were small. We had a lot of six-dog races. We didn't have enough dogs in those days for eight-dog races."[62] The shortage of greyhounds at one Florida track forced the dogmen to run the same dogs night after night.[63] Miami resident Boyd H. Rhodes later described the days of early dog racing in the 1920s as "hard times." After the manufacturing company where he worked went bankrupt, he spent the next ten or twelve years racing "everywhere there was a track to race."[64] Trainer Merrill Blair reflected on the sport's perilous beginnings, stating that "it's a wonder all the greyhound owners didn't get each other killed in those days. We would do some of the wildest, foolhardiest things. The men in those days knew how to have a good time to the fullest. It's not like that at all anymore."[65] Some of the pioneer dogmen found lucrative earnings on the side through bootlegging, especially in the Miami area.[66]

Quite a few dogmen chose to break ties with INGRA and follow other promoters. The track in Tulsa opened by R. J. Allison, for example, enjoyed some success, even though it closed in 1923. Smith's former partner, Heintz, with whom Smith had split in 1922, also sought to pave his own way. Smith and Heintz's partnership had soured while they were seeking to refine the so-called electric rabbit. One challenge—and point of contention—involved the creation of an effective braking apparatus to stop the device and to place it out of harm's way once the race was over.[67] As things turned out, Smith and Heintz had different solutions, which led to legal battles between the two men. Heintz developed a retractable arm for the rabbit and an escape for the motor to come to a safe stop. He also used an "inside" lure that ran along the inside lane of the track. Smith's apparatus, in contrast, was positioned along the outside lane. The inside lure eventually caught on and is still in use today.

In business on his own, Heintz, a Californian who had ties with the NCA, had attempted to set up a track in Detroit but failed, then he turned to Atlantic City, New Jersey.[68] Two separate efforts in Ohio ensued, as did a track in Huntington, West Virginia, and later in New Orleans, Louisiana, around 1927. Heintz had established the American Electric Rabbit Racing Association, Inc. (AERRA), favoring the inside lure rather than Smith's outside model, and used colored blankets for the hounds rather than collars to differentiate them from one another. He promoted his device in greyhound publications, such as the NCA stud book, and boldly claimed that his version, patented in 1929, was the "only successful lure for greyhound racing."[69]

The disintegration of the partnership between Smith and Heintz led to a schism in dog track management that continued throughout the 1920s.[70] Significantly, some facilities were even built by promoters other than Smith and Heintz. For instance, a group of four men known as the "Big Four" combined forces to open a track in Tampa, Florida. Made up of J. Homer Ellis, Jack Chambers, Dr. A. L. Spindler, and a man from Memphis now known only as "Parton," the four were able to attract a number of kennels that had previously been associated with Smith.[71] Hartwell acknowledges that it took "considerable courage" for the group to part ways with INGRA, given the strong likelihood that their efforts to open the Tampa track and other planned racing facilities would fail. In Hartwell's view, if Smith had succeeded in his efforts to control dog racing, dogmen who raced at non-INGRA tracks would have had a major obstacle to overcome: the threat of permanent banishment from dog racing by its governing association.[72] Because of their own bold move, dogmen who switched allegiance to the Big Four were tagged the "Outlaw Bunch" by Smith and his followers.[73]

Regardless of track ownership or management, obtaining a "booking" at a dog track was initially an informal affair and was often finalized with little more than a handshake. The term derived from the standard practice at early tracks. The facility manager or promoter would ask a greyhound owner if he wanted to race his dogs; if he did, his name was entered into a small book.[74] Tracks booked entire kennels rather than individual racers.[75] The booking system favored established partnerships since the track operators were understandably inclined to prefer a safe choice and generally knew who had already furnished and could still furnish a reliable kennel of dogs. For instance, dogman Charles R. Sterling's kennel was strong enough to instill confidence in racing officials: Sterling kept forty-five of his racing greyhounds in his Clay Center, Kansas, breeding facility and selected seventeen of them to travel to the St. Louis dog track.[76] Dogmen engaged in greyhound racing from the beginning thus enjoyed an inherent advantage, which in turn rendered it difficult for newcomers to gain entrance into the business.

At the same time, track management also tended to retain bookings with dogmen whom they already knew even if the quality of their dogs had deteriorated. For example, even the best kennels could be wiped out after an outbreak of distemper or pneumonia, leading to problems with already arranged bookings. The booking system itself also began to spark tensions as the number of owners and greyhounds grew larger in proportion to the number of available tracks, although in the early years most racing kennels had remained small, at times maintaining as few as four to ten dogs.[77] Promoters also initially arranged for racing kennels to be placed in proximity to the track. Turnout pens—enclosed areas for the dogs to romp around and relieve themselves—did not yet exist. Dogmen were thus obligated to walk the greyhounds, sometimes even three to four times a day. Leading a small group of leashed greyhounds, the dogmen could cover distances up to several miles during the morning or evening workout. This physically

Dogman Forbe Spencer with boy and greyhounds in Taunton, Massachusetts, 1938. (Greyhound Hall of Fame)

Derby Lane Kennels in St. Petersburg, Florida, ca. 1925. (Derby Lane Archives)

intensive aspect of greyhound care was obviously demanding and required diligent attention.[78]

From its beginnings greyhound racing was a seasonal sport that required travel from venue to venue. Florida served as the sport's winter headquarters. When Smith opened the Hialeah track in Miami in 1922, he unknowingly established the lasting pattern of the dogmen's annual winter migration to Florida. Summer bookings could be more difficult to secure; the dogmen were often forced to drive long distances to locate available venues during these months. The term "racing circuit" is still widely used in the greyhound racing industry to describe the traveling and booking patterns of the dogmen. For instance, a dogman's kennel might be awarded one racing contract at Derby Lane in Florida during the winter season and another at Multnomah in Oregon during the summer. Eventually many dogmen would be able to adhere to a regular traveling circuit, but in the early years very little was firmly established.

These men faced significant obstacles in transportation as they traveled from track to track in search of racing opportunities. The roads of the 1920s were a far cry from the superhighways constructed after World War II. Many roads were narrow, muddy, and poorly maintained. Driving on them could be not only uncomfortable but unsafe; driver's examinations were not

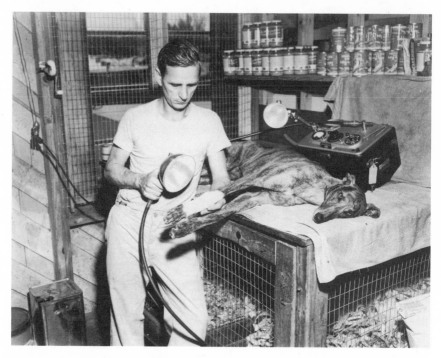

Dogman George Alder caring for his racing greyhound, ca. 1947. (The Wolfsonian-Florida International University, Miami Beach, Florida, Gift of Bliss Van Den Houvel and Linda La Rocque)

widespread until the 1930s.[79] As difficult as it was to travel across the country, it was far more challenging to bring along kennels of greyhounds. There was no established system of hauling dogs from track to track; each dogman had to devise his own way. According to one source, Forbe Spencer pulled the first dog trailer, "a flat trailer with crates on [sic] covered by canvas, from Wichita, Kansas, to St. Louis. Everyone told him he would kill himself and his dogs but he didn't, and now dogs are hauled in trailers all over the country."[80] Trucks, like automobiles, had only lately come into existence, with the small pickup truck an even more recent development.[81] Some men used cut-down cars or flatbed trucks with crates piled on the back. Dogman Jack Lucas created a dog-hauling truck out of a hearse.

Trips that would be considered insignificant today required planning and skill in the 1920s. Maps of rural roads were unreliable, and service stations could be difficult to locate. Even changing a tire was an ordeal: flats had to be fixed by removing the tire from the rim and repairing the inner tube with patching equipment. Dogmen traveling in Florida had to avoid hitting both open-range cattle, known as "Swamp Dogies," and alligators.[82] For the dog-men, completing a trip of 300 to 400 miles was a major achievement, and a 500-mile journey was almost unheard of, a tale to be passed down from generation to generation as family folklore.[83]

Greyhounds were sometimes transported by train. A group of dogmen would often travel together after checking in the hounds as excess baggage.[84] Trainers rode with the dogs, sometimes even on top of the crates. The selection of food for both man and dog was spartan; many dogmen relied on canned salmon. If they ran out of cash, they resorted to sharing meals with the dogs. Commercial dog food was already available at the time, but it does not appear to have been widely used within this community.[85] When times were tough, dogmen could turn to odd jobs during layovers. Many were chronically short on supplies. When Gene Randle first arrived at a track at the age of nineteen, he and his partner were armed with two or three racing muzzles, two leads, some rope, no money, and no transportation.[86] At the other extreme, one 1930 photograph shows two men next to an airplane in Oklahoma holding two greyhounds. The hounds are nattily attired in plaid coats, leading one to presume that they were valuable racers preparing to travel to their next competition.[87] Transport by air was unusual, however, and belies the dogmen's typically more humble means of transportation.[88]

The day-to-day work of the dogmen was usually mundane.[89] The industry was only beginning to take shape and the rules were still being established. The responsibilities of the dogmen were gradually formalized, and their role as animal caretakers became more and more systematized. Duties included feeding the dogs (often a mixture of hamburger meat with some combination of dog biscuit, bread, barley porridge, and vegetables), exercising them, and, once their workouts were over, rubbing them down and checking them for soreness. Of the kennels listed in INGRA's *Racing Greyhound Stud Book,* the vast majority were located in St. Louis, East St. Louis, and New Orleans. A fair number were also in Florida, Kentucky, Oklahoma, Texas, Ohio, and Kansas.[90] Like the coursers before them, many dogmen retained deep ties to the countryside despite their frequent travel from city to city. They were often former or current farmers or ranchers, or persons associated with agriculture in some other capacity. A number were butchers or meatpackers, and most were white males. Quite a few hailed from Ireland or Scotland, whether by ancestry or by immigration. This may be one reason why the birth of American dog racing is so often credited directly to the Irish.

To be sure, some dogmen did not fit the mold. Some were not farmers, having left jobs in the oil industry, construction, or sales to pursue a completely new way of life. Very few were African Americans, with Texan Willie Hiblow one of the notable exceptions. Hiblow coursed greyhounds, a pastime that was usually limited to whites in the 1920s.[91] Some later referred to him as the "Jackie Robinson of greyhound racing," declaring that like his counterpart in baseball, Hiblow broke the color barrier. But Hiblow was a rare exception and had gained access to the coursing community only through his friendship with the owner of a coursing park in Waco, Texas.

A number of dogmen were actually women, but they, too, were exceptions to the rule. Most early photographs of dogmen show large groups of white men with their greyhounds; only occasionally are women present. A large group of greyhound owners photographed at the Emeryville track features two stylishly dressed flappers. Although they are far outnumbered by the men, their presence at the races is significant, especially considering that Emeryville was one of the first dog tracks established. Yet given their attire, it seems unlikely that these women played any significant role in handling animals at the track. Greyhound publications sometimes did include photographs of women who owned greyhounds, but in many other cases women were associated with greyhounds because of their husbands' work in the business. For instance, Mrs. Ray Page of Lincoln, Nebraska, is featured in 1932 in the NCA stud book. She is listed as the owner of a top coursing greyhound, Princess Capitola. Page did in fact work with greyhounds as a consequence of her husband's position: he was president of the NCA in 1932. A few authentic rogue female pioneers did exist, however. "Ma Carroll" won a major coursing classic in 1905 (the National Waterloo Plate) and continued into track racing in the 1920s.[92]

Involvement in dog racing, even at its periphery, might have been one way for women to enjoy new social freedoms. With the exception of a few interviews, no extensive firsthand accounts documenting the role of women in greyhound racing appear to exist.[93] Given the marginal nature of the dogmen's life, many could in all likelihood succeed only by relying upon the support of their families. Wives undoubtedly helped out at the kennels, given the time-consuming and demanding nature of animal husbandry.[94]

Family involvement in greyhound racing is, in fact, a hallmark of the industry. A core group of families has been involved in the business since its beginnings, and it is difficult to imagine greyhound racing without them. Certain family names are instantly recognizable to industry insiders: Alderson, Ewalt, Hartwell, Randle, Sutherland, and Wootten, to name just a few. The story of the Randle family is a classic example. Born in central Kansas in 1889, B. E. "Boyd" Randle fathered five boys, Duane, Ned, Ray, Gene, and Arvin, all of whom became well-known dogmen. As Duane Randle has related, "He [Boyd] raised dogs and it went on from there. When my brother, Gene, got out of school and was old enough, he went to the racetrack. As each one of us boys got old enough, we entered into the business. We were all raised with greyhounds from the very start, since dad raced them before any of us even came to the racetrack."[95]

Another family dynasty in the industry is the Hartwells. Patriarch Paul Hartwell, Sr., began his career in Thornton, Illinois, at the Illinois Kennel Club.[96] He remained in the business until 1942 or 1943. His father-in-law, E. C. "Butch" Sanders, born in 1878, had resided in Texas and Oklahoma and worked as a butcher. Paul C. Hartwell, Jr., believes that his grandfather's association with ranchers put him into contact with greyhounds. Paul Jr. was immersed in the business from his earliest years. He began as a cool-out boy at age eleven at the dog track in Hollywood, Florida, and he worked at sixteen tracks in nine states in the course of his career.[97] His jobs covered the entire spectrum of the business, from mutuel manager to scale clerk, paddock judge, trainer, general manager, and racing secretary.[98]

The model and the reality of family involvement in the greyhound industry have fostered a feeling of friendship and informality among the dogmen, an atmosphere that continued for many years. Although the dogmen of today often lament the loss of camaraderie within the greyhound racing community, the dogmen of the early years were nonetheless competitive and tough. That said, even though they were competing for bookings with each other, they were likely to offer assistance to a downtrodden pal. In 1950, James "Dreamy" Conlen recounted, "In the early days if a dogman ran out of gas and was pushing his car or truck through town, all the other dogmen would come and help him push it to the kennel area. Nowadays, if the same thing happened, they'd watch him pushing the truck by himself, all the while muttering, 'How'd that sonofabitch get booked?'"[99]

The pioneer dogmen, many of whom were related or at least maintained tight bonds of friendship, continued to wander from track to track in search of bookings throughout the 1920s. Despite a banner year in 1928, with about thirty-four tracks in business, the sport was far from secure as a fixture of American cultural life. Moralistic demands for legal reforms were taking their toll on the industry. Moral crusaders continued to argue that the element of gambling in greyhound racing rendered it entirely undesirable. Tracks in Arkansas, Kentucky, Louisiana, Michigan, New York, Texas, and Wisconsin all "succumbed to pressure groups" that effected their closure, although some reopened in subsequent decades.[100] Competitors for the gambling dollar resented the dogmen's presence in the marketplace. To the horse-racing industry they had become an unwelcome distraction. At times it seemed as if the dogmen could find few supporters outside of the industry.

Moreover, greyhound racing increasingly faced opposition from those who not only objected to gambling but also perceived a threat of infiltration by organized crime. Some dog track operators were criticized for associating with dubious characters, often referred to at the time as "hoodlums." The gambling population often did not belong to "respectable" society and was therefore more readily associated with sordid company. And even though the dogmen themselves were usually from rural working-class environments and were rarely involved in promotional efforts, they were generally painted with the same brush. Given this cast of characters, the popular media have often been ready and eager to associate dog racing with organized crime.

Alleged links between greyhound racing and crime syndicates could rarely be proven and prosecuted, but the accusations permanently stained the reputation of the sport. The most frequently cited criminal association was with Chicago mobster Al Capone during the 1920s. After gaining a stranglehold in Chicago, Capone extended his grip to suburban areas, including Cicero, located west of the city. Reform pressures instigated by Chicago mayor William Dever had forced Capone to expand his operations outside of the city proper.[101] Cicero soon became the center of Capone's criminal business undertakings. The Hawthorne track, located in Cicero and managed by future INGRA head Edward Joseph O'Hare, opened in 1927 and was widely believed to be associated with organized crime. Such suspicions were solidified when, on one occasion, Capone walked across the track and changed the outcome of a dog race on the result board while accompanied by his bodyguards.[102] Capone was not the only gangster with his hands supposedly in dog racing. Another Chicago-area track with links to organized crime was the Fairview Kennel Club, located north of Cicero near Maywood. Mobster George "Bugs" Moran was believed to be involved with this facility.[103]

Deeply held concerns about the perils of gambling were sometimes addressed through the cinema. In the popular book and subsequent movie *Dark Hazard* released in the early 1930s, the downfall of the central character, a gambling man named Jim "Buck" Turner, begins in Chicago and unfolds in Barrowville, Ohio, where the protagonist returns to his gambling ways when a dog track opens nearby. After going to the races and even

Greyhound racing trophy presentation. Al Capone may be pictured in the back row smoking a cigar, ca. 1930. (Greyhound Hall of Fame)

buying a greyhound, aptly named Dark Hazard, Jim once again falls into a disreputable lifestyle, ruining any possibility of returning to respectability in Ohio.[104] This story is fundamentally a morality tale about a man forced out of decent midwestern society because of his habit of gambling on the dogs. In reality, dog racing was not uncommon in Ohio beginning in the late 1920s, although it was stamped out by 1940. Toledo, Cleveland, Akron, Canton, Warren, Steubenville, Dayton, Columbus, and Bainbridge, among other Ohio cities and towns, all experimented with the sport. The reputation of Ohio's greyhound tracks was mixed. The Grove City track was reportedly financed by Al Capone.[105] Dogman Thomas Karsten described early dog racing in Steubenville as "wide open." He recalled that "you had everything right there, after the track closed you could go to the clubs and shoot craps, roulette, and if that wasn't your thing, you could go to the nearest street corner for anything else."[106]

Objections to gambling ran deep in American culture. Historian David G. Schwartz notes that there have been specific periods in American history when antigambling sentiments have either waxed or waned. At the height of Progressive reform, gambling was widely criminalized. Even when gambling started to regain a degree of respectability after World War I, some moralists continued to campaign against it. States did begin to consider regulated pari-mutuel wagering as an acceptable source of revenue as early as the 1920s. This shift accelerated in the following decades when more and more state governments began to embrace legalized gambling for its potential as a generous source of state income for use in relieving economic hardships.[107]

Nonetheless, newspaper coverage throughout the early and mid-twentieth century frequently focused on local community complaints about dog tracks as harmful: they supposedly took money from the poor, fueled crime, caused traffic congestion, and led to work absenteeism.[108] Greyhound racing faced such animosities and prejudices in both urban and rural environments. Gambling in the urban sphere was linked with organized crime, prostitution, bootlegging, excessive drinking, petty crime, and general moral decay, whereas dog racing in its rural form (specifically, the training of racing greyhounds with live quarry) was occasionally criticized for being distasteful and, most obviously, cruel to rabbits and other small animals used as prey. During this period objections centered on the cruelty inflicted on the live quarry rather than the welfare of the dogs.

In fact, complaints about greyhound racing's toxic effects on society often went hand in hand with the claim that the sport was inhumane to animals. The criticisms evolved through the years but chiefly began with concerns over the welfare of the rabbits being chased. Coursing contests usually resulted in the deaths of small quarry, but dog racing with a mechanical lure was supposed to eliminate this problem. During the 1920s and 1930s the primary criticism relating to racing dogs arose from the widespread concern that they were underfed and looked half starved.[109] This belief probably stemmed more often from a lack of knowledge of greyhound anatomy than from accurate perception. Unlike today, the dogs were infrequently seen by the mainstream urban public away from the racetrack. Greyhounds are naturally lean, and even those that are healthy and well fed sometimes appear gaunt and bony, especially alongside other breeds more popular in the United States over the past century, such as German shepherds, cocker spaniels, Boston terriers, beagles, Labrador retrievers, and poodles.[110]

Americans in the 1920s were in fact far more familiar with breeds other than greyhounds, such as German shepherds. As a result of the tremendous popularity of the canine actor Rin Tin Tin, and the blockbuster success *Where the North Begins* (1923) and numerous other films featuring "Rinty"

"Mission Boy," Champion at Greyhound Races, Hialeah, Fla.

Postcard of Mission Boy, ca. 1925. This is a rare example of a champion racing greyhound featured on a postcard. In 1924 he was photographed with boxing great Jack Dempsey at a trophy ceremony after a racing victory in Hialeah, Florida. (Collection of Tim O'Brien)

that followed, the German shepherd became the most popular breed in the United States from 1925 to 1928.[111] Historian Susan Jones observes that during the post-World War I era, canine heroes, including military dogs, were valorized by the American public and became "cultural figures of note."[112] The original Rin Tin Tin was allegedly taken from the ruins of a bombed-out dog kennel in France during the Great War. Canine fame and glory was not limited to dogs that could charm audiences on the silver screen. Balto and Togo, Alaskan sled dogs, captured the nation's attention when they delivered lifesaving medicine to Nome, Alaska, during the dead of winter.

These well-known canines helped launch a film genre known affectionately as "flea features," but even as Americans became more inclined to acquire a dog—and valorize heroic ones—greyhounds were not a part of this cultural shift. A growing consumer apparatus accompanied the rise of pet keeping, but when greyhounds were admired, Americans were far more likely to express their enthusiasm for the breed by gambling on them. A few remarkably successful racing greyhounds achieved some name recognition, such as Mission Boy, but his popularity never reached the fame accorded to Rin Tin Tin or, for that matter, the celebrity dogs that followed, such as Asta, Toto, and Lassie.

Still, greyhound racing made tremendous strides toward acceptability in the 1920s. The image of the sleek racing greyhound would gradually become more and more recognizable to the American public. After a brief period of resistance (launched by antigambling moralists) to all forms of gambling in Florida in 1927, the sport began to receive its greatest welcome in that state. The Sunshine State soon proved to be the ideal environment for racing; its balmy climate was only one of its many appeals. A growing tourist market was increasingly drawn to the state, a dynamic vacation spot where Americans could dabble in a wide array of sporting and leisure activities. Here, greyhound racing would find its niche. Owen Patrick Smith did not live long enough to see the sport flourish, although his goal of eliminating the cruelty of the chase had largely been accomplished. Given coursing's long history, this was no small victory for all involved.

The sport's warm welcome in Florida, however, was not echoed in horse-friendly states such as Kentucky and New York. A new challenge awaited the sport of greyhound racing: thoroughbred horse racing. Purists who accepted only horse racing as legitimate were decidedly unenthusiastic about the prospect of unwanted canine competition. The chasm between the two sports continued to grow deeper as dog racing sought to acquire new strongholds. Horse racing periodicals such as the *Daily Racing Form* and *The Blood-Horse* rather nervously tracked greyhound promoters' legalization efforts as they were taking place at high levels of state government across the country. Horse writers tended to describe the canine competition on the oval as "not a sport, but a mechanical gambling device," all the while betraying a certain degree of anxiety.[113] Florida's rich tourist market continued to expand at a healthy rate and was amenable to the growth of both sports, but this arrangement was atypical. In states where horse racing was already well established, powerful state leaders were often adamantly opposed to the presence of dog racing. In other locations, promoters of the two sports simply sought to gain an advantage over one another in order to expand their own markets. One of the most startling political encounters—the legal battle that took place in the heart of bluegrass country—began, not surprisingly, when O. P. Smith opened a dog track in Erlanger, Kentucky, in 1925. There the story of dog racing's struggle for legitimacy had evolved into a direct competition between horses and hounds.

CHAPTER THREE

HORSES, HOUNDS, AND HUSTLERS

The racing dog is to the Thoroughbred about what the flea is to the dog, and horsemen's interest in dog racing is based completely on what chance it has of injuring horse racing.
The Blood-Horse, April 1, 1939

Greyhound racing has been maligned and abused by uninformed "crackpots" for years, yet none of them can truthfully accuse the sport of being crooked.
Dogman F. B. "Happy" Stutz, *Greyhound Racing Record*

In a political and legal battle reminiscent of David and Goliath, greyhound-racing promoters, beginning in the late 1920s, dared to challenge the powerful horse-racing industry in Kentucky by attempting to establish dog racing in that state. Unlike David, they lost, but not without a fight—one that ended unceremoniously with the crack of the gavel in the U.S. Supreme Court. In Kentucky—and later, in other key states—greyhound racing was denied a "square deal" in the political, legislative, and judicial realms. In American popular culture, greyhound racing was understood, then and now, not as the sport of elites but as a working- and middle-class spectator sport inextricably linked with gambling. In contrast, horse racing was privileged both in the houses of government and in the courts. Its gambling component was portrayed—somewhat disingenuously—to be of minor importance. Rather than a mere game of chance, the "Sport of Kings" was understood as a noble and refined sport, one that could almost be characterized as a divine romance between man and flying beast.[1] Regardless of these differences, however, greyhound racing was forced to compete with thoroughbred horse racing from the beginning, largely because both sports shared the pari-mutuel market. Within this social and economic framework, dog racing found itself to be the poorer cousin. More than eighty years later, little had changed: one dog track executive complained that the relationship between horse- and dog-racing leaders was similar to the dynamic once seen between aristocrats and peons. He admitted, with some frustration, that he "felt like he was at the leper table" when attempting to mingle with the horsemen at professional conferences.[2]

Still, failure in Kentucky in 1927 did not preclude proponents of dog racing from attempting to establish legal operations in other states equally sympathetic to horse racing and suspicious of the "half-starved" greyhounds.[3] For some skeptics dog racing was somehow unnatural, like "horse racing gone mad," with frenzied greyhounds turning on one another in their quest for the elusive rabbit, the "grotesque shadows of their doubled-up bodies . . . like some macabre drawing by Doré."[4] Horsemen repeatedly claimed that there was no "sport" in greyhound racing, that it was little more than a numbers game. They argued that dog racing lacked the foundation of animal breeding that distinguished thoroughbred racing from imitators of the sport. The feeling was perpetuated by members of The Jockey Club, the thoroughbred horse-racing authority established in 1894 by wealthy sportsmen such as August Belmont, Jr., and William Collins Whitney, and trickled all the way down to the horses' groomsmen.[5] Greyhound historian Paul Hartwell notes that "even if a horse trainer had holes in his pants, he still considered himself the elite and dog people were the poor relations."[6]

At stake were money and power. Typically, more money was gambled at horse tracks than dog tracks, yet greyhound racing began to show signs that it might consistently draw in larger crowds than its rival. The sport's overwhelming success in the late 1920s among the working class (as well as across a broad swath of society, including women) in London and in other industrial cities in England such as Manchester and Liverpool would not have gone unnoticed.[7] The difference between horse- and dog-racing venues centered again and again on the clientele: journalists routinely referred to dog racing as "the sport of the common man."[8] In addition to these deeply entrenched cultural assumptions, those in a position of power believed that they could dictate and control who could gamble, and where. Sensing a potential loss of revenue, politicians aligned with horse-racing interests were eager to eliminate the competition and threat to their own power and authority posed by the greyhound tracks. One New York racing commissioner fretted in 1937 that, as "racing rivals, the dog will be the death of the horse."[9] Despite its cherished identity as the "Sport of Kings," horse racing in fact drew in the gambling dollar from all classes of bettors. Some prominent politicians and citizens voiced objections to gambling operations based on moral grounds; others exploited this platform to justify their distaste for dog racing even when their moral reservations did not extend to horse racing.

Even outside of the powerful thoroughbred racing establishment, promoters intent on establishing legalized greyhound racing were forced to navigate a labyrinthine political process. Encountering political favoritism and in some cases the intrusion of organized crime, antigambling and other critics decried the behind-the-scenes deal making necessary to establish legal venues for gambling on the dogs. Track operators accepted it as part of the normal process required to stimulate interest in the sport, even if unsavory business practices took place. Moreover, savvy promoters with political clout could in fact make the critical difference between success or failure in the halls of state government.[10] Massachusetts serves as a case in point: beginning in the 1930s key politicians in the state were aligned with the dog tracks; horse-racing interests had not accrued the power they enjoyed in Kentucky and New York.[11] Pro-dog-racing forces were then able to triumph in the Bay State despite widespread grassroots community opposition.[12]

At the same time, the legalization of gambling in a number of states in the 1930s unquestionably bolstered the institution of greyhound racing: pari-mutuel wagering on dogs was legalized in 1931 in Florida, 1933 in Oregon, 1935 in Massachusetts, and 1939 in Arizona. The horse- and dog-racing industries were rarely partners in such legalization efforts. Hartwell has noted that the horse lobby's support in the early 1930s for legalized betting on both horse and dog racing in Florida was "just about the first and last incidences [sic] of voluntary cooperation between the two industries."[13] Legalization of pari-mutuel wagering allowed for state regulation of the tracks, which in turn translated into tax profits. Other forms of gambling were already being conducted at both horse- and dog-racing facilities—in addition to various illegal offtrack betting parlors—but the shift to legalized gambling offered both racing organizations and state governments the possibility of generous earnings. Pari-mutuel wagering could be tremendously lucrative: one industry analyst later observed that in earlier years securing a license to operate a legalized pari-mutuel facility—especially a dog track—was equivalent to obtaining a "license to print money."[14] Given this reality, the key issue remained: would the pari-mutuel pie go to the horses, or to the dogs, or to both? This was answered state by state, vote by vote.

The story behind the lengthy battle to establish dog racing in the heart of Kentucky horse country sheds light on the politically treacherous path to legalization; no less important, it exposes a class-based bias widely held against dog racing. Above all, the battle shows just how effectively opponents of greyhound racing could block the sport even in a state sympathetic

"Kings of the Turf," postcard, ca. 1909. This image presents horses and greyhounds as equals and was printed about a decade before greyhound racing was established. (Author's Collection)

to another, essentially equivalent form of gambling. The fact that a court case over the legalization of dog racing in Kentucky eventually reached the U.S. Supreme Court speaks to the enormity of the struggle.[15]

The conflict began in Erlanger, Kentucky, located east of Louisville on the Ohio River across from Cincinnati, Ohio. On August 4, 1925, a dog track operated by O. P. Smith and his associates opened in Erlanger in the heart of bluegrass country. Thousands of people attended, causing traffic jams on nearby roads. One reporter described the crowds as "cheerful" and "good-natured"—for the era, an uncharacteristically benign assessment of the dog-racing audience.[16] The same correspondent also commented that it "seemed as though all Cincinnati and a large part of Covington and Newport were there [at the greyhound track]."[17] The track grounds included an entranceway arch with the words "Erlanger Kennel Club," a grandstand that seated 4,000 persons, offices, and a restaurant. Greyhound kennels, all of which were surrounded by fencing, were also maintained at the facility. Racing took place between 8 and 11 p.m., daily except Sunday, and was electrically illuminated. The track itself was a quarter-mile long and included a mechanical lure and starting boxes; the operators followed the standard INGRA rules of dog racing. Patrons were charged an admission fee of 99 cents and could approach the "betting sheds" to buy tickets for each race "bearing numbers corresponding with the number given the dog."[18] Tickets were sold for $2, $5, or $10. After the race, the person with tickets on the winning dog could collect his earnings, minus a commission taken by the Erlanger Kennel Club. Lawyers for the racetrack later denied, however, that purses or prizes were paid to the owners of the winning dogs.

The jubilation over the new track was short-lived. The initial legal battle began when the Commonwealth of Kentucky sought an injunction in Kenton County Circuit Court restraining the Erlanger Kennel Club and its officers, Owen P. Smith, George Sawyer, and Martin J. Hyland, from operating greyhound races and selling pools.[19] The greyhound racing proponents in turn sought an injunction restraining the state from interfering with their business, a dog track, which they claimed was perfectly legal.[20] The two cases were adjudicated at the same time; the trial judge ruled in favor of the state, denying the dog track's request for an injunction. This counterstrategy of filing their own injunction had often succeeded previously, at least temporarily, in restoring greyhound racing at tracks in other states, but it did not work in the circuit court of horse-friendly Kentucky.[21]

The battle continued unabated, however. The Commonwealth of Kentucky filed a civil suit in the Kenton County Circuit Court on December 1, 1925, arguing that the state law granting an exemption for gambling at horse-racing events did not include dogs. The crux of the state's argument held that according to sections 1960 and 1961 of Kentucky Revised Statutes, the sales of French pools (pari-mutuel wagering) were unlawful. Section 1961, which had been passed in 1893, exempted from the penalties of gambling laws those "persons who sell combination or French pools on any *regular race track* [emphasis added] during the races thereon." Additionally, the "pool room" act of 1908 dictated that horse racing and any other contest between man and beast was forbidden unless conducted during "regular race meetings" or "enclosures" supervised by the State Racing Commission. Attorneys for the state argued that there had been no intention to include dog racing when the horse-racing exemption was codified. Lawyers for the Erlanger Kennel Club objected. They argued that any construction of the law that claimed that the gaming statutes apply to dog racing but not to horse racing was "contrary to the Constitution of Kentucky and of the United States." Attorneys for the Erlanger Kennel Club may have known from the beginning that they were fighting an uphill battle, although early on they did manage to have stricken from the record the state's prejudicial language about the crowds that attended the dog races, described as "large numbers of sporting men, disorderly, idle and evil disposed people."[22]

Despite their efforts, they were unable to convince the trial judge that dog tracks were "regular race tracks" or "regular race meetings" within the meaning of the law. Attorneys for the greyhound industry believed that when section 1961 exempted "regular race tracks," it was referring to the track itself and not to a species of animal. Because the dog track would then be legal under this construction of the law, gambling could take place. But the judge ruled that because dogs were not specifically exempted from the 1908 Pool Room Act, gambling at the Erlanger Fair Grounds was illegal. The court of appeals in Kentucky later unanimously affirmed the judgment of the lower court.[23] In his ruling the appellate judge made a number of oblique references to the "moral depression" that dog racing would encourage and declared that to rule in the Erlanger Kennel Club's favor would "also throw open wide the door for the collection of assemblies and bodies of people to engage in gambling and which experience has taught always results in more or less disorderliness."[24]

Undaunted, Smith and his Erlanger Kennel Club associates (many of whom were leaders in INGRA) relentlessly pursued their goal to establish Kentucky as a center for dog racing. The case thus ended up before the U.S. Supreme Court. The oral arguments were not recorded or even transcribed at this early date, but the briefs that were filed still exist.[25] Augustus Owsley Stanley, a former U.S. senator from Kentucky, argued the case for the dog-racing industry. In a lengthy brief he maintained that when the words "regular race track" were used, dog racing was within the spirit of the law, arguing that "race" and "track" were generic terms used to describe any contest of speed. He claimed that the dog-racing industry had been deprived of its use of property and had consequently suffered great pecuniary loss.[26] His primary argument, however, was that the law as construed by the appellate court in Kentucky served to "monopolize and confine the enormously rich rewards . . . to certain especially favored corporations engaged in a particular industry (horse racing)."[27] He charged that this constituted blatant discrimination and was, moreover, legally indefensible, in that it denied dog racing equal protection under the law.

The state countered, arguing that a "reasonable classification" did not violate the Fourteenth Amendment. Attorneys for the state submitted that horses and dogs had only superficial similarities and were thus not subject to identical legislative control. Although both creatures were animals, they had been categorized differently in previous Supreme Court rulings. Whereas horses were like "cattle, sheep, and other domesticated animals," dogs were in a category with "cats, monkeys, parrots, singing birds, and similar animals kept for pleasure, curiosity, or caprice." Most important, previous case law had established that dogs had no "intrinsic value" and were not useful as beasts of burden, for draft (with limited exceptions), or for food. Because horses and dogs belonged to two fundamentally different categories of animals and only exhibited an "artificial similarity," a legislative classification "including the one and excluding the other" was "entirely reasonable." Dogs themselves were even difficult to classify because they were "peculiar in the fact that they differ among themselves more widely than any other class of animals." While some were esteemed for their good qualities and companionship, others were little better than a "public nuisance." All canines were also "more or less subject to attacks of hydrophobic madness [rabies]."[28] Attorneys then pointed out another crucial difference between horse racing and dog racing: the former was only legal between sunrise and sunset, but the latter was regularly conducted at night. This, too, they argued, was an important distinction and a proper basis for legislative classification.

The Supreme Court heard the oral arguments but did not reverse the decision of the appellate court. As a result of this action the Kentucky dog-racing industry was dealt a fatal blow: on December 14, 1927, gambling on greyhound racing was eliminated altogether as a legal enterprise in the Bluegrass State. According to a journalist present during the hearing, one judge asked why gambling was allowed for horse racing yet prohibited for other types of racing. Justice Oliver Wendell Holmes responded that it might be to promote the industry of breeding thoroughbred horses. Attorneys for the state again pointed out that dogs belonged to a different classification than horses, a comment the reporter declared "must have been an irritating statement to dog-lovers who read it."[29] Regardless of how dog lovers and greyhound-racing advocates responded to this line of reasoning, the case established a precedent by which each state would have to legalize dog racing separately. By ruling in this fashion the U.S. Supreme Court ended up helping states promote horse racing without the threat of competition from greyhound racing.[30] A *New York Times* reporter declared more broadly that because of this ruling, "any state can permit wagering in one sport and deny it to another."[31]

Greyhound-racing advocates had known from the beginning that they were fighting thoroughbred horse-racing interests. A *New York Times* article published on December 9, 1927, immediately after the court had heard the arguments in the above dispute between dog track operators and Kentucky state officials, noted that the attorney for the pro-dog-racing forces "vigorously attacked" the monopoly of the Kentucky Jockey Club and related associations over racetrack gambling.[32] The sole remaining means of legalizing dog racing in Kentucky would have been through state legislative reform, and despite several attempts this never occurred.[33] Greyhound racing in Kentucky had officially ended. O. P. Smith and INGRA's desire to use Erlanger as a training center and distribution point for dog tracks around the country was essentially quashed.[34]

The horse-racing industry mounted a similar campaign against greyhound racing in New York State beginning in the late 1920s.[35] The issue of class—thinly veiled as a desire to protect public morals—was once again in the forefront of the debate. The *New York Times* reported on the newly opened Dongan Hills track at the old Richmond County fairgrounds on Staten Island beginning in July 1928, with ten races planned for each evening except for Sundays. The article noted that the "ever-spreading sport" had finally reached the Empire State, in addition to "all over Europe and even in Shanghai, Singapore, and Cairo." Races at Dongan Hills were held at night so "all elements of society" could attend the contests, where spectators could watch the "lean, tense, straining dogs in their futile chase."[36] This time the sponsoring agency was the American Greyhound Racing Association (AGRA), led by Douglas G. Heintz.

Betting at Dongan Hills was conducted through the system of picture selling (or "cards"), which were sold for $2 each.[37] Gambling, technically illegal, was protected at this track by an injunction issued by New York Supreme Court Justice Selah B. Strong in Brooklyn, who restrained police from arresting employees who sold "cards" for money.[38] The police, however, alleged that photographs of racing greyhounds sold at the tracks were actually gambling tickets. In defiance of the injunction, police officers arrested two men from AGRA who were ostensibly only selling photographs of dogs but in reality appeared to be involved in illegal betting. A Richmond County grand jury later upheld the sale of greyhound "picture cards" or "postcards," submitting that it did not constitute gambling.[39] Richmond County Judge Harry J. Tiernan warned against future police intervention, noting that officers would be breaking the law if at subsequent races they attempted another arrest without solid evidence. The question of whether or not gambling was taking place at Dongan Hills took an even more bizarre turn in 1931 when two winning greyhounds, Flirty Meadows and Hood, were subpoenaed to appear in county court; authorities wanted to determine whether the hounds were real or "merely a camouflage" to evade the gambling laws. Without offering further detail the *New York Times* simply noted that the canines "attracted much attention" when arriving at the district attorney's office and "like all other witnesses the dogs waived immunity" before appearing in front of the grand jury.[40]

After tensions abated at Dongan Hills, the battle over legalized gambling on greyhound racing heated up once again in New York during the mid–1930s.[41] Several other tracks were in operation by 1935, including the Batavia Kennel Club, the Buffalo Kennel Club, the Mineola Fair Grounds in Long Island, the Nassau Kennel Company in Albany, and the Orangeburg Kennel Club.[42] At about the same time a number of bills were introduced to legalize greyhound racing in the state, even though the governor, Democrat Herbert H. Lehman, was known to be unsympathetic to dog racing. In 1936 the New York State Racing Commission unanimously came out in opposition to a proposed law to legalize betting on dog racing statewide.[43] The Bronx Democrat who introduced one of the first bills, Senator Julius S. Berg, noted, "Logically there can be no objection to wagering on dog racing if wagering on horse racing is allowed. The Jockey Club is a rich man's organization and seems determined to maintain a monopoly on racing in New York State and to eliminate all competition."[44]

The commission responded by drawing a clear line between dog racing and horse racing, a distinction clearly defined by class. In a published letter the commission claimed that dog racing was "anti-economic and opposed to the best interests of all sports" and also likely to fall victim to fraud. The body argued specifically that night racing coupled with unsavory characters in attendance could pose a danger to the public, and would also take their patronage away from other legitimate businesses such as theaters. In its letter the commission stated bluntly that the "class of patrons" found at dog tracks was "not high."[45] One commissioner, John Sloan, declared that horse racing and dog racing did not mix; he claimed, in fact, that the latter was not a sport at all. He questioned the value of an enterprise that required dogs to be "sufficiently starved to be hungry for the chase" and maintained that the "essential breeding industry—which is the backbone of horse racing, the reason for the existence of the sport, and of inestimable value to the farmers and the military of this nation—is entirely lacking in dog racing."[46] The commission chairman, Herbert Bayard Swope, stated that "dog racing is unsportsmanlike and detrimental to the ancient sport of horse racing."[47] Racing commissioners were joined in their crusade against dog racing by various civic, religious, and social-reform organizations.

The greyhound-racing constituency was sharply critical of what they perceived to be a class-based bias held by horse-racing interests. One judge, commenting on a court case that would allow greyhound races to continue at the Mineola Fair Grounds, agreed with them:

> I think it is no more inimical to society for the good people of Nassau County to bet on dogs than it is for the Vanderbilts and the Belmonts to bet hundreds of thousands of dollars on what a few horses are going to do. . . . I can't understand why it's all right to bet at Belmont . . . and yet after dark it becomes a crime to come to Mineola and help promote the Queens-Nassau Agricultural Society and put $2 on a greyhound.[48]

Other supporters of dog racing asserted that the legalization of dog racing would give poor men unable to attend horse racing a break in the form of their own recreation. A former district attorney of Nassau County, Elvin Edwards, concurred, plainly stating that "only the wealthy can attend horse racing; dog racing is a poor man's sport, and thousands want it legalized."[49] Another defender of greyhound racing charged that horse-racing interests controlled state racing commissions and legislators, a claim that was to be repeated in many other states in the years to follow.[50]

Dog racing as it existed in Nassau County in 1936 was upheld for the time being in a judicial ruling allowing greyhound races to continue at the Mineola Fair Grounds.[51] New York Supreme Court justice Paul Bonynge pointed out that the board of supervisors in Nassau County approved of dog racing, as did various other public officials, organizations, and citizens. With a touch of bitterness he observed that when horse racing had been legalized, the state legislature had "suddenly discovered" the need to improve the "breed of horses." Bonynge noted further, "In a backhand way, this Legislature restored racetrack betting by removing the criminal penalties. But let no one suspect that our best citizens repair to Belmont Park and other near-by tracks for the purpose of betting or gambling. Perish the thought, for their brains rest on higher things. Improving the breed of horses is their aim."[52]

The victory of the pro-dog-racing forces was short-lived, however. In 1937 the governor of New York vetoed a bill that would have legalized greyhound racing statewide and allowed open betting at dog tracks.[53] An article in the *New York Times* published shortly before Governor Lehman issued his veto had contained a number of unsavory details—many of which would have been angrily contested by the dogmen—about the life of racing greyhounds. The reporter declared that the underfed dogs raced because they were "hungry for meat." This claim was followed by an even more disturbing statement: "Because of his diet, and the strain of training, the dog soon loses his usefulness. The telltale signs are meanness and a tendency to fight. Frequently, when dogs are discarded, they die of pain because of contraction of the muscles. The dogs raced have an average life of only about three and a half years."[54] Even though the correspondent was deeply skeptical about the welfare of the greyhounds, this point of view was not driving the debate in New York.[55] His observations regarding the short life span of the racers, including the statement that many greyhounds were so inbred as to be valueless, were in fact unusual for the time.[56]

AS THE DOG RACING BILL IS DEBATED

"Troy's Wooden Horse Had Nothing on Him," or "As the Dog Racing Bill Is Debated," political cartoon drawn by Elmer R. Messner, originally published in the *Rochester Times-Union* and *New York Times*, May 16, 1937. (New York State Library and Rochester Institute of Technology Archive Special Collection)

In contrast, a political cartoon published in the *New York Times* shortly before the above ruling symbolically reflected the anxieties and fears of the public. A "Trojan horse" in the shape of a racing greyhound, which represents legalized dog racing, is being led by a man representing the State Legislature legislators, and is positioned to enter New York and endanger the people with gambling, racketeering, and political machinations.[57] Greyhound racing critics—the most prominent of whom were state racing commissioners—claimed to be acting on behalf of the public good: "certain features of dog racing are not conducive to the betterment of social conditions in this country."[58] Once again, the thinly veiled subtext was class. Commissioner Swope claimed that dog-racing facilities were harmful in that they, unlike horse tracks, "do not require . . . any such qualitative or quantitative analysis of the preliminary financial status of a patron."[59] He and other racing commissioners were berated by Nassau County district attorney Martin W. Littleton, Jr., for "hypocrisy to the core."[60]

Both New Yorkers and others throughout the country were watching this political theater with great interest. Although most of the discourse in New York (at least ostensibly) related to the preservation of public morals, there were also a few references to the standard industry practice of "blooding" the dogs on live rabbits during training. More unusual was an editorial in the *New York Times* that drew attention to the short life span thought to be in store for the greyhounds: "[They] have a life of racing usefulness of only about fifteen months. Then they are chloroformed so that an inherently vicious dog, and one so trained, will not be loosed on the community."[61] A writer for the Boston-based Massachusetts Society for the Prevention of Cruelty to Animals (MSPCA) publication *Our Dumb Animals* jubilantly declared that with this defeated New York bill, the "death knell" had sounded for the "so-called 'sport'" in the Empire State.[62] Despite the efforts of the Nassau County Kennel Club (located at the Mineola Fair Grounds), which took its lawsuit to New York's highest court in order to continue its operations, legalized dog racing in New York was essentially extinguished by 1937.[63] Another lawsuit filed by the Orangeburg Kennel Club against prominent horse-racing interests (as well as the governor and attorney general) was similarly unsuccessful.[64] In contrast, pari-mutuel wagering on thoroughbred horse racing was legalized in New York in 1939.[65]

Much of the East Coast establishment had proved to be hostile to dog racing, but the sport's reception on the West Coast was little better. Greyhound racing had existed sporadically in California since Emeryville had opened in 1919 for a brief period, but gambling on the sport was never legalized in the state. Murray Kemp, best known for his decades-long management of the Multnomah Kennel Club in Portland, Oregon, later recalled that the greyhound industry missed a key opportunity for legalization in California in the early 1930s. At the time horse-racing interests were contriving to have pari-mutuel wagering legalized by referendum. Dog racing was intentionally excluded from their proposal. In a 1983 interview Kemp reflected on the lost opportunity, noting that the horsemen had said it would be preferable if only horses were named in the 1933 racing act, at least initially:

> We foolishly acquiesced to the proposal. We agreed to wait until the next session of the legislature at which time we were promised full support from the horsemen to be included in the pari-mutuel racing act. We fell for it. The clout of the movie people, who were also part of the horse racing act, became anti-greyhound. . . . We were flimflammed. So ended the dream of greyhound racing in California.[66]

Despite this failure, a number of dog tracks in California ran with "relatively little opposition" through 1938.[67] Kemp characterized the Baden Kennel Club and Belmont Kennel Club, both in the vicinity of San Francisco, as quite successful during the 1930s. Greyhound tracks also operated in Los Angeles and Sacramento. But as the decade progressed some Californians began to grapple with the perceived downsides of greyhound racing. Newspaper reports from the late 1930s testify to a strong opposition force that included church groups, veterans' associations, civic leaders, parent and teacher organizations, small businesses, and even the Screen Actors Guild.[68] The greyhound industry believed that the horse-racing industry itself was an equally powerful albeit less visible member of this campaign.

Most objections to dog racing in California were based on the perceived threat to community morals, but some complaints were already centering on animal welfare. The San Francisco Society for the Prevention of Cruelty to Animals (SFSPCA) published articles in the mid–1930s in its journal, *Our Animals,* condemning the use of live rabbits at dog training tracks in Los Angeles and Santa Clara County.[69] While early critics of greyhound racing allied with the humane movement tended to focus on the cruelty of the chase and the fate of the rabbits or other small animals used in training, some Californians raised another type of complaint. These critics expressed discomfort with what they believed to be the unnatural use of greyhounds in sport. They claimed that dogs were not competitive animals but cooperative ones, and should therefore serve only as pets. Critics also expressed reservations about exposing children to racing greyhounds. A Los Angeles editorial written several years after the controversy in California had died down warned that dog racing created vicious dogs. Exposure to the sport was thus a menace to children, who "look upon all dogs as friends and pets and are unable to understand that those beautiful animals have been transformed into brutal beasts."[70]

In 1939 California attorney general Earl Warren, who later became the state's governor and then the fourteenth chief justice of the U.S. Supreme Court, launched a major effort to stop illegal greyhound racing. His aggressive campaign was in all likelihood not fueled by moral opposition to racing or protective sentiments toward animals. Instead, he was focusing his attention on an illegal activity that could easily be eliminated because it was practiced so openly.[71] His supporters, however, were likely motivated by other reasons. Letters poured in to Warren's office praising him for his "fearless moral courage" in shutting down the greyhound tracks.[72] Numerous organizations and businesses supported his decision, including the Young Men's Christian Association (YMCA), the Sacramento Federation of Churches, the Young Democratic Clubs of California, and the Twentieth Century Fox Film Corporation, the last of which likely feared dog-track competition for the entertainment dollar. The State Humane Association of California praised Warren for having "declared war" on the dog tracks in protest against the cruel treatment of animals as well as the loss of family income through gambling.[73]

Warren had targeted the dog track in El Cerrito, which had been in operation since 1932.[74] John J. "Blackjack" Jerome owned the facility, which was one of seven greyhound racing venues in the state at the time, and had been warned by Warren to discontinue his open violation of state criminal laws.[75] The banner headline in the *San Francisco News* on March 14, 1939, announced Warren's crackdown on dog racing, reporting that greyhound tracks had been operating for years in defiance of state law.[76] In later years Warren reminisced that Jerome had had the reputation for being a tough strikebreaker, but Warren did not believe that he was associated with "larger gambling interests," undoubtedly a code phrase for organized crime.[77] Rather than launching a raid on El Cerrito, Warren adopted a more restrained approach. In addition to sending Jerome a warning letter, he spoke with him personally, stating, "You can stop on your own accord and get out without any cost to you or without any trouble of any kind, or it can be done the hard way."[78]

Warren's warning had the desired effect. He never had to have the track (or any other track in the state) raided after the spectators at El Cerrito

"Derby Night" racing program cover, September 1939. (Greyhound Hall of Fame)

Kennel Club were informed that gambling at the greyhound track was illegal and the upcoming Saturday would be the last day for racing.[79] Speaking in the early 1970s, Warren acknowledged that as a result of these events in the 1930s, "we've never had a dog track in California to this day."[80] A subsequent attempt in 1948 to legalize gambling on greyhound racing in California had also failed, but a massive effort would be launched in the 1970s to try once again to legalize the sport.[81] In contrast, pari-mutuel wagering on horse racing had been continuously legal in California since 1933.

Because greyhound racing had faced such strong opposition in the Golden State, efforts to expand and promote the sport had shifted to Arizona, which in 1942 did authorize pari-mutuel gambling on dog racing. Additionally, the city of Portland, Oregon, likely absorbed a measure of the pro-racing sentiment that had captured the hearts of some Californians. A few of the individuals who had supported legalized racing in California in the early 1930s had transferred their efforts to Oregon when they realized that they might meet with greater success there. Murray Kemp, investment broker Pete P. O'Connor, and several other promoters learned that a bill to legalize pari-mutuel wagering on horses was to be introduced in the 1933 Oregon legislative session. O'Connor was able to convince the legislature that dog racing, too, would boost state revenues and provide new opportunities for employment. State senator J. M. McFadden, a horse breeder who operated a sizable stable, championed the successful bill. Although horse racing did not actually commence in Oregon until 1947, greyhounds were able to begin a long tradition of racing in Portland at the Multnomah track on May 23, 1933, only a short time after the bill was passed.

Of all the dog-racing venues on the West Coast, Portland's Multnomah Greyhound Park was the most successful. Its popularity even induced a few members of the Portland management team to pursue expansion into Colorado.[82] All the while, some Oregonians were displeased with the existence of dog racing in their state and charged that outside interests, especially those from California, were profiting from legalized racing to the detriment of Oregon's working people. Richard L. Neuberger, an Oregon state senator and journalist and later a Humane Society of the United States board member, published a scathing article in the September 8, 1951, issue of *The Nation*. In it he implied that the racetracks had employed a nefarious and highly successful scheme that would ensure the continuation of pari-mutuel wagering in the state. Rather than supporting the state's general fund, revenues from racing were to be distributed to the state's thirty-six county fairs and other similar agricultural events, thus ensuring loyal rural support. Whenever the continuation of racing was threatened, gambling supporters would raise the prospect of lost funding for 4-H clubs, livestock exhibitors, rodeo riders, and farming organizations. Neuberger charged that the racetracks had built up an "irresistible phalanx of beneficiaries" that Oregon's politicians were afraid to oppose.[83] The brouhaha came to a head in 1952 when the state's entire electorate was called to the polls to decide whether or not to retain racing. Kemp stated that opposition came mostly from churches and from the movie industry, the latter of which was threatened by the nighttime competition that greyhound racing was posing.[84] Still, the people of Oregon voted approximately nine to five in favor of permitting pari-mutuel wagering to continue. This vote of confidence heralded a long period of success and prosperity at the Portland greyhound track.

In contrast to Kentucky, New York, and California, the horse-racing industry was not a strong political force in Massachusetts. The Bay State legalized pari-mutuel gambling on greyhound racing in 1935, but not before overcoming energetic and widespread opposition from detractors of the sport outside of horse-racing interests.[85] A number of factors tainted the reputation of dog racing as it struggled to emerge in New England, only one of which was the charge that racing greyhounds lived "artificial and repressed" lives contrary to their nature.[86] Francis H. Rowley, the president of the MSPCA, issued this objection in a letter sent to every Boston daily newspaper in 1938. This was already several years after dog racing had been legalized, but shortly before a new referendum allowing the voters to decide whether racing would continue in Massachusetts was presented. None of the newspapers printed his protestations, and the letter was finally published in 1939, only in the MSPCA's *Our Dumb Animals*. In this forum it was probably only read by limited audiences who already subscribed to a demanding code of humane principles regarding animals.[87] With specific reference to dog racing, such viewpoints were not aired widely during the 1930s and were usually overshadowed by other concerns about the emerging sport.

The lion's share of opposition in Massachusetts to legalized pari-mutuel wagering came not from animal protectionists but from moralists who bore an especially strong bias against gambling on dog racing and the criminal activity that they believed would accompany it. A persistent belief that organized crime controlled elements of the sport dominated much of the public discourse on greyhound racing in the state.[88] Religious forces were also speaking out adamantly against legalized pari-mutuel wagering, especially dog racing, although horse-racing interests were also battling the same critics as they tried to secure legalization in Massachusetts.[89] A further component of the drive for legalized dog racing was political, reflecting the economic challenges and class conflicts that characterized the New Deal years. In 1934 Massachusetts, like the rest of the country, was suffering from a severely depressed economy. The textile industry had long been failing, and industrial cities such as Lowell, Lawrence, and Fall River were struggling.[90] New dog tracks were frequently located in working-class towns: the track in Springfield, Massachusetts, for example, specifically targeted Connecticut River Valley mill workers. Some observers believed that greyhound racing promised to become a viable means of economic development. Others, however, were not so sure. One critic indicated that greyhound track operators "ingeniously" tied racing legislation to charity; another called attention to the industry's "cunning propaganda" that led the public to believe that racing was a form of public philanthropy.[91]

Although some of the early canvassing to establish greyhound racing in Massachusetts was carried out by local enthusiasts who went door to door to bolster support, the real battle over legalization took place in the statehouse in the mid–1930s.[92] The allure of a major new state revenue source brought the possibility of pari-mutuel wagering to the forefront despite Governor Joseph Buell Ely's personal objections to dog racing.[93] In office from 1931 to 1935, the year pari-mutuel wagering was legalized in his state, the governor represented the socially traditional and fiscally conservative current in New England society that looked down on racing as "demoralizing" and anathema to proper, healthy government.[94] After he left office Ely pointed his finger in blame at New Dealers for failing to address the economic downturn appropriately. He charged that President Roosevelt and his followers had "tried to annihilate the bankers and the public utilities and are giving us horse racing, dog racing and lotteries. This 'more abundant life' seems to be horse racing." After criticizing the president's inheritance tax proposals and disincentives to save money, he charged that "we can't have a Sunday school picnic and go on handing out the ice cream forever."[95]

Governor Ely's distaste for raising state revenues through gambling operations was not echoed by the majority of Massachusetts voters, or at least not by their elected representatives in the statehouse. Horse track operator Bill Veeck later charged that the legislature had always been under the sway of pro-dog-racing interests, and that especially the track in Revere enjoyed its "long and many-tentacled reach into the halls of power." Greyhound racing benefited initially from the support of what Veeck described as an all-powerful lobbyist, Clarence King, along with the considerable political clout of George Reynolds, the owner of the Revere track.[96] On June 26, 1934, the state senate adopted a measure to provide for a statewide straw ballot to determine the will of the voters on the question of legalizing horse and dog racing.[97] Several days later the legislature passed a pari-mutuel betting bill for both horse and dog racing.[98] An emergency preamble attached to the bill stipulated that it became law at once unless vetoed by Governor Ely.[99] On July 29, 1934, a *New York Times* headline declared a "revival of racing" in New England, since similar proposals had also recently been passed in New Hampshire and Rhode Island.[100]

While racing proponents had reason to be jubilant, a number of newspaper reports revealed cracks in the plan. One article indicated that some Massachusetts citizens were reconsidering their decision to support legalization of dog racing as questions arose about the logistics of establishing tracks and distributing profits.[101] Critics also continued to raise moral objections. Some warned that greyhound racing would prove to be even more toxic to communities than horse racing because people who could not afford to go to the horse races during the day could still manage to gamble at the dog tracks at night. Theater owners were also wary of the added competition and voiced their opposition.[102] A hearing scheduled for early March 1935 in the Massachusetts statehouse, at which church organizations planned to plead for the repeal of the dog-racing law, was expected to draw one of the "largest crowds ever to attend a legislative hearing," according to the *Boston Herald*.[103] In early March 1935 a hundred Boston clergymen voiced their public disapproval of greyhound racing; other churchmen throughout the state spoke out repeatedly against both dog and horse racing.[104] A *New York Times* article pointed out that Massachusetts voters did not fully realize the details of the law rendering greyhound racing legal. A number of cities, such as Cambridge, objected to the development of a local dog track even though a countywide vote had supported the development.[105] City leaders in Quincy, Readville, Methuen, Marshfield, Hanson, and numerous other small Massachusetts municipalities all objected to the introduction of local dog tracks and successfully prevented their establishment.[106] In general, however, Boston residents were not as strongly opposed to pari-mutuel wagering as were some citizens from smaller towns.

State, county, and municipal governments were not the only entities that grappled with controversies accompanying the establishment of greyhound racing. Before some New England townsfolk had even begun their struggle to prevent the introduction of dog racing in their own communities, the president of the Boston Braves baseball team, Emil Fuchs, had declared in late 1934 his ambition to introduce dog racing into Braves Field. Although Fuchs had shown interest previously in a Florida dog track, the driving motive behind this declaration was to obtain a new source of revenue. Since 1934 the baseball club had been undergoing a serious financial crisis. The response from the National League to Fuchs's plan was immediate and clear: the idea of including a dog track at the stadium was "absolutely preposterous" and "entirely at variance with the principles for which baseball has battled so strenuously."[107] The 1919 Chicago Black Sox scandal involving the fixed World Series was also still in recent public memory. It was thus unlikely that his idea would ever assume legitimacy, but it does illustrate the initial jostling for racing licenses (and, by association, for new tracks and revenue opportunities) that took place during the early years of legalization.

Greyhound racing's drive for legitimacy in Massachusetts continued to the end of the decade. Republicans bitter about the 1934 election of Democratic governor James Curley, the flamboyant Irish Catholic politician often compared to Al Smith and Huey Long, pointed to the "emotional recklessness" in Massachusetts that had brought about both "Curleyism" and dog racing.[108] Curley was associated with urban boss politics and the immigrant vote.[109] Critics were once again both ready and able to associate dog racing with the lower class. Robert T. Bushnell, the president of the Republican Club of Massachusetts, linked the running greyhounds with desperate voters:

> In an era of depression and economic chaos . . . it is not unusual for people to be controlled emotionally rather than through common sense; hence, it is not at all surprising that in the year Massachusetts voted for dog racing it also elected Curley. . . . The poor beasts, trained in puppyhood to mangle the bodies of live rabbits and later kept at a point of starvation so that they will dash blindly and hungrily after a fake rabbit, are in precisely the same situation as the voters of Massachusetts in 1934. One goes with the other. It represents a state of mind.[110]

Bushnell and his party believed that these "twin evils"—Curleyism and dog racing—could be eliminated when the voters regained their senses and voted for the Republican ticket, although his hope for returning the Republicans to office was not realized until 1939, when Governor Leverett A. Saltonstall was elected to office.

The Saltonstall administration inherited dog racing at a time when many observers believed that organized crime had already infiltrated the parimutuel industry and, still worse, various branches of the government. In the face of these earlier rumors the Massachusetts State Racing Commission had already issued its first report in 1935, which gave credence to its position that pari-mutuel racing was being conducted free of criminal interference. It listed licenses issued to the Bay State Greyhound Association and the Old Harbor Kennel Club in Revere, the Bristol County Kennel Club in Dighton (Taunton), and the Crescent Kennel Club in West Springfield.[111] Attendance reports were included, which recorded about 4,000 to 6,000 spectators per event. The total pool for all dog-racing meetings was listed at $15,458,072, and the distribution of funds to states and counties was calculated and reported as well. The meticulous accounting reflected in the report flew in the face of accusations that unscrupulous forces were actually pulling the strings. The 1939 Racing Commission report submitted to the newly elected Saltonstall included the confident statement that "it is the unanimous opinion of the Commission that during the year of 1939 racing was conducted on a high plane in this commonwealth" and also attested that it practiced strict supervision over pari-mutuels, but others were not so sure.[112]

For a time the governor received urgent, pleading letters from Leland Bickford, a journalist who worked for the Yankee Network.[113] The problem with greyhound racing in Massachusetts, according to Bickford and other critics, was not any evil inherent in the sport but rather the corruption within its present management. One question was repeatedly raised: who really owned and controlled the tracks?[114] Bickford was convinced that organized crime had polluted greyhound racing in Massachusetts, and he was adamant that the governor should take action. Bickford's charges ranged from rigged bookkeeping to allegations that dog-racing managers and promoters were front men working for crime bosses, but the complaints were all variations on the same theme of mob infiltration and corruption.[115] Bickford was especially troubled by the integrity of the stockholders at Wonderland in Revere, the Bristol Kennel Club in Dighton (Taunton), and the Raynham track, which opened in 1940. He further claimed that Raynham was "built on credit from top to bottom, and is still insolvent."[116]

Writing in 1940, Bickford declared that for the past five years, dog racing had been a "cancer eating away the vitals of good government, due to some of the highly unscrupulous political figures behind it."[117] He claimed that these forces had "done more to corrupt and destroy decency in government than any other thing in the Commonwealth."[118]

The accusations were quite effective in tarnishing the reputation of the sport and underscored the challenge of opening new dog tracks while keeping them "respectable." Evidence was often circumstantial, although a number of the men accused of shady involvement, such as the Republican floor leader of the Massachusetts House of Representatives in 1936, Martin Hayes, were in fact later convicted of financial crimes.[119] Many of those who were involved with dog tracks were criticized as men of questionable integrity even when no evidence could be unearthed and claims could not be proven in court.[120] Bickford later complained that as a result of his campaign against dog racing, he and his family had received anonymous threats.[121]

Accusations of corruption did not cease. A lengthy article published in early 1940 in the *Saturday Evening Post* was insistent in its allegation that dog racing in Massachusetts (and Florida) was a mob import from Chicago, courtesy of one Eddie O'Hare, who was long believed to be an associate of Al Capone and who took over INGRA in 1929.[122] The author went so far as to declare: "So powerful did Capone become in dog racing that he soon dominated the International Greyhound Association [INGRA], which [Owen Patrick] Smith had organized."[123] A similar charge had been levied in 1939 when another journalist observed that "with Capone out of the way, O'Hare rapidly became the undisputed czar of dog racing."[124]

Banner headlines announcing the murder of Eddie O'Hare (i.e., "Gang Slays Taunton Dog Track Man") had done little to assuage public concern about the integrity of greyhound racing.[125] O'Hare had been deeply involved in the dog-racing business on a number of fronts. Owen Patrick Smith's successor at the head of INGRA, O'Hare helped establish a number of dog tracks around the country, including the Miami Beach Kennel Club, the Madison Kennel Club, and the Lawndale Kennel Club.[126] In Massachusetts he maintained a penthouse apartment at the track in Dighton, an arrangement similar to that presented in the fictional Hollywood film *Johnny Eager*. Known as "Artful Eddie," O'Hare was well known in organized crime. Before his abrupt death he managed to find himself "inextricably entangled" in Capone's activities, despite his deep dislike for him.[127] According to a Capone biographer, O'Hare avoided social interaction with mob members and mistakenly believed that this distance would protect him, but on November 8, 1939, O'Hare was murdered just a few days before Capone was to be released from Alcatraz federal prison. O'Hare was gunned down after leaving his office at Sportsman's Park in Cicero, just outside of Chicago. Shortly before his death, he had indicated that he wanted to get out of the racing business because "there was too much heat."[128] After his murder Governor Saltonstall declared that henceforth "only reputable Massachusetts citizens" would be permitted to conduct racing in the Bay State.[129]

Some accusations leveled by the media contradicted stated positions of other Massachusetts political figures. Governor Ely, who had held office from 1931 to 1935, had professed to be no fan of gambling schemes, but the 1940 *Saturday Evening Post* exposé claimed that he, as well as Martin Hayes, James Curley, and other politicians, were responsible for luring dog racing to the state.[130] Other critics, including fellow politicians, were not adverse to drawing attention to the hypocrisy of political figures perceived as beholden to dog-racing interests. In 1937, several years after gambling on the sport had been legalized in the Bay State, one Boston legislator groused with unabashed bitterness that the Massachusetts legislature "has shown itself to be completely under the power of the dog track operators." His wry suggestion (summarily rejected by the rules committee) was to replace the symbol of the Massachusetts Bay Colony—the codfish—with a greyhound. In the same spirit, senators unwaveringly supportive of dog racing were assigned a special moniker, "Swifty," the local nickname for the mechanical rabbit. When one of these senators would walk by, others would wryly comment, "there goes Swifty"—the same refrain used to announce the start of the artificial lure around the dog track.[131]

The legitimacy of dog racing was also contested in New Jersey. The most promising venue for racing appeared to be Atlantic City. Here, gambling and alcohol were both largely unregulated. In 1923 the state's first dog track opened for business in the booming resort town. Within a few years a more favorable (and indoor) venue in Atlantic City was selected, a new $15 million convention hall that even featured a "luxurious clubhouse."[132] Beginning in 1934, pari-mutuel betting on dog racing was legalized in New Jersey, but only as an emergency measure to provide debt-burdened municipalities with much-needed additional revenue. Operations were subject to supervision by the State Racing Commission, a body that in all likelihood was more committed to the goal of establishing legalized horse racing in the state. That year, $10 million were wagered by 910,000 patrons at New Jersey's four dog tracks: Atlantic City, Long Branch, Camden, and Linden.[133]

As it turned out, the windfall was temporary. Objections were raised about unfair business practices (such as the distribution of free tickets) in addition to the more serious charge of racketeering.[134] One detractor, a theater owner, claimed that races were held in the morning in order to educate children how to gamble.[135] The State Racing Commission even sued the Atlantic City Kennel Club because track operators refused to pay state taxes. Absent from the public discourse was any commentary about the treatment of the dogs; instead, state leaders appeared to be more concerned about the moral well-being of its citizens. In reality, however, this platform had often been used before to abolish greyhound racing when other reasons were actually in play. On April 8, 1935, the state supreme court ruled that dog racing was unconstitutional in New Jersey, citing the corrupting influence of gambling.[136] The history of legalized greyhound racing in the state was over, having lasted little more than a year.

Objections to dog racing that had plagued the sport in New Jersey persisted in American popular culture well before animal advocates began to change the primary focus of public conversation about dog racing to the treatment of the greyhounds themselves. This wide range of problems continued to poison the well that sustained greyhound racing, namely, the support of Americans who loved to gamble at the dog tracks. The troubles that continued to plague the industry arose from conflicting cultural ideas about gambling, acceptable modes of public entertainment, the place of animals in society, and the regulatory function of state government.

But despite a widening and at times seemingly insurmountable array of challenges, the greyhound racing industry in the United States managed to achieve considerable success over extended periods. In some cases promoters were able to twist the specter of organized crime into a playful marketing ploy; Americans could enjoy a little bit of "naughty" fun while betting on the dogs.[137] Any guilt about taking part in gambling was softened by the knowledge that some of the money taken in at the dog track would enter state coffers and fund charitable causes. At other times state-sanctioned "mutt derbies" at greyhound tracks put a family-friendly face on the industry.[138] Another strategy was the appointment of upstanding community members such as teachers to serve seasonally as pari-mutuel clerks at the dog tracks, or the appointment of school athletes to work as lead-out boys to represent the wholesomeness of the industry.[139] The state most effective in casting aside any remaining doubts about the viability of racing was Florida. After a brief prelude of fits and starts, greyhound racing was to reach its apotheosis in the Sunshine State, America's growing vacation wonderland.

CHAPTER FOUR

HALCYON DAYS AND FLORIDA NIGHTS

*At this [Miami Beach Kennel Club greyhound] track, famous as
a gathering place for smart enthusiasts of the sport, are seen the
exquisite gowns which identify their lovely wearers as patrons of
the finest shops of the fashion world.*
"Rusty's Glimpse of Fashion Road," *Miami Daily News,* 1936

*Dog tracks are to the horse parks what slot machines are to the
night clubs: a poor man's recreation.*
"Paradise Regained," *Fortune* magazine article on tourism in
Miami, January 1936

When Florida's first greyhound track, the Miami Ken-
nel Club in Hialeah, opened in 1922, one reporter observed that northern
audiences had discovered a "new thrill" watching "long, lithe, swift" greyhounds racing just like horses on the turf.[1] Within a few years, however, the
Miami Kennel Club failed as a dog track and was converted into a horse-
racing venue. The property where the dog track was situated became part of
the stabling area for horses; the greyhounds were forced to find other, more
promising sites for racing. And in fact, whereas dog racing may have foundered in Hialeah, other cities and towns in Florida beckoned, and the state
soon proved to be greyhound racing's most fertile ground for expansion.

Once pari-mutuel wagering in Florida was legalized in 1931, the Sunshine State welcomed the sleek racing dogs with unbridled enthusiasm and
eagerly promoted the "Sport of Queens" as one of its main attractions for
visitors. In one 1932 film, dog racing is even referred to as the "new sport of
kings and presidents," an unsubtle attempt to catapult dog racing into the
elite sphere of thoroughbred horse racing.[2] Although in most cases more
money was wagered annually at horse races than at greyhound tracks in
Florida, dog racing still attracted far more spectators than thoroughbred
horse racing through the 1930s and up to American entry into World War
II, when cumulative year-end figures are tallied.[3]

Still, the uneasy relationship between horse and dog racing inevitably gave rise to comparisons, only one of which centered on the two animals in question. The racing greyhound's disposition was not always characterized in a consistent fashion, but it was nonetheless repeatedly likened to that of the thoroughbred racehorse. At the time, the greyhound was often described as "highly strung," a statement that many aficionados of the breed would certainly contest and a description that more accurately describes the behavior of a racehorse. A 1943 Warner Brothers Vitaphone production titled *Tropical Sportland* claimed that greyhounds are "beautifully cared for, as such obvious aristocrats should be" and worth "fabulous sums to their owners."[4] The continued desire to mimic the culture of horse racing is made even more obvious when the program announcer declares that the dogs are watched for "form and breeding" as close as Kentucky Derby horses are, with all the pomp of the horse-racing establishment.

To be sure, even though dog tracks drew in large audiences and hosted many more racing days per year than the horse tracks, the thoroughbred horse as king of the turf was a powerful icon in American sporting culture and one not easily dethroned. Promoters thus sought to characterize the greyhound as an elite athlete of the same caliber as the racehorse. The importance of the purebred greyhound—promoted as a canine aristocrat and referred to as a true "thoroughbred"—was a key component in the equation.[5]

The emergence of dog racing in Florida was a direct consequence of aggressive development and creative marketing designed to attract northern and midwestern visitors to the Sunshine State. Owing to the monumental dimensions of the task at hand, Florida became a tourist haven only gradually.[6] Promoters, land developers, and entrepreneurs such as Henry Morrison Flagler, John Collins, and Henry B. Plant seized the opportunity to create the infrastructure required for Florida—especially the southern region—to become a national tourist destination.[7] Flagler's efforts were buttressed by the chairman of publicity at the Miami Chamber of Commerce, Everest G. Sewell, who aggressively used his office and its resources to establish the city as the foremost tourist destination in the United States.[8]

Despite a growing national transportation network perfectly designed to boost visitation in America's new vacationland, the challenge of developing Miami Beach still remained. Indiana promoter Carl Graham Fisher tackled with gusto the monumental task of converting acres and acres of undeveloped swampland into a tourist paradise.[9] Fisher was a gifted promoter who understood the importance of devising incentives to draw in vacationers. He lured President-elect Warren Harding to the newly built Flamingo Hotel on Biscayne Bay in January 1921, shortly before Harding was sworn into office. He brought national sports icons to the area and even imported a polo team from the United Kingdom and established a venue where they could play. The so-called bathing beauties of Miami Beach were an enticement for visitors. Parades highlighting changing fashions in women's swimwear were another means of attracting crowds.[10]

Buoyed by Fisher's vision and drive to create a tourist mecca, Miami Beach grew tremendously during the Florida land boom of the 1920s. Many new landowners were nouveaux riches from the Midwest, whereas many of the East Coast elite still favored the more exclusive Palm Beach. Several of the newly wealthy midwesterners—auto industry barons and other northern manufacturers with now-familiar names such as Firestone, Hertz, and Annenberg—settled in Miami Beach on Millionaire's Row, located on the east side of the peninsula above Lincoln Road.[11] The price of lots in Miami Beach skyrocketed.[12] Yet this rate of growth, while impressive, was not sustainable and was already beginning to weaken by the fall of 1925. The flurry of development was also accompanied by some ominous signs. The culture of the building boom was plagued by a worrisome degree of lawlessness. Land speculation was rampant and eventually caught the eye of the federal Bureau of Internal Revenue, which launched an investigation. A vibrant black market for alcohol was clear evidence of the failure of Prohibition in the region. The coup de grace was the catastrophic hurricane of September 1926, which burst the bubble. The "orgy of speculation" fueling the land boom was over, and it took several years of recovery before Miami Beach was resurrected.[13]

Despite this colossal setback, the cultural elements that defined Miami Beach for much of the mid-twentieth century were firmly established in the course of the 1920s.[14] Florida historian Gregory Bush asserts that "Miami's winter tourist industry . . . created images of popular engagement with leisure that lingered for decades and functioned as an important component in defining modern consumer culture."[15] It was Carl Fisher who created and solidified Miami Beach's association with a broad spectrum of entertainment offerings, including grandiose hotels, lavish parties, an array of sports, and the iconic bathing beauties. Large, fashionable crowds from the North eager to spend their newly acquired riches sought a pleasant but also exciting winter destination. They thronged to fast-paced activities such as racing, sports contests, parades, and festivals, all the while creating a culture of display and consumption throughout southern Florida. The whirlwind combination of swimming casinos, ferry rides, masquerade parties, and parades on Flagler Street created an amusement park atmosphere in the entire Miami area.[16] Journalist Herbert Hiller argues that Florida's trademark cultural image of bared bodies and tropical adventure ultimately emanated from Miami Beach.[17] National celebrities including sports figures and emerging Hollywood stars began to flock to Miami Beach. The confluence of speed, status, and spectacle transformed the image of South Florida and fueled its burgeoning development.[18]

The culture of around-the-clock entertainment and excess inevitably came at a price. Although on the surface the city was run by "old-guard WASPS" who retained economic and political control, other forces were also at work.[19] The money, glamour, and excitement attracted both social parvenus and underworld elements. Bootleggers supplied locals and tourists alike with alcohol. A number of the dogmen in South Florida were themselves involved in illegal liquor sales.[20] Prostitution thrived and illegal gambling operations, including betting on greyhound racing, also flourished. Various other forms of gambling drew in additional tourists; slot machines and table games were popular in local hotels and clubs.

Organized crime allegedly controlled some of the area gambling operations as well as some of the racetracks themselves. Miami Beach became the new home of Al Capone in the late 1920s. One local chronicler claimed that Capone maintained a controlling interest in an unnamed Miami dog track, in all likelihood the Miami Beach Kennel Club.[21] Mobster Meyer Lansky, who was a close friend of Charles "Lucky" Luciano and Benjamin "Bugsy" Siegel, was also headquartered in Miami Beach. Nearby communities in South Florida were no less susceptible to incursions by organized crime. The Hollywood Kennel Club, which opened in 1934 in Hallandale, was rumored to have fallen under the influence of Meyer and his brother Jake Lansky.[22] These men continued to exert their authority throughout the 1930s and into the following decades.[23]

English journalist T. H. Weigall wrote in his 1932 book *Boom in Paradise* that government did little to combat this wild atmosphere, noting that the "state legislature, in abolishing with one superb gesture the state income and inheritance taxes and in abandoning any attempt whatever to enforce the Prohibition and anti-gambling laws, joined in the chorus and definitely adopted the policy of making the wealthy and pleasure-seeking visitor its primary consideration, and practically its only one."[24] For decades to come, gambling reigned as the main social activity in Miami Beach.[25] Bookmakers continued to seek customers interested in betting on horses or dogs, but there is little to no evidence to suggest that underground betting parlors were established specifically for gambling on greyhound racing. Rather, the illegal betting rooms were geared toward profiting from horse racing, undoubtedly because the amount of money bet on thoroughbred horses was significantly higher.

Even though the specter of underworld influence continued to cast its shadow, the legalization of pari-mutuel betting on horse and dog racing in 1931 was a critical victory for both industries. In 1925 the drive for legalization had come under threat, even in adventure-rich Florida. There were still plenty of detractors who resisted the introduction of any form of legalized gambling—Florida governor John W. Martin declared in 1927 that laws against pari-mutuel wagering were to be rigidly enforced—but after a series of court challenges, such opposing concerns were overpowered by pro-racing constituencies.[26] The Florida State Racing Commission, whose members were appointed by the governor, was given the highly politicized and contentious task of assigning the starting and ending dates of the racing season for each track. But before this could take place, the tracks were first required to apply to the commission for a racing permit. Not all permits were granted. In the first year, out of thirty-three applications for dog-racing permits, twenty were accepted, twelve were denied, and one was withdrawn.[27] No reasons were cited for the denials in the commission's annual reports, although the meeting minutes reveal a cutthroat environment. An attorney representing the Clay County Kennel Club complained that some permit applications were being filed with the sole purpose of "shaking down the operators who have been legitimately operating."[28]

Once accepted, each track sought to obtain the selection of racing dates that would ensure the highest profits. The Miami area was generally the most competitive and lucrative, since its three dog tracks—Biscayne, West Flagler, and Miami Beach—commanded the highest attendance numbers for most of the 1930s.[29] In 1935 the state legislature decided to prohibit the establishment of new greyhound tracks within twenty miles of existing dog-racing facilities in order to "properly restrict the number of additional dog tracks in any given locality."[30] Throughout the decade and many years thereafter, both the assignment of race dates and the issuance of new racing licenses continued to be sore subjects among track operators as well as local business owners.[31] After the legalization of betting on horse and dog racing, the negotiations for racing dates became a part of the racing commission's official record, but there were undoubtedly behind-the-scene machinations—in Florida and elsewhere—as operators sought to obtain the most advantageous racing days.

Beginning in the 1920s an unusual and critical compromise had gradually been established in Florida between dog- and horse-racing interests. Thoroughbred horse racing had traditionally coveted and dominated the afternoon slots, although this pattern was not codified until the early 1940s.[32] Horse racing had always been granted this privileged position, whereas greyhound racing was relegated to the evenings unless a matinee opening was available on a day when the horses did not run. Wealthy patrons could afford to attend the races in the afternoon because they did not have to report to work. In contrast, patrons of the dog tracks could complete a full day's shift and still attend the greyhound races at night. This balance was certainly not permanent, nor did it necessarily occur in other parts of the country, but it unquestionably established the early pattern of nighttime greyhound racing in Florida.

Once all of these factors were in place—the legalization of racing and the selection process for race dates at each track—Florida was well positioned to take the new sport of greyhound racing and "reach for the stars": stars from Hollywood, the baseball diamond, the boxing ring, and other popular entertainment venues. From its legalized beginnings in the 1930s, promoters sought to link Florida greyhound racing with plentiful leisure, high fashion, high living, and an emerging celebrity culture associated with sports, cinema, radio, and other forms of popular entertainment.[33] Several dog tracks flourished in the Miami area, including the West Flagler Kennel Club, Biscayne Kennel Club, and Miami Beach Kennel Club, the latter promoted with flair by Frank Anderson, who employed a wide array of savvy marketing strategies to bolster the popularity of the sport and entice larger crowds to his track.[34] Miami Beach Kennel Club consistently enjoyed the highest attendance numbers of all three Miami dog tracks prior to World War II.

In 1925 two other tracks opened in Florida, the Six Mile Creek Kennel Club in Tampa and the St. Petersburg Kennel Club, which was eventually known as Derby Lane. Like Miami, St. Petersburg experienced its own land boom in the 1920s, also attracting tourists looking for new modes of entertainment. St. Petersburg Kennel Club's founding patriarch, T. L. Weaver, was a successful businessman and developer who had made his fortune in the lumber industry.[35] Before the land boom exploded, he had purchased property north of town near Gandy Bridge, a site that proved to be an ideal venue for dog racing. The opening of Gandy Bridge across Tampa Bay in 1924 reduced the drive from Tampa to St. Petersburg from forty-three to nineteen miles. Not unlike Miami Beach, the Sunshine City "flirted with

Babe Ruth and winning greyhound Racing Ramp at trophy presentation in Florida, 1925. (Derby Lane Archives)

decadence" in the 1920s, and had its own share of bootlegging, speakeasies, nightclubs, and prostitution.[36]

When the St. Petersburg Kennel Club opened it attracted a celebrity audience almost immediately. A surviving photograph from its inaugural year shows an awards ceremony with baseball great Babe Ruth, two fashionably dressed women, and the winning greyhound.[37] In the years to come St. Petersburg proved to be one of the most successful and longest-lasting greyhound-racing venues in the United States. The facility was impressive in its own right, with an art deco judge's stand and a two-story clubhouse with a porch that "looked almost like a plantation home," according to Mary Margaret Winning, the granddaughter of T. L. Weaver, Derby Lane's founder.[38] Along with Hialeah, the track was one of the earliest to pioneer the use of night lighting to bring in evening crowds.[39] Promotions and attendance at the St. Petersburg Kennel Club were buttressed by the frequent presence of baseball stars in the area. Babe Ruth enjoyed his status as the "toast of the town" and was known to place bets on the dogs, as did Lou Gehrig, Dizzy Dean, and Walter James Vincent "Rabbit" Maranville.[40] The Boston Braves conducted spring training in St. Petersburg from 1922 to 1937, and the New York Yankees also arrived for yearly spring training in 1925. For decades these teams practiced seasonally at Crescent Lake Park, with the dog tracks providing the perfect evening diversion for many baseball players.[41]

Both for baseball players in training and for the general public, Florida proved to be an ideal venue for leisure activities of all sorts, with greyhound racing enjoying an increasing share. A promotional feature airing in 1933 boasted that "legalized betting [at the Florida dog tracks] rivals that at the horse track, running as high as $250,000 a week at some places."[42] While thoroughbred horse racing especially appealed to the blue-blooded elite, greyhound racing consistently attracted a broader swath of society. Miami chronicler Ann Armbruster maintains that dog racing was the main event at South Beach for decades, where "a quarter's admission could buy Hialeah-style excitement."[43] And even though working-class spectators were the regulars at the dog tracks, special efforts were put forth by management to attract a more exclusive crowd. An early printed promotion captures the essence of what the Miami Beach Kennel Club—"more than a racetrack, a Florida show place"—was trying to sell, boasting of its luxuriously appointed club rooms, broad verandas, and soft music: "From all over the world smartly clad men and women gather at the MIAMI BEACH KENNEL CLUB to watch the fleetest of greyhounds run on the brilliantly lighted course of the world's most beautiful dog racing track. . . . Truly the MIAMI BEACH KENNEL CLUB is the meeting place of the fashionable in dress and sports. Dog racing here IS the sport of the elite."[44]

These claims include prime examples of the language and imagery used by promoters to create the overwhelming impression of exclusivity. In reality, the so-called social elite continued to favor the thoroughbred horse tracks. During the 1936 winter season the *Miami Herald* social column printed lists of socialites spotted at Hialeah, but no mention is made of individuals patronizing the Miami Beach Kennel Club or any other dog track, for that matter.[45]

The history of the Miami Beach Kennel Club was painstakingly documented from its beginnings, likely by a track employee, in a series of oversized scrapbooks. The earliest volumes reflect a superbly ambitious and successful marketing strategy that employed a wide array of techniques to draw people to the tracks. The publicity worked. The brainchild of boxing promoter Tex Rickard, who died just hours before his track opened, the Miami Beach Kennel Club became tremendously popular. Rickard also managed Jack Dempsey, the world-champion heavyweight, who was an

enthusiastic supporter of dog racing.⁴⁶ In the late 1930s the facility functioned as a popular showplace for a range of entertainment in "America's
Winter Playground." The Miami Beach Kennel Club promoted itself first
and foremost as the intersection of glamour and excitement. A poster advertisement for the December 28, 1937, gala season opening announced that
as an "architectural masterpiece patterned after an old Spanish mission,
lapped by the blue Atlantic's rippling waves and set amid gently swaying
palms, the Miami Beach Kennel Club presents a picture of unforgettable
beauty and charm and serves as a fitting background for the 'Sport of
Queens' presented throughout the winter season by America's pioneer greyhound racing organization."⁴⁷

The social lounge in the clubhouse was particularly impressive, with
wood-beamed ceilings, an ornate chandelier, and stately furniture, all with
a distinctly European feel. A painting of two greyhounds framed by a dark
curtain was prominently featured above the fireplace. The clubhouse was
thus designed as the oasis for fashionable society, a "mecca for the elite of
sportdom."⁴⁸ Clothing was given special prominence: a full-page 1936 newspaper advertisement featured "Southern Fashions at Miami Beach" and a
drawing of the Miami Beach Kennel Club. The long, clean lines of the wom-
en's gowns visually echo the shape of the lean greyhound pictured in profile
at the top of the promotion.⁴⁹ Another article from the same year described
the scene: "SMARTLY CLAD sophisticates from Broadway, Michigan Boulevard
[sic], Beacon Street, or like haunts of boulevardiers lolling in a luxurious
clubroom lounge listening to the strains of a tempting orchestra or crowd-
ing out on the wide veranda to see eight of the fleetest greyhounds in the
world spin madly around the brilliantly lighted course under the magic of
a moon lit tropical sky."⁵⁰ A third promotion, also from 1936, boasts, "the
brilliance of the social contingent which attends, plus nightly races by the
world's fastest greyhounds over a perfect race course, are the reasons for the
Miami Beach Kennel Club being listed as 'tops' on the resorter's spectator
list."⁵¹

While the area's thoroughbred horse races did attract the highest echelon
of East Coast society, as evidenced by dispatches printed in the society column of the *Miami Herald* in the late 1930s, greyhound racing was in fact
also able to generate appeal to some wealthy customers. Yet even though an
upper-class contingent evidently did frequent the Miami Beach dog races
at the time, newspaper promotions describing an exclusive clientele at the
Miami Beach Kennel Club betray a robust measure of wishful thinking and
fanciful exaggeration. The fact is that Palm Beach society looked down on

the parvenus of Miami Beach. The first wife of Carl Fisher, Jane Fisher, later confessed that "Palm Beach society . . . thought we were scum."[52] Miami Beach residents with "new" money earned from manufacturing were often written off by the press as "minor capitalists."[53] Newly wealthy midwesterners who frequented the Miami Beach Kennel Club were often joined by sizable crowds of ordinary, working-class spectators. In truth, the cost of admission to the clubhouse—50 cents—was not especially prohibitive. The clubhouse entrance fee for the thoroughbred races at Hialeah Park, in contrast, was $4.[54]

Fashionable dress and company were just one part of the evening's attractions offered at the Miami Beach Kennel Club. Music and radio broadcasts also formed an integral part of the show. The radio program "There Goes Rusty" ("Rusty" is one nickname often given to the fake rabbit serving as the mechanical lure) was broadcast every night at the Miami Beach Kennel Club at 6:35 p.m. on WIOD and 7:15 p.m. on WQAM, except for Sundays. The show featured musicians and singers performing live in the clubhouse. In April 1936 the Clarence McIntyre Orchestra was photographed in the lounge of the clubhouse for a special radio program.

Music had become an important component of the entertainment package available at greyhound tracks. For instance, Bob Crosby, one of Bing Crosby's brothers, performed with his orchestra at the Biscayne dog track in 1936. Describing him as a radio idol with 30 million fans, the Hollywood greyhound track featured Chet Brownagle the same year. The St. Petersburg Kennel Club, later renamed Derby Lane, featured a large bandstand next to the track; it continued to showcase live music for decades.[55] Band music entertained patrons before the races and during post time, a short interlude showcasing the dogs as they were ceremoniously marched to the starting boxes. Instead of the thirty-minute break customary between horse races, only a fifteen-minute lull separated races at the greyhound tracks. When live music was not available, there was often an opportunity to see a radio star in person. In 1939 dog-racing patrons were encouraged to come to the Miami Beach Kennel Club for a chance to see well-known performers who would be singing later the same night at the nearby Plaza Theatre.

Apart from the musical interludes and featured stars, promoters also devised other, more inventive ways to create an entertaining spectacle for audiences. They took full advantage of the brief period between races; the grooms walking the dogs to post were dressed in smart, military-like uniforms. One promotional film raved, "The classiest greyhounds in the South, each with his own valet, are parading to the post, like a lot of thoroughbreds

Derby Lane marching band, St. Petersburg, Florida, 1934. (Derby Lane Archives)

at the Kentucky Derby." Another announced, "Here they come, the parade of the 'Greyhound Soldiers.'"[56] A 1935 photograph of the Miami facility pictures a snappily dressed marching band parading down the track led by a uniformed bandleader with knee-high leather boots, military cap, and baton. Other extant footage of action at the greyhound tracks shows similar pomp and ceremony, a display likely meant to assure the public that the races were conducted on the highest plane, without a hint of trickery or corruption. Once the race was made official, the grooms saluted the track stewards, another gesture signifying military precision, order, and reliability.

Still, such mimicry of officialdom was sometimes oddly juxtaposed with more circuslike modes of entertainment. For a time, monkeys were used as "jockeys" atop greyhounds, a phenomenon that appears to have been less than agreeable for both parties involved. One dogman recalled, "They'd hold a special race with the poor things strapped to the backs of the greyhounds. A lot of times some of the monkeys would be dead at the end of the race. They had literally been shaken to death."[57] The monkeys were outfitted with jockey silks and positioned on special saddles. This gimmick was employed at a number of dog tracks in the 1930s, even including some outside of Florida, but the forced partnership between canine and simian was nonetheless short-lived. Hoye Perry, who worked as a lead-out boy at the Palm Beach Kennel Club, recalled that the monkey races always drew in a crowd, but the humane society eventually put a stop to the peculiar practice.[58] Reports from elsewhere stated that the monkeys "bit and clawed their steeds" during the competition, adding to the mayhem.[59] There is no doubt that several state racing commissions became wary of the practice.[60] An application to conduct betting on races with monkey jockeys in Florida was denied in 1933, but more significantly, four years later, an applicant seeking to race his greyhounds with monkey jockeys was turned away altogether, with the curt response that the Florida State Racing Commission's rule number 85 now disallowed the practice. It sanctioned only true greyhound racing, with all other types of "freak races," including those with monkey jockeys, strictly forbidden.[61]

Likely one of the most highly anticipated events to take place at the Miami Beach track in 1937 was a vigorously promoted film shoot for an upcoming movie starring Shirley Temple, *His Master's Voice*. The movie was never completed, even after the leading role was reassigned to Jane Withers, but a great publicity effort was put forth to ensure large crowds at the track on the day that the crew was scheduled to commence filming.[62] A number of advertisements had featured Rusty the rabbit inviting patrons to attend the event and to "participate in the production of the Twentieth-Century-Fox picture." Racing scenes as well as the "colorful crowd" were scheduled to be filmed.

Two different versions of the film's story line exist. According to a contemporary newspaper report, Temple's character arrives from the North in Miami, where she decides to visit the dog track. After the little girl feeds a racing greyhound a hamburger, the dog loses the race and his "cruel owner" is furious. The greyhound escapes from the kennel and ends up at the city pound. Temple's character is able to reclaim the dog after she earns money by dancing and singing. Eventually, she enters him in a stakes race, and the greyhound wins.[63] However, the original script, written by Bess Meredyth, reads rather differently. The narrative focuses on an Ohio family's quest to collect an inheritance that had been stolen from them by a Miami-based criminal. This man is a greyhound kennel owner, the proprietor of the track café, and the head of an illegal betting ring. It appears that the dog, with the innocuous race name of Twinkle Toes (but to the little girl, he's known as "Skinny"), never actually races and is in fact adopted by the young girl.

Monkey jockey astride racing greyhound, ca. 1930. (Greyhound Hall of Fame)

This plotline stands in stark contrast not only to the version described in the newspapers but more important to the characterization of the racing dog as vicious and bloodthirsty. Such an assessment of the racing greyhound's temperament was not uncommon at the time and for the most part had the effect of excluding these dogs from mainstream pet adoption programs for decades. Even so, there are very few contemporary reports of serious greyhound attacks on their owners, trainers, or members of the general public.[64] In all likelihood, such fears were unfounded, mistakenly based on the breed's "bloodlust" for small prey. On the other hand, some pioneer dogmen did allege that racing greyhounds were mean and unsuitable to keep as pets. Still, given that *His Master's Voice* was never released, the public was obviously never exposed to this unusually sentimental view of the racing greyhound as a child's pet.

Another short film featuring racing greyhounds, *Never Catch the Rabbit*, was shown numerous times in the mid–1930s.[65] This RKO short narrated by Bill Corum portrays greyhounds as "blue-blooded" and temperamental, inclined to fight even when loaded up into the starting boxes.[66] Still, the mood of the production is fairly lighthearted, with the standard jokes about hungry greyhounds eager to chase the rabbit even though it is fake. The RKO piece was paired in local cinemas with prominent feature films such as *The Garden of Allah,* starring Marlene Dietrich and Charles Boyer.[67] Newspaper advertisements promoting the films featured Rusty the rabbit encouraging Miami Beach Kennel Club patrons to attend the afternoon showing at the movie theater because "its color matches the gay throng at the Beach Kennel Club every night."[68] Any connection of the feature to dog racing is undoubtedly a stretch; Rusty's real purpose was to bring crowds to the film short that followed, *Never Catch the Rabbit,* and thus encourage audiences to patronize the evening races at the track.

This example of collaboration, or at least cooperation, between cinema and greyhound racing is noteworthy because most local downtown stores, especially restaurants and theaters, were wary of the competition posed by state-sanctioned pari-mutuel gambling. Numerous references in the meeting minutes of the Florida State Racing Commission of the time indicate that competing entertainment markets such as hotels, restaurants, and gambling establishments were struggling to find a comfortable coexistence in "America's winter playground." A letter submitted by the Dade County Chamber of Commerce for the October 3, 1936, commission meeting reported "much dissatisfaction among business men in the Greater Miami area over the racing schedule."[69] Word of the problem even reached the *New York Press,* which in 1939 published an article with the dramatic headline "Miami Dog Tracks Steal Play from Rivals for Night Trade."[70] The relationship between local businesses and greyhound tracks could certainly have a part in a track's success or failure. Letters from angry owners of competing businesses undoubtedly swayed politicians and other influential players who were already skeptical about the introduction of dog racing into their communities.

Yet by encouraging vacationers and tourists to frequent a broad spectrum of popular venues in their area, Miami dog tracks sought to use the competition for the entertainment dollar to their own advantage. The Miami Beach Kennel Club thus repeatedly sought to link greyhound racing with other leisure activities available nearby. Its advertising encouraged visitors to enjoy other attractions in the afternoon, such as motorboat racing, followed by its dog track at night. One newspaper promotion proposed a full day's schedule for Miami visitors: horse racing at Tropical Park in the morning, an Orange Bowl football game in the afternoon, and the dog races at Miami Beach in the evening. Advertisements provided information on the many options for transportation to the track available to patrons, including trolleys from downtown Miami, jitney sedans, deluxe coaches, and taxis.

Even though greyhound tracks remained aggressive about courting the upper echelons of society, or at least wished to project the image of exclusivity, they continued to reach out to the working class. In 1932 Miami merchants complained to the racing commission that dog track operators were leaving free admission tickets at stores, drink stands, and filling stations for "any and everybody" in order to boost attendance at the races. They bemoaned the "promiscuous distribution" of free tickets as a form of unfair competition.[71]

Track promoters also cleverly filled local newspapers with appreciative acknowledgements to various organizations within Dade County. The Miami Beach Kennel Club tipped its cap to "organized labor of Miami," offering "good wishes to such a splendid organization" in a 1935 half-page advertisement in the *Miami News,* the self-described organ of the Florida Federation of Labor.[72] The relationship between track management and labor could work in other mutually beneficial ways as well. Construction companies that were helping build sections of the Miami Beach Kennel Club published announcements noting their involvement. The Jeffrey Lumber Yards declared in a 1936 advertisement that "we are happy to have furnished the lumber for the remodeling of the grandstand of MBKC."[73] In the same year the Hollywood Kennel Club, located in nearby Hallandale and self-titled the "aristocrat of greyhound tracks," featured a special night at the track honoring firemen.[74]

Some dog-track marketing was geared specifically toward attracting members of the working class to the races by making them feel as if they were associated with, or at least witness to, a facet of upper-class society. The *Miami Herald* ran a serial cartoon featuring the exploits of Rusty the rabbit and his master Ebony, a character in blackface. In this and other such cartoons Rusty himself represents a working-class fellow who is sometimes a little overwhelmed by the glamour of Miami Beach. In another cartoon the rabbit smokes a cigar and marvels, "Miami Beach sure beats Tulsa, where grandpa usta' run."[75] Supposedly the working-class audience could identify with Rusty's comic wide-eyed appreciation of the spectacle at the track since many of the advertisements were pitched from his point of view. The mechanical rabbit frequently appeared as a playful spokesperson in racetrack marketing efforts. In one promotion, Rusty declares, "Oh Boy! If these hounds wouldn't chase me so fast I'd sit right down on the track and gaze at those glamorous ladies in their gorgeous gowns over in the club house."[76]

Nor did advertisers neglect to target middle-class audiences as well. Men and women of comfortable means with some extra spending money were also potential dog-racing fans. Early Miami Beach promoters created a cartoon series that tracked the shopping activities of a comely cartoon figure named Tillie. The *Where's Tillie?* series featured an attractive, smartly dressed young lady patronizing a local beauty salon, clothing store, and hotel; her outings inevitably concluded with a trip to the Miami Beach Kennel Club. This run of advertisements also employed a male figure, Jerry, in a similar manner.

While some marketing efforts featured stereotypical middle-class consumers such as Tillie and Jerry patronizing the dog tracks, greyhound racing promoters were still relying primarily on images of celebrities and nubile bathing beauties in magazines and newspapers to entice visitors. The number and range of promotional images of race-winning greyhounds pictured with celebrities and attractive women at the south Florida tracks attests to the degree in which the sport was being integrated into other facets of mainstream American popular culture. In the early years the stars (e.g., Babe Ruth, Jack Dempsey, Primo Carnera, and John Pesek) had often hailed from the professional sports arena, but as the industry grew dog racing did in fact begin to attract an even broader spectrum of popular cultural icons.[77] Hoye Perry, a lead-out boy at the Palm Beach Kennel Club from 1936 to 1939 and thereafter a mutuel clerk, recalled seeing Cary Grant, Errol Flynn, and other movie stars at the track in the late 1930s and the 1940s.[78]

In addition to associating the sport broadly with glamour, sophistication, and an elite lifestyle, greyhound racing promoters linked the sport's image specifically with the female body.[79] Even apart from commercial greyhound racing, the sleek form of the greyhound was often paired visually with the elegant lines of a well-dressed woman, as seen for example on the cover of the March 20, 1937, *Collier's Weekly* magazine. A popular motif in art deco drawings and paintings of the era also featured pairings of women and greyhounds.[80] The motif was also used in jewelry, sculpture, and architectural ornamentation. Even household items such as lamps and bookends sometimes incorporated the image of the sleek racing dog. In fact, according to one scholar, the greyhound became a "quintessential image and symbol of the Jazz Age."[81]

Paradoxically, even as the greyhound began to symbolize wealth, glamour, and sophistication, the racing dogs themselves were sometimes portrayed in ways that emphasized their animality. This is evident in the significant difference between the cultural and aesthetic images of the greyhound and the manner in which the animal itself was often described to racing fans. A 1932 sports promotion narrated by Ted Husing describes the supposedly vicious nature of the breed quite vividly, noting that the animal was instinctively a killer and inclined to "jump a fallen leader in a race in an effort to kill him."[82] Husing makes it clear that the greyhound is trained using live jackrabbits and encouraged to make the kill and acquire the taste for blood. The darker instinctual elements of the greyhound temperament are likely being emphasized for dramatic effect, but the viewer is left with little doubt that these "moody" and "delicately formed" animals are a class apart from friendly Fido, the average family pet. Characterization of the racing greyhound as aggressive, even dangerous, was not altogether unprecedented. When dog racing debuted in the early 1920s, one headline announced the accidental destruction of the mechanical rabbit during a race, noting ominously that after the greyhounds caught the lure, "what the dogs did not do to the rabbit is not worth telling."[83] Despite (and perhaps also because of) this image of the greyhound as threatening and even vicious when provoked, visitors to Florida flocked to the greyhound tracks in ever greater numbers in the years before World War II.

More than 3 million tourists a year were visiting South Florida by 1940, but the growing threat of the war in Europe was an obvious interruption. Not long after the bombing of Pearl Harbor on December 7, 1941, and the subsequent U.S. entry into the war, the footprint of World War II was already evident in advertisements for greyhound racing. The Miami Beach Kennel Club began to emphasize winning in a new sense: victory over international threats. The track offered numerous victory nights, where U.S. defense bonds were awarded to the winners of each race in addition to regular purses. During a brief period in the early 1940s, dog racing triumphed over thoroughbred horse racing and in 1943 even boldly (albeit only briefly) declared itself the "New Sport of Kings." On January 10, 1943, a Miami newspaper asserted that "greyhound racing has taken the Miami sports spotlight since the suspension of horse racing last week."[84] Wartime restrictions on travel had deeply affected the horse-racing industry because horses could no longer be legally transported to and from racing facilities by railroad or truck. The dogmen, in contrast, were not as handicapped by the wartime travel ban. They used privately owned trailers—which were still permitted—to transport their greyhounds.

In 1943 the Florida State Racing Commission acknowledged the adverse effects that blackouts, gasoline shortages, and restricted public transportation services were having on pari-mutuel earnings but concluded that "dog racing was not as seriously affected as horse racing."[85] Many fans could continue to attend the dog races by means of alternative transportation. Numerous photographs of horse- or mule-drawn buggies taking visitors to the dog tracks in Florida during World War II testify to the industry's popularity despite uncertain times.[86] By 1945, however, the director of war mobilization and reconversion called for the cessation of racing in order to aid the war effort further. From January 3, 1945, to May 12, 1945, no racing was conducted in Florida.

The postwar years in Florida, including the Miami area, were characterized by recovery and remarkable growth. The state's tourist trade doubled in the 1950s, growing from 4.5 to 9 million visitors by the end of the decade.[87] A number of factors contributed to this boom, including technological advances, the GI Bill, and a strong automobile, housing, and durable goods market. In addition to the social elite who had paved the way for luxury tourism in southern Florida, "Tin Can" tourists who had roamed the state's new highways before the war were gradually eclipsed by a broader spectrum of Americans in bigger cars and with larger budgets. Americans not only enjoyed more leisure time but were also more able and willing to spend money. Florida historian Gary Mormino characterizes this shift to consumerism as the "rise of modern Florida tourism."[88]

Now more than ever, working- and middle-class Americans could afford to vacation in the Sunshine State. What once had been the privileged domain of the elite was now being democratized and made available to average consumers. Midwestern millionaires gradually abandoned Miami Beach for more prestigious locations and were replaced by an estimated 2.5 million visitors who flocked to the Miami area every year during the 1950s. New hotels—382 in 1955—now housed average American tourists. The Miami Beach social scene still continued to draw vacationers with its eager displays of excess and virtually limitless menu of leisure activities. Mormino asserts that Miami and Miami Beach "mirrored popular culture" more than any other place in Florida.[89] Entertainment reporter Jeanne Wolf noted that Miami Beach in the 1950s was the "center of the world's entertainment industry," while comedian Shecky Greene reminisced that "there will never be anything like Miami Beach in the 1950s."[90] Judging from dog racing's rising popularity in this dynamic environment, those in the greyhound industry believed that the sport still had tremendous potential to become a major American pastime.

The growing allure of Florida as a tourist destination also launched a boom in nearby Cuba. During the 1950s Miami served as a springboard to Cuba, which became a mecca for American tourists as well as for associated illegal activities. More than 100,000 visitors frequented the island during the winter season at the beginning of the decade, and numbers were expected to increase dramatically in the future. Journalist T. J. English argues convincingly in *Havana Nocturne* that mobsters Meyer Lansky, Santo Trafficante, Jr., and Charles "Lucky" Luciano exerted tremendous authority over the gambling empire in Cuba in the decade before Castro's revolution.[91] These crime bosses hoped to capitalize on the corruption of Fulgencio Batista's government and create an unrivaled tourist nightlife fueled by gambling, prostitution, and alcohol. Through the efforts of greyhound entrepreneur Bill Huntley, Sr., who had successfully launched several dog tracks in Miami, greyhound racing was introduced to Cuba in 1951. The *Greyhound Racing Record* crooned about the sport's expansion, eagerly publicizing a canine airlift managed by Pan American Airways: "600 Greyhounds to Cuba in Greatest Mass Air Flight of Dog Racing History." The destination track was described as a "priceless jewel" on the shores of the Gulf of Mexico, located near the National Casino and directly across from the Havana Yacht Club, where the "elite of Cuban aristocracy" socialized.[92]

Florida greyhound track operator and circus owner Jerry Collins purchased the Havana Greyhound Kennel Club soon after its establishment.[93] Collins had assumed management of the Sarasota Kennel Club in 1945 and the dog track in Daytona Beach in 1949. Before his foray into dog racing, he had served four terms in the Florida state legislature earlier in the decade.[94] A savvy marketer, Collins used promotional giveaways, a bevy of female dancers, and the occasional visit from an important politician such as Florida governor Fuller Warren to keep the spotlight on his Havana track. In 1952 the Havana Carnival featured a parade float with live racing dogs attended by "señoritas." The rolling display was decorated with the track's trademark: a large silhouette of a female rumba dancer holding a brace of greyhounds. Collins himself managed to pull out of Cuba before the 1959 revolution, later claiming that he knew well in advance that the country was on the verge of a Communist takeover, but despite this setback he continued to expand his empire of tracks around the United States.[95] After acquiring ownership in 1954, he transformed the Sanford-Orlando Kennel Club from a facility with a handle under $3 million a year into a highly successful track that boasted a handle of more than $54 million thirty years later.[96]

Greyhound racing in Florida continued to flourish in the 1950s and subsequent decades. Outside of South Florida, Derby Lane was still one of the top bookings, but Tampa and Sarasota also attracted large crowds. The dog track in Tampa, which had first opened for the 1932–1933 season, benefited from extensive renovations in 1954.[97] Likewise, the struggling Sarasota greyhound track was resurrected after being purchased in 1946 by Jerry Collins, who rapidly turned the venue into a thriving operation. Also owned and managed by Collins, the Volusia County Kennel Club in Daytona Beach was another track to burst onto the scene with renewed vigor in the early 1950s. Given the diversity of these venues, the face of the gambling public varied considerably from track to track in Florida just as it did throughout the country. The fan base drawn to each facility was partially a reflection of local demographics, but it was also shaped by its track management and its own marketing strategies. One former lead-out, Wes Singletary, who worked at the Tampa Greyhound Track from August 1976 to January 1977, recalls a rather seedy, "carnie-like" atmosphere filled with colorful characters and a decidedly blue-collar crowd. The occasional mobster also frequented the track, such as Epifano Trafficante, who patronized the clubhouse. Singletary recalled that differences between the clientele at the Tampa track and at Derby Lane were noticeable and were even reflected in the fancier outfits worn by the lead-outs at Derby Lane. While the Tampa lead-outs wore simpler clothing, those at Derby Lane wore more traditional, quasi-military uniforms seen in the early years of greyhound racing.[98]

Baseball players continued to patronize the Florida tracks, just as they had before the war. Many lived in Tampa, where the Cincinnati Reds held spring training, or in St. Petersburg, where the New York Mets practiced.[99] Well-known players were often present at the dog races, including Pete Rose, who was later disgraced for gambling on his own games and convicted of tax evasion.[100] The Cincinnati Reds were not the only team at the tracks: a reporter claimed in 1950 that the dog races were a "favorite March nocturnal haunt of the Yankees and Cardinals." The coach of the Yankees, perhaps foreseeing trouble, allegedly restricted his players to one night a week at the greyhound track.[101]

Greyhound racing eventually spread to the Florida panhandle, sometimes referred to as the "Miracle Strip" or "Emerald Coast," or, to quote others, the "Redneck Riviera." The area around U.S. Highway 98 experienced a tremendous boom after the war and according to some critics acquired a distinctly garish appearance.[102] This region largely attracted white southerners from surrounding states, many of whom belonged to the working class.[103] The Pensacola Kennel Club, Washington Kennel Club in Ebro, and Jefferson County Kennel Club in Monticello opened in 1946, 1955, and 1959, respectively. The track at Ebro established a nursery and play area for children, an indication that the track's management knew it could draw in more regular, working-class families if child care were available when one or both parents gambled at the races. "Experienced attendants" were available to watch the children, who were entertained at the playground and able to enjoy candy, popcorn, soda, and hot dogs at the snack bar.[104] Historian Andrew Hurley notes that in the 1950s, sites where consumers spent money were often redesigned and refurbished to accommodate all family members.[105] This drive for family-centered entertainment was, ironically, even taking place at a gambling facility.

Ebro's appeal to mainstream Americans characterized much of Florida's postwar (and in some cases, prewar) tourist culture. The state's tourist trade doubled in the 1950s and had doubled again by 1967. The average visitor in 1956 spent $5.95 a day and stayed for eleven days. Almost three-quarters of the visitors traveled by car.[106] According to Gary Mormino, vacation destinations in Florida also often "reinforced one's identity," attracting visitors based on their class, age, religion, and ethnicity. For example, working-class midwesterners favored Ocala, Gulfport, and Lakeland; southern whites preferred Destin and Panama City; older Americans settled in St. Petersburg; Jews flocked to the Miami area; and the moneyed class continued to gravitate to Palm Beach.[107]

After decades of development the landscape of Florida now beckoned to all Americans who were ready to travel, with a vacation destination available for virtually everyone. Consumerism had become an integral part of Florida tourism. Entertainment options for Florida's visitors thus went far beyond the dog tracks. They could enjoy "goofy golf," water parks, haunted houses, and "Wild West" shows on their vacations. All over the state diverse roadside attractions continued to spring up, many of which used animals as a means of entertainment. Parrot and monkey jungles, alligator wrestling, dolphin performances, and other such novelties drew in tourists who motored along Florida's scenic routes and stayed at newly built motels.[108]

Tourists frequently purchased souvenirs during their travels and sent family and friends postcards of Florida that documented quirky vacation adventures. Some of these postcards celebrated the excitement of the dog tracks: greyhounds competing in a hurdle race, taking a sharp turn on the track, or charging out of the starting box. Others focused on the popularity of the sport and showed packed grandstands. One tourist sent a postcard of the nightly crowd at the "World's most modernistic dog track," the

Volusia County Kennel Club in Daytona Beach, in 1952, writing, "I'm at the races for the third straight nite [*sic*]. Getting to know these greyhounds very well."[109] Such greyhound-themed postcards proved to be especially popular in the 1940s and 1950s.

Promoters persisted in their association of greyhound racing with glamour and exclusivity despite the changing reality of its increasingly broad appeal. As a consequence of aggressive marketing, dog racing was catapulted into Florida's burgeoning popular culture and, over time, into other regions in the country. This was a dynamic process designed to attract both rich and poor to the races, but promoters continued to rely on images of prosperity and pleasure to lure middle- and working-class Americans to the track. Even if a wealthy clientele was in short supply, advertisements for the dog races would often strive to project an elite atmosphere. The link between sophistication, glamour, and greyhounds, first promoted at the Miami tracks in the 1930s and so visible in numerous art deco designs and artworks from this era, remained a theme in greyhound racing promotions well into the 1960s and beyond. The Palm Beach Kennel Club ran an advertisement on December 31, 1960, in the *Greyhound Racing Record* that featured a drawing of a fur-clad woman and her husband at the races.[110] Three years later, a Palm Beach promotion for the gala season opening announced that "it's all new, it's exciting, it's glamourous, it's thrilling, it's wonderful, superb clubhouse service . . . in fact every luxury and convenience you would expect at the world's newest and most modern greyhound course."[111] These claims were not limited to the Florida tracks. A 1960 advertisement for the "Magnificent" Mile High Kennel Club in Denver, Colorado, repeatedly used the word "glamorous" to describe the new box seating along with its drawing of a well-dressed couple enjoying the races.[112] The link between glamour and dog racing could also reach the level of the patently absurd. One advertisement for three Miami-area tracks (Biscayne, Flagler, and Hollywood) presented a drawing of a nattily dressed couple: the long-necked female, with pearls and a feathered, décolleté evening gown, and the male, sporting a derby and bowtie. The lovely pair was, in fact, two long-nosed greyhounds.[113]

The greyhounds themselves were not always meant to be the center of attention, however. In fact, marketers persisted in their long-standing reliance on images of attractive women in beach attire to bolster attendance at dog races. The popular image of greyhound racing, originally a product of southern Florida, remained a simple "sun and fun" bathing-beauty aesthetic. Women were often featured playing with racing greyhounds on the beach, in the kennels, or at the track.[114] Young ladies in bikinis or swimsuits were sometimes included in the awards ceremony. The cover of the *Grey-hound Racing Record* frequently pictured young women, often in bathing suits and heels, frolicking with greyhounds. These women were playfully described as "Palm Beach Pretties," "Hollywood Honeys," or "Phoenix' Phairest." Greyhounds are sometimes shown pawing at the female cover model or gently nibbling on a woman's ear.[115] One early Miami Beach promotion pictured a bathing-suit-clad woman in heels whispering "advice" to the mechanical lure, which looked like a stuffed bunny rabbit.[116]

This cultural association of greyhound racing, attractive females, and fun originated in Florida, but it was adopted by other tracks throughout the country to promote their races. A 1962 photograph in the *Greyhound Racing Record* revealed women dressed as Playboy bunnies with the "Playboy Club Special" race-winning greyhound at the races at the Phoenix Greyhound Track.[117] A cartoon printed in the same magazine playfully exposed the irony of showcasing girls rather than greyhounds at the dog track. In the image two racing greyhounds warily eye a bathing beauty posing for a photograph, and they place their own bet: "I'll lay you seven to five we're cropped out of the picture."[118]

At times the women included in greyhound promotions were newly crowned sports queens or beauty contestants. Queens of the Florida Orange Bowl, an annual college football bowl game held in Miami since 1935, were pictured with some frequency. For instance, the Orange Bowl queen and her "maids of honor" participated in opening night celebrations at the Miami Beach Kennel Club in the mid–1940s. On another occasion, the queen presented the trophy for the Miami Beach Kennel Club inaugural stakes race winner. Not surprisingly, various football teams competing in the Orange Bowl were photographed at the Florida dog tracks as well, in addition to famous professional athletes—both retired and active—including Joe DiMaggio, Willie Mays, Joe Theismann, and Doug Flynn.

Sports heroes had been spotted at dog tracks since the 1920s, but the association of greyhound racing with beauty pageants did not emerge until shortly after World War II. The Miss America contest, which was first held in 1921 in Atlantic City, New Jersey, became the most famous beauty pageant in the United States. Nurtured in an era that valued more conservative roles for women, the competition blossomed in the 1950s. Miss America evolved into a much larger enterprise, one that eventually became a major televised event. Sports journalist Frank Deford, in his book *There She Is,* hints that the competition was a type of "debutante ritual for the masses."[119] The contest and parade, together with its festival setting, had the additional

"A Dog's Life Can Be Great," Phoenix, Arizona, $50,000 Phoenix Futurity, March 1, 1960. (Bettmann/Corbis)

purpose of sanctioning the public display of women's bodies. Greyhound-racing promoters eagerly embraced this chance for publicity: Miss New Hampshire graced the cover of the *Greyhound Racing Record* in 1955 along with two brindle greyhounds.[120]

Miss Universe was also a frequent guest at the Florida dog tracks. This beauty contest, held at Miami Beach from 1960 to 1971, generally placed an even greater emphasis on the swimsuit competition over the other qualifications. The Miss Universe event had been launched in 1952 by a swimsuit manufacturer after the 1951 Miss America winner refused to pose in a bathing suit. Miss Universe presented the winner's trophy at Derby Lane on a number of occasions during the 1960s. Other tracks also cashed in on the publicity generated by Miss Universe, including the Palm Beach Kennel Club, which ran a feature race in her honor in 1959. The *Greyhound Racing Record* pictured the recently victorious Miss Universe in 1963 with a champion greyhound at the Miami Beach Kennel Club.[121] On the occasion of her visit to the track, the magazine did not opt for subtlety in its account of the event. The article declared that "Dog players became girl watchers" during the awards presentation of the Miss United States Trophy Race in 1963.[122]

Along with beauty queens, sports stars, and bathing beauties, the greyhound-racing industry embraced another means of advertising the races: participation in parades. These grand spectacles could capture the public eye with an appeal that was nothing short of a promoter's dream. Parades had long been associated with the Miss America contest, and the "queens" showcased in greyhound-racing floats bore a clear resemblance to those seen in beauty pageants and debutante balls. Floats that featured attractive women together with racing greyhounds further linked the sport with ideals of feminine grace and glamour, a vision of beauty that could appeal to women of all classes. In 1952, for instance, the American Greyhound Track Operators Association (AGTOA) float in Daytona featured women competing in the Miss Dixie Beauty Contest. Similarly, floats for the St. Petersburg Kennel Club (widely known as Derby Lane after 1950) aggressively promoted the idea of the "Sport of Queens."[123] These displays typically included women dressed like debutantes in elegant ball gowns, often with white gloves, with an appointed "queen" seated on a covered throne. Live greyhounds—sometimes wearing their racing silks and muzzles—also rode the floats and were presented by smartly uniformed lead-out boys. The message was clear: greyhound racing in Florida signified sexy, glamorous, sporting fun.

Miss Universe Kiriaki Corinna Tsopei and War Penny at Derby Lane greyhound track, ca. 1964, photographed by Maddock Photography in St. Petersburg, Florida. (Derby Lane Kennel Club and Greyhound Hall of Fame)

Greyhound racing in Florida parade float, 1949. (Derby Lane Kennel Club and Greyhound Hall of Fame)

Hollywood celebrities, such as Jimmy Durante, Jerry Lewis, Jackie Gleason, Janet Leigh, Tony Curtis, Burt Reynolds, and Jayne Mansfield, were often pictured in the winner's circle or at promotional events at the Florida dog tracks.[124] Some, like Gleason, who broadcast his show from Miami Beach, the "sun and fun capital of the world," were even owners of racing greyhounds. Dog racing's connection with celebrity culture emerged in Florida, but its footprint was seen elsewhere. Many stars were pictured at dog-racing venues in other areas of the country, especially Arizona, and occasionally Oregon: Paul Newman was photographed studying a racing program at the Tucson Greyhound Park; Merv Griffin was pictured with a racing greyhound wearing a special "Hi! Merv Griffin" racing silk at the Multnomah Kennel Club in Portland; Dean Martin participated in the trophy presentation at Washington Greyhound Park in Phoenix; and John Wayne was a track guest in Tucson, also in the greyhound winner's circle.[125] Florida dog track promoters had in all likelihood instigated this trend and were the driving force behind its dispersal, although another factor was the simple fact that many stars were already on set in Arizona filming upcoming movies.

Celebrities continued to roll into South Florida, especially Miami Beach. Former talent agent Jerry Grant observed that "every superstar in the world came to Miami Beach in the 1950s."[126] Frank Sinatra, accompanied by the "Rat Pack" of Dean Martin, Jerry Lewis, Peter Lawford, Joey Bishop, and Sammy Davis, Jr., partied there and added more than a hint of male swagger and naughtiness to a vibrant social scene one historian has described as "awash in temptation."[127] In 1959 Sinatra even appeared on the cover of the *Greyhound Racing Record* along with a young woman newly crowned as the "Queen of American Greyhound Racing" together with the canine victor in the year's Frank Sinatra feature race.[128]

Only the year before, award-winning director Frank Capra had filmed Sinatra at the Flagler Kennel Club in Miami in his movie *A Hole in the Head*.[129] In this film Sinatra plays a down-on-his-luck hotel owner searching for a way to pay off his debts. Accompanied by Jerry Marks, an old friend from the Bronx who has met with success in Miami by courting ties with shady businessmen, Sinatra's character, Tony Manetta, wins big at the dog races but promptly loses it all again. The footage of the evening races at the Flagler Kennel Club reveals that greyhound racing is still linked with glamour and excitement: Jerry's entourage of beautiful, fashionable ladies (as well as bodyguards and local politicians) watches the races from reserved box seats. Attendants come to them to take their bets so that these high rollers won't miss any of the action. Not much love for the dogs is in evidence, however; one of the wealthy gamblers nonchalantly refers to the racing greyhounds as "miserable beasts." The scene is primarily about gambling and excess, and attendance at the dog races is chiefly a demonstration of wealth and social display. Nor was *A Hole in the Head* the first Hollywood movie to feature the pitfalls of gambling on dog racing. When *Dark Hazard* was released in 1934, betting on greyhound racing was also depicted as a moral danger, a vice that brings down a man who is dogged by his gambling problem and consequently fails to attain respectability in his small midwestern town. Capra's *A Hole in the Head* exudes an altogether more lighthearted feel than *Dark Hazard* and succeeds in capturing the easy, relaxed atmosphere of southern Florida.[130]

The role of television publicity in greyhound racing has long been a thorny issue for the industry. In early years, racetrack operators feared that television would take bettors away from the tracks. Put simply, the perceived risk of the new medium was that fans would passively watch (and soon

Frank Sinatra pictured with brindle racing greyhound, 1959. (Greyhound Hall of Fame)

grow to prefer) televised races rather than attend them in person and participate in sanctioned pari-mutuel betting. They feared losing on-site gambling revenues, but instead they failed to capture the interest of an entire new generation of fans. Other reasons factored in as well, however. NGA's Gary Guccione admits that the greyhound-racing industry probably did not face the prospect of televised dog racing with "undivided attention," but he still feels that it would not have been able to compete with the more monied horse-racing establishment for airtime.[131] Network television executives may also have been nervous initially about showcasing a sport with a strong component of gambling. One gaming analyst has argued that industry leaders in dog racing were even more focused on the gambling customer than the horse-racing operators, who were often thoroughbred owners themselves. These horse owners "focused much more on the horsemen, and took their position as 'sport of kings' with concomitant noblesse oblige."[132] Greyhound racing leaders may have missed out on securing a strong television presence (and increased popularity in the sport) in their single-minded pursuit for profit.

Still, some track promoters were eager to cultivate national attention through the new medium. Greyhound racing, especially in Florida, did benefit occasionally from national television coverage, which, along with journalists in the print media, "fell in love with the Sunshine State in the 1950s and 1960s," according to one historian.[133] Millions of Americans were able to watch the greyhounds compete on seventy-seven NBC stations in an evening feature race held at the Miami Beach Kennel Club in early 1955.[134] One year later, racing greyhounds from Miami appeared on the *Steve Allen Show*. The *Greyhound Racing Record* boasted, "It is seldom that greyhound racing gets a chance like this for national TV publicity."[135] An estimated 45 million viewers watching the show were treated to the spectacle of a pack of greyhounds exiting a Greyhound bus.[136] Greyhounds from the West Flagler Kennel Club had been transported from Miami to New York on a Riddle Airlines cargo plane; once on set, they rehearsed for their big moment.[137]

The greyhound was not often used as a marketing image in American corporate culture, with only a few notable exceptions. The Miami Beach Kennel Club featured an Aviation Night Winner after World War II; in the 1950s it was not unusual to see photographs of racing greyhounds posed with uniformed stewardesses in front of Pan American or National Airlines planes. At this point air travel was still strongly associated with exclusivity and status, a link certainly welcomed by the Miami tracks.

But far better known is the iconic use of the sleek racing dog on the Greyhound bus line. For a time, the company did use a racing greyhound, named Lady Greyhound, for promotions.[138] The Greyhound Corporation had, in fact, established both its bus line and its logo in 1929, independently of the dog-racing industry.[139] Lady Greyhound made her own television debut on April 7, 1957, and reigned for about a decade. She appeared on a number of popular television programs, including shows of Art Linkletter, Steve Allen, Jack Benny, Gary Moore, and Ed Murrow. The mostly white greyhound with patches of gold on her coat often sported a bejeweled collar and diamond-studded tiara. Even she was a beauty queen adorned like her human counterpart, Miss America. Lady Greyhound received a number of honors, including that of "Lady-in-Waiting to Mrs. America," the "Queen of National Transportation Week," and other such titles and awards loosely associated with animal advocacy, including one from the American Humane Association.[140] Lady Greyhound's ultimate purpose, however, was to boost ridership on Greyhound buses, not to increase spectatorship in the sport of her compatriots.

Still, given its numerous promotional successes in the postwar period, many in the industry had hoped to see greyhound racing enter the national sports scene. But instead, gambling on the dogs (as well as the horses) fell under a different type of national scrutiny. U.S. Senator Estes Kefauver's campaign against criminal syndicates captured the national spotlight in 1950 when he formed the Special Committee to Investigate Organized Crime in Interstate Commerce.[141] Many of the committee hearings were aired live on national television, affording most Americans their first glimpse into the machinations of organized crime. The scope of the investigation was broad, and greyhound racing managed to catch the eye of investigators: in its second interim report, the committee charged that Chicago mobsters had succeeded in infiltrating some Florida dog track operations.[142] The committee members eventually concluded that the Florida State Racing Commission had not effectively "removed the cloud" hanging over dog racing in the state as a result of links to Capone's associates. In its final report of 1951, the committee charged that dog track operator William H. Johnston, along with other financiers, had funneled illegal contributions to the 1948 Florida gubernatorial campaign. It was pointed out that Johnston, president of the Miami Beach Kennel Club in the late 1940s and early 1950s, was allegedly an "old-time associate of Al Capone's legatees." Equally troubling, the commission argued, was that Johnston and his tracks "seem to enjoy immunity from State level inquiry."[143]

Those who followed the dog-racing industry were aware of other problems with its public image. In 1953 *Greyhound Racing Record* editor Robert Burtt assessed the current state of dog racing in an article titled "The Sport of Queens Comes of Age." In it, he lamented that the industry had failed to promote itself effectively. Industry leaders had been unable to find a suitable slogan or symbol to focus their marketing efforts, with advertising generally limited to the efforts of individual tracks.[144] Burtt observed with evident frustration that greyhound racing still suffered from a perplexing lack of

Lady Greyhound, ca. 1959. "Lady Greyhound" was the mascot for the Greyhound bus, but she was registered with the National Coursing Association (later the National Greyhound Association). She was promoted as the "famous living symbol of the greyhound corporation" and made her television debut in 1957. (Greyhound Hall of Fame)

national recognition. His attitude reflected the mindset of many of those within the greyhound racing business, one that remains to this day: a sense that they would always remain second-class citizens forced to live in the shadow of horse racing and other big-league sports.

The industry's lack of confidence was not entirely unfounded, however. *Sports Illustrated,* too, noticed greyhound racing's peculiar situation: a 1961 article pointed out that dog racing was Florida's biggest spectator sport, but horse tracks and spring baseball training still received the lion's share of national publicity.[145] A number of industry experts believed that greyhound racing, like horse racing, ought to be and needed to be attracting sustained national media coverage. Yet neither dog nor thoroughbred horse-racing promoters were able to take advantage of the growing power of network television to help popularize their respective sports. Although horse-racing promoters were eventually able to secure a presence on national television (most notably for the Triple Crown and the Breeders' Cup), the thoroughbreds enjoyed an advantage over the greyhounds.[146] Horse racing, unlike dog racing, was legal in leading media markets, such as California, New York, and Illinois. Top venues for greyhound racing—Boston, Denver, Miami, to name a few—were usually only able to garner local and regional publicity. In dramatic contrast, television catapulted the popularity of professional football and basketball in the 1960s. Even sports with a more modest fan base in the United States, such as ice hockey, golf, and tennis, were eventually able to claim a continuing presence on network television.[147]

Burtt pointed to other troubles as well. He bemoaned the fact that greyhound racing was always forced to take a defensive stance, "maneuvered by its enemies into explaining its right to exist."[148] Although this statement called attention to all detractors of the sport, the subtext was no less clear: thoroughbred horse-racing interests had for years watched the growth of greyhound racing with a wary eye. Greyhound racing leaders, too, had rather obsessively compared themselves with horse racing, not only because of their obvious similarities but also because dog and horse racing were the only sports in the United States—with the exception of jai alai, which was only legal in Florida—with sanctioned pari-mutuel wagering.[149] A 1965 article in *Time* magazine, which acknowledged that dog racing had "almost" achieved respectability, captured the chilly relationship between the dog and horse racing: "Talk about greyhound racing to a horseman, and his lip curls in contempt."[150]

Hostility had been felt on both sides of the fence from the beginning. A headline in the *Greyhound Racing Record,* an organ of the Florida racing industry, complained that the horse-racing lobby had resorted in 1955 to a "vicious whispering campaign" with the aim of eliminating the possibility of dog racing in New Hampshire.[151] Suspicions that horse-racing interests were working against dog racing behind the scenes were supported in a confidential FBI report from the 1970s. In it, one federal agent noted, "Whenever greyhound racing attempts to obtain a state license, usually thoroughbred racing interests make an effort to block their attempt to obtain a license, inasmuch as thoroughbred track owners believe greyhound racing would take wagering money away from the thoroughbred business and thus cause a decline in their mutual [sic] handle."[152]

What remained after all of the industry's efforts and frustrations over several decades was a considerable disconnect between image and reality in greyhound racing. In Florida and throughout the United States, dog racing was still hampered by a number of persistent problems with its public image. To begin with, greyhound racing's self-proclaimed identity as the elite "Sport of Queens" did not, in fact, mirror reality: dog-racing fans were largely middle and working class, and the glamorous image associated with some of the early tracks, such as the Miami Beach Kennel Club, was gradually fading. One reporter cynically described this track as early as 1964 as filled with "noisy people sloshing frothy beer on their gaudy shirt-fronts," adding that "there is a sameness about them," a comment virtually unthinkable in the exuberant dispatches broadcast from South Florida in the 1930s.[153] The drive for expansion into new markets, even those in low-income areas, muddied the industry's efforts to maintain its would-be high-brow reputation. If more and more Americans were attending dog racing at new venues in Florida and elsewhere in the country, how could all of the fans be a part of a so-called elite culture? Historian Gary Mormino observed that a vacation in the Sunshine State, "once a luxury for the conspicuous few, has become commonplace for millions of working- and middle-class Americans."[154] Following the opening of Disney World in 1971, much of Florida entertainment was increasingly controlled by corporate giants. Florida tourism, defined by corporate mass culture, could no longer be credibly linked with elite pastimes.[155]

Nonetheless, for millions of fans and other pleasure-seekers, the sport of greyhound racing reached its apogee in the Sunshine State. Flush with profits, industry leaders gushed to any and all that dog racing had become Florida's top spectator sport.[156] The greyhound-racing industry was also expanding, drawing tourists to regions that had previously been untapped for dog racing. With attendance at the tracks still on the rise and pari-mutuel handles on the upswing, most experts in the industry had good reason to believe that racing in Florida—and elsewhere—would continue to flourish. A winning combination of sun, fun, and a hint of naughtiness had propelled the sport to new heights. By 1970 the integration of greyhound racing into Florida's tourist menu would be complete.

This spirit of optimism shared by promoters and fans of the sport would, in due time, be quashed. Dog racing soon faced a new foe: animal advocates eager to eliminate greyhound racing altogether. Initially, many industry insiders underestimated the potential political strength of their opponents. But beginning in the 1970s, the growing animal protection movement was gradually beginning to succeed in its attempts to scratch off the patina of glamour, sun, and fun attached to the sport of dog racing and expose a hitherto invisible darker side, the racing industry's widespread "disposal" of otherwise healthy greyhounds once their running careers were over and they were no longer considered useful. With the simultaneous rise of pet keeping in the United States and the multi-million-dollar industry that grew up to support and perpetuate it, traditional, utilitarian attitudes toward animals (many of which were still embraced by the dogmen charged with caring for the greyhounds) were rapidly falling out of favor in the United States. Animal protectionists began to cast much of the blame for the poor treatment of the greyhounds on the dogmen, an attack that may not have been free from class overtones, in light of the thoroughbred horse-racing industry's relative immunity from similar criticism at the time. Despite the fact that thousands of ex-racing horses were also being discarded after they were no longer "useful," the public eye was now fixed on the dogs. Internal and external difficulties facing the greyhound-racing industry would soon threaten the very existence of the sport—and those who made their living from it—throughout the United States. For animal protectionists, however, it was the dawn of a new era, and anti-racing activists were poised to strike at greyhound racing's very core: the use of animals for entertainment.

CHAPTER FIVE

DOGGONE MAD

You would have dogs coming out your ears . . . if you didn't destroy them.
Greyhound kennel owner Bill Maloney, speaking to the disposition of ex-racing greyhounds, *Inside Edition*, 1990

In 2009 Wayne Strong, a veteran dogman headquartered in Abilene, Kansas, the heart of the dog-racing industry, agreed to discuss his experiences in the industry and his commitment and willingness to "pet out"—find adoptive homes for—his own racing greyhounds once they were ready for retirement. He acknowledged that there was a dark side to the sport, but he believed that racing dogs lived a "golden life" while in the business. Strong admitted that as he grew older, he had become more sensitive to the needs of his animals and almost felt as if he could see into their minds. But when he looked at a picture of an adopted greyhound sprawled out on a queen-sized bed in deep repose, he shook his head in disgust and muttered to himself, "That dog has nothing to live for."[1]

For Strong, greyhounds are meant to race. In his mind, it was unfair to subject this canine athlete, bred for centuries as a sight hound, to a sedentary life in an urban apartment. Like Strong, the community of dogmen has never questioned their own use of greyhounds for sport. Put simply, their lifestyle is fundamentally based on the utilitarian use of animals, fostered by an agricultural mindset. Animals are viewed as a type of property vital to one's livelihood and treated accordingly; their value is economic rather than sentimental.[2] By the end of the twentieth century, however, Strong's views—and those of his fellow dogmen—were increasingly out of favor in the United States.

Strong's views are not unique among those working directly with breeding, training, and racing greyhounds. In 1992 Joseph E. Sullivan III, the owner of the Hinsdale, New Hampshire, dog track, declared, "There are 2,000 years of philosophy and human development that say man is superior to animals and animals can be used by man. . . . You find it in the Book of Genesis and in Aristotle, Thomas Aquinas, St. Augustine, and Descartes."[3]

He acknowledged that he was bothered by the euthanasia of ex-racing grey-hounds, but as a track owner he had been doing all he could do to ensure that they were treated well while racing.

British historian Keith Thomas has observed that Western philosophers in the early modern period (1500–1800) began to grapple with the idea that animals were entitled to some degree of moral consideration. The an-thropocentric tradition enshrined by Aristotle was gradually replaced by a more "modern sensibility" toward animals. Put simply, there was a grow-ing tendency to challenge long-held beliefs that honored man's central posi-tion over animals. Christianity, as it was widely interpreted at the time, had placed man in a position of authority over all other creatures. But during this shift toward a broader sensibility, nonhuman animals were increasingly credited with "reason, intelligence, language, and almost every other hu-man quality."[4] While the dogmen (and their counterparts) have still tended to honor the Old Testament edict granting man's dominion over animals, animal protectionists operate under a different set of beliefs and standards.[5] Animal activists have professionalized and institutionalized the concept of compassion toward animals symbolized by St. Francis of Assisi.[6] They have also been influenced by Enlightenment thinkers who recognized that all sentient beings are capable of feeling pain, a notion most famously ar-ticulated by the British social reformer Jeremy Bentham, who stated, "The question is not, Can they *reason?* nor, Can they *talk?* but, Can they *suffer?*" Some animal protectionists have taken this line of reasoning a step further and maintain that animals deserve certain rights, an argument advanced by contemporary philosophers such as Tom Regan and attorneys such as Steven M. Wise and Gary Francione.

These Western ideas about the rights of animals, which were strength-ened by the Victorian emphasis on kindness toward animals and the sub-sequent rise of pet keeping in American society, have led many families to consider their dogs as individuals with unique, valuable lives, as special family members who deserve soft beds, superior medical care, and a happy, comfortable existence.[7] As more and more Americans became detached from agrarian lifestyles, dogs were increasingly viewed solely as pets rather than as working animals. As a consequence the utilitarian outlook of grey-hound breeders, owners, and trainers eventually—and perhaps inevitably—came under fire.

Greyhound racing has thus become a point of conflict among Ameri-cans of decidedly diverse ideological persuasions about the role of animals. While for some, a utilitarian attitude toward animals may still be accepted as a fixture of daily life, others have concluded that their use inevitably leads to abuse. In 1986 Jill Hopfenbeck was a veterinary student at Tufts University; she had never been exposed to greyhounds. When she entered the anatomy lab, however, she was taken aback by the sight of twenty preserved corpses of ex-racing greyhounds on dissecting tables. Their ear tattoos revealed that none was older than three years. After this rather surprising discovery Hopfenbeck began to feel that something larger was amiss, and from that point on she was gradually transformed into an anti-racing activist.[8]

The awakening of Hopfenback's critical interest in the world of greyhound racing was no isolated event. Damaging media reports and exposés beginning in the late 1970s had unleashed a period of aggressive criticism of the dog-racing industry by the 1980s. Detractors declared that the sport was inherently cruel and that no level of reform could rid greyhound racing of its evils. Both the dogmen and the promoters had seen it coming, but as one industry insider has admitted, "The track operators were arrogant."[9] The resulting media assault, prominently launched in 1978 by a damaging exposé on ABC's premiere broadcast of its news magazine *20/20*, left the industry on the defensive and many animal advocates eager to eliminate dog racing altogether, a pattern that continues today. Indeed, over the final three decades of the twentieth century, animal protectionists effectively planted seeds of doubt in much of the broader American public about the very feasibility of a cruelty-free greyhound-racing industry.

Contrary to the assertions of some anti-racing activists, greyhound racing has never been entirely free of criticism from the news media, which for many years before 1978 had questioned the morality of gambling and also occasionally found fault with the industry's treatment of animals.[10] The focus and tenor of media criticism gradually changed from mildly critical to graphic and confrontational. A notable early exception was an exposé printed in 1958 in *Argosy,* a popular men's magazine. An article covering the welfare of the ex-racing greyhound came as somewhat of a surprise given the magazine's previous incarnation as a pulp publication, but *Argosy* had recently shifted its focus and included a wider range of serious subjects. The May 1958 cover shows four racing greyhounds and poses the question, "Must These Dogs Die?"[11] The article revealed one consequence of greyhound racing little known to the public at the time: dogs who were poor racers were likely to be killed.

The stark reality of euthanasia was presented directly to *Argosy*'s readers and included a picture of a dead greyhound being removed from a decompression chamber. Graphic photographs of dead greyhounds were rarely, if ever, in circulation at this time, but in this case the disposal of ex-racing dogs was addressed with complete openness and honesty. A range of individuals involved in dog racing were interviewed and quoted in the article. Dogman Clyde Boyd stated that three types of greyhound exist in each litter: those who race, those who breed, and those who are destroyed. A prominent Miami veterinarian admitted that he euthanized hundreds of greyhounds every year, but he, too, felt that there was no alternative. Another person simply remarked, "It's not the dog's fault and it's not the owner's. It's just the way things are." The purpose of the *Argosy* article was, however, not to propose the discontinuation of dog racing but to document that the widespread "slaughter" of greyhounds was "unavoidable, and nobody's fault."[12]

Argosy's public critique of the industry did not go unnoticed in Abilene, Kansas, where the National Greyhound Association (NGA) had been headquartered since 1945. Minutes from the organization's 1958 spring meeting reveal that its members found the article "detrimental," even though it addressed a subject that the industry itself had already identified as a concern.[13] In fact, much of the industry-supported press such as the *Greyhound Racing Record* was fairly open about the consequences of large-scale greyhound racing: dogs that were too slow for racing because of age or injury as well as those not talented enough to train in the first place were simply put to death.[14] Complaints about the breeding of too many dogs began to appear in industry publications in the early 1950s.[15] The statistics were unsettling: a 1952 article in the *Greyhound Racing Record* openly admitted that fewer than 30 percent of greyhounds were "usable" for track racing.[16] Bob Burtt, the lead editor, while readily acknowledging a range of problems in the burgeoning industry, focused on the loss of money involved with raising dogs that would never make the track rather than the inevitable loss of life. Burtt noted that in earlier years, when kennels were smaller, greyhounds were raised around a farmhouse in the open rather than in pens. The dogs trained in open fields, and, most important, only higher-quality greyhounds were bred. Burtt clearly recognized the hazards of breeding for quantity rather than quality. He was not alone in his observations; many dogmen were also complaining about this growing problem.[17]

The problem only worsened. During the 1970s, new states legalized dog racing, more Americans attended the races, and more greyhounds had to be bred. In order to meet the increased demand for racing dogs, breeding operations grew significantly during the second half of the twentieth century, sometimes putting the "mom and pop" operations in competition with kennels up to ten times their size.[18] The business of greyhound racing was changing, and the industry recognized its own growing pains. The number of greyhounds no longer "useful" after their racing careers had ended was steadily increasing. From the perspective of the dogmen it was not viable economically to care for the animals that were no longer earning their keep. This was a simple fact of the business, and the decision to discard ex-racers was, for them, a simple necessity.

The NGA has not kept data on kennel size, but the evolution of greyhound kennels can still be broadly outlined. Breeding farms can loosely be categorized into three classes: "mom and pop" businesses with fewer than 40 dogs, medium-sized operations with fewer than 100 dogs, and large compounds with more than 100 and sometimes up to 400 greyhounds.[19] As early as the 1950s, a few greyhound kennels were already fairly large, such as Ned Randle's farm near Wichita, Kansas, with its nearly 100 animals.[20] In the 1960s the Kirkpatrick family ran a large greyhound business in Texas, and the O. K. Duke farm in Lee, Florida, was also of significant size. A number of large kennels expanded during the 1970s and 1980s— some farms managed more than 400 greyhounds—and were able to acquire a large number of bookings at a variety of tracks around the country. The Beckner farm in Florida had between 400 and 700 greyhounds.[21] Dick Andrews estimated that between 500 and 600 dogs were cared for at his farms in Abilene, Kansas, and Jacksonville, Florida, in addition to those that were leased in his racing kennels.[22] Gordon Davis, Jr., owner of Kansas Kennels, was another major kennel operator at the time.[23] In 1980 Tom Sellman was managing two farms, nine employees, and, in his words, 400 "head" of dogs, a term commonly employed to indicate the number of cattle.[24]

Not everyone who worked directly with the dogs was comfortable with these rapidly growing breeding operations. Clarence Connick, a greyhound trainer highly respected by his peers, observed in 1982 that greyhound racing had evolved into a "mass production system" in which owners unreasonably expected one man to care for forty dogs.[25] He considered it impossible for one individual to care for so many greyhounds, a situation made worse by the fact that as the first generation of experienced trainers retired, many were replaced by inexperienced kennel help.[26]

Moreover, some dogmen believed firmly that too many greyhounds from inferior bloodlines were being bred. This created a glut of dogs in the market, a significant number of which had limited racing talent.[27] At the same time, the eventual quasi-industrialization of greyhound kennels dramatically changed the work of many dogmen from that of skilled trainers into little more than kennel janitors, according to one retired dogman, and further sullied their already tarnished reputation.[28]

Modernized greyhound breeding practices also contributed to the increasing overproduction of racing stock. In the 1970s the NGA began to allow racing greyhounds to be artificially inseminated; frozen sperm was first used in the following decade.[29] Instead of transporting brood bitches for breeding, semen was shipped to them. With frozen semen a greyhound bitch in heat could be bred to a stud at any time without requiring the bitch's owner or trainer to schedule an appointment and travel along with the bitch to the kennel where the stud was kept.[30] The top greyhounds were increasingly used for more and more breedings, which for some critics risked contributing to "compressed pedigrees," or a lack of genetic diversity.[31] Prior to 1970, the top ten stud dogs might partake in 25 percent of matings, but by the end of the century they were responsible for about half. Additionally, the market for frozen semen was globalized beginning in the twenty-first century.[32] In prior years, greyhounds from Ireland or Australia had to be imported in order to diversify the gene pool and thereby improve the level of racing, but the introduction of frozen semen simplified the process enormously. These developments all made it possible for more greyhounds to be bred with greater ease and at a lower cost.[33]

Not surprisingly, the size of racing kennels—as opposed to breeding and training farms—was increasing at the same time. Craig Randle, an NGA inspector, attests that "megakennels" began to emerge by the 1980s, some with as many as 200 dogs.[34] Complicating the problem was a decision by track owners to permit kennels to race with "open lists" rather than "closed lists," the latter traditionally limiting participation to around twenty-four preselected dogs.[35] The new system, which emerged in the mid–1980s, allowed for frequent substitutions or replacements on the "open list" of eligible racing dogs and thus reinforced the growing preference that injured or race-weary animals requiring additional care and rest should be replaced instead of rehabilitated. Randle believes that the tracks simply thought it would be easier to work with fewer racing kennels, but the end result was the frequent disposal of dogs that would, at one point, have had a chance to develop and excel on the track.

As the dogmen well know but the betting public may not all realize, the racing quality of dogs at each track varies considerably. Simply put, not all tracks are alike. A grading system was institutionalized in the late 1940s and early 1950s by Paul Hartwell, Sr., an experienced and highly respected racing secretary. Responding to widespread complaints that the method of selecting dogs for races was unfair and arbitrary, he devised the Hartwell Grading System to systematize the process. His design is still in use today with only minor differences. Current versions do vary slightly according to place and time, but Hartwell's system allows the racing secretary to classify each dog in a racing kennel into one of five or six categories depending on its past performances. The skill categories range from grade A, which is reserved for the best racers, gradually down through grades B, C, and D, and ending with E. Most tracks also include grade M ("maiden") for dogs entering competition for the first time.[36]

Hartwell's system was designed to establish industry-wide consistency of racing quality by increasing the likelihood that greyhounds of equal or similar ability would be placed in the same racing grade. His modifications did improve the perpetually strained relationships between dogmen and track officials; most agreed that it resulted in fairer competition for all parties involved. Unfortunately, it also created a hierarchy by which some greyhounds were more valued than others. As one director of racing succinctly explained the problem, "As you move down the [hierarchy of] tracks, there's an increasing problem of disposing of dogs."[37]

There were other unexpected consequences of increased greyhound production. Animal protectionists had long been troubled by the growing problem of pet overpopulation in the United States, and they now felt that the rapidly expanding greyhound industry was making the situation even more desperate.[38] The Humane Society of the United States (HSUS) estimated in the early 1970s that 13.5 million unwanted dogs and cats were euthanized each year in the nation's shelters.[39] Animal advocates contended that the influx of ex-racing greyhounds at animal shelters—already overrun with homeless but often healthy animals slated for euthanasia—was an added burden that shelter personnel could not handle. Animal protectionists were outraged by the dogmen's practice of having greyhounds euthanized, but they were even angrier when they were asked to complete the task for them. Carter Luke, CEO and president of the Massachusetts Society for the Prevention of Cruelty to Animals (MSPCA), stated that for a time large numbers of ex-racing greyhounds were being taken to his agency's facilities to be killed humanely. When critics complained, the dogmen stopped bringing in their greyhounds and instead found other means of disposing of them.[40] Many suspected that the alternative methods used to destroy greyhounds were less than humane. Like many other animal protectionists, Luke resented being forced into the system of disposal, stating that he did not like making a "deal with the devil" to euthanize ex-racing hounds.[41] MSPCA shelter manager Joe Silva stated in 1992 that "at some point, we have to ask whether we're really providing humane deaths or are part of the problem."[42]

At one time many greyhound owners, breeders, and trainers had hoped that larger kennels would lead to a more robust industry with heftier profits, but the economy of scale proved to be a double-edged sword. Dogmen were, in fact, able to raise more dogs and in some cases make more money. But as more and more greyhounds were bred, more and more were slated to die. This quasi-industrialized version of greyhound production eventually reached a level that industry critics deemed intolerable.[43] When kennels were small, most Americans could not or did not take notice of the scale of greyhound breedings and disposals, but the expanded industry produced a huge surplus of ex-racing dogs that was increasingly hard to miss. Angry animal advocates responded to the crisis by publicizing the grim consequences of bulk killing, often distributing pictures of dead, recently euthanized greyhounds, sometimes even stacked in piles.[44] A number of exposés even documented the act of killing by filming lethal injections.[45] Invariably, the greyhounds featured in the press were killed at animal shelters and humane societies, the very facilities that were supposed to protect animals from harm. Animal protectionists, frustrated by their forced involvement in the system, often placed the blame squarely on the dogmen.

As a consequence of these problems, the dog-racing industry has supported, although did not conceive of, the now widely popular movement to have ex-racing greyhounds adopted into permanent family homes. Initially, however, both animal advocates and dogmen resisted the idea. The concept of widespread greyhound adoption by American families (as an alternative to euthanasia) was at this point unheard of. In fact, the executive secretary of the Humane Society in Miami, Mrs. Charles W. Pusey, specifically and confidently stated in 1958 that the racing greyhound "can't be adjusted to ordinary household standards. He's strictly a kennel dog, and can't be anything else."[46] She declared that her agency had tried placing greyhounds in homes, without success, because "racing dogs are vicious and completely unmanageable. . . . They kill smaller animals and bite everything in sight, including people of all ages."[47] If greyhounds were adopted in American homes, the article warned, owners would be driven crazy with lawsuits filed by butchers, bakers, milkmen, mailmen, and mothers of "chewed-up" children. This view was held by some prominent humane organizations well into the 1970s. The HSUS contended in a 1975 article that greyhounds were destroyed after racing because they did not make suitable pets. Specifically, their upbringing made it "difficult for them to relate with people" and their "killer instinct" forced them to bite anything that moved, including people.[48]

As for the dogmen, they themselves often preferred to see their dogs euthanized rather than placed in homes where they might live dull, sedentary lives or, worse, suffer from abuse.[49] In recounting her family's history in the greyhound business, Leslie Wootten writes that her uncle Robert felt it was "not only expedient, but humane" to shoot a racing greyhound between the eyes when its career was over. In this way, he knew "without a doubt it was taken care of, something he could not guarantee if it was handed over to someone else."[50] In essence, the dogmen felt that they would still be held responsible even for what happened to the dogs once they were out of their care. In their experience families outside of the industry could not handle the idiosyncrasies of the breed. Furthermore, dogmen could often not afford to devote time or money to the time-consuming task of finding homes for ex-racers. Individual practices varied, but initially there was a fair amount of resistance to greyhound adoption in the dog-racing community.

Another theory explaining the industry's initial unwillingness to embrace adoption is decidedly cynical: the dogmen and their associates did not want outsiders to know just how many dogs were being disposed of as part of standard business practice. Adoption pioneer Ron Walsek stated in 1992 that the biggest reason why adoption was slow to catch on was because "greyhound tracks just wanted to keep it a deep secret that thousands of dogs are killed each year." Walsek suspected that when more dogs were adopted, Americans would want to know what had happened to the rest. At first, only the racing industry was aware that an overabundance of dogs was a problem. Outside the public space of the track, greyhound racing remained a closed society, and most Americans knew little to nothing about breeding practices or other aspects of the industry. Adoption opened a door that many now believe has, somewhat unexpectedly, contributed to the industry's steady decline.[51]

A miniscule number of greyhounds had been placed into homes before 1980, but the process had rarely been a coordinated effort. Beginning in the early 1980s, a few concerned individuals who objected to the high number of greyhounds discarded after their careers were over began to establish adoption groups.[52] Their goal was both to rescue ex-racers slated for euthanasia and to prepare them for daily life as domestic pets in permanent, loving homes. Greyhounds trained for racing had little or no knowledge of the family home environment, including glass doors, stairs, and furniture. But adoption leaders soon realized that greyhounds could overcome their unfamiliarity with domestic life (e.g., learn to climb stairs) after several days or weeks of training. With time and patience most ex-racing dogs could be smoothly integrated into family homes.

The relationship between the greyhound industry and adoption groups was often tense since the latter were often openly anti-racing and viewed their mission as a "rescue" operation designed to "save" ex-racing greyhounds.[53] Some early adoption pioneers wanted nothing to do with the industry and criticized its practices quite openly. Hugh Geoghegan made certain that he operated independently of it: he established the Greyhound Rescue Association (GRA) out of his Cambridge, Massachusetts, home and later helped found the Greyhound Project, a New England adoption group. Organizations such as the GRA, with an unbending anti-racing ideology, upset industry leaders. In response the industry established the American Greyhound Council (AGC) in 1987, to "fund and manage greyhound welfare, research and adoption programs for the racing community."[54] That same year, independent adoption groups and greyhound owners created Greyhound Pets of America (GPA); local chapters of GPA were soon set up throughout the country. Working in tandem with GPA, the AGC disbursed grant monies to its eligible adoption groups.[55] Persons associated both with GPA and with other groups that partnered in some way with the industry, such as Retired Greyhounds as Pets (REGAP), were generally expected to maintain a "racing-neutral" public platform and devote their energies to finding homes for greyhounds rather than criticizing the industry. This policy of "muzzling" adoption volunteers continues to be a controversial albeit loosely policed rule.

Now that the adoption of ex-racing greyhounds has become a mainstream phenomenon in American culture, there is a certain social cachet to adopting a "rescue" animal. Australian sociologist Raymond Madden believes that the image of the greyhound has shifted from a "glamour pedigree sport dog" to a working-class emblem (as a racer) and finally to a regular family dog with a "rescue" label. The last concept, according to Madden, is represented in popular culture by Homer Simpson's rescue greyhound, Santa's Little Helper. Here, the "racing" and "rescue" narratives overlap; a dog once vulnerable to exploitation by gamblers (greyhound as "racer") is released into the safe domestic sphere (greyhound as "rescue"). The greyhound has long signified "class," but throughout history, it has paradoxically functioned both as a prized companion of the elite and as a victim "enslaved in the 'sordid cruelty' of working-class recreation and gambling." Examples of the former abound in popular narratives of the greyhound, most prominently Cynthia Branigan's *The Reign of the Greyhound,* an example of the "ancient and noble" trope of the racing greyhound. Rescuers can borrow from both ideals. They can feel rewarded for removing an animal from peril and enjoy their brush with aristocracy if they are inclined to consider their pet's bloodlines as elite.[56]

The evident overproduction of greyhounds was not the only concern facing the industry. The use of jackrabbits (and other small live animals) for training and for coursing threatened to discredit it further. In fact, the use of jackrabbits for coursing, which had only occasionally been criticized at the turn of the nineteenth century, continued to be the primary target of sporadic negative media attention, albeit primarily within animal advocacy circles. *Sports Illustrated* had occasionally covered coursing and greyhound racing in a positive light in the 1960s and 1970s, but a 1975 article focused entirely on the use of live rabbits during training.[57] The HSUS had already taken notice of this practice in the early 1970s when it announced that its most severe criticism of the dog industry was directed at the use of live rabbits as lures.[58] Several other articles followed in the HSUS bulletin that tracked the problem, but the number of Americans who read the publication was likely rather low; in 1976 the HSUS had only around 30,000 members.[59]

The visibility of the issue increased dramatically when Geraldo Rivera, reporting for ABC's *20/20,* joined HSUS investigator Frantz Dantzler to film a public coursing event in Abilene, Kansas. Rivera's decision to focus on the topic may have been inspired by his concern for animals, but he also probably realized that "animal rights" was becoming a hot-button topic and would attract audiences for his brand-new show. Immediately distancing himself from the label of animal rights zealot, Rivera opened the segment (which aired in 1978) with the statement that you "don't have to be . . . 'animal crazy' to know that the way we treat animals is a reflection of the way we treat each other."[60] Rivera pointed out that 20 million Americans bet more than $2 billion at dog tracks in 1977, but then he wondered out loud "how popular greyhound racing would be if fans knew just how the greyhounds were trained."

Several spectators at the coursing meet were interviewed on camera. One unidentified individual stated that if live coursing was cruelty, it was "necessary cruelty," and that jackrabbits had long been regarded as pests by farmers and ought to be killed.[61] HSUS's Dantzler attacked this reasoning head on, stating that this line of justification was "pure nonsense." Dantzler maintained that jackrabbits no longer lived in the wild in Kansas and were in fact shipped in from West Texas for coursing events at the cost of $6 a head. To the American public this could not have been common knowledge, even though *Greyhound Racing Record* had long been printing advertisements placed by jackrabbit suppliers.[62] The ABC exposé concluded with an interview with Bob Dole, then a U.S. senator from Kansas, who called coursing an act of "inhumanity" and "cruelty" and vowed to introduce legislation to make public coursing illegal. Indiana senator Birch Bayh submitted an even more aggressive bill; he proposed to halt all training practices using live animals.[63]

The broadcast, like others that followed, contained a secondary unspoken dimension: the issue of class. According to one dogman, the story unfairly portrayed the people at the coursing event as lowly and crass. Specifically, he complained that the editing made it appear as if the attendees at the coursing event were eating rabbits rather than barbecued chicken. After the feature aired, "people wouldn't look at us at the grocery store"; he and his family long felt shunned by the local community.[64]

Kansas dogmen were not the only ones to experience backlash generated by the report. The public response to the 20/20 story was immediate and damaging to the NGA and greyhound racing as a whole. According to the NGA, it received the "most 'hate' mail this Association has ever seen," stating further that "the scars inflicted from a public-relations standpoint could take years to heal." The industry admitted in the *Greyhound Review* that "never in the 58-year history of Greyhound racing has the sport in this country received as much detrimental publicity as it has in the last 30 days."[65] Critics of greyhound racing were referred to in industry publications as "maniacs" as well as "do-gooders," a term that had long been used to describe animal advocates in public discourse. Even more interesting was the industry's acknowledgment that some members of the racing community had been warned about these "fanatics" but no one had taken them seriously.[66] Despite its initial failure to ignore signs of trouble, the NGA did eventually respond to the publicity storm that followed and decided to discontinue the use of live rabbits at public coursing events. Private coursing events continued, however, as did the use of live rabbits in these venues.

Even within the industry, opinions varied about the viability of continuing the use of live prey. In 1973 an NGA committee discussed the possibility of eliminating public coursing events, partially because of the poor quality of jackrabbits but also due to the association's fear of adverse publicity.[67] Three years later a letter from the president of the Kansas Greyhound Breeders Association, Gordon Davis, Jr., was read at an NGA board meeting. Attendees were informed that unless public coursing with live rabbits ended, legislation would be enacted that prohibited their use for any reason, including training. The *Greyhound Review* conducted a poll of NGA members in 1976 inquiring whether public coursing with live rabbits sponsored by the organization should continue in Abilene; 96 members voted yes, 173 voted no.[68]

A lengthier discussion took place at the NGA's regular fall meeting in 1976, at which point internal division within the greyhound community over the issue was increasingly evident. Ed Craig stated to the membership that a diminishing jackrabbit population in Kansas was the main problem faced by coursing enthusiasts. To make possible their use in an event, they had to be shipped in by the hundreds from western Texas and New Mexico, confined in holding pens on site before they were used, and, in his words, left exposed to the elements all night. The conversation inevitably turned to humane organizations, which, according to Dean Childress, were the least of their worries. He questioned why it was acceptable to use 600 rabbits a week for live lure training but unacceptable to use 400 rabbits twice a year for a coursing meet. Another member tersely responded that one was public and the other, live lure training, was not. This individual, who is only referenced as "Hooper," claimed that killing a jackrabbit in a coursing event was more humane than any other way it was killed in the world. He also maintained that humane societies "had never won a battle anywhere if you fought them."[69] Hooper's statement may have reflected some ineffectiveness of humane societies in past attempts to eliminate dog racing and coursing, but it certainly did not foresee the relationship between the two factions that was to emerge in the future.

The HSUS was behind yet another damaging episode for the greyhound industry in the late 1980s. In 1988 Gail Eisnitz, then a novice undercover agent for the HSUS, posed as an animal illustrator and gained the trust of several dogmen in Lee, Florida, a small town sixty miles east of Tallahassee.[70] What she learned about their treatment of animals—the use of live lures—led to a joint raid with the Florida Game Commission and Madison County law enforcement. The first of its kind, the raid resulted in the arrest of a dozen dogmen, including lead trainer Robert Mendheim.[71] He groused that during the raid, "You'd have thought they were after Bonnie and Clyde or John Dillinger."[72]

In addition to their importation of jackrabbits, which was illegal under Florida law, Mendheim and the others were caught using live lures during training. Unaware of their being under surveillance, they had tied a rabbit onto the training track's mechanical lure for the greyhounds to chase.[73] Four men, including Mendheim, were charged with a felony and the remaining eight with a misdemeanor. They were later acquitted but were nonetheless suspended from greyhound racing by the Florida Division of Pari-Mutuel Racing.[74] The HSUS had long suspected that greyhound trainers were using live lures even though their public statements were met with fierce denials. In 1989 former HSUS investigator Robert Baker stated that two years before the sting in Lee, Florida, "Robert Mendheim telephoned our Tallahassee office to boast that he was no longer using live lures in training. Look where he is today."[75] Writing for the *Greyhound Review* in 1993, Tim Horan declared that the industry itself had never suspended anyone for the use of live lures but was instead focused on the well-being of greyhounds rather than playing "detective like the HSUS does." The industry has continued to struggle with the issue.[76] In 2011 an Abilene veterinarian admitted that he knew of a prominent trainer who still used live lures, even though their use for training is no longer allowed in Kansas, Oklahoma, Texas, Florida, or any other state where greyhounds are trained or raced.[77]

The campaign to abolish greyhound racing sometimes even appeared to harbor a class-based bias against the persons who worked directly with the animals, namely, the dogmen, and also against the gamblers who bet on the dogs. In recent years sociologists have started to grapple with the demographics of animal rights activism and have observed that the majority of activists are female, white, well educated, and often middle-class or affluent.[78] In contrast, their targets often, although not always, belong to a lower socioeconomic demographic. Dogmen frequently complain of biased treatment solely because of their trade.[79]

Indeed, the dogmen believe that dog racing is criticized with greater vigor than its American counterpart, thoroughbred horse racing. For more than a decade, greyhound racing has been faced with an animal protection organization—GREY2K USA—devoted exclusively to eliminating it.[80] In contrast, horse racing, dog racing's closest cousin, has never been confronted with a comparable anti-racing opponent, one that is solely charged with ending the industry. Similarly, while the HSUS firmly speaks out against all greyhound racing, it is noticeably more circumspect when criticizing various aspects of thoroughbred horse racing. The organization acknowledges the many problems in the sport but does not call for its elimination altogether.[81] Long the domain of wealthy families such as the Belmonts, Guggenheims, Whitneys, and Woodwards, horse racing is a much more powerful and intimidating target than the working-class dogmen of more humble origins. This uneven treatment of greyhound racing versus horse racing may stem from a class-based bias against the former, but it may also derive from the perception that dogs are essentially pets while horses are simply livestock, even in those cases in which they are tremendously valuable.[82] Another possibility is that there is a stronger association between greyhound racing and gambling than that between thoroughbred horse racing and gambling, thus accounting for some of the cultural biases.[83] HSUS president Wayne Pacelle does not believe that his organization's differing stance on the two sports is "explicitly a class issue"; instead, he maintains that the approach of the HSUS has more to do with "the visibility and acceptance of the [greyhound and horse racing] industries. Greyhound racing is not nearly as entrenched in this country as horse racing."[84]

That being said, horse racing has in recent years come under increasing fire for animal welfare concerns. To cite three more prominent examples, the highly publicized breakdowns and deaths of Eight Belles (2008) and Barbaro (2007), and decades earlier, Ruffian (1975), all grabbed national headlines. Recent articles in the *New York Times* have exposed appalling injury rates in thoroughbred horses, especially at certain tracks where claiming races are held. It is statistically more dangerous to be a thoroughbred racehorse than an average racing greyhound, but dog racing is often painted as altogether crueler and more destructive.[85]

Greyhounds, too, can and have been fatally injured while racing, but in truth the thoroughbred horse is a considerably more fragile animal than the racing greyhound and is thus at greater risk of a catastrophic breakdown. As veterinarian Larry Bramlage has observed, thoroughbreds "run right on the edge of their physiology" given the tremendous weight and force that their fragile ankle bones are required to support.[86] Greyhounds, in contrast, are equipped with an altogether more robust physiology, their lean physiques notwithstanding. Dogs are certainly at risk of injury when they race, or, for that matter, when they compete in any other athletic competition, such as flyball, but most injuries sustained on the track can be repaired with proper medical treatment.[87] Nonetheless, GREY2K USA bases much of its anti-racing ideology on the premise that greyhound racing is a high-risk enterprise for the dogs. The fact remains that a broken ankle in a thoroughbred racer is potentially far more devastating.

Likewise, dog racing was for years criticized for its failure to find permanent homes for ex-racers. While greyhound adoption rates have now improved dramatically, the disposition of thoroughbred horses that are no longer raceworthy remains a serious problem. The most famous example is Ferdinand, the 1986 Kentucky Derby champion who is believed to have met his end in a Japanese slaughterhouse.[88] A 2012 photograph in the *New York Times* of a dead racehorse—Teller All Gone—dumped in a junkyard was eerily reminiscent of photographs of dead and discarded greyhounds published in the late 1980s and early 1990s.[89] At that time Americans were bombarded with such images of deceased greyhound racers, but the spectacle of a dead and carelessly discarded thoroughbred horse is altogether new. Retirement farms for thoroughbred horses, such as Old Friends in Lexington, Kentucky, are the exception rather than the rule, although they are increasing in popularity.[90] Moreover, the use of drugs to mask the pain experienced by sore or injured horses has proved to be devastating for the animals; acclaimed sportswriter William Nack blames the use of corticosteroids beginning in the 1970s for the rise of catastrophic breakdowns in horses.[91] None of these problems in thoroughbred racing has gone unnoticed, but until recently they have been subject to less rigorous public scrutiny from animal protectionists.

A class-related bias may be evident in the fight to eliminate other "sporting" events, such as cockfighting. In a related example anthrozoologist Hal Herzog argues that the battle to end cockfighting is about cruelty but that the "subtext is social class" because participants in the activity are "easy groups to pick on" such as Hispanics and rural, working-class whites.[92] Herzog cites a long-standing tradition of social bias, also evident in England, regarding certain sporting activities. Blood sports that appeal to the working class, such as bullbaiting, were more aggressively targeted by animal advocates, while sports favored by the landed gentry, such as fox hunting, were for many years overlooked and thus permitted to continue.

While there may be no overt connection between blood sports (such as cockfighting) and greyhound racing, sociologists Atkinson and Young argue that there is, in fact, a link.[93] In their view, even though dog racing is conducted in the public sphere according to a carefully defined set of rules, unsavory practices such as the use of live lures in training do occur outside of the public eye. Furthermore, although no live animals are chased during an actual race, the pursuit is nonetheless a "mock" violent social activity. They see the subtext of greyhound racing as the imagined killing of the prey. In their study on sports violence, Atkinson and Young assert that racing's civilized façade (first institutionalized by INGRA) is designed to minimize and even obscure the often harsh experience of the sport. To illustrate their point, they cite as one example a Texas dogman who admits that the race stirs up some "hunting feelings" in him, leading him to wish that the lure were real so that the hounds could catch it and tear it apart.[94]

A particularly cutting political cartoon that characterizes this undercurrent of bloodlust was printed in the *Arizona Republic* in 1992. Titled "Arizona's Ultimate Blood Sport," the image pictured several men—quite obviously characterized as disreputable—conducting a cockfight; instead of two fighting gamecocks, however, a snarling racing greyhound is positioned to fight a rather startled-looking rooster. In the back two trash cans labeled "Dead Greyhounds" and "Dead Gamecocks" are pictured; both are piled up with animal corpses.[95]

Dogmen are not the only targets of overt class-based criticism. Greyhound-racing fans themselves have also been subject to derision. One political cartoon, printed in 1978 in the *Hartford Courant*, features an ominous-looking audience of greyhounds betting on a pack of men running as if they were greyhounds, chasing a dollar bill dangling from the mechanical lure. Two of the men in the pack are even wearing muzzles, while the others are grimacing and panting. Their very animality is emphasized by crouched postures, hanging tongues, and ravenous expressions. Such a cynical image linking gambling and greed to dog racing is virtually inconceivable in other contexts, such as thoroughbred horse racing, where the core audience is conventionally too well heeled to exhibit such levels of depravity.

Given these harsh critiques of the sport, greyhound industry proponents often complain that they are unfairly singled out for their use of animals. They point out that their breeding operations are not puppy mills and their animals are cared for according to strict industry standards. They charge that many dogs in the United States suffer from neglect and abuse, including the hundreds of thousands of dogs that are euthanized in shelters each year. Pet overpopulation—made worse by the failure of many Americans to spay and neuter their pets—is indeed one of the most overwhelming dilemmas faced by animal protectionists. Other problems in canine welfare persist in addition to high euthanasia rates in shelters. An underground culture of dogfighting continues to plague poor neighborhoods in American cities; this blood sport exploits both the fighting dogs (usually pit bulls) and the hapless bait dogs that are used for training. Still another debate over canine welfare centers on purebred dogs: some argue that the health of certain breeds (e.g., cavalier King Charles spaniels, bulldogs, German shepherds, boxers) is in jeopardy because of excessive and irresponsible breeding. One veterinarian, Dr. Mark Evans of England's Royal Society for the Prevention of Cruelty to Animals (RSPCA), described the Crufts dog show in England (similar to the Westminster Kennel Club dog show in the United States) as "a parade of mutants"; likewise, Florida veterinarian (and greyhound orthopedic specialist) Dr. Jon Dee used the term "genetic disasters" to describe some of the purebred dogs in circulation in the United States.[96]

Given this wide array of problems, dog-racing proponents often question why they are so aggressively targeted. But many animal advocates have joined the struggle for improved animal welfare (or rights) for ideological reasons; to them, animal exploitation crosses social, economic, racial, and cultural boundaries. Animal advocates believe that abuse and neglect comes in many shapes and forms; varying circumstances are often of little import. They charge that a greyhound expected to earn his keep by racing on the tracks is little different from a dog abandoned at a shelter. Pro-racing advocates would hotly debate this point, reiterating their core belief that greyhounds love to race, but animal activists feel that regardless of the specifics, all dogs deserve a better life, period. The definition of what this exactly constituted gradually began to change as the century progressed.

To that end, anti-racing advocates found increasing mainstream support during the late 1970s and 1980s and were ready for a full assault on the industry by the 1990s. At first, most of the negative publicity regarding greyhound racing was generated by publications of animal protection alliances. In May 1986 *Animals' Agenda* published a lengthy article that excoriated greyhound racing.[97] This report, given the oft-repeated title "Running for Their Lives," decried the persisting use of live lures, the widespread killing of "unusable" greyhounds, and, a new element in the equation of abuse, the sale of ex-racers to research labs. Once again some industry insiders suspected that their public image was deteriorating and something needed to be done. Kennel operator Pat Dalton noted in 1982 that "the number one priority for greyhound racing is to make peace with the humane societies."[98] Two years later dogman Herb "Dutch" Koerner admitted that sitting down and talking with humane societies would be "a step in the right direction."[99] In the *Greyhound Review* in 1981, Greg Farley had been even more blunt. He wrote that no one is

buying the "goody two shoes" image we have been trying to sell to the public. We are fooling no one with our phony propaganda about how well we treat our animals. . . . Nobody likes a hypocrite. The fact is that greyhound racing is considered a dirty word by the general public, ranked behind bullfighting and cockfighting, right where it belongs. It's a miracle that humane societies all over the country aren't picketing our tracks every night of the week. But that day may yet be coming.[100]

Farley saw that the tide was turning and he was right. Beginning in the late 1980s and reaching a feverish pitch by the 1990s, greyhound racing received the worst pummeling in the mainstream media that it had ever experienced. Public criticism of dog racing had always circulated, but the attacks in the closing years of the twentieth century were different in character. A new generation of explicit exposés recounted horrific abuses in the industry often supported by disturbing photographs of mangled rabbits and dead, diseased, or mutilated greyhounds. *Inside Edition* ran a story on March 5, 1990, titled "Greyhounds: Running for Their Lives," in which a featured dogman, Bill Maloney, spoke frankly about the euthanasia of racing greyhounds after their careers were over.[101] A *National Geographic* exposé airing in 1993 showed matter-of-factly animal control officers euthanizing ex-racing hounds and then disposing of them. The mainstream magazine *Reader's Digest* featured a story in 1992 about the "Hidden Shame of an American Sport," while *Life* headlined a 1991 exposé with the words "Run or Die."[102] The strong anti-racing theme in this article represented a strong reversal of a *Life* feature published in 1947 that seemed to accept coursing as a respectable pastime.

Horror stories began to emerge. In 1991 the so-called Chandler atrocity made headlines throughout the state of Arizona: more than 100 ex-racing greyhounds had been shot, dumped, and carelessly buried in an abandoned lemon grove near Chandler.[103] Members of NGA, including greyhound breeder Janet Allen, who was also on the agency's board of directors, condemned the brutal act publicly, but the damage to the industry's reputation was already done.[104] Criticism from the press was scathing: one political cartoon pictured Garfield the cat, representing the greyhound industry, standing on a mound of dead hounds, holding an assault rifle.[105]

The brouhaha was not limited to Arizona. Publications elsewhere were criticizing the underbelly of the industry with equal zeal: one anti-racing image in a Miami newspaper showed a drawing of a greyhound at the starting line with a gun held to his head.[106] Greyhound burial grounds were being discovered near racetracks, including one in Hinsdale, New Hampshire. In 1991 the *Denver Business Journal* stated that 50,000 greyhound racers were being put to death every year, a number also cited by the HSUS and often repeated and even increased. A reporter writing for *Animals* subsequently claimed that 50,000 to 90,000 greyhounds were killed each year.[107] One article deeply critical of the industry was highlighted in the *Village Voice;* in this instance the "hard numbers" were 45,000 to 50,000 "surplus" greyhounds "slaughtered annually."[108] Both male and female readerships were

"Benson's View of the Greyhound Racing Industry," drawn by Steve Benson. This political cartoon was created in response to the discovery in Chandler, Arizona, of a large number of dead greyhounds that had been shot and dumped in an abandoned lemon grove. (January 12, © 1992, *Arizona Republic*)

targeted by print media across the country: publications as diverse as *Ladies' Home Journal* and *Penthouse* featured articles on the cruelty of greyhound racing, and, in the latter case, the figure of 50,000 is cited again.[109]

Anti-racing forces and the greyhound industry have long battled over such statistics. Each side has alleged that the other has kept incomplete, inaccurate, or intentionally misleading records, has manipulated breeding statistics, or has failed to disclose other critical information.[110] Much to the chagrin of the racing industry, the negative press appeared to be ubiquitous. Damaging statistics were printed again and again and, according to the industry, gained a life of their own irrespective of the truth.[111] NGA's Gary Guccione has called this negative publicity "a multi-decade hatchet job" and stated that "for many years, the number of dogs 'killed,' as reported by critics, was more than were being bred."[112] He stated, in fact, that "if we killed that many greyhounds every year, we wouldn't have any greyhounds left to race."[113] There is still no consensus today about these statistics. As recently as 2012, one of the most active anti-racing organizations, GREY2K USA, has claimed that thousands of greyhounds are still being killed each year when they are no longer profitable as racers.[114] The Greyhound Protection League (GPL) has estimated that more than a million greyhounds have been killed in the industry's seventy-five-year history.[115]

Before the bad publicity metastasized, the pro-racing and anti-racing camps had attempted sporadically to work together. In 1984, for instance, the two sides met face to face to discuss their differences at an American Greyhound Track Operators Association (AGTOA) meeting. According to Guccione the NGA had been trying to open up discussions with the HSUS. As Guccione recounts it, John Hoyt, the executive director of HSUS, gave a speech to the track operators expressing his organization's position on dog racing. In effect, he stated that even if the industry never euthanized another racing greyhound, the HSUS would still be fundamentally opposed to the sport. Guccione recalls the moment vividly, stating that "you could feel the air going out of the room."[116] But on the opposite side of the table, Hoyt had already been blasted by his own colleagues for negotiating with greyhound-racing representatives. Robert Baker later said he believed it had been "naive" of Hoyt to meet with the industry, and he felt along with other staff members that Hoyt was just being used by the greyhound business to bolster its own image. According to Baker, an unnamed official from the Florida Division of Pari-Mutuel Wagering also told the HSUS that they were inadvertently lending respectability to greyhound racing simply by showing up at the meeting.[117]

Not surprisingly, many examples can be cited to illustrate wrongdoings of an industry that has involved thousands of people for a period of more than 100 years. Some of the problems raised by critics attracted immediate attention when deficiencies in animal care spilled into human health issues. The state of Florida eventually shut down the Key West track after a number of violations, one of which was an accumulation of liquid canine feces in a public parking lot; the track responsible was called a "veritable cauldron of animal abuse."[118] Public discourse reached a fever pitch in 2002 when the remains of hundreds of racing greyhounds, most likely from the Pensacola greyhound track, were discovered shot and buried at a landfill in Lillian, Alabama. In an article printed in USA Today, Baldwin County district attorney David Whetstone stated that the find was "almost a Dachau for dogs."[119] The language describing greyhound abuse was now evoking a historical framework of imprisonment and genocide.

A related set of horrors emerged when reports surfaced that ex-racing greyhounds were being used in medical research. As a result of aggressive sleuthing by Susan Netboy of the GPL in cooperation with other activists, including In Defense of Animals (IDA), a number of cases of ex-racing greyhounds sold for laboratory research were documented and brought to public light.[120] Vivisection—the use of live animals for medical research—has long been a controversial practice in the United States, and the revelation that ex-racing greyhounds were being used for such purposes further tarnished the reputation of the industry.[121] In some cases, the owners were not aware that their greyhounds were being used for research but instead believed that their dogs had been "petted out"—placed for adoption—into homes. But according to a USDA memo commenting on one such case in 1989, most of the greyhound owners the agency had spoken with knew where their dogs were going and had no objection to their being used for research.[122] This assertion is corroborated by Netboy, who later asserted that around 75 percent of the dog owners she contacted did not appear to care that their dogs had been sold to medical labs.[123]

Cases of this sort have caught the attention of noted politicians, including Congresswoman Barbara Boxer, who helped stop the use of greyhounds for invasive bone experiments at the Letterman Army Institute of Research in 1989.[124] Netboy campaigned aggressively for their release and, in her words, was able to get those in the army who were holding the greyhounds to come out "with their hands in the air" because they could not justify legally their possession of the dogs. Greg T. Ludlow of Goodyear, Arizona, classified by the USDA as a Class B or "random source" animal dealer, was later charged with illegally obtaining greyhounds to sell for $350 apiece for medical experimentation.[125] Under pressure from the Animal Welfare Institute (AWI), the USDA withdrew Ludlow's Class B license in 1989, but after his license was reinstated he was caught again in 1994 illegally selling greyhounds for research purposes.[126]

Other documented cases have involved experimentation on ex-racing greyhounds at prominent universities, including Arizona State University, the University of Arizona, Kansas State University, Mississippi State University, and Iowa State University.[127] Cathy Liss, the president of the AWI, stated in 2008 that she had personally seen ex-racing greyhounds being used in medical laboratories in the 1980s, but she no longer believed that this was common practice.[128] Isolated cases of their more recent use have been documented, however, most notably in 1998, at Auburn University, and in 2000 at a cardiac research lab, Guidant Corporation, in Saint Paul, Minnesota.[129]

Veterinary schools, too, were at one point not unwilling to use greyhounds for experimentation. Two separate memoranda sent from the University of California, Davis, School of Veterinary Medicine's Animal Resources Services in 1989 praised the viability of ex-racing greyhounds for research purposes. Staff veterinarian Sallie B. Cosgrove noted that the greyhounds available had had "unsuccessful" racing careers and would have been euthanized at the racetrack had they not been purchased for research.[130] Colorado State University's veterinary school received hundreds of dogs from dogman Bud Frank in the early 1990s; at the time, he openly admitted that he had previously killed and buried his unusable greyhounds himself, but now "we use CSU to pass the buck." A student whistleblower documented on videotape that many of these animals suffered in poor conditions at the veterinary school before they were euthanized.[131]

The NGA had issued a statement in November 1989 opposing the use of greyhounds in research when explicit written permission has not been given by the registered owner. The association agreed to "provide information as to ownership of the greyhounds so as to prevent any criminal or civil liability with respect to fraudulent acquisition of greyhounds or stolen greyhounds."[132] Although it would be difficult to prove that the disposition of ex-racing greyhounds to universities and laboratories for medical experimentation was widely practiced within the industry, Joseph Wilson, Jr., a track owner in Mobile, Alabama, and former AGTOA president, admitted during a Tennessee legislative hearing in 1983 that before adoption had been established as a satisfactory solution, "we were trying to get the different labs and universities and medical centers to take these dogs to use them for experimental animals, but that got to be a problem. . . . People don't like that, certain people."[133] But ten years later, AGTOA issued a strong statement to the contrary and voiced its opposition to this practice.[134]

The disposition of ex-racing greyhounds continued to be a major concern, but the quality of their daily care and nutrition while still on the tracks was another point of contention. One issue plaguing the industry in recent decades has been the use of cheap, raw "4-D" meat to feed greyhounds. The USDA identifies meat derived from dead, dying, diseased, or disabled animals as 4-D.[135] Critics argue that the meat is a "pathogenic smorgasbord" often loaded with bacteria and other microbes that can cause severe vomiting and diarrhea, known as kennel blowouts.[136] In addition, they maintain that it is unsafe for kennel personnel to handle this meat because of potential health hazards.[137] However, to be clear, nonhuman consumption of 4-D meat, which is legal to sell, buy, and use, is sanctioned by the USDA.

Anti-racing organizations such as GREY2K USA are deeply critical of the use of 4-D meat to feed racing greyhounds, calling it the "poorest meat available."[138] Implying that economic interests outweigh the welfare of the dogs, the group points to racing handbooks that acknowledge 4-D meat as the most cost-effective for the industry. The greyhound industry itself maintains that 4-D meat is inappropriate for human consumption but "healthy and nourishing" for animals, and that it is the same meat used in most commercial pet foods.[139] The latter claim is specifically rebutted by the HSUS, which maintains that there is no evidence to verify the use of 4-D meat in commercial pet food. Many in the industry readily point out that dogs are willing to eat just about anything, a fact of nature that in their view justifies the use of this low-grade meat. The cost of feed has also risen, so the use of higher-quality beef is said to be cost-prohibitive for most kennels.[140]

Dr. Brad Fenwick, a board-certified veterinary microbiologist, believes that 4-D meat has been unfairly maligned, noting that it is fed to zoo animals around the world without detrimental consequences or, for that matter, negative publicity. He espouses a pro-racing industry platform and actively promotes this point of view when he is asked to speak to veterinary students across the country. Fenwick asserts that there is "no scientific evidence" indicating that 4-D meat is harmful to greyhounds and that the claim of harmfulness has its origin in a political campaign against racing. He believes that minor management changes in racing kennels, such as thawing 4-D meat in the refrigerator rather than at room temperature, can virtually eliminate kennel blowouts.[141]

Dr. Linda Blythe, one of the authors of *Care of the Racing and Retired Greyhound*, is in general agreement with Fenwick's point of view. The book is often cited by GREY2K USA as evidence that 4-D meat is harmful, but Blythe herself counters that it is a "far reach" for anti-racing proponents to cite 4-D meat as a problem point in the industry. She states, "I think to use it as a thing to block greyhound racing is crazy because it is grasping at straws." In her view, if the meat is fed to healthy, adult greyhounds, contaminated 4-D meat at its worst can cause a "transient diarrhea" for several days. She explains that the use of 4-D meat is a "purely economic thing," given that it can be purchased at only 50 cents a pound. Similarly, Fenwick notes that if the meat were in fact hazardous and reduced racing performance, it would not be economically logical for the dogmen to continue using it.

Independent testing has revealed the presence of salmonella and *E. coli* bacteria in some 4-D meat, a situation made more serious because dogmen do not cook the food before giving it to the dogs.[142] There has long been a belief in the greyhound industry, hailing back to the early coursing days in

England, that raw meat is better for racing greyhounds than cooked meat. Veterinarian and greyhound expert John R. Kohnke notes that the feeding and nutrition of greyhounds is an art and a science that has long been "overshadowed by tradition and folklore."[143] Moreover, raw meat has sometimes been associated with virility and manliness in American culture, and it appears that this relationship, at least in part, has been projected onto racing greyhounds as well.[144] The reasons for the continued use of raw meat could also be more mundane. Fenwick argues that if cooking the meat actually improved performance, the dogmen would long ago have taken pains to incorporate this time-consuming step into their feeding practices.

Greyhound trainers have not always used 4-D meat purchased from large slaughterhouses or meatpacking companies. In the very early years some greyhound owners fed their dogs meat they had secured themselves, such as meat from wild jackrabbits, which were abundant and easy to obtain.[145] As the industry became more systematized, feeding patterns gradually changed. Because their breeding kennels were usually located in rural areas, dogmen were often able to obtain feed from nearby farms or local butchers. A survey of twenty-five top dogmen from 1979 to 1980 revealed that the major protein source in racing greyhounds' diets was usually some combination of beef and horse meat, and occasionally lamb, chicken, or fish.[146] This high-protein meal was then often supplemented with vegetables, milk, or vitamins.

The fact that for many years horse meat has often formed part of the diet for the racing greyhound eventually raised a new set of questions for animal advocates. Many advocates believed that using ex-racing horses to provide horse meat for racing dogs was a further, extreme example of systemized cruelty to animals. Dogman Ed Souza unabashedly justified this feeding practice in 1975, stating, "There is no room for sentiment in this business. . . . Horse racing, dog racing, same basic thing. What do you think happens to the losers at Pompano Harness Track? What do you think my dogs are eating right now?"[147]

Perhaps because of the failure of the organized humane movement and the greyhound industry to work together, the industry attempted to effect reforms on its own. When criticism of greyhound racing was continuing to increase but before negative publicity reached its apex, the American Greyhound Council (AGC) was jointly established by NGA and AGTOA.[148] In addition to a stated commitment to greyhound adoption, the AGC sought to create standardized guidelines for the care of greyhounds and maintenance of their kennel facilities. The industry also established an inspection program. Breeding farms and kennels became subject to both announced and unannounced visits to ensure compliance with the industry's own animal welfare guidelines. One full-time inspector, Craig Randle, together with part-time inspectors from all of the nine AGC districts nationwide, were responsible for the visits. At his busiest Randle—who himself hails from a long line of dogmen—would visit 700 to 750 farms per year. NGA members who violated AGC rules were subject to warnings, fines, and even permanent expulsion from the NGA.[149]

The AGC guidelines enacted in October 1993 and revised in 2000 and 2001 specified the proper care of greyhounds, including kennel housing, appropriate dog runs and run housing, turnout pens and exercise areas, and requirements for crates, sanitation, farms, and personnel. A significant change in the protocols added in 1993 was the industry's insistence upon using carpeting or bedding in kennel crates.[150] Some members are expelled from the association each year for egregious violations of AGC guidelines, but more typically violations are minor and dogmen are simply required to clean up their kennels.[151]

Also in response to criticisms from animal advocates, the greyhound industry has produced instructional videos on the proper care and training of greyhounds. A video narrated by veterinarian J. R. Gannon of Melbourne, Australia, advises trainers how to conduct a "soundness exam" on a racing greyhound.[152] He encourages dogmen to pay close attention to their greyhounds' physical condition, stressing that this is a short and easy process that will prevent injuries. In 1990 an instructional video featuring Herb "Dutch" Koerner's successful kennel in Hays, Kansas, was released. It discusses the stages of greyhound development and training and the methods of training greyhounds without live lures.[153]

A larger project was the creation of the video *Ensuring the Welfare of the Racing Greyhound,* a production jointly created by NGA, AGC, and a public relations consultant, Marsha Kelly, who has partnered with NGA since 1995.[154] *Ensuring the Welfare of the Racing Greyhound* is shown to all interested visitors at the Greyhound Hall of Fame in Abilene, Kansas, which is located directly across from the Eisenhower Presidential Library.[155] The production highlights the exceptional lineage of the greyhound, noting its beginnings in the era of Egyptian pharaohs. The narrator states that the video's aim is to help "reasonable people" learn the facts about greyhound racing without the interference of "media hype." Viewers are then shown the development of a racing greyhound from its beginnings on a farm to its final disposition, adoption in a loving home—"tangible evidence of the industry's conscientious commitment to humane care and responsible animal management."[156]

Perhaps the best-known improvement in training methods championed by the industry had come much earlier: veteran dogman Keith Dillon's creation of the Jack-A-Lure in the early 1970s. This device differs from the mechanical lure in that it is used only for training, but, more important, it is designed to teach the greyhound to run after a moving object in a straight line without the use of a live animal.[157] After the greyhound masters the Jack-A-Lure (or similar drag lure), he graduates to the whirlygig. This mechanism also employs a fake lure, but instead of running after it in a straight line, the greyhound must now run in a small circle. The trainer stands inside the circular area and pushes a long pole that is attached to a center pivot. A lure is attached to the other end of the pole, but it is kept at eye level and does not drag on the ground.[158] Only after mastering the whirlygig is the greyhound ready to run on a racing track, this in a training exercise known as schooling. All subsequent track training can then proceed with the standard mechanical lure, thus allowing the entire process to be completed by the trainer with no use of live prey.

Dillon made and sold hundreds of Jack-A-Lures himself.[159] At first there was much resentment toward artificial lure training. Critics believed that greyhounds would not respond to the Jack-A-Lure, but Dillon asserted, "I haven't trained any other way since 1973, and I've had seven All-Americans." The NGA and AGTOA hired the public relations firm Hill and Knowlton to help Dillon promote training with the new device. Dillon narrated a training video on its proper use, maintaining that greyhounds would just as willingly chase a "Post toasty" on the Jack-A-Lure as they would a live rabbit.[160] Nonetheless, even though his training approach was popular, it was not adopted by all dogmen.[161]

In addition to supporting adoption programs, the AGC also partnered with the veterinary school at the University of Florida to promote research in greyhound sports medicine.[162] In 2007 the organization published a manual on greyhound care written by veterinarians and other experts.[163] While the more traditional dogmen were generally disinclined to seek professional veterinary care for their greyhounds and in many cases managed most or all of their own vetting, a second book, *Canine Sports Medicine and Surgery* (1998), reflected how much the business had changed.[164] Edited by three veterinarians, this publication explored topics of interest regarding the health and performance of racing greyhounds: track biomechanics and design, track care and first aid for racing greyhounds, proper nutrition, and general kennel management. Despite its technical language, the intended audience of the book is clearly not only veterinarians but also the dogmen themselves.

Partly as a result of such efforts, the quality of veterinary care for racing dogs has unquestionably improved in recent decades, although not all greyhounds have benefited from the advances. As kennels have grown larger, individual dogs have tended to receive less attention, whereas before World War II most kennels were smaller and individual care had higher priority.[165] And although veterinarians played an increasingly important role after the war, much of the health care (such as deworming) was still managed by the breeder or trainer.

Some humane societies have maintained that industry-spearheaded efforts such as increased self-regulation and instructional videos and books are publicity stunts rather than honest attempts to effect change. They were quick to point out that in 1988, when AGTOA was seeking a public relations firm to help it improve its public image, one company was unwilling to take AGTOA on as a client.[166] Ketchum Public Relations, based in Washington, DC, sent a letter on September 16, 1988, to George D. Johnson, Jr., the executive director of AGTOA. In it, Ronald R. Mueller, the senior vice president and director, stated,

> Your members have made it clear to us that they are unwilling to get actively involved in the live lure issue, and both the members and the association have expressed only an interest in "passive cooperation" with organizations seeking to find homes for greyhounds whose racing careers have come to an end. What we want your members to know is that the image of greyhound racing *can* be significantly improved, but *not* by an *agency* doing it for them. . . . If at some point your members decide they want to *change* the *circumstances,* you might then want to decide which of the large national public relations firms can best implement a program to *communicate* the *changes* to the American people, with the goal being to *change* their *opinions* based on *changed reality.*[167] (emphasis in original)

Portions of this damaging memo were reprinted in a number of magazine articles critical of the dog-racing industry soon after it was written.[168]

The notion that the greyhound industry would or could police itself has been widely ridiculed by animal advocates. Skeptics argue that if state racing commissions are expected to investigate animal welfare violations at the tracks, this is tantamount to the "fox guarding the henhouse." They maintain that such an arrangement will never prove effective in protecting

Aerial view of modern racing greyhound farm, ca. 1980. The kennels and dog runs can be seen behind the main house. (Courtesy of Air Photo, Inc., and the Greyhound Hall of Fame)

greyhounds.[169] And while critics charge that the industry's efforts to improve its own standards are disingenuous and ineffective, they are equally concerned that existing legislation fails to protect the greyhounds adequately. The legal landscape surrounding racing dogs is, in fact, constantly evolving, and greyhounds are protected by a range of laws, yet not necessarily by laws that Americans might expect. First passed in 1966 and amended repeatedly since then, the federal Animal Welfare Act (AWA) protects animals including dogs that are being used or are intended for use for research, testing, experimentation, or exhibition purposes. Yet racing greyhounds and racehorses were both specifically excluded from the exhibition category by USDA regulations in 1972.[170] Greyhound breeders, trainers, and owners are therefore not subject to AWA standards of care but are instead bound only by state and local anticruelty laws like any other dog breeder or owner in their respective states.[171] Such laws vary considerably, but animal cruelty, however it may be defined, is considered a felony in forty-seven states.[172] Thirty-one of these states have increased the severity of animal cruelty violations from misdemeanors to felonies within the past ten years.[173]

All persons handling greyhounds at racetracks are obliged both to obey anticruelty laws and to adhere to specific regulations concerning animal care issued by the state racing commission. The most significant external (i.e., non-racing greyhound industry) regulation of greyhound welfare thus falls not under federal law but to the oversight of state racing commissions, which are governmental agencies responsible primarily for overseeing dog and horse racing on a procedural basis.[174] These agencies, whose members are usually appointed by the state governor, seek to ensure that dog (and horse) racing is conducted fairly and that wagered money is managed appropriately. The majority of rules issued by them thus dictate the responsibilities of track workers, namely, the pari-mutuel manager, racing director, chart writer, lure operator, paddock judge, patrol judge, veterinarian, and other lower-level employees, all of whom must follow strict protocols. Only a fraction of the regulations pertain to the protection of the animals that are racing, and even then they usually protect animals only while on the track premises. When they include criteria for appropriate care and handling of greyhounds, the language tends to become quite broad. In Texas, for instance, the track veterinarian is expected to monitor the kennels on race day to evaluate "the general physical condition" and "general manner of handling" of the greyhounds.[175] These rules exist first and foremost to ensure that the public is wagering on animals that have not been drugged or otherwise tampered with in any fashion, even though their wording may suggest otherwise.

Regulations in Florida, the state with the most greyhound tracks, have simply declared since 1992 that "it is the intent of the Legislature that animals that participate in races . . . be treated humanely both on and off racetracks, throughout the lives of the animals."[176] Arizona, by contrast, has issued regulations applying specifically to greyhounds both at the breeding kennel and the racing farm.[177] Alabama rules require kennel workers specifically to treat racing greyhounds humanely, borrowing its description of inhumane treatment from its own state anticruelty law.[178] In more recent years some states (such as Wisconsin) mandated adoption programs, whereas others simply recommended their implementation or continued use.[179] State pari-mutuel regulations are thus characterized by their variability, their focus on track operations, and their tendency otherwise to employ broad language that may or may not specifically stipulate the "humane" treatment of greyhounds or the mandate to follow state anticruelty laws.

This heterogeneous external regulatory system has proved to be imperfect. Greyhounds may be protected by a broadly framed racing commission law in one state and a broadly framed anticruelty law in another. A former track veterinarian from Iowa, Arthur Strohbehn, has pointed out weaknesses inherent in such legal protections. Strohbehn was troubled by the quality of the meat fed to greyhounds at Iowa tracks but discovered that the state regulatory system left him with little recourse to resolve his concerns. The Iowa Racing Commission told Strohbehn that he should not be concerned with the matter, and the Bureau of Animal Industries in Des Moines indicated they had no intention of enforcing racetrack laws, leaving it to the state veterinarian instead. The state veterinarian, however, said that he had no jurisdiction over the matter and that it was the responsibility of Strohbehn himself, who had a contract with the racing commission, to see that the laws were followed.[180] In this case, the regulatory system designed to protect animals had broken down.

A number of state racing commissions prohibited the use of live lures beginning in the 1980s, but a complete, industry-wide ban never became a part of federal law.[181] In 1987 U.S. Representative Bob Dornan of Orange County, California (along with fifty-two cosponsors), introduced H.R. 1433, a bill to amend the AWA to prohibit dog racing and training involving the use of live animals as lures. Known as the Anti-Live Animal Lure Act of 1987, it was first referred to the Committee on Agriculture and then sent to a subcommittee on March 10, 1987, where it was ignored and never resurrected.[182]

At the time one industry magazine, *Greyhound USA,* urged subscribers to write Congress and ask that the bill be rejected.[183] Reflecting on his years as an HSUS inspector, Robert Baker complained in a 2009 interview about the hypocrisy he perceived in the industry. He stated that when he exposed publicly the continued use of live lures, industry spokespersons repeatedly denied that they were still used, but when a bill was submitted to the Florida legislature to make the practice a felony, the industry still opposed the bill. Baker decided that the only way to combat his opponents effectively was to enact clear, targeted legislation to fix the problem and require prosecution of those who did not comply, because persuasion clearly did not work.[184]

Another regulatory issue identified by critics involves interstate travel. Although greyhounds are frequently moved across state lines, there are no regulations stipulating how the dogs must be transported. This is a valid concern, since travel is inherent in the system of seasonal bookings at different tracks. For instance, dogs that race in Florida for a winter season are likely to compete in another state during the following summer. The dogs are thus periodically subjected to long road trips. They are usually transported in trailers designed specifically for greyhounds, only some of which include climate control. Conscientious dogmen are often willing to travel for long hours without stopping in order to prevent their dogs from overheating; this is a voluntary measure on their part, however, and not required by law.[185] Travel from track to track within a single state is also likely, of course, and this, too, may involve long distances in a single season. As of 1991, Arizona and Oregon were the only states that had issued standards for the intrastate transport of greyhounds.[186]

For most of greyhound racing's history, injuries that occurred on racetracks were neither reported nor compiled in any systematic or coherent manner. GREY2K USA actively campaigned to change that practice and successfully lobbied the Massachusetts and New Hampshire state legislatures to force dog tracks to release injury reports, in 2001 and 2004, respectively. Other states soon followed suit as a consequence of the group's activism. Today GREY2K USA aggressively publicizes data from these reports, putting it forth as evidence of the cruelty of the sport, a tactic that has in turn sparked much controversy in the industry. Track employees complain about the paperwork, arguing that it consumes too much time given that even minor injuries, such as a stubbed toe, must be reported. The adjectives used by the industry to describe GREY2K USA's presentation of the injury reports range from "bogus" to "exaggerated" to "misleading," but the organization stands by its evidence.[187] GREY2K USA founder and president Christine

Standard greyhound transport truck with attached hauler trailer, 2010. (Ray Wong, photographer)

Dorchak notes, "Our greatest accomplishment has been to document the reality of dog racing and to use the industry's own information to make the case against it. This fact-based approach, I believe, has changed the face of anti-dog racing activism."[188]

By the end of the twentieth century and even well into the next decade, pro-racing and anti-racing factions had become even more deeply divided. Bitterness between the two camps has only continued to fester. In 2008 NGA's Guccione stated, "They'll do anything to paint the industry in a bad light," whereas in 2009 Baker commented, "These people [referring to the industry] are not sincere."[189] Even though the industry is clearly in decline, the fight is not over. The most visible national anti-racing activist, Christine Dorchak, vowed in 2011 to "keep working until everyone knows the truth about dog racing and this cruelty ends nationwide."[190] The greyhound industry charges that animal rights activists are ideologically inflexible and refuse to accept the legitimacy of institutionalized greyhound racing even if all dogs are well cared for and adopted into loving homes when their careers are over. The industry complains specifically about its opponents' repeated use of allegedly wildly inflated and otherwise highly inaccurate statistics. It maintains that animal advocates recycle old stories of abuse in order to drum up new opposition to greyhound racing. Some dogmen claim that animal rights activists are motivated by greed and are seeking more donations for their cause only so that they can increase the size and membership of their organizations. They rage that animal advocates have little or no knowledge of greyhound racing and rely only on newspaper accounts that document the occasional abuses perpetrated by "bad apples." Their greatest anger is often reserved for activists who charge that the dogmen themselves are abusing their animals by keeping them muzzled and caged for long hours and then forcing them to run. The dogmen counter that it is they, in fact, who take good care of their dogs, while humane associations house animals in crates or on hard kennel floors.[191] Many also claim that animal rights activists working for humane societies are militant hypocrites because they are the ones who euthanize thousands, even millions, of unwanted shelter animals each year, however unwillingly.[192] This complaint has long been one of the most frequently raised by dogmen seeking to defend their own practices.

American public discourse about the ethics of greyhound racing has failed almost completely to unravel the complexity of the issue. Both camps are now stubbornly entrenched and essentially unwilling to work with each other, and both engage at times in media tactics or other behavior that are deeply problematic. The greyhound-racing industry repeatedly oversimplifies the issues; while the animal advocacy movement has always been a complex one informed by differing perspectives, the industry has frequently portrayed it as a monolithic, united front intent on removing some of life's daily pleasures from mainstream American families, such as circuses, rodeos, and barbeques.[193] Animal advocates are not only driven by starkly differing viewpoints; in many cases, they are themselves deeply divided. Rather than accepting the heterogeneity and complexity of the animal protection movement, the industry claims that mainstream Americans who love animals but believe that they can be "used" responsibly for entertainment, work, and food all actually support "animal welfare." Those who believe that animals should never be eaten, never used for entertainment, and never be made to serve humans in any way supposedly believe in "animal rights."[194] Those who support "animal welfare" can accept greyhound racing, whereas those who embrace "animal rights" do not and never will. This simplistic polarization of the animal advocacy in the United States serves only to obfuscate the issues.

In like manner, some animal protectionists have relied on generalities about greyhound racing that deserve deeper reflection. Although it is true that some greyhounds do not thrive in the racetrack environment, most do like to run and to chase moving objects. While at the track many racing dogs exude great excitement and frequently vocalize and wag their tails. Dr. Brad

Fenwick, who has worked with the industry for fifteen years, believes that the dogs actually become stressed when they do not run. Some of its critics tend to paint the industry as a monolithic evil, but conditions from kennel to kennel and racetrack to racetrack vary dramatically. Indeed, they differ from dog to dog, depending on the day, the weather, the track, the kennel, the trainer, the diet, and other variables as well. Direct observation suggests that some racing greyhounds are comfortable and happy, whereas others are not. One Arizona-based animal control advisory board member noted that greyhound operations "range from the sublime, where the dogs are treated like royalty, to the tragic."[195]

Some activists are evidently not fully informed about the current workings of the industry, and some may be relying too heavily on media accounts to shape their own views. Some have little or no firsthand knowledge of the business. It is also safe to say that the responsible people within the industry—those who ensure that their greyhounds receive good care and, in recent years, permanent homes after their racing careers are over—are frequently overlooked. The horror stories from the past—the atrocities in Chandler, Arizona; the claim that greyhounds from the Coeur d'Alene, Idaho, racetrack were electrocuted by means of the "Tijuana hot plate"; the putrid conditions at Key West that led to the track's closure—do seem to resurface in media discourse over and over, even when conditions at a specific farm, kennel, or racetrack in question are not comparable.[196] Moreover, many dogmen of the new generation are visibly conscientious about the disposition of their stock and track the welfare of their adopted greyhounds long after the dogs have left their care.

Like most ethical conundrums, there are complex, variable factors to consider when deciding whether greyhound racing is an acceptable sport. Would the sport be viable even if all greyhounds remained healthy and happy and were ensured an injury-free life and comfortable retirement home after their careers are over? Some say no and cling fiercely to their anti-racing positions. People for the Ethical Treatment of Animals (PETA) is one such animal advocacy group. The organization's president, Ingrid Newkirk, argues that animals should never be used in any capacity for human entertainment or other benefit. Significantly, this includes the institution of pet keeping. Critics such as she have also contended that racing in its cleanest and finest form can never and will never exist; therefore, the entire enterprise must be shut down. As the veteran animal activist Robert Baker has stated about the sport, "The cruelty is so inherent, there is no way you could clean it up and regulate it effectively."[197]

GREY2K USA has undoubtedly been the strongest anti-racing force in recent years and is certainly responsible, at least in part, for orchestrating the demise of greyhound racing in Massachusetts. Wayne Pacelle, the president of the HSUS, positioned his organization squarely in the anti-racing camp when he endorsed GREY2K USA's aggressive state-targeted legislative and political campaign against the sport, noting that its work was the "best news greyhounds have had in decades."[198] There are also those in the middle, those who concede that injuries and occasional abuses occur while acknowledging that as in any sport or activity, this is inevitable. The American Veterinary Medical Association (AVMA) supports the use of animals in sport, including dog racing, as long as precautions are taken against "negative welfare impacts" on the animals in question.[199] Even within the community of dogmen there are widely differing opinions. Some dogmen simply view greyhounds as livestock, animals to be cared for only as long as they have economic value, whereas other dogmen are more sensitive to their needs. And finally, there are the thousands of views in between, beliefs held by each and every individual who has participated in or otherwise encountered greyhound racing in some capacity.

Despite this range and complexity of opinions, the sport has enjoyed periods of impressive acceptance and success in Florida as well as at other dog tracks in states as distant and diverse as Oregon and Massachusetts. Individuals who have harbored doubts have nonetheless been able to put aside their concerns and enjoy a day at the races, despite incessant, recurring public criticisms. But from the beginning there have also been those who have insisted on grappling with the moral complexities present in the institution of greyhound racing, and their moral objections have continued to fuel disagreements and debates in American society. While anti-racing activists may agree with the simple premise that greyhounds love to run and people like to gamble, they maintain that any economically driven enterprise is bound to reward some but exploit others, however unintentionally. In the sport of greyhound racing, greyhounds are ultimately the commodity and vehicle with which wagering has operated. This commodity may be widely loved, in different ways and for different reasons, but in the sport of dog racing it is a commodity nonetheless. Americans have long received conflicting messages about the appropriate use of animals, and the greyhounds have undoubtedly been caught in the crossfire.

CHAPTER SIX

THE FALL

Our intention is to keep working until everyone knows the truth about dog racing and this cruelty ends nationwide.
Christine Dorchak, founder and president of GREY2K USA

Aggressive anti-racing campaigns launched by animal advocacy groups such as GREY2K USA had cut to the marrow of the greyhound-racing industry, but an increasingly competitive national market for mass entertainment was yet another behemoth facing the sport. Televised sports such as football and basketball—along with other professional and college sports broadcasts—were drawing gamblers away from the tracks. NASCAR, which held its first major televised race in Daytona Beach in 1961, eventually became the country's most popular spectator sport.[1] Inexorable change in the gambling market—namely, the gradual loss of the pari-mutuel monopoly in American gaming—was also clearly evident, although still difficult for many in the greyhound-racing industry to accept. Other gambling options gradually drew spectators away from the dog tracks: newly legalized state lotteries, casinos, and Native American gaming establishments all loomed large as competitors for a piece of the entertainment dollar.[2]

In the face of these changes, greyhound-racing advocates still sought to expand the sport into new states. Dog-racing interests had fought bitterly to legalize gambling on greyhound racing in the key state of California in 1976, but their efforts were thwarted by a well-organized opposition force. Kansas—the heart of the American greyhound-breeding industry—managed to legalize the sport in 1989, rewarding dog-racing enthusiasts with an important symbolic victory. But the closure of the Kansas dog tracks less than twenty years later was devastating to all of those involved.[3] Other industry changes were equally troublesome. Greyhound tracks in western states (e.g., Arizona and Colorado) had enjoyed long periods of prosperity, but new corporate management had become a destabilizing force. In addition to these problems, even the bugaboo of organized crime continued to threaten the reputation of dog racing as a "clean" sport—the industry liked to say that dog racing was "cleaner than a hound's tooth," but not everybody was convinced.[4]

External factors affecting the entire entertainment and gambling market were not the only concerns facing the greyhound-racing industry. Internal discord was a continuing problem. Track operators and dogmen were constantly at odds and rarely worked together in pursuit of common goals, namely, more fans, new legalized venues, better tracks, increased publicity, and, most critically, more money for everyone involved. On a number of occasions some of the dogmen decided to strike their tracks for a larger percentage of purse winnings, but they had little success. All of these factors contributed to greyhound racing's gradual decline and fall in American culture, even though, paradoxically, the industry by all accounts was in "prime growth mode" in the 1980s.[5]

At its height in the late 1970s and early 1980s, dog racing was frequently touted as the sixth most popular sport in the United States, following the established national favorites, including horse racing, baseball, football, basketball, and hockey.[6] Florida hosted a number of popular stakes races with large purses and continued to draw devoted fans from all over the country. After the Sunshine State, the undisputed leader in greyhound racing, Massachusetts, posted the second highest attendance numbers nationwide in 1974, reaching a total of 2,228,137 visitors.[7] Million-dollar handles were recorded at Wonderland on four separate occasions in the 1980s: August 29, 1981 (Derby Night); May 5, 1983; August 11, 1984 (the fiftieth anniversary); and April 30, 1988 (the grand reopening).[8] The 1980s were for many leaders in the business the golden years of greyhound racing in the United States: in 1989 national dog-racing attendance reached 26.6 million.[9] But as National Greyhound Association (NGA) executive director Gary Guccione later admitted, underneath this veil of abundance, the "decaying process was already starting." Average attendance was actually dropping, but according to Guccione, "we were just getting more tracks," thus shielding the extent of the decline.[10]

Given these circumstances, the lack of effective positive publicity remained a serious problem for the dog-racing industry. Steven Crist, publisher and editor of the *Daily Racing Form*—a major thoroughbred horse-racing publication—declared recently that the greyhound industry has been absolutely "terrible" in public relations. He believes that GREY2K USA successfully orchestrated the elimination of dog racing in Massachusetts in 2009 by means of a "historic misinformation campaign" and a "completely lie-based platform," while the greyhound industry itself failed to respond appropriately.[11] Even before GREY2K USA had emerged, however, industry leaders were nervous about working with the media given the damaging exposés about animal cruelty that had begun to surface in the 1980s. The NGA and other industry leaders were likely wary of the press: stories about racing dogs that were meant to be positive could theoretically spiral into publicity disasters.[12]

For a period, however, several decades before animal advocates gained public prominence, the American Greyhound Track Operators Association (AGTOA) had taken an active lead in promoting the sport. Created in 1946, the group was initially made up solely of Florida track operators but was expanded by 1961 to include all states with dog racing. The organization published the *Greyhound Racing Record,* which allowed it to better control the manner in which the sport was being portrayed to racing fans.[13] It also came out with the *American Greyhound Racing Encyclopedia* in 1963. In it, AGTOA asserted that a clear narrative about greyhound racing could finally be put "on the record," declaring that its "history [from] this point will be perpetuated accurately and completely. For the first time, greyhound racing has its 'Bible.'"[14]

Undaunted by animal advocates who were trying to alert Americans to abuses in the sport, some within the industry were still agitating for expanded press exposure in order to attract new fans. In 1981 dogman Aubrey Wallis echoed the belief of many in the business when he declared that the industry needed to become more aggressive about cultivating the sports media. Observing that greyhound racing received no television coverage even though it was the sixth largest spectator sport in the United States, Wallis suggested that AGTOA fund televised race coverage to bring greyhound racing before the masses.[15] Arthur Watson, who served as NBC sports president from 1979 to 1989, stated in 1982 that dog racing suffered from "limited national awareness of what greyhound racing really is. . . . You're very regionalized as a sport." He suggested exerting more pressure on national sports publications and television networks, noting, "It's up to you [the dog-racing industry] to put together a package and try to sell it to the network. . . . You have to help the people you're pitching to get a feel for that event."[16] Marketing experts generally agreed that greyhound racing, although growing in certain markets, urgently needed to strengthen the voice of its leadership and cultivate its relationship with the national media.

While dog-racing interests were occasionally granted opportunities for promotions by the national media, most publicity and fan support remained regional or local. With occasional exceptions, including a story on the champion greyhound Never Roll in *Life* magazine in 1942, a number of articles in *Sports Illustrated* in the 1950s, 1960s, and 1970s, and several short features on television programs such as the *Merv Griffin Show*, greyhound racing retained its regional character even as it experienced significant expansion into new states.[17] *Greyhound Review* writer Ryan H. Reed characterized dog racing outside of Florida during the 1970s as "a collection of individual local attractions."[18] The booking system could sometimes limit the appearance of a given greyhound—including an especially talented racer—to a particular track, preventing the dog from competing in special derby races and thereby developing a wider fan base.[19] Despite such obstacles, some racers were still able to attract a significant regional following. One dogman recalled the greyhound Tell Jimmy, who competed at the Plainfield, Connecticut, track and enjoyed a broad and loyal fan base. Many children collected his picture, and the dog's photograph was also often seen posted in bars and cafes throughout the state.[20]

Other greyhounds achieved tremendous popularity and fan loyalty. Exceptional racing dogs were eventually inducted into the Greyhound Hall of Fame in Abilene, Kansas. Established in the early 1960s, the Hall of Fame was a sign and symbol of the industry's desire to define and promote its own history.[21] Later relocated directly across from the Eisenhower Presidential Library, the new Hall of Fame (and museum) was the first public venue for fans to learn about the history of the sport. Florida greyhound track promoter Carl Timothy Hoffman declared that the site would serve as a "permanent monumental shrine" where people could pay tribute to the Sport of Queens.[22] During the dedication ceremony dogman Keith Dillon, a key supporter of the project and the NGA president at the time, asked, "Why shouldn't we stand alongside other great sports like football, basketball, and horse racing that maintain Halls of Fame here in America?" Gary Guccione, writing for the *Greyhound Review*, was perhaps more realistic when he admitted several years later that as "badly as people in general are misinformed about greyhounds and greyhound racing, it [the Hall of Fame] has to be worthwhile."[23] The industry could now both honor the "pioneers" who had nurtured the sport from its beginnings and induct greyhound racing's leaders and stars—both human and canine—into its own Hall of Fame. By 1976 attendance numbers had reached 28,000 per year, a respectable accomplishment for a facility located close to the middle of Kansas.

Still, despite these efforts, not one of the most celebrated racing greyhounds of the twentieth century—not Mission Boy, Rural Rube, Real

Huntsman, Traffic Officer, Downing, Flashy Sir, Miss Whirl, Marathon Hound, or Keefer, to name but a few—ever achieved the level of name recognition seen repeatedly in thoroughbred horse racing.[24] In her 2007 book, *Keefer: The People's Choice,* Leslie Wootten chronicles the Florida-based popularity of a talented greyhound racer from Keith Dillon's breeding kennel who achieved great recognition in the sport after a number of wins, including a 1986 victory in front of record crowds at the Derby Lane Distance Classic. Keefer then dominated in a number of major races despite occasional setbacks, solidifying his reputation as "the people's greyhound," according to Wootten.[25] Fans even wore "I Saw Keefer Run" T-shirts and displayed homemade signs that read "We love you Keefer" at the track. In 1986 he was featured in a front-page article in the *Wall Street Journal.* But even this prized example of positive national media coverage resulted from a serendipitous discovery. The *Wall Street Journal* reporter had actually traveled to Florida to cover a different story; while there she encountered the ballyhoo over Keefer and only then opted to learn more about the greyhound races.[26]

Even Guccione has acknowledged that dog racing will never be a sport that can "create the Seabiscuits." Noting that horse racing at least has the option of featuring and interviewing star jockeys, *Sports Illustrated* senior writer Frank Deford pointed out, "Where are the personalities in greyhound racing? They bark. It's difficult to create a cult when you have no one to interview." Deford in fact advised AGTOA in 1989 that garnering regional rather than national media attention was the best strategy for promoting greyhound racing. He argued that every major sport in the United States developed more than 100 years ago, and that they were "in the same pecking order then that they are today." In essence, because greyhound racing was a relative newcomer in the United States, it lacked a mainstream following with deeply entrenched social traditions.[27]

Expansion remained a key goal for the dog-racing industry, even in the face of increasing opposition from animal advocates and a national media establishment that evinced little interest in the sport itself. This relentless drive to expand flew in the face of those who had long believed it was more productive to nurture local and regional markets. Some greyhound-racing promoters continued forth, unwilling to accept that their chief competitor for the pari-mutuel dollar—the thoroughbred horse-racing industry—wielded significantly more political and financial power. Despite these odds, they held tenaciously to the belief that more greyhound tracks could catapult the sport to new heights and, in turn, could yield considerable riches for track owners.

California was a case in point: if dog racing were legalized in the Golden State, a huge media market could be accessed, not to mention the potential windfall in gambling profits. The political scenario in California in the mid–1970s played out much differently than it had in Earl Warren's era. The legalization effort was launched when California assemblyman Leon Ralph, a Democrat from Los Angeles, introduced a bill to permit greyhound racing in his own district and four other California counties.[28] The bill failed, in large part because of the powerful horse-racing lobby.

Undaunted, greyhound-racing proponents realized that gambling on the sport could also be legalized by means of a direct ballot initiative. This legalization effort in California was spearheaded by George Graham Hardie, a former harness-racing driver and businessman who managed a public relations firm that also assumed responsibility for promoting the initiative. He conceived of what was in 1976 referred to as Proposition 13—an initiative statute to establish legalized gambling on greyhound racing—which gave California voters the opportunity to bypass the legislature and legalize dog racing directly.[29] Hardie quickly amassed a team of supporters who then obtained the required 600,000 signatures to qualify the initiative for the ballot. In Hardie's somewhat modified proposal, instead of directing state gambling revenues into a general fund, he created a series of so-called motherhood funds that would receive the money, including aid for children, senior citizens, and others in need.[30] He argued that greyhound racing would also create 10,000 new jobs in the state, establish a billion-dollar state industry, generate $60 million in new tax revenues, and keep California money circulating within the state rather than allowing it to hemorrhage into nearby Las Vegas.[31]

Greyhound tracks would be established in eight heavily populated California counties and thereby could be readily patronized by fans from major cities such as San Diego, Los Angeles, San Francisco, and Sacramento.[32] Hardie promised that strict animal welfare guidelines would be enacted; he assured the public that greyhounds would not be trained using live animals and that healthy racers would not be destroyed. He also proposed the creation of a farm for retired racing dogs. Hardie noted that dog racing was the fastest growing spectator sport in the United States and benefited from the most rigid security and public protection.

Critics disagreed vehemently with Hardie's claims. Branding greyhound racing as a "volatile industry" with great potential for corruption, they argued that Hardie himself would be the primary beneficiary of the new law, since he stood to gain millions.[33] Hardie owned the Golden State

Greyhound Association, which many believed would enjoy disproportionate profits should legalization be achieved. Critics even charged that Hardie would exert excessive influence on the selection of state racing commission members.[34] Los Angeles district attorney John Van de Kamp summed up Proposition 13 with the accusation that the initiative was a "sweetheart measure . . . aimed at enriching one man and his associates."[35] The Los Angeles city attorney concurred, wondering whether "a small group of promoters will be able to fool the public into giving them a monopoly over a billion-dollar business."[36]

The lobbying group People Against Proposition 13 was organized, launched an aggressive campaign, and secured the support of major newspapers including the *Los Angeles Times, San Diego Tribune, Sacramento Bee, San Francisco Chronicle,* and *San Francisco Examiner.*[37] The supporters of People Against Proposition 13 included animal advocacy organizations, representatives from law enforcement, labor organizations, and various civic and religious groups.[38] Television advertisements launched against Proposition 13 were blunt, leaving little room for doubt about the fate of greyhounds whose careers were over: the dogs were "doomed" and will "join other greyhounds in death. . . . When they lose, they're destroyed." The advertisements also decried the use of live lures—"rabbits, often kittens"—to cultivate a killer instinct in the racers. The closing message was clear: "Dog racing isn't a sport. It's the cruelty nobody talks about. Don't make it legal, too." Voters were urged not to make California the "newest killing ground" for the "plunderers and promoters."[39]

An interim hearing was conducted on October 15, 1976, at which Senator Ralph Dills, chairman of the Committee on Governmental Organization, laid out the potential benefits of introducing the "fastest growing spectator sport in the country" to California.[40] Hardie himself maintained that greyhound racing had a "philosophical right" to exist in California, and he expounded the ways in which the public could be ensured of a clean sport. He complained that Proposition 13 had encountered the "strongest harassment of any initiative in the history of California" and that he was being outgunned by well-financed and self-interested opposition groups, including the horse-racing industry. He acknowledged that dog racing was essentially a poor man's gambling opportunity, as one senator had worded it, and would thus likely draw a different crowd than would thoroughbred horse racing.[41] One of Hardie's supporters from the Golden State Greyhound Association, dogman Mervin Roberts, praised the business precisely because it was a "poor man's industry" that average working men could enjoy.[42] An opposing speaker testified that most of the organized labor movement in California rejected legalized dog racing because it feared working people would lose money at the tracks.[43] This argument had been used extensively in the 1930s and revealed the social discomfort many felt about sanctioning an additional form of gambling targeted specifically at the working class. What was, for some, a suitable and viable entertainment option for the poor was for others one more means of exploitation that offered little more than a convenient and speedy route to financial suicide.[44]

Animal advocates testified that dog racing was cruel. They cited Danny Williams of the Palm Beach Kennel Club in Florida, who had admitted in a recent *Sports Illustrated* article that thousands of greyhounds that could no longer run were gassed.[45] They denounced the use of live rabbits for training purposes and claimed that ex-racing greyhounds would make poor family pets and even posed a danger to the community if they were placed in private homes. They maintained that Hardie's safeguards, supposedly designed to protect greyhounds, were filled with loopholes. For example, the provision that trainers could not race dogs that had been trained with live animals was weakened with the phrase "knowingly use." Furthermore, there was no mandate forcing owners to turn over their dogs to retirement farms once their careers were over.[46]

In the run-up to election day Governor Jerry Brown criticized the proposition's "unsavory odor," although he made it clear that he was commenting only on the proposal itself and not on dog racing in California in general.[47] The people of California voted overwhelmingly against Proposition 13: only 25 percent were in favor, whereas 75 percent were opposed.[48] At the time, the California secretary of state's office stated that no ballot initiative had been so soundly defeated in the past fifteen years.

Industry advocates blamed the animal rights movement, the horse-racing lobby, and the film industry for the failure. Veteran greyhound breeder Jack Sherck, who had worked side by side with Hardie in support of Proposition 13, recalled in 2009 that the opposition "obliterated us," in part because of their larger arsenal: a high-powered public relations company, a sizeable budget, and superior ancillary support. He singled out groups that rejected dog racing outright, including horse-racing interests and animal advocacy organizations.[49] Not long after the initiative failed, dogman F. B. "Happy" Stutz decried the "diabolical propaganda program" financed by critics of dog racing in California, namely, the horse racing and movie industries, and charged that they presented a "distorted propaganda blitzkrieg of the type used by Joseph Goebbels, Hitler's propaganda minister."[50]

Dogman Campbell Strange, who was himself not yet involved in greyhound racing in 1976, later stated that the campaign against dog racing was so effective that he had "second thoughts about getting involved with it after reading and listening to what the humane societies and the horse industry had to say about it." He acknowledged that if a dogman like himself could become skeptical, the "average man on the street" was not likely at all to support legalized greyhound racing.[51] In 1977 Guccione labeled the defeat as the disappointment of the year, but he later acknowledged in retrospect that it was nowhere near as demoralizing to the industry as the blows that were to come much later, when major tracks such as the Multnomah Kennel Club in Portland and the Mile High Kennel Club in Denver closed permanently in 2004 and 2008, respectively.[52]

The struggle to legalize dog racing in Kansas emerged as another serious challenge facing the industry as it attempted to expand its national presence. Greyhound racing advocates knew that Kansas was the historic heart of the industry; the state had always been an important greyhound breeding center, joining Florida, Oklahoma, and Texas as a top breeding state. The unwillingness of the people of Kansas to legalize greyhound racing in their home state was a festering sore spot for the dogmen. They felt that "greyhounds . . . with no racing" is like "wheat . . . with no bread."[53] An attempt to legalize greyhound racing in Kansas had been initiated after World War II by Dr. Al M. Bissing, a Wichita dentist and dog-racing enthusiast. After returning from army service in 1946, he purchased 35 acres to raise and train greyhounds. By 1954 he was ready to advocate for legalization. He later recalled that when the local newspaper broke the story, "It was like a bomb, radio stations, televisions, and all the newspapers in the state went berserk. All the way from Kansas City to Denver. The County Attorney tried to arrest us, but to no avail."[54]

Yet Bissing did meet with some initial success. After he testified in a district court over the legality of dog racing, the judge ruled that an 1895 Kansas statute permitted gambling within a racing enclosure for no more than two weeks a year. This exemption had originally been created to pave the way for horse racing at fairs, but the judge decided that the track proposed by Bissing for Wichita would be covered as well.[55] Not long thereafter, however, the Kansas attorney general overruled the decision, likening the situation to "a law which would permit murder for two weeks in the year."[56] The Kansas supreme court eventually ruled that the statutory exemption under which dog racing in Wichita had formerly been conducted was unconstitutional.[57]

The legalization effort in Kansas was not revitalized until the 1980s. The

Kansas Greyhound Breeders' Educational Association, Inc., had declared decades earlier that "nothing is more Kansas than greyhounds," invoking the usual list of legalization's benefits, most significantly the added revenue for state coffers.[58] Around this time, the Kansas Greyhound Breeders' Association (led by dogman Gene Randle) had taken a large group of Kansans to the Mile High Kennel Club in Denver. After meeting with Colorado civic dignitaries they were reminded that "if you knew the number of Kansans who come here each summer and the amount of money they wager, I'm sure you'd want to keep them in your state." The visitors were schooled by their hosts in the business of greyhound racing and were assured that it took place on the highest, cleanest level.[59] By 1981, when the campaign to legalize dog racing was resurrected, the *Kansas Business News* calculated that the 150 greyhound farms in the state added up to a $14 million investment. That year, Dickinson County (where Abilene and the Greyhound Hall of Fame are situated) was the number one greyhound-producing county in the United States.[60] In 1986 a constitutional amendment was passed that authorized pari-mutuel wagering. Both the Wichita Greyhound Park and the Woodlands in Kansas City, Kansas, opened three years later.

Guccione later characterized the 1980s as the "golden days" of dog racing in the United States, largely because the industry's aggressive expansion into midwestern and southwestern states (for instance, Wisconsin, Iowa, and Texas) seemed so promising.[61] The Woodlands in Kansas City enjoyed some early successes and for a time ranked as one of the top five greyhound tracks in the country.[62] But despite its hard-earned legalization victory and auspicious beginnings in Kansas, the industry had unknowingly picked a precarious time to legalize the sport in the state. The boom that greyhound racing had experienced in the 1980s came to an abrupt halt the following decade when Indian gaming and state-sanctioned casinos began to squeeze out their competition.[63] In testimony given in Topeka in 1992, the executive director of the Kansas Racing Commission, Dana Nelson, pled for the reduction of pari-mutuel tax rates on track revenues in the state of Kansas and observed that since 1986, "not a single greyhound track in this country has shown a five-year trend of increasing handles. . . . To the contrary, many tracks have shown a continued downward spiral over the same five-year period."[64] Later, in a last-ditch effort to save the tracks, the industry fought for a bill legalizing slot machines at the dog tracks. It passed but ultimately proved ineffective.[65] Wichita ended live racing in 2007, and the Woodlands closed in 2008.[66]

Legalization, expansion, and their aftermath were not the only challenges facing dog racing. In recent years many industry experts have complained that the "purists" no longer run the tracks.[67] Most greyhound-racing traditionalists agree that corporate track owners have often failed to perform as well as some of the sport's pioneers, many of whom managed day-to-day operations directly and with careful attention.[68] Arizona and Colorado, two states where greyhound racing once thrived, are such cases. Brothers David K. Funk and Arthur Funk launched the sport in Arizona soon after legalization in the late 1930s, opening a track at the Western Greyhound Park located in Phoenix and later one in Tucson.[69] In 1954 they unveiled a new, million-dollar track in Phoenix that drew a record crowd of almost 10,000 fans on its opening day.[70] By the late 1960s, the brothers were managing six greyhound facilities in the state.[71] Through their efforts, Arizona had rapidly become a stronghold of dog racing.

In 1980, after thirty-eight years in the industry, the Funks sold their ownership share of their Arizona tracks to the company Delaware North and Wisconsin business executive George Gillette.[72] Greyhound historian Leslie Wootten argues that this move precipitated a "long, slow decline" in Arizona greyhound racing.[73] The new corporate owners, according to Wootten, were unable to provide the same personal involvement that the Funks had delivered. Instead of direct management by one family with local and regional ties, the majority of Arizona greyhound tracks were now operated by an out-of-state company. Bill Georgantos, a friend of the Funks and longtime general manager of their racing circuit, reportedly resented the heavy-handed corporate control, particularly in financial matters. Wootten notes that the dog tracks were just one of many interests overseen by Delaware North, whereas "greyhound racing was the primary focus—the heart, if you will—of the Funk family."[74] In 2009 the Phoenix Greyhound Park closed permanently.[75] The gradual decline of greyhound racing in Arizona suggests that the sport flourished more readily when bolstered by locally or regionally based leadership with a targeted interest in greyhound racing.

As was the case in Arizona, day-to-day operations at the Colorado tracks were for years handled by individuals who not only lived in Colorado but also belonged to and interacted with the local communities. The first president of the Mile High Kennel Club in Denver was a mortician from Pueblo, George McCarthy; the Pueblo Greyhound Park was funded by local physicians.[76] Arden Hartman, who worked as general manager at three Colorado dog tracks, was widely regarded as an experienced greyhound man with a demonstrated interest in and dedication to the sport.[77] Bill Lee, who began his career as a lead-out at Mile High, eventually shared management duties with Hartman at a number of dog-racing facilities. The community attachment to greyhound racing had a financial component as well: several Colorado tracks, including the Mile High, Pueblo, and Cloverleaf Kennel Clubs, even held a public offering of stock. Fans who became stockholders, even with smaller investments, could feel a sense of ownership. They, in turn, passed down their stock (and their loyalty to the track) to their children, thus promoting a continuing fan base.[78]

In 1990, however, five Colorado facilities, including the Mile High Kennel Club, the Pueblo Greyhound Park, and the Interstate Kennel Club in Byers, were sold by current owner Joe Linsey and his nephew Alfred S. Ross to the British company Wembley PLC.[79] By the time the Mile High Kennel Club was sold by Wembley, USA (controlled by Wembley PLC) to BLB Investors, LLC, in 2005, the track was already in trouble. Hartman faulted Wembley for ruining Mile High, noting that the company hired individuals who had never even met its customers. Lee, too, criticized the successive corporate management, observing that its accountants acted as bean counters who neither demonstrated love for the sport nor evidenced any real knowledge of it. He was particularly troubled when Wembley reneged on a promise to give former public stockholders free season passes in perpetuity.[80] Mile High's closure in 2008 revealed that even a track that had enjoyed many years of popularity and success could fail when faced with an onslaught of new challenges brought about by corporate ownership.

Greyhound racing had also continued to face allegations well into the 1970s and beyond that the sport was somehow connected to crime syndicates. In addition to dog tracks in Florida and Massachusetts, establishments in North Carolina, Arizona, Arkansas, and Nevada were all rumored at one time or another to be operating under the influence of organized crime, according to contemporary media reports. The rumors alone—despite the fact that this type of criminal activity rarely, if ever, was proved—have nonetheless managed to cast a shadow over the sport's reputation.[81]

Even prominent greyhound track operators such as Joe Linsey have seen their reputations called into question. A 1981 inductee into the Greyhound Hall of Fame, Linsey's importance as a founding father of American greyhound racing cannot be doubted. He served as chairman of the board at the Taunton, Massachusetts, dog track as well as at the Mile High Kennel Club and Pueblo Greyhound Park in Colorado and at Lincoln Park in Rhode Island. Additionally, he helped organize and then lead AGTOA, serving as its president for three terms.[82] By the time he died in 1994, he was a multimillionaire who could boast of numerous prestigious associations: founding trustee of Brandeis University; recipient of the Brandeis Medal for Distinguished Service to Higher Education; member of the Board of Governors of the Humane Relations Center of Boston University; president of the Jewish Memorial Hospital; and, perhaps ironically, member of the executive committee of the National Council on Crime and Delinquency.

During the Prohibition era, however, Linsey had acquired a criminal record. Linsey was a Russian immigrant who had been arrested for bootlegging in 1927 and sentenced by the Bristol County Superior Court to one year in jail.[83] Many years later, in 1957, the FBI concluded that he was acquainted with "local hoodlums and racketeers."[84] In 1968 the bureau reported finding a "low power radio frequency transmitter" on the Taunton Greyhound Association's phone line.[85] Mobster (and top government witness) Vincent Teresa revealed in a 1973 tell-all memoir that Linsey was an associate of Mike Rocco ("Mike the Wiseguy"), who in turn worked for mobster Joe Lombardo ("Joey the Clown") and Raymond Salvatore Loredo Patriarca, who was sentenced to federal prison for conspiracy to murder.[86] Still, despite such suspicions, Linsey was never arrested or convicted of any crime during his reign as a greyhound track operator.

North Carolina grappled with comparable criticism of the dog tracks in Moyock in Currituck County and Morehead City in Carteret County in the late 1940s. The *Raleigh News and Observer* printed a number of stories critical of greyhound racing, claiming that a 1951 investigation had found that at least three men associated with the North Carolina tracks had "questionable histories."[87] One reporter pointed out that Paul Cleland, the director of the Morehead City track, had previously served time in prison for fraudulent sales in a stock deal. In 1953 a number of North Carolina newspapers claimed that the state's tracks were controlled by the Frank Costello crime syndicate. During a trial in Freehold, New Jersey, a female witness had testified that the Costello family held sizeable interests at the North Carolina tracks and that her husband had profited from the operation.[88] An editorial in the *Raleigh News and Observer* decried the continued existence of greyhound racing in North Carolina, noting that both of the state's dog-racing venues were "acquiring a nation-wide reputation as gambling centers. . . . When enough persons of underworld character get together, they form the nucleus for organized crime."[89]

Both North Carolina tracks closed permanently in 1954, but attempts were made to reopen them in the following years. North Carolina attorney general Malcolm Seawell weighed in, firmly stating that the return of dog racing would be "an invitation to organized crime and crime syndicates."[90]

In 1959 the Norfolk (Virginia) County Board of Supervisors sent letters to politicians in neighboring North Carolina complaining that the Moyock track had caused not only traffic jams but also an increased volume of welfare cases and other social woes in their state.[91] The same year, greyhound racing took a lethal hit in North Carolina when a bill to legalize dog racing on a local-option basis was voted down by the House Finance Committee, 28–17. One journalist declared that as a consequence of this ruling, for this session "the dogs are dead."[92] Greyhound racing was never revived in North Carolina.[93]

Arizona track operators David and Arthur Funk also found themselves under media scrutiny as a result of their partnership with a large sports conglomerate known as the Emprise Corporation (later reorganized and renamed Delaware North), a company that frequently had to fight accusations of ties to organized crime.[94] The Funks came into the spotlight after an investigative reporter, Don Bolles, died from injuries sustained in a car bomb explosion in June 1976.[95] Bolles had been pursuing allegations that the Arizona greyhound tracks were associated with organized crime, namely, the Emprise Corporation. Bolles had not been killed instantly in the explosion; his last words were reportedly, "They finally got me," then interpreted as an ominous reference to criminal elements. The Funks were never implicated in the murder but their public reputations were tarnished nonetheless.[96]

The public eye often associates such problems with the greyhound industry as a whole, operating under the assumption that the industry is a united front, but in truth greyhound racing has been plagued by friction between the dogmen and the track operators from the beginning. The dogmen have long been discontented with their bargaining position when hammering out booking contracts and gambling purses: they have even compared the track owners' relationship to the dogmen to that between the "landed barons and the vassal[s] of the middle ages."[97] This undercurrent of tension was not readily evident to the betting public, however. In 1975 F. B. "Happy" Stutz summarized the problem for his fellow dogmen: "It's a healthy industry from everybody's but the kennel owners' viewpoint."[98] Profits were increasing, but where was the money going?

The dogmen claimed that, with few exceptions, it was not going to them. They were deeply dissatisfied with the way in which the "pari-mutuel pie" was distributed at tracks in Florida and elsewhere. Large purses gave the appearance of a thriving industry. For instance, the Biscayne Irish-American purse was $125,000 in 1970, and the Hollywood World Classic was $125,000 in 1975.[99] Special charity races that raised money for organizations such as the March of Dimes had the added benefit of generating positive publicity for dog racing. But underneath this ready flow of cash, troubles were brewing. Communication between dogmen and track operators had always been strained, and the relationship only continued to sour.

From the sport's beginnings the racing kennel owners had chafed under the restrictive provisions of their bookings with track management. They complained that they had little or no say in the creation of their contracts and that track operators wielded too much power and control over the entire booking process. Because all contracts were individually awarded and there were more dogmen than bookings, track management invariably had the upper hand at the bargaining table. The dogmen routinely complained that contracts were presented to them on a "take it or leave it" basis. If a racing kennel rejected the terms of a contract or attempted to negotiate for better terms, a long line of dogmen was waiting eagerly to obtain a booking for their own kennels. Reflecting on his long career in the business, dogman Jim Frey has stated that contracts were the "greatest obstacle that kept us under the heel."[100]

The dogmen's numerous attempts to establish their own advocacy groups—and thereby increase their bargaining power—have had limited success. To their own detriment, when faced with problems, they have been disinclined to unite with one another and find strength in solidarity.[101] Instead, each dogman has faced the consequences of his (or her) weak bargaining position alone. The dogmen had long been allied with the National Coursing Association (NCA) in Kansas, renamed the National Greyhound Association (NGA) in 1973, but this organization served primarily as a registry for greyhounds, although it publishes its own magazine about the sport as well.[102] Over the years the dogmen established a number of associations designed to improve their occupational status and working conditions across the country, generally with mixed results.[103] One such group, the Greyhound Owners Benevolent Association (GOBA), was designed in part to remedy the weakness of their bargaining position.[104] Membership reached approximately 650 in early 1948.[105] The dogmen associated with this group decided to strike eight Florida dog tracks that same year, a failed effort that lasted only one week.[106] GOBA disbanded soon thereafter.[107]

In 1973, still disgruntled with their financial outlook and embittered by their low status, the dogmen resurrected GOBA in an attempt to improve their position in the industry, even though their membership numbers reached only about 315.[108] GOBA's stated goal was to "dignify and elevate the role of the greyhound man as an equal partner with the state and the racetracks in Florida's greyhound racing industry." Its leadership focused on what it perceived to be a fundamental threat: even though the business itself appeared to be thriving, its foundation—the dogmen themselves—was in financial distress. The dogmen blamed spiraling kennel costs and inadequate purse returns for their woes. In 1974 GOBA enumerated in a formal report the many problems facing the dog owners, most notably their failure to secure a minimum guaranteed purse at Florida racetracks.[109] GOBA declared that the greyhound tracks enjoyed a monopoly and that profits were disproportionately and unreasonably higher for the track operators.[110] The fact that the horsemen had also initiated a strike in the early 1970s that had resulted in improved purses did not go unnoticed. Paul Discolo, one of the dogmen to participate in the forthcoming protests, later complained, "If the horseman gets seven percent [of the handle], why can't we?"[111]

In the mid-1970s the dogmen orchestrated a series of strikes that threatened to shut down operations in Florida. Trouble erupted in Miami when the dogmen threatened to boycott the July 3, 1975, opening at the Flagler Kennel Club. Owner David Hecht, who had assumed management of the family business after his father Isadore "Izzie" Hecht died, later blamed "strike fever" that had broken out at the New England tracks for the problems that erupted in Florida.[112] Unlike earlier strikes in the industry, the 1975 crisis in South Florida attracted sustained attention from the press because of the headlines garnered by the eighteen striking dogmen, known as the Flagler Eighteen.[113] After the men launched their strike, Hecht filed suit in the U.S. District Court and Dade County Circuit Court seeking an injunction forcing the dogmen to race their dogs.[114] His injunction was granted, but when the dogmen refused to comply with the court order, they were incarcerated in the Dade County Stockade. The situation was unprecedented: Wayne Strong later recalled that "none of us believed they'd put us in jail," but "they put us [in] with hardened criminals."[115] Florida Supreme Court Chief Justice James Adkins ordered the dogmen to return to the track. After a swell of media attention, they eventually complied, ending the strike.

In retrospect, the repercussions of the dogmen's actions in Florida were fairly damaging, although there may have been a few lingering benefits. NGA's Guccione later observed that the strikes led to "greater sensitivity from the tracks' standpoint to the issues that were affecting the greyhound people." He acknowledged that even though track officials had refused to make certain other concessions at the time, they did increase purse percentages for the next five years.[116] Other assessments were not so upbeat. Greyhound historian Paul Hartwell concluded that the entire industry was damaged by the strikes of the 1970s because tracks brought in substandard kennels to replace those that were protesting.[117] Dogman Wayne Strong stated that the strikes unintentionally set off a cycle of greed from which the industry never again recovered, a cycle in which every party involved in the business of greyhound racing—the kennels, the track operators, and the state—began to demand a higher cut of the handle. As a result, they "killed the goose that laid the golden egg."[118]

Dogmen with booking contracts in other states, including Massachusetts and Arizona, had also agitated for better conditions but had met with equally poor results.[119] Breeders on strike in Arizona alienated the public when they threatened to kill twenty-five greyhounds a day until track management agreed to negotiate. The Arizona Greyhound Breeders Association (AGBA) financial chairman stated, "We intend to start putting away dogs every week to demonstrate to the public how the tactics of the race track has [sic] affected 47 small Arizona businessmen."[120] Miami reporter Bill Braucher wrote that the "bizarre action" was halted by the state's assistant attorney general, who obtained a ten-day restraining order to prevent the killings. Braucher maintained that until the restraining order was issued, spokesmen for AGBA had threatened to carry out the destruction of 300 dogs worth an estimated $1 million. Although the Arizona breeders later claimed the threat was a publicity stunt, their strategy backfired. Arizona governor Raul Castro and state attorney general Bruce Babbitt used the words "senseless, repulsive, inhumane, unjust, immoral" to describe the failed ploy.[121]

The 1975 strikes were the last major uprising mounted by the dogmen. Ignored by labor advocates, and in their own view exploited by track operators, the men who bred, raised, and trained racing greyhounds felt as if they were a marginalized group of workers with no effective voice or representation. Their actions often left them without work altogether. Like several other dogmen who had been involved in the 1975 Florida strikes, Jim Frey permanently lost three bookings in South Florida: Miami Beach, Biscayne, and Flagler.[122]

Despite their continuously evolving struggles with track operators, the dogmen have rarely elicited any sympathy from the public. Instead, these greyhound owners, breeders, and trainers, stung by broad public disapproval over animal welfare issues, have seen their reputations sullied and their commitment to their animals questioned. Those who run their businesses conscientiously and according to industry standards—and, in their view, treat their greyhounds humanely—are often put in the same category as those who egregiously violate animal welfare laws. Despite their maligned image, however, the dogmen view their trade as a legitimate means of earning a living. They have long taken pride in their work and relish its unique character. Commenting on anti-racing organizations such as GREY2K USA, one breeder, Gina Dalton, recently complained, "They're ruining a whole industry, they're ruining people's lives."[123] To greyhound breeders, trainers, and owners, it often appears as though their critics care more about the welfare of animals than the human beings who raise them. The attack on dog racing is interpreted as a cultural assault, an attempt to eliminate a way of life altogether. Given these circumstances, the dogmen have felt increasingly powerless to confront the changing landscape before them, witnessing as they are a cultural transformation in the way Americans relate to greyhounds—animals that are no longer considered commodities but pets and family members. Anger and defensiveness have won the dogmen little public sympathy or support.

To their detriment, the dogmen have been poorly positioned and fundamentally ill equipped to respond to such challenges to American greyhound racing. The introduction of simulcasting in the early 1980s is a prime example of another change that further weakened their bargaining position and undermined their way of life. Simulcasting allows bettors to gamble on races taking place at other tracks via a closed-circuit broadcast or, more recently, through high-quality video by satellite or live web streaming. Once simulcasting was introduced, the potential for strikes decreased significantly: the dogmen knew that if they rejected the booking arrangements at a track, the facility could easily continue with simulcasts of races conducted elsewhere in the absence of live racing on site. However, simulcasting altered the economic landscape of the sport in still more critical ways. Some experts in the industry perceived simulcasting to be a serious threat to live racing—especially at smaller tracks—but the issue was complicated, and not everyone agreed on the degree and scope of its impact.

Either way, greyhound owners were frustrated that they had no part in the negotiation of simulcasting agreements, and they sought to remedy the situation. In 1989 they attempted to secure new federal laws modeled on legislation previously passed by the horsemen, the Interstate Horse Racing Act (IHRA) of 1978, by proposing the Interstate Greyhound Racing Act.[124] One provision of IHRA required horse owners to be represented in negotiations between track owners and the racing commissions of states entering into an interstate simulcasting agreement. Similarly, the proposed legislation would prohibit interstate offtrack wagering on greyhound racing unless all parties involved, including the dog owners, agreed to the terms and conditions of the wagering. Simply put, tracks had been simulcasting races without the permission of the greyhound owners whose dogs were racing, and few, if any, benefits issuing from the racing had been accruing to the owners.

The dogmen knew that their failure to secure a place in these business negotiations meant another lost opportunity to improve their earnings. During his appearance before a subcommittee of the House Energy and Commerce Committee in August 1990, Guccione, representing the NGA, testified that individuals who raised, trained, and raced greyhounds were suffering financially. He stated further that fewer than 50 percent of NGA members were breaking even or earning profits. Guccione asserted that while the outlook for dog racing was bright, the proprietary rights of greyhound owners were being "denied under the current practice of interstate simulcasting." He urged, therefore, that Congress grant to the dogmen the right to join the negotiating table. Other NGA supporters submitted testimony as well. Greyhound breeder Janet Allen emphasized the point that the proposed legislation was not an anti-simulcasting bill. But she, too, bemoaned the "blatant unfairness" of permitting the transmission of races without the permission of the dog owners.[125] AGTOA, however, was decidedly unsupportive of the legislation.[126]

The distance separating state racing commissions, greyhound tracks, and offtrack betting (OTB) corporations from the individual dogmen was starkly illustrated by the testimony of Ross Lingle, a greyhound breeder and owner from Altus, Oklahoma. He recalled that, at first, he did not even know that Lincoln Greyhound Park in Rhode Island, where he and his son had secured a booking, had already started to simulcast its races. Lingle stated,

> The way I found out about it, in Oklahoma, I live out in the country and I don't have cable TV, so I have a satellite dish. I ran across it on the satellite one day. I hollered at my wife and said, hey, lookey here, here is greyhound racing on the satellite. I didn't know where it was from, and all of a sudden I saw one of my dog's names on the screen, why this is Lincoln Greyhound Park. So we watched it and thought it was very thoughtful of them to put our dogs on TV so we can watch them way back in Oklahoma, kind of got a kick out of it.[127]

But later, Lingle spoke with his greyhound trainer, who informed him that the races had been on the air for six weeks. Only then did Lingle begin to wonder whether he would receive any money for the use of his greyhounds. After initially being told that he would not receive any remuneration, he eventually did manage to secure a small payment, although, according to his testimony, he learned nothing about how the proceeds from the simulcast were divided.

More congressional hearings followed, but the NGA and its allies never succeeded in making their case. Guccione later speculated that the legislation would never have passed until all segments of the industry were united in their support for the proposal; in particular, he felt that AGTOA's refusal to back the proposal was especially damaging. He maintained further that it would have required millions of dollars to lobby Congress effectively, funds that his organization did not have. Guccione concluded that NGA's failure to win the passage of the Interstate Greyhound Racing Act was "huge"; had it become law, it "would have given greyhound owners much more control of their fate and destiny with respect to simulcasting."[128] Although the bill did not pass, some greyhound owners did see their earnings from simulcasting rise slightly. But marginally improved purses coupled with a tiny fraction of simulcasting profits did little to improve their overall financial situation. National greyhound racing handles had already been on a steady decline since the late 1980s or early 1990s, depending on the method of calculation.[129]

Simulcasting may have been a welcome addition for racing enthusiasts, but its impact on the industry as a whole has been a subject of debate. Too many racing dates can weaken fan support. Before simulcasting even began, year-round racing threatened to dilute the excitement generated by a defined racing season with a clear-cut opening day and a firmly established final race of the season.[130] Oregon track operator Murray Kemp may have been right when he maintained that a greyhound track could sustain the fans' enthusiasm if the season opened and closed within a clearly defined period of sixty days, but interest would drastically wane if the season were extended, even by a bit.[131] In some cases, increasing the number of dog races for the public to bet on has offered a quick fix—namely, a temporary growth of profits—but the widespread, almost universal availability of parimutuel wagering via Internet gambling hubs, OTB establishments, and simulcasting has been a mixed blessing for the sport.[132]

Even beyond simulcasting, the gaming market was undergoing tremendous changes. The monopoly enjoyed by pari-mutuel wagering operations since the early 1930s was slowly eroding, progressively replaced by new forms of gambling that were easier to understand and faster to execute.[133] Along with the other challenges to traditional mores during the social revolutions of the 1960s, the old prohibitions against gambling were also steadily eroding.[134] Florida was the first southern state to succumb to the trend: its citizens voted in favor of a lottery amendment in November 1986 and officially instituted the new game in 1988.[135] Operation of the state lottery in Florida weakened greyhound-racing revenues almost immediately.[136] In large part the generation of individuals—in Florida and beyond—who were willing to devote the time to pore over racing forms and "handicap" dogs or horses was also dwindling, replaced by younger gamblers who were often unwilling to grapple with such challenges.[137] Moreover, new and simpler gaming options were rapidly emerging throughout the country, especially once Native American gaming entered the picture.

In the late 1980s Congress had reexamined the possibility of legalizing diverse forms of gaming on tribal reservations.[138] Amid increasing calls for greater self-determination and new revenue sources, Indian tribes began to consider establishing legalized gambling for the general public on native lands. But state governments felt threatened by the possibility of the tribes circumventing the established system of state racing commissions and, more important, by the potential loss of state tax proceeds: because tribes enjoyed sovereignty, Indian gaming establishments were not required to turn over a percentage of the betting handle for state taxes. Nonetheless, after a series of congressional hearings, interested parties hammered out what would eventually become the legislative backing for legalized American Indian gaming: the Indian Gaming Regulatory Act of 1988, known as IGRA.[139]

The subsequent launch of Indian gaming in the wake of IGRA's passage in 1988 profoundly damaged the dog-racing industry.[140] Even twenty-one years after the passage of the act, Guccione was still decrying the uneven playing field on which state-regulated gaming was heavily taxed while Indian gaming was not taxed at all. This view was also advanced by a longtime Washington, DC, lobbyist for AGTOA, Henry Cashen, who stated that Indian gaming was a "constant water-drag" affecting all legal gaming establishments in the country, including racing.[141] In 2009 gaming analyst Will Cummings asserted, "Indian gaming has been the biggest of all the blows that have landed on greyhound racing over the past twenty years . . . because it launched a chain reaction of subsequent events."[142] After IGRA was passed, state governments began to realize that state-sanctioned casino gambling could be a lucrative revenue source. When they saw that Native American tribes were enjoying burgeoning profits, the states wanted their own piece of the gaming pie. Together with Indian gaming, the spread of state-sanctioned casino gambling further stunted the growth of greyhound racing.[143]

Before the passage of IGRA, however, the NGA had considered joining forces with Indian gaming interests rather than competing against them.[144] A very real possibility of establishing a greyhound track on Indian lands had emerged by 1985, when the NGA testified during congressional hearings that it was backing an effort to work with the Pueblo of Santa Ana in New Mexico to establish the Santa Ana Greyhound Park.[145] But not all parties interested in promoting greyhound racing supported this proposal. AGTOA recognized that dog tracks on Native American reservations could easily outperform state-regulated tracks simply because they would not lose money to state taxation. It thus demurred, arguing not only that added federal oversight was unnecessary but also that the absence of state regulation would allow unsavory elements to infiltrate the Native American tracks. In response, AGTOA invoked the specter of organized crime, arguing that unregulated (i.e., Indian-run) tracks would act as a "magnet for criminal elements frustrated at their lack of success" at tracks regulated by state racing commissions.[146] An industry that had previously boasted of the incorruptibility of greyhound racing rapidly changed its tune when it realized that competition from Indian pari-mutuel operations could pose a real economic threat. AGTOA was more than willing to raise the bugaboo of organized crime when it served a particular political and economic purpose. The idea of dog racing on tribal lands was eventually abandoned altogether.

Instead, greyhound tracks have tried to stay afloat by establishing "racinos," which are a combination of a casino with a dog track.[147] Initially, racinos benefited a number of greyhound-racing operations, including Iowa's Bluffs Run Greyhound Park and Dubuque Greyhound Park, and West Virginia's Wheeling Downs and Tri-State racetracks. The racino combination did improve purse revenues for the dogmen, especially after Iowa and West Virginia enacted statutes that diverted a portion of slot machine revenues to greyhound purses.[148] But Guccione, when evaluating the long-term efficacy of racinos as a means to save greyhound tracks, stated in 2009 that the "jury is still out."[149] The so-called racino compromise did initially bail out a number of failing tracks, but the long-term consequences of the partnership between tracks and casinos are no longer looking good for dog-racing enthusiasts. A 2012 *New York Times* headline declared, "Greyhound Races Face Extinction at the Hands of Casinos They Fostered." In the article, Florida racetrack operator Isadore Havenick is quoted as observing that the "only time there's a large crowd of people watching dogs is when people get up from the poker table to smoke."[150] Dog tracks now complain that they are forced to subsidize a pastime—greyhound racing—that has been almost entirely abandoned by the public.

Initially, tracks had included casino operations at their racing facilities only on the condition that live racing would continue and a portion of the casino profits would subsidize purses. Now, so-called decoupling legislation pending in several states seeks to separate the mandate for live racing at tracks where casinos are in operation. In Iowa the corporate owners of Bluffs Run Greyhound Park, Harrah's Entertainment, Inc., offered in 2010 to pay the state $7 million a year to end the requirement that casinos at dog tracks subsidize racing purses. Iowa casinos have been required to pay these subsidies since the mid–1990s.[151] Some constituencies in Florida are now seeking a measure to allow casinos to operate without live racing.[152] This reversal requires political clout and has resulted in strange bedfellows: GREY2K USA (in partnership with HSUS and the ASPCA) and the majority of Florida track operators are all lobbying in favor of the change.[153] Those who resist decoupling legislation include the dogmen—largely because they would lose coveted bookings should tracks close for live racing—as well as those tracks that likely would not survive if the changes are enacted.

It is difficult to imagine a more peculiar pairing than GREY2K USA and Florida greyhound track operators, but the present gaming environment has forced some industry leaders to resort to purely pragmatic methods of survival. HSUS president Wayne Pacelle acknowledges that partnering with dog tracks to end live racing in Florida may at first seem surprising, but "we are always trying to turn adversaries into allies."[154] Most individuals in the dog-racing business understand that the sport is nearing its end, but they still decry and resent the methods used by their opponents, especially GREY2K USA. A fact sheet issued by the organization (available on its website) highlights the many reasons why its leaders believe the dog-racing industry is inhumane and needs to be eliminated: greyhounds "endure lives of terrible confinement" and "suffer serious injuries while racing," all the while needlessly participating in a "dying industry."[155]

Greyhound racing's eventual demise in the United States is a predictable reality that both pro- and anti-racing forces generally agree upon, even when they can find no other common ground.[156] The reasons why dog racing drew in crowds during its early years have become increasingly irrelevant in the twenty-first century. Once, the sport held the promise of an inexpensive and entertaining night out, an evening where fans could gamble on the races

Kennels for racing greyhounds at a breeding farm, 2010. (Ray Wong, photographer)

and enjoy a bit of fun at a new and exciting public venue. Stars from the silver screen and the athletic field were an additional draw on certain occasions: their very presence legitimized the sport and in some cases gave it a patina of glamour. But the novelty and excitement of dog racing, especially as it was packaged for consumers in Florida, was gradually superseded by an overwhelming array of new entertainment options. NASCAR was only one of several spectator sports that eventually drew in larger crowds than dog racing ever could or did. There is no doubt that visitors to the Sunshine State loved and still love to watch racing, but by the end of the twentieth century they preferred stock cars to greyhounds.

But beyond this evolution of the popular entertainment market, the shifting role and status of the dog in the United States may have had an even greater impact: changing attitudes toward all canines, including the racing greyhound, formed a major part of the equation. With the rise of animal advocacy in the 1970s, new questions were raised about the role of animals. Some of these issues were addressed across the entire range of public discourse, including even television sitcoms, as in the episode of *The Odd Couple* that featured an adopted racing greyhound living for a brief period in the household of Oscar and Felix. The two divorced roommates engage in a continuing comic dialogue that anticipates many of the issues that will surface when working dogs such as racing greyhounds are introduced into the family environment; as Felix advises a rather skeptical Oscar, "There are three of us now."[157] Oscar is baffled by Felix's insistence that their greyhound, Golden Earrings, is a pet destined to live his life in their small New York apartment, and he mocks Felix for having bought the dog an array of matching collars and leashes, indulging the dog with fresh meat rather than packaged kibbles, and talking to the dog as if he were a baby.

What baffles Oscar most of all is Felix's insistence on treating the greyhound as if he were a beloved family member. Felix criticizes Oscar for wanting to race the dog and states quite simply, "You don't love Golden Earrings—all you want to do is exploit him."[158] This became the philosophical position adopted by more and more Americans as greyhound racing gradually came under fire for its perceived exploitation of animals. Before the adoption movement was in place, the number of ex-racing greyhounds that were euthanized prematurely was undoubtedly quite high; the exact numbers will never be known. But even after the drive for the adoption of ex-racers became increasingly successful, an unanticipated consequence surfaced: a growing number of Americans became convinced that greyhound racing should be eliminated altogether. These Americans began to realize that even under the best circumstances possible, within the market system of dog racing, ex-racing greyhounds are ultimately discarded goods—a canine commodity. Only in recent decades have they been identified as valuable for another use: that of beloved pet.

Americans once gambled on greyhounds; now they snuggle with them. Claude Levi-Strauss famously said that "animals are good to think with." When we look into the eyes of the greyhounds, they may reflect more about ourselves as Americans than anything else. One of the mantras commonly spoken by greyhound enthusiasts, be they industry insiders or greyhound adopters, is that "it's all about the hounds." Is it about the dogs, or is it really about us?

APPENDIX

LIST OF ALL GREYHOUND TRACKS
THAT HAVE OPERATED (LEGALLY AND
ILLEGALLY) IN THE UNITED STATES
(LIVE RACING ONLY)

Author's Note

Every effort has been made to ensure accuracy, but an exact and complete compilation of all greyhound tracks that have operated in the United States (including the exact years of operation) is essentially impossible. Before legalization many tracks existed "on the fix," leaving no official records documenting their existence. Many records have been lost, and the only "proof" of a track having operated is the oral and written accounts of those who raced their greyhounds there. Even then, memories are notoriously unreliable, and one person's account often conflicts with those provided by others.

In the list below, each track is listed under the state in which it operated; however, many tracks were located on state borders and the track's "home state" is occasionally unclear. In the cases in which a track was known by a number of different names or, in all likelihood, changed ownership, all of the track names are usually listed together under one listing. In other cases, it was difficult to determine whether references to greyhound racing in a particular city referred to one or two different tracks. To further complicate the issue, some tracks operated at fairgrounds or different locations within the cities in which they are listed depending on the year. In a few cases a track with the state license to race is not necessarily the track where races are held. Finally, dog tracks may have only operated for one or two days in the years that they are listed; however, in other cases, they operated seasonally or at least on a more regular basis.

All of these factors should be taken into account when using this list as a resource.[1]

In the United States

Alabama
Birmingham Racing Club/Jefferson County Racing Association (Birmingham),
    1992–present
Greenetrack (Eutaw), 1977–1998
Mobile Greyhound Park (Mobile/Theodore), 1973–present
Victoryland Greyhound Park/Macon County Greyhound Park (Shorter), 1984–2011

Arizona
Amado Greyhound Park (Amado), 1963–1984
Apache Greyhound Park (Apache Junction), 1962–2004

Benson Kennel Club (Benson), 1966
Black Canyon City Greyhound Park (Black Canyon City), 1967–1984
Desert Greyhound Park (Apache Junction), 1957–1962
Fairgrounds Kennel Club (Phoenix), 1939
Manzanita (Phoenix), 1949
Phoenix Greyhound Park (Phoenix), 1954–2010
Tucson Greyhound Park (Tucson), 1944–present
Washington Park/Arizona Kennel Club (Phoenix), 1947–1953
Western Greyhound Park/Western Greyhound Kennel Club (Phoenix), 1942–1953
Yuma Greyhound Park (Yuma), 1961–1993

Arkansas
Riverside Kennel Club/Riverside Greyhound Club (West Memphis), 1926, 1928,
    1935–1941
Southland Park Gaming and Racing/Southland Greyhound Park/Southland Racing
    Corp. (West Memphis), 1956–present

California
Alviso Kennel Club (San Francisco), 1932
Baden Kennel Club (South San Francisco), 1932–1938
Bayshore Kennel Club (Belmont/San Francisco), 1933–1938
Belmont Kennel Club (San Francisco), 1931–1932
Beverly-Fairfax Kennel Club (Los Angeles), 1932
Blue Star Amusement Racing (Emeryville), 1919–1921
Capital City Kennel Club (Sacramento), 1932
Compton Kennel Club (Los Angeles), 1932
Culver City Kennel Club (Culver City/Los Angeles), 1931–1932
Culver City Southwest Kennel Club (Culver City/Los Angeles), 1938
El Cerrito Kennel Club (El Cerrito), 1932–1939

Colorado
Cloverleaf Kennel Club (Loveland), 1955–2006
Denver Greyhound Racing Association (Denver), 1924
Interstate Kennel Club (Byers), 1971–1991; 1992–2008 in Commerce City
Lakeside Park Kennel Club (Denver/Lakeside Park), 1927, 1929
Mile High Kennel Club (Commerce City/Denver), 1949–2008
Pueblo Kennel Club/Pueblo Greyhound Park (Pueblo), 1949–2002; 2007–2008 in
    Commerce City
Rocky Mountain Kennel Club/Rocky Mountain Greyhound Park/Post Time Grey-
    hound Racing (Colorado Springs), 1949–2005
Uranium Downs (Grand Junction), 1955–1958

Connecticut
Plainfield Greyhound Park (Plainfield), 1976–2005
Shoreline Star Greyhound Park (Bridgeport), 1995–2005 (closed 1996–1997)

Florida
Biscayne Kennel Club (Miami), 1926–1995
Clay County Kennel Club (Orange Park/Jacksonville), 1931–1934

Daytona Beach Kennel Club/Volusia County Kennel Club/Seminole Racing/West
  Volusia (Daytona Beach), 1948–present
Derby Lane/St. Petersburg Kennel Club (St. Petersburg), 1925–present
Ebro Greyhound Track/Washington County Kennel Club/Washington Kennel Club
  (Ebro), 1955–present
Flagler Greyhound Park/West Flagler Greyhound Track/West Flagler Kennel Club/
  Flagler Kennel Club/Flagler Dog Track (Miami), 1932–present
Jacksonville Kennel Club (Jacksonville), 1934–2007
Jefferson County Kennel Club (Monticello), 1959–present
Key West Kennel Club/Berenson's Key West Greyhound Track (Key West), 1953–1963,
  1968–1991
Mardi Gras Race Track/Hollywood Kennel Club/Hollywood Greyhound Track/Bro-
  ward County Kennel Club (Hollywood/Hallandale Beach), 1934–present
Melbourne Greyhound Park (Melbourne), 1991–present
Miami Beach Kennel Club (Miami Beach), 1929–1980
Miami Kennel Club (Hialeah/Miami), 1922–1928
Naples-Ft. Myers Greyhound Track/Bonita-Ft. Myers Greyhound Track (Bonita
  Springs), 1957–present
Orange Park Kennel Club/Clay County Kennel Club (Orange Park), 1946–present
Palm Beach Kennel Club (West Palm Beach), 1932–present
Pensacola Greyhound Track/Pensacola Kennel Club (Pensacola), 1946–present
Sanford-Orlando Kennel Club/Longwood Kennel Club (Longwood/Orlando), 1931,
  1935–present
Sarasota Kennel Club (Sarasota), 1926, 1929, 1944–present
Seminole Greyhound Park (Casselberry/Orlando), 1981–2001
Seminole Kennel Club (Orange Park/Jacksonville), 1928–1930
Six Mile Creek Kennel Club (Tampa), 1925–1932
South Miami Kennel Club (Coral Gables), 1929
St. John's Greyhound Park/Bayard Raceways (Jacksonville), 1977–2000
Tampa Greyhound Park/Associated Outdoor Clubs/West Florida Racing & Athletic
  Association (Tampa), 1932–2007
Vero Beach Kennel Club (Vero Beach), 1929

Georgia
Atlanta Kennel Club/Dixie Lakes Greyhound Racing Association/Dixie Lakes Kennel
  Club (Union City/Atlanta), 1927–1929

Idaho
Coeur d'Alene Greyhound Park (Post Falls), 1988–1995

Illinois
Calumet City Kennel Club (Chicago), 1929
Elgin Kennel Club (Elgin), 1927
Fairview Kennel Club (Chicago), 1927–1929
Hawthorne Kennel Club (Chicago), 1927–1932
Illinois Kennel Club (Homewood/Thornton), 1926–1932
King's Highway Kennel Club (East St. Louis), 1930
Lawndale Kennel Club (Cicero/Chicago), 1927

Madison Kennel Club (East St. Louis), 1926–1931
Ogden Kennel Club (Chicago), 1927–1928
Peoria Kennel Club (Peoria), 1928
Peoria Racing Association (Peoria), 1930
Riverview Kennel Club/Riverside Kennel Club (Chicago), 1922–1923
Silver Heels Kennel Club (East St. Louis), 1928
St. Louis Kennel Club/St. Clair Kennel Club/St. Clair Amusement Company (East St. Louis), 1921–1925

Indiana
Ft. Wayne Kennel Club (Ft. Wayne), 1929
Harrison Kennel Club (Harrison), 1929–1932, 1936–1938
Indianapolis Racing Association (Indianapolis), 1929
Jeffersonville Kennel Club (Jeffersonville), 1928–1934, 1936–1937
New Albany Kennel Club (New Albany), 1934

Iowa
Bluffs Run/Horseshoe Casino and Bluffs Run Greyhound Park/Iowa West Greyhound Association (Council Bluffs), 1986–present
Dodge Park Kennel Club (Council Bluffs), 1941–1943
Dubuque Greyhound Park/Dubuque Racing Association/Mystique-Dubuque Greyhound Park and Casino (Dubuque), 1985–present
Waterloo Greyhound Park (Waterloo), 1986–1996

Kansas
Camptown Greyhound Park (Frontenac), 1995–2000
Chanute Kennel Club (Chanute), 1921
Wichita Greyhound Park (Wichita), 1989–2007
Woodlands Greyhound Park (Kansas City), 1989–2008

Kentucky
Erlanger Kennel Club (Erlanger), 1925–1927
Tacoma Park (Dayton), 1936–1937

Louisiana
Metairie Ridge Kennel Club/Metairie Kennel Club (New Orleans), 1925–1928
New Orleans Kennel Club/Heinemann Park (New Orleans), 1926–1928
Shreveport Kennel Club/Jewella Kennel Club/Tri-State Kennel Club (Shreveport), 1927–1928
St. Bernard Kennel Club (New Orleans), 1936

Maryland
Riviera Beach Dog Track (Riviera Beach), 1935

Massachusetts
Bristol County Kennel Club/Sportsmen's Park (Dighton/Taunton), 1935–1939
Crescent Kennel Club (West Springfield), 1935–1938
Lawrence Kennel Club (Lawrence), 1934
Raynham/Taunton Greyhound Park/Massasoit Greyhound Association at Raynham (Raynham), 1940–2009

Wonderland Greyhound Park/Bay State Greyhound Association/Old Harbor Kennel
   Club (Revere), 1935–2009
(Note: County fairs are not included, but they often involved pari-mutuel wagering on
   greyhound racing, such as the Topsfield Fair in Essex County)

Michigan
Detroit Kennel Club (Detroit), 1927
Jackson Kennel Club (Napoleon), 1928

Minnesota
Minneapolis Kennel Club (Savage), 1930

Mississippi
Gulf Coast Kennel Club (Biloxi), 1947–1948, 1951

Missouri
Electric Holding Company Kennel Club (North Kansas City), 1927–1928
Kansas City Kennel Club (Kansas City), 1927
Ramona Kennel Club (St. Louis), 1926–1928
Wellston Kennel Club (Wellston/Overland/St. Louis), 1927

Montana
Butte Kennel Club/Montana Greyhound Racing/Montana Greyhound Racing Asso-
   ciation/Montana Kennel Club (Butte), 1941–1944, 1946–1947
Glacier Greyhound Park/Glacier Greyhound Dog Racing Park/Great Falls Dog Track/
   Cascade Kennel Club/Cascade County Kennel Club (Great Falls), 1960–1964
Great Falls Kennel Club (Great Falls), 1947
Highland Kennel Club/Montana Sportsman's Kennel Club (Butte), 1926–1932
Montana Kennel Club (Great Falls), 1941–1944
Western Montana Kennel Club/Copper City Race Track/Western Montana Club/Cop-
   per Kennel Club (Butte), 1957–1959
Yellowstone Kennel Club/Yellowstone Kennel Club Racing Association/Greater Bill-
   ings Greyhound Racing Association/Midland Empire Racing Association (Bill-
   ings), 1954–1956, 1959

Nebraska
Ravenna Kennel Club (Ravenna), 1937

Nevada
Las Vegas Downs (Henderson/Las Vegas), 1981

New Hampshire
Hinsdale Greyhound Park/Hinsdale Dog Track (Hinsdale), 1973–2008
Lakes Region Greyhound Park/Lakes Region Greyhound Club/The Lodge at Bel-
   mont/Berenson's Belmont Greyhound Track (Belmont), 1975–1978, 1981–2009
Seabrook Greyhound Park/Yankee Greyhound Racing Association (Seabrook),
   1973–2008

New Jersey
Atlantic Kennel Club/Auditorium Kennel Club/Atlantic City Kennel Club (Atlantic
   City at the Indoor Convention Hall), 1933–1934

Atlantic Park/Atlantic City Kennel Club (Atlantic City), 1922–1924, 1926
Camden Kennel Club/Pennsauken Central Airport Sporting Club/Pennsauken
    Kennel Club (Camden), 1933–1934
Essex Kennel Club (Newark), 1926
Linden Kennel Club/Union Kennel Club (Linden), 1933–1934
Long Branch Kennel Club/Long Branch Kennel Association (Long Branch),
    1933–1934, 1936

New Mexico
New Mexico Kennel Club (Hobbs), 1930

New York
Batavia Kennel Club (Batavia), 1930, 1935
Buffalo Kennel Club (Buffalo), 1935
Celtic Park/New York Greyhound Racing Association (Queens), 1928
Dongan Hills Track (Staten Island), 1928–1930
Gloversville Kennel Club (Gloversville), 1934
Island Kennel Club (Staten Island), 1931
Middletown Fairgrounds (Middletown), 1931
Mineola Fair Grounds/Nassau County Kennel Club (Mineola/Garden City),
    1929–1937
Monroe Greyhound Association (Rochester), 1927–1928
Monticello Kennel Club (Monticello), 1933
Nassau Kennel Company (Albany), 1935–1937
Nyack Kennel Club (Nyack), 1931, 1936
Orangeburg Kennel Club (Orangeburg), 1934–1938
Queens Kennel Club (Queens), 1936

North Carolina
Carolina Racing Association, Inc. (Morehead City), 1948–1953
Cavalier Kennel Club (Moyock), 1949–1953

Ohio
Akron Greyhound Racing Association (Akron), 1926
Bainbridge Kennel Club (Bainbridge), 1934–1938
Bellaire-Wheeling Kennel Club (Bellaire), 1928
Brimfield Kennel Club (Brimfield), 1931–1932, 1939–1940
Canfield Kennel Club/Mahoning County Fair (Canfield fairgrounds), 1933–1936
Canton Kennel Club (Canton), 1930
Cleveland Kennel Club (Cleveland), 1930
Fairfield Dog Track (Cincinnati), 1929
Franklin Kennel Club (Grove City/Columbus), 1926–1928
Fort Miami Fairgrounds (Toledo), 1937
Fowler Kennel Club (Fowler), 1938–1939
Geauga Greyhound Association (Bainbridge), 1938
Indian Lake Kennel Club (Indian Lake), 1928–1929
Jefferson County Kennel Club (Steubenville), 1927
Kent Kennel Club (Kent), 1939
Lake Milton Kennel Club (Lake Milton), 1939–1940

London Dog Track (London), 1931
Proctorville Kennel Club (Proctorville), 1936
Ravenna Kennel Club (Ravenna), 1931–1932
Springdale Kennel Club/Springdale Amusement Park/Harrison Kennel Club
    (Hamilton/Cincinnati), 1926–1931
Steubenville Greyhound Kennel Club (Steubenville), 1937–1940
Tobasco Dog Track (Tobasco/Cincinnati), 1931
Toledo Kennel Club/Toledo Greyhound Club/Dixie Kennel Club (Toledo), 1926–1928
West Jefferson Kennel Club (West Jefferson/Columbus), 1928–1931, 1934

Oklahoma
Magic City Kennel Club (Tulsa), 1927–1930
Mid-Continent Park (Tulsa), 1921–1923
Oil City Kennel Club (Tulsa), 1925–1926, 1930

Oregon
Multnomah Greyhound Park/Fairview Park/Murray Kemp Greyhound Park
    (Portland/Wood Village), 1933–2004

Pennsylvania
Aspinwall Kennel Club (Aspinwall/Pittsburgh), 1930
Bridgeport Kennel Club (Bridgeport/Philadelphia), 1930
Bridgeville Dog Track (Bridgeville), 1930
Erie Kennel Club/Expo Kennel Club (Erie), 1930
New Kensington Kennel Club (New Kensington/Pittsburgh), 1930, 1933–1936

Rhode Island
Lincoln Greyhound Park/Twin River (Lincoln), 1977–2009

South Carolina
Myrtle Beach Kennel Club (Myrtle Beach), 1937

South Dakota
Black Hills Kennel Club (Rapid City), 1949–1991
Sodrac Park (North Sioux City), 1954–1993

Texas
Alamo Greyhound Association/All-Texas Racing Association (San Antonio), 1927–
    1928, 1935
Arlington Kennel Club (Arlington/Fort Worth), 1936
El Paso Kennel Club (El Paso), 1932
Galveston Kennel and Fair Association (Galveston), 1927–1928
Gulf Coast Greyhound Track/Corpus Christi Greyhound Race Track (Corpus Christi),
    1990–2007
Gulf Greyhound Park (La Marque), 1992–present
Missouri City Kennel Club/South Main Kennel Club (Houston), 1932–1935
Oak Downs Kennel Club (Dallas), 1935
Sportsman's Greyhound Racing Association (Dallas), 1936–1937
Valley Race Park/Valley Greyhound Park (Harlingen), 1990–2009

Utah
Salt Lake City Kennel Club (Salt Lake City), 1933

Vermont
Green Mountain Race Track (Pownel), 1976–1992

Washington
Olympic Kennel Club (Seattle), 1933, 1935
Vancouver Kennel Club (Vancouver), 1933–1935

West Virginia
Capitol City Kennel Club/Capitol Kennel Club (Charleston), 1927, 1929
Ceredo Kennel Club/Ceredo Amusement Company (Huntington), 1926–1929
Kanawha Kennel Club/Kanawha Exhibition Company (Charleston), 1926, 1928
Tri-State Greyhound Park/Mardi Gras Casino and Resort/Cross Lanes Dog Track
    (Cross Lanes), 1985–present
Wheeling Downs Racing Association/Wheeling Island (Wheeling), 1976–present

Wisconsin
(Blue) Mound Kennel Club (Milwaukee), 1927–1928
Dairyland Greyhound Park (Kenosha), 1990–2009
Fox Valley Greyhound Park (Kaukauna), 1990–1993
Geneva Lakes Kennel Club (Delavan), 1990–2005
St. Croix Meadows Greyhound Racing Park (Hudson), 1991–2001
Tri-State Kennel Club (Superior), 1927
Wisconsin Dells Greyhound Park (Lake Delton), 1990–1996

Near the United States

Canada
Canadian National Kennel Club (Montreal), ca. 1928

Cuba
Havana Greyhound Kennel Club (Havana), ca. 1951–1957

Mexico
Agua Caliente Greyhound Club (Tijuana), ca. 1947–present
Juarez Greyhound Club (Juarez), ca. 1964–2005
Tijuana Greyhound Club (Tijuana), ca. 1927–1929

NOTES

INTRODUCTION: ROVER OR RACER?

1. Martin Cohan, "And Leave the Greyhounds to Us?" *The Odd Couple*, season 2, directed by Hal Cooper, aired December 31, 1971 (Hollywood, CA: CBS Paramount Network Television, 2007), DVD.

2. *Dark Hazard*, directed by Alfred E. Green (1934), DVD transfer at UCLA Film and Television Archive; *Johnny Eager*, directed by Mervyn LeRoy (1942; Burbank, CA: Warner Home Video, 2009), DVD; *Hole in the Head*, directed by Frank Capra (1959; Beverly Hills, CA: MGM Home Entertainment, 2001). DVD.

3. "Puttin' on the Dog at Miami Beach,"Hearst Metrotone News 1, no. 244 (1930), DVD transfer at UCLA Film and Television Archive.

4. "Canine Tracks Do Rushing Business," Hearst Metrotone News 4, no. 240 (1933), DVD transfer at UCLA Film and Television Archive.

5. "Salute to Baseball," *Steve Allen Show*, aired October 7, 1956, DVD transfer at UCLA Film and Television Archive. When Allen hops off the bus, he declares with an ironic smile that it was "quite a ride" with all of those greyhounds.

6. "Greta, the Misfit Greyhound," *Walt Disney's Wonderful World of Color* 9, no. 18, directed by Larry Lansburgh, aired February 3, 1963, VHS.

7. "Simpsons Roasting on an Open Fire," *The Simpsons*, season 1, directed by David Silverman, aired December 17, 1989, at UCLA Film and Television Archive. See also "Two Dozen and One Greyhounds," *The Simpsons*, season 6, directed by Bob Anderson, aired April 9, 1995. Sam Simon, cocreator of the show with Matt Groening, later stated that this first episode was designed to show Homer's "progressive degradation" as he tried to save Christmas, almost an "anti-Christmas special" that hinged on a decisive moment at the dog track. Simon only became directly involved with animal activism several years later when his friend Drew Carey filmed an episode of his sitcom titled "Dog Soup" in 1994. Disturbed by stories of abuse in the greyhound industry while directing the show, he experienced what he later described as a "crisis of conscience." Simon characterizes himself as an animal lover who became an animal rights activist at the time of this Drew Carey episode. His earlier decision to create an episode sympathetic to racing greyhounds—even in a comic series—was in keeping with the direction in which many other Americans were gradually heading in their attitudes toward dog racing. Sam Simon, telephone interview with author, September 21, 2011.

8. See also Bruce Horowitz, "Even without Kardashian, Skechers Ad Stirs Controversy," *USA Today*, January 12, 2012. In many cases the difference in quality between greyhound tracks depends on one key factor: money. The size of a track's pari-mutuel handle is dependent on how much money is bet at the track. Larger handles translate into better purses, which in turn draw in faster racers. Tracks with higher handles tend to invest in superior facilities and devise more sophisticated promotions.

9. Jim Twigg, Kansas City Retired Greyhounds as Pets (REGAP) board member, interview on KCTV, Kansas City, Missouri, February 9, 2012.

10. For an analysis of Victorian sentimentalism, the ethos of kindness toward animals, and human dominion over animals, see Katherine C. Grier, *Pets in America: A History* (Chapel Hill: University of North Carolina Press, 2006), 127–139. For a discussion of early animal advocacy organizations, most of which were located in large urban areas, see Diane L. Beers, *For the Prevention of Cruelty: The History and Legacy of Animal Rights Activism in the United States* (Athens: Swallow Press / Ohio University Press, 2006), 60–90. Regarding evolving ideas of animal use and humanitarianism as well as related issues, see Susan Jones, *Valuing Animals: Veterinarians and Their Patients in Modern America* (Baltimore: Johns Hopkins University Press, 2002).

11. The term "Sport of Queens" was likely derived from Queen Elizabeth I's interest in greyhound coursing in the sixteenth century. Other royal women, according to legend, also owned greyhounds, including Cleopatra.

12. The "dogmen" are the men (and occasionally women) who breed, raise, train, and race greyhounds. This unusual term is widely used by the dogmen themselves and has long been employed to describe a diverse group of individuals whose commonality lies in their sustained involvement with the hands-on work of racing greyhounds. Some dogmen are breeders who own farms, whereas others work solely as trainers. Still others manage or own racing kennels that set up contracts, or "bookings," with racetracks. In the early years these individuals, typically from rural, agrarian roots, often lived a gypsy lifestyle traveling from state to state with their greyhounds, eking out a living. The term "dogmen" is thus used here to describe the men and women who work directly with racing greyhounds. Some individuals in the greyhound business see "dogmen" as a term of endearment, although others resist its use. The word is employed throughout this book because of its long-standing use within the greyhound community, but the term is used here as a neutral moniker describing a group of individuals with no judgment intended.

13. "Hanson Board Bars Dog Track," *Boston Herald*, February 7, 1939.

14. In this case as well as in future references, gambling on greyhound racing is what is being legalized, not the sport itself. The dates of legalization in key states include Florida (1931); Oregon (1933); Massachusetts (1935); and Arizona (1939).

15. Owen P. Smith, George Sawyer, Martin J. Hyland, et al. v. Commonwealth of Kentucky, 275 U.S. 509 (1927).

16. Miami Beach Kennel Club 1937 scrapbook, Miami Beach Kennel Club Scrapbook Collection, Wolfsonian Collections, Florida International University, Miami Beach, Florida (hereafter MBKC scrapbooks, FIU).

17. The total amount of money bet on a race at a pari-mutuel track (the gross wagering) is known as the handle. The method of distributing the handle varies from state to state and even from track to track. The majority of funds are returned to successful bettors as winnings. The remaining money is disbursed to a number of recipients. A percentage is turned over to the state for taxes and a portion is reserved for the gambling facility. The track then distributes a percentage of these funds to the contract kennels as purses. Purse distribution to racing kennels in the United States generally follows a standard formula: the winner receives 50 percent of the purse, the kennel with the

second-place dog receives 25 percent, the third-place dog earns 15 percent, and the final 10 percent goes to the fourth-place finisher.

18. Some kennels specialized in breeding, others focused entirely on training, and still others were exclusively racing kennels. Breeding operations today are centered in Kansas, Oklahoma, and Texas, but at one point Florida was a prime breeding state. Greyhounds have long been imported from the United Kingdom and, in later years, from Australia as well. As time passed, greyhounds in the United States have been bred more and more for speed.

19. Before racing greyhounds are ready for competition, they are put through a training process known as schooling. The racing distance has varied but is usually $5/16$, $3/8$, or $7/16$ of a mile, with marathon races reaching $1/2$ and super marathon races reaching $9/16$ of a mile.

20. A number of cultural theorists have established the groundwork for interpreting leisure and consumerism as an expression of class, including Michael Kammen, Jackson Lears, Warren Susman, Andrew Hurley, Lawrence Levine, and Joan Shelley Rubin.

21. Clubhouses for wealthy patrons, similar to those seen at horse-racing facilities, allowed well-heeled attendees to separate themselves from the crowds.

22. Walt Bogdanich, Joe Drape, Dara L. Miles, and Griffin Palmer, "Mangled Horses, Mangled Jockeys," *New York Times*, March 25, 2012. Humane Society of the United States (HSUS) president Wayne Pacelle also observed that horse racing has come under increased scrutiny in recent years for abuses. Wayne Pacelle, telephone interview with author, August 13, 2012.

23. One such market research survey focused on the demographics of the Seabrook, New Hampshire, dog track in the late 1970s. See Starr F. Schlobohm, University of New Hampshire, "Market Research Survey of Patrons of Seabrook Greyhound Park 1981," prepared for Yankee Greyhound Racing, Inc., March 31, 1981. Another example is an ethnographic case study of the Victoryland track in Shorter, Alabama, in the late 1980s. See Douglas J. Rentz, "Winning Talk and Losing Stories: An Ethnographic Case Study of the Gaming Social World at Victoryland Greyhound Park" (PhD diss., Auburn University, 2001). The question of race deserves further consideration. Before the civil rights movement seating at many southern tracks was segregated. Other dog tracks catered to a different patron base; the facility in Greene County, Alabama, for instance, chiefly attracted working-class African Americans. A number of individuals have referred to segregated tracks during personal interviews with the author. According to Myra Sullivan, who began working at the West Memphis track in 1955, African American fans frequented the "canine club," whereas the white fans spent time in the greyhound "kennel club." These two clubs were in separate but attached buildings. Whether this segregated track seating was by choice or mandated by track management is unclear. Myra Sullivan, personal interview with author, August 6, 2008. Louise Weaver of the Derby Lane Kennel Club has also indicated that seating was segregated at the Florida tracks before the civil rights movement. Louise Weaver, personal interview with author, February 20, 2009. See also William M. Adler, "The Bear Trap," *Esquire* (September 1989): 204–212.

24. For a review of scholarship on greyhound racing in England, see Norman Baker,

"Going to the Dogs—Hostility to Greyhound Racing in Britain: Puritanism, Socialism, and Pragmaticism," *Journal of Sport History* 23, no. 2 (Summer 1996): 97–119; Mike Huggins, "Going to the Dogs," *History Today* 56, no. 5 (May 2006): 31–36; "Racing Greyhounds after the 'Tin Rabbit,'" *Literary Digest* (October 22, 1927): 54–60; "British Greyhounds and Gambling," *Literary Digest* (January 7, 1928): 18–19; Mike Huggins, "'Everybody's Going to the Dogs?' The Middle Classes and Greyhound Racing in Britain between the Wars," *Journal of Sport History* 34, no. 1 (Spring 2007): 401–444.

25. See Keith Thomas, *Man and the Natural World: A History of the Modern Sensibility* (New York: Pantheon, 1983).

26. Animal advocates often mark the (nascent) ethos of kindness to animals as emerging during the Axial Age, the period between 800 and 200 BCE. A number of key figures articulated their views at this time, including Confucius and Lau Tzu in China; Mahavira and the Buddha in India; Zoroaster in Persia; and Pythagoras and Socrates in Greece, to name a few. See Norm Phelps, *The Longest Struggle: Animal Advocacy from Pythagoras to PETA* (New York: Lantern, 2007), 14.

27. See Noralee Frankel and Nancy S. Dye, eds., *Gender, Class, Race, and Reform in the Progressive Era* (Lexington: University of Kentucky Press, 1991); Lori D. Ginzberg, *Women and the Work of Benevolence: Morality, Politics, and Class in the Nineteenth-Century United States* (New Haven, CT: Yale University Press, 1992); Leigh Ann Wheeler, *Against Obscenity: Reform and the Politics of Womanhood in America, 1873–1935* (Baltimore: Johns Hopkins University Press, 2004); Carol Mattingly, *Well-Tempered Women: Nineteenth-Century Temperance Rhetoric* (Carbondale: Southern Illinois University Press, 1998); Nell Irvin Painter, *Standing at Armageddon: A Grassroots History of the Progressive Era* (New York: W. W. Norton, 1987); and Robert H. Wiebe, *The Search for Order, 1877–1920* (New York: Hill & Wang, 1966).

28. "Coursing Trials," *Life* 22, no. 20 (May 19, 1947): 97–100.

29. See "State-by-State News Update: Arizona," *Greyhound Network News* 2, no. 1 (Spring 1993). Otis McClellan's greyhound kennel was described by witnesses as a "canine concentration camp." See also "Man Says He Killed Thousands of Dogs for $10 Each," *USA Today*, May 22, 2002; *Prime Sports—Press Box* television news program from Coeur d'Alene, Idaho, ca. 1992, VHS; Karyn Zoldan, Arizona Greyhound Rescue, interviewed on KOLD news program, October 24, 2006, VHS. All VHS tapes provided to the author by Susan Netboy of the Greyhound Protection League.

30. Harriet Ritvo, *The Animal Estate: The English and Other Creatures in the Victorian Age* (Cambridge, MA: Harvard University Press, 1987), 87, 90.

31. Grier, *Pets in America*. See also Katherine C. Grier, "Buying Your Friends: The Pet Business and American Consumer Culture," in *Commodifying Everything: Relationships of the Market*, ed. Susan Strasser (New York: Routledge, 2003), 43–70.

32. Grier, "Buying Your Friends,"43, and Jones, *Valuing Animals*, 115.

33. Jones, 116.

34. Grier, *Pets in America*, 34–35. See also Hal Herzog, *Some We Love, Some We Hate, Some We Eat: Why It's So Hard to Think Straight about Animals* (New York: Harper Perennial, 2010), 122. He notes, "Between 1900 and 1939, annual AKC registrations went from 5,000 puppies to 80,000. The big craze for purebreds came after World War II, when the proportion of American dogs that were purebreds jumped from 5

percent to 50 percent, and registrations were growing fifteen times faster than the human population of the United States."

35. Michael Schaffer, *One Nation under Dog: Adventures in the New World of Prozac-Popping Puppies, Dog-Park Politics, and Organic Pet Food* (New York: Henry Holt, 2009), 18–19.

36. In the last several decades, scientists have finally accepted the premise that canines are worthy of study, and as a result, specialists from a range of disciplines are learning more and more about their origins, behaviors, and needs. We now know definitively that dogs descended from grey wolves, *Canis lupus,* sometime between 15,000 and 30,000 years ago, possibly from East Asia. It is likely, although not entirely certain, that they came to small human settlements as opportunistic, curious scavengers and, according to one wit, have been running the greatest scam in human history ever since. James Serpell, "Dog Origins: The How, When and Why of Dog Domestication" (lecture, National Sporting Library Conference, *Lives of Dogs: Origins and Evolution of Hunting and Sporting Breeds,* Middleburg, VA, October 23, 2010); James Serpell, "Canid Evolution: From Wolf to Dog," reprinted from *Grzimek's Online Encyclopedia of Animal Life,* 2009; John Bradshaw, *Dog Sense: How the New Science of Dog Behavior Can Make You a Better Friend to Your Pet* (New York: Basic Books, 2011); Alexandra Horowitz, *Inside of a Dog: What Dogs See, Smell, and Know* (New York: Scribner, 2009); Mark Derr, *How the Dog Became the Dog: From Wolves to Our Best Friends* (New York: Overlook, 2011); Xiaoming Wang and Richard H. Tedford, "How Dogs Came to Run the World," *Natural History* 117, no. 6 (July/August 2008): 18–23; *Nature: Dogs that Changed the World,* DVD (New York: Thirteen/WNET & Tigress Productions Limited, Educational Broadcasting Corporation, 2007); and James Serpell, ed., *The Domestic Dog: Its Evolution, Behaviour, and Interactions with People* (Cambridge: Cambridge University Press, 1996).

37. See Cynthia A. Branigan, *The Reign of the Greyhound* (Hoboken, NJ: Wiley, 2004); Kristin Mehus-Roe, ed., *The Original Dog Bible: The Definitive Source for All Things Dog* (Irvine, CA: Bowtie Press, 2005); D. Caroline Coile, *Greyhounds: Everything about Purchase, Care, Nutrition, Behavior, and Training* (Hauppauge, NY: Barron's, 2001).

38. Paul C. Hartwell, *The Road from Emeryville* (San Diego: California Research Publishing, 1980); Leslie A. Wootten, *Keefer: The People's Choice* (Sedona, AZ: Memory Works, 2007); Ryan H. Reed, *Born to Run: The Racing Greyhound from Competitor to Companion* (Lexington, KY: A Thoroughbred Times Book, 2010); Robert Temple, *The History of Greyhound Racing in New England* (Bloomington, IN: Xlibris, 2011); James Smith, *History of the American Greyhound Derby: The Kentucky Derby of Greyhound Racing* (Seattle: CreateSpace, 2012).

39. The invention of the electronic totalisator, or tote, by Henry Straus in the late 1920s was a landmark development in pari-mutuel gambling. Eliminating the need for tedious calculations completed by hand, this new device electronically calculated the odds as wagers came in from bettors. The machine made continuous adjustments as new bets were placed. See David G. Schwartz, *Cutting the Wire: Gaming Prohibition and the Internet* (Las Vegas: University of Nevada Press, 2005), 34–35.

40. John Hervey, *Racing in America,* 3 vols. (New York: Jockey Club, 1944); Laura Hillenbrand, *Seabiscuit: An American Legend* (New York: Ballantine, 2001); William

Nack, *Secretariat: The Making of a Champion* (New York: Da Capo, 2002); T. D. Thornton, *Not by a Long Shot: A Season at a Hard-Luck Horse Track* (New York: Public Affairs, 2007); Jane Schwartz, *Ruffian: Burning from the Start* (New York: Ballantine, 2002); Lawrence Scanlan, *The Horse That God Built: The Untold Story of Secretariat, the World's Greatest Racehorse* (New York: St. Martin's Griffin, 2008); Dorothy Ours, *Man o'War: A Legend Like Lightning* (New York: St. Martin's Griffin, 2007); Linda Hanna, *Barbaro, Smarty Jones, and Ruffian: The People's Horses* (Moorestown, NJ: Middle Atlantic Press, 2008); Nan Mooney, *My Racing Heart: The Passionate World of Thoroughbreds and the Track* (New York: HarperCollins, 2002); Joe Drape, *The Race for the Triple Crown: Horses, High Stakes and Eternal Hope* (New York: Grove Press, 2002); Charles Leerhsen, *Crazy Good: The True Story of Dan Patch, the Most Famous Horse in America* (New York: Simon & Schuster, 2009).

CHAPTER ONE: CHASING RABBITS

1. Dogs have been domesticated for thousands of years and have long occupied an important niche in American society, although their roles have changed significantly with time.

2. Theodor de Bry's images were based on the drawings of French artist Jacques Le Moyne.

3. H. Edwards Clarke, *The Greyhound*, 6th ed. (London: Popular Dogs, 1978), 25. See also Evan Ratliff, "Mix March Morph: How to Build a Dog," *National Geographic* 221, no. 2 (February 2012): 35–51; Heidi G. Parker et al., "Genetic Structure of the Purebred Domestic Dog," *Science,* new series 304, no. 5674 (May 21, 2004); Bridgett M. vonHoldt et al., "Genome-wide SNP and Haplotype Analysis Reveal a Rich History Underlying Dog Domestication," *Nature* 464 (April 8, 2010).

4. *Xenophon & Arrian, On Hunting*, trans. and ed. A. A. Phillips and M. M. Willcock (Warminster, UK: Aris & Phillips, 1999).

5. Clarke, *Greyhound*, 25. Arrian worked under the Roman emperor and also used the pen name Xenophon.

6. Thomas Goodlake, *The Courser's Manual or Stud Book* (Liverpool: Harris, 1828), xiii.

7. Gervase Markham, *Country Contentments: or, The Husbandmans Recreations*, 4th ed. (London: Thomas Harper, 1631), 255. See also Ainsty, "A History of Coursing," in *British Sports and Sportsmen, Racing and Coursing* (London: Hazell, Watson & Viney, 1908), 241.

8. Ainsty, "History of Coursing," 236.

9. Clarke, *Greyhound*, 26. In this context "pothunting" refers to market hunting, which gentlemen sportsmen in the United States denounced.

10. There were significant differences between hunting hare across open land and the related sport of hare coursing.

11. See *British Sports and Sportsmen, Racing and Coursing*, part II, vol. 2 (London: Ballantyne, 1911), 554.

12. The first coursing club was organized by Lord Orford in 1776 at Swaffham. Other coursing clubs soon followed, including the Ashdown Park Club (1780), Malton Club (1781), Newmarket Society (1805), Amesbury Club (1822), and Altcar Society

(1825). The Duke of Norfolk's original coursing rules remained in use and were later even adopted by American coursers. See also Jonathan Magee, "Coursing and Upper Classes in Victorian England," *Sport in History* 28 (September 3, 2008): 2; Dennis Brailsford, *A Taste for Diversions: Sport in Georgian England* (Cambridge: Lutterworth, 1999), 24; Clarke, *Greyhound*, 27; and Ainsty, "History of Coursing," 245.

13. Magee notes that the National Coursing Club used Thacker's Rules, which were an updated version of Norfolk's Laws of the Leash. Magee, "Coursing and Upper Classes," 2.

14. Clarke, *Greyhound*, 28.

15. Irish coursers were also in attendance. See John Martin, *Tales of the Dogs: A Celebration of the Irish and Their Greyhounds* (Belfast: Blackstaff, 2009). The Waterloo Cup was coursing's equivalent to Wimbledon in tennis and Epsom in horse racing. Clarke, *Greyhound*, 27. See also Charles Blanning and Sir Mark Prescott, *The Waterloo Cup: The First 150 Years* (Winchester, UK: Heath House, 1987). In 1836 the Altcar Club inaugurated a small, eight-dog race. The contest was held on the estate of the Earl of Sefton in Altcar. The event grew from a sixteen-dog- to a thirty-two-dog stake, and finally, in 1857, to a sixty-four-dog competition. It remained a popular event for many years. Hare coursing was banned in 2005 in the United Kingdom.

16. Hugh Dalziel, *The Greyhound; Its History, Points, Breeding, Rearing, Training, and Running* (London: A. Bradley, London & County Printing Works, 1886; Warwickshire, UK: Vintage Dog Books, 2005), 17. Citations refer to the Vintage edition. In this context the word "pothunter" refers to one who hunts game for food.

17. *A Treatise on Greyhounds, with Observations on the Treatment and Disorders of Them*, 2nd ed. (London: T. Gosden, Sportsman's Repository, 1825), 39.

18. "Death of 'Stonehenge,'" *Forest and Stream* 30, no. 6 (March 1, 1888).

19. Stonehenge [John Henry Walsh], *The Greyhound in 1864*, 2nd ed. (London: Longman, Green, Longman, Roberts & Green, 1864), 330. In his essay on coursing, Harding Cox also endorses "good sound horseflesh" as sufficient nourishment for the greyhound. See Harding Cox, *Coursing and Falconry* (London: Longmans, Green, and Co., 1892), 72.

20. Dalziel, *Greyhound*, 46–48. Dalziel's use of the term "unearned increment" is a clear reference to Henry George's single-tax theory as articulated in his 1879 book *Progress and Poverty*. The phrase would likely have been an esoteric metaphor even in its own time. The term refers to profits earned from rising land values, specifically property value that rose not on account of the owner's doings but rather because of community improvements in the area.

21. Ibid., 49.

22. Ibid., 47.

23. Ibid., 13. See also chapter 9 in Emma Griffin, *Blood Sport: Hunting in Britain since 1066* (New Haven, CT: Yale University Press, 2007).

24. Dalziel, *Greyhound*, 41–42.

25. Huggins dates the growth of middle-class interest in coursing to the 1850s. See Mike Huggins, "Coursing in Britain," in *American Encyclopedia of Sports*, forthcoming.

26. References to greyhounds in the antebellum period are fairly scattered, but at this point a few arrived in the United States. Dispatches from England printed in

American newspapers occasionally commented on the breed, in one case reporting on a race between a horse and a greyhound over a course in Doncaster in 1800 (the greyhound lost), and in another to note what knowledgeable gentlemen fed their running hounds. See "Anecdotes of the Greyhound, Selected from the Sportsman's Cabinet," *Daily National Intelligencer,* October 26, 1819. See also Editorial, *New York Morning Herald,* May 12, 1838. A few were mentioned for sale by auction in Philadelphia along with other goods, but such references are relatively rare. See Auction Sales, *Philadelphia North American and United States Gazette,* April 14, 1859. In 1856 a new book was released in London that detailed ways to train coursing greyhounds. See Advertisement, *Charleston Mercury,* January 3, 1856. This advertisement was repeated in a number of newspapers.

27. W. S. Harwood, "Coursing on Western Prairies," *Sports Library Outing Magazine* 37, no. 1 (October 1899): 45–50. See also Joseph A. Graham, *The Sporting Dog* (New York: Macmillan, 1904), 113.

28. The officers are listed as James Adams, C. Dixon, N. Curry, C. L. Place, H. Buchanan, and M. Kelly. The first meeting was in Alameda County. See "California Coursing," *Daily Evening Bulletin,* September 20, 1879.

29. Samuel Hubbard, Jr., "The Greyhound in Sport," *The Californian* 3, ed. Charles Frederick Holder (San Francisco: Californian, 1893), 655.

30. "Hare and Hounds," *Milwaukee Sentinel,* November 11, 1874. The article noted, "Dog-racing is rapidly gaining in popularity among the people of California, and, doubtless, as in the English realm, will ere long rival and take precedence of horse-racing."

31. Graham, *Sporting Dog,* 120.

32. Ibid., 113. Graham later notes that wire fences "checked" the open plains coursing events (124).

33. Ibid., 123.

34. Harwood, "Coursing on Western Prairies," 50.

35. Daniel Justin Herman, "From Farmers to Hunters," in *A Cultural History of Animals,* vol. 5, *The Age of Empire (1800–1920),* ed. Kathleen Kete (Oxford: Berg, 2009), 47–71.

36. Harwood, "Coursing on Western Prairies," 47.

37. Ibid., 49.

38. "The Royal Sport of Coursing," *Forest and Stream* 22, no. 3 (February 14, 1884).

39. Bulletin, *Forest and Stream* 28, no. 13 (April 21, 1887). The 1896–1897 edition of the *California Coursing Review* estimated that about 200 greyhounds were registered in the state of California in 1894. See the *Greyhound Stud Book,* vol. 3 (Denver: American Coursing Board, 1894), 124, Greyhound Hall of Fame, Abilene, KS (hereafter GHF). This same article also indicated that "on the coursing fields of this country the day of the Jack and Jill greyhound has passed, never to return," indicating the growing importance and value of thoroughbred greyhounds. On November 11, 1900, the *San Fran Call* reported that there were more than 2,500 greyhounds in San Francisco that would now be subject to the tax assessor.

40. Harwood, "Coursing on Western Prairies," 45.

41. Photograph Collections, GHF. The picture includes D. C. Luse, R. H. Smith, Colonel David Taylor, Dr. P. Van Hummel, C. G. Page, Edward Kelley, H. Boyd, S. K.

Dow, and J. V. Brinkman. The American Coursing Club held annual meetings at Cheyenne Bottoms, near Great Bend, Kansas, through 1892. In 1894 and 1895 the event took place in Huron, South Dakota.

42. "The American Coursing Club Meet," *Forest and Stream* 20, no. 14 (October 25, 1888).

43. Ibid.

44. "American Coursing Club Meet," *Forest and Stream* 33, no. 16 (November 7, 1889).

45. Founded in 1871, Hutchinson, Kansas, was a temperance community and was originally known as Temperance City.

46. "National Coursing Association," *Forest and Stream* 33, no. 14 (October 24, 1889).

47. "Greyhounds and Coursing," *Forest and Stream* 32, no. 8 (March 14, 1889).

48. "An Eastern Coursing Club," *Forest and Stream* 19, no. 15 (November 9, 1882).

49. "Eastern Coursing Club," *Forest and Stream* 32, no. 8 (March 14, 1889).

50. "The Long Island Coursing," *Forest and Stream* 33, no. 22 (December 19, 1889). See also "Eastern Coursing Club's Meet," *Forest and Stream* 33, no. 22 (December 19, 1889).

51. The organization had been formed in 1866; most historians consider it to be the first animal protection society in the United States, followed shortly thereafter by the MSPCA in Boston. The articles refer to the organization as the "S.P.C.A.," but in all likelihood the ASPCA in New York City is the organization being referenced.

52. The slip is a special collar and leash device that allows a handler to release two dogs (preparing to hunt or chase prey) simultaneously.

53. "The Long Island Coursing" (see n. 50).

54. "That Rabbit Baiting," *Forest and Stream* 31, no. 21 (December 13, 1888).

55. Graham, *Sporting Dog*, 121.

56. One searches in vain for evidence of early large-scale Irish immigration to the west. By 1885, even though more than 14,000 immigrants from the British Isles had settled in Kansas, this was only 2.7 percent of the foreign-born population. Specifically, there were 4,718 Irish, 360 Welsh, 2,143 Scots, and 6,802 English settlers in 1885. These census data thus reveal that only .9 percent of the foreign-born population was Irish. James R. Shortridge, *Peopling the Plains: Who Settled Where in Frontier Kansas* (Lawrence: University Press of Kansas, 1995), 81.

57. John P. Davis, *The Union Pacific Railway: A Study in Railway Politics, History, and Economics* (New York: Arno, 1973), 140. Originally published in 1894.

58. An article published by the Kansas Greyhound Owners for Economic Development, Inc., noted that immigrants imported greyhounds from Ireland and England before the days of Texas cattle drives. Dogman C. N. Lambert comments, "The roots came from the Irish who settled here. When the railroad came through here many of the Irishmen who worked on the railroads stayed and settled in the area." See "Bringing More 'Ahs' to Kansas," Greyhound Owners for Economic Development, ca. 1986, Kansas State Historical Society, Topeka, KS (hereafter KSHS). Another Kansas publication dates the importation of greyhounds somewhat later: "Early settlers who homesteaded in Western Kansas in the 1880s and 1890s found thousands of jackrabbits

over-running the land. . . . Remembering how greyhounds were used to hunt rabbits in England and Ireland, many of the homesteaders sent for dogs to help bring the rabbits under control. The fleet dogs proved to be a boon to the pioneers." See "The Hounds of Kansas," *To the Stars*, May/June 1956, 9, KSHS.

59. "Greyhound Racing Pioneer," *Greyhound Racing Record*, January 31, 1947.

60. See Hugh Geoghegan, "Greyhound Project," ca. 1992, provided to the author by Robert Baker.

61. John E. Baur, *Dogs on the Frontier* (San Antonio: Naylor, 1964), 84.

62. For another view, see Roger D. McGrath, *Gunfighters, Highwaymen, and Vigilantes: Violence on the Frontier* (Berkeley: University of California Press, 1987). For an excellent history of the American West, see Richard Slotkin's trilogy: *Regeneration through Violence: The Mythology of the American Frontier, 1600–1860* (Norman: University of Oklahoma Press, 2000); *The Fatal Environment: The Myth of the Frontier in the Age of Industrialization, 1800–1890* (Norman: University of Oklahoma Press, 1998); and *Gunfighter Nation: The Myth of the Frontier in Twentieth-Century America* (Norman: University of Oklahoma Press, 1998).

63. Robert R. Dykstra, *The Cattle Towns: A Social History of the Kansas Cattle Trading Centers* (New York: Knopf, 1968), 103, 112.

64. Graham, *Sporting Dog*, 115.

65. David Dary, *Seeking Pleasure in the Old West* (New York: Knopf, 1995), 137–138.

66. During the 1880s a number of town settlements were established by wealthy Englishmen in states such as Iowa, Kansas, and Tennessee. Many of these settlers were the second sons of noblemen seeking new opportunities. See Curtis Harnack, *Gentlemen on the Prairie* (Ames: Iowa State University Press, 1985), 46. See also George Meltzer, "Social Life and Entertainment on the Frontiers of Kansas, 1854–1890" (MA thesis, University of Wichita, 1941), 101.

67. Robert W. Richmond, *Kansas: A Land of Contrasts*, 4th ed. (Wheeling, IL: Harlan Davidson, 1999).

68. E. Hough, "In the Cherokee Strip, VII," *Forest and Stream* 29, no. 2 (August 4, 1887).

69. Baur, *Dogs on the Frontier*, 82.

70. Eugene D. Fleharty, *Wild Animals and Settlers on the Great Plains* (Norman: University of Oklahoma Press, 1995), 31.

71. One contemporary described hunting expeditions with Custer as not unlike the "days of chivalry" when some "feudal lord went out to war or to the chase, followed by his retainers." James Potter, "The Use of Dogs for Hunting on the Frontier," *Montana: The Magazine of Western History* 55, no. 3 (Autumn 2005): 36–47. Custer eagerly cultivated this image, drawing partially upon the model of the European aristocrat and writing extensively of his exploits.

72. George Armstrong Custer, *My Life in the Plains, or, Personal Experiences with Indians* (New York: Sheldon, 1876), 37.

73. Elizabeth B. Custer, *Tenting on the Plains or General Custer in Kansas and Texas* (New York: Harper & Brothers, 1895), 129–132.

74. Elizabeth B. Custer, *Boots and Saddles, or Life in Dakota with General Custer* (New

York: Harper & Brothers, 1885), 55–56. See also Brian Patrick Duggan, "Our Dogs Give Us Such Pleasure," in *Family Dog* (March/April 2012): 30–33.

75. Graham, *Sporting Dog*, 115.

76. Related examples include a letter written in 1876 by an officer while stationed in the Indian Territory; he referred to a large group of greyhounds taken on a wolf hunt. See "Bypaths of Kansas History," *Kansas Historical Quarterly* 13, no. 1 (February 1944): 98–106. A Texas cavalryman, H. H. McConnell, also noted that there were a number of valuable greyhounds with his regiment, although most of the regiment's dogs were mongrels. See H. H. McConnell, *Five Years a Cavalryman, or, Sketches of Regular Army Life on the Texas Frontier, 1866–1871* (Jacksboro, TX: J. N. Rogers, 1889), 132.

77. Kevin Adams, *Class and Race in the Frontier Army: Military Life in the West, 1870–1890* (Norman: University of Oklahoma Press, 2009), 85.

78. Dogs involved in these activities in the Great Plains frequently died from fatigue, literally running themselves to death. See Meltzer, "Social Life," 102–103.

79. Adams has asserted that such sporting activities "appealed to a self-conscious officer elite because they expressed notions of upper-class masculinity and gentility." Adams, *Class and Race*, 84–86. One expedition involving the legendary Buffalo Bill (William Frederick Cody) was led by Lieutenant Hayes, who brought along five greyhounds for coursing antelopes and rabbits. The meals were prepared by French chefs, with the dinner waiters clothed in fine evening dress. Don Russell, *Lives and Legends of Buffalo Bill* (Norman: University of Oklahoma Press, 1960).

80. Richard Irving Dodge, *Hunting Grounds of the Great West: A Description of the Plains, Game, and Indians of the Great North American Desert* (London: Chatto & Windus, 1878), 203.

81. Ibid., 210.

82. John Mortimer Murphy, *Sporting Adventures in the Far West* (London: Sampson Low, Marston, Searle, & Rivington, 1879), 368–370.

83. Grantley F. Berkeley, *The English Sportsman in the Western Prairies* (London: Hurst & Blackett, 1861).

84. Murphy, 14. See also Baur, *Dogs on the Frontier*, 85.

85. "Bypaths of Kansas History," *Kansas Historical Quarterly* 6, no. 3 (August 1937). See "Kansas in 1854," *New York Daily Tribune*, June 23, 1854.

86. Editorial, "Raid of the Nimrods," *Rocky Mountain News*, December 20, 1874. McCarty was a veteran of the Mexican War and held a position in the western Department of Mines and Mining.

87. Charles Frederick Holder, "The Crown of the San Gabriel Valley, Pasadena," *The Californian* 2 (1892): 432. Palmer notes that women participated in coursing in the Los Angeles Coursing Club. See T. S. Palmer, Department of Agriculture, Division of Ornithology and Mammalogy, *The Jack Rabbits of the United States* (Washington, DC: GPO, 1896), 66.

88. Francis Fenelon Rowland, "Cross-Country Riding," *The Californian* 1, no. 2, ed. Charles Frederick Holder (1892): 2–3.

89. Ibid., 5.

90. Palmer, *Jack Rabbits of the United States*, 66.

91. Hares were known to be detrimental to farmers' crops; they devoured melons, cabbage, carrots, alfalfa, cotton, grape and sweet potato vines, and grain. Ibid., 30.

92. It took only five jackrabbits to consume the same amount of food as one sheep. Accounts of damage could be shocking: a Prescott, Washington, man reported in 1895 that white-tailed hares had inflicted "vast" damages upon orchards, vineyards, and grain fields. Three years before, however, the assault had been even worse; the jackrabbits had destroyed entire "bearing orchards." Even earlier, in 1887, a Beaver County, Utah, farmer wrote that black-tailed rabbits devoured entire fields of cereals and caused some farmers to lose their entire crop. Palmer, *Jack Rabbits of the United States*, 31.

93. Ibid., 58. Palmer notes that bounties were not effective.

94. Photograph Collections, 1894, KSHS.

95. The USDA reported that as a consequence of rabbit drives and/or hunts, 370,195 hares were killed in California from 1875 to 1895; 12,202 in Oregon from 1894 to 1895; 37,215 in Utah from 1849 to 1895; 21,829 in Idaho from 1894 to 1896; and 28,666 in Colorado from 1893 to 1895. Palmer, *Jack Rabbits of the United States*, 64. Before white settlers took control of the plains, rabbit drives had even been conducted by Native American tribes. Such a drive was noted in 1839 and involved men, women, and children. Ibid., 47.

96. Ibid., 50. Palmer notes that the town regularly celebrated its birthday in this fashion.

97. Ibid.

98. Ibid., 59.

99. Many have remarked that the sounds emitted by a hare while in its death throes are similar to that of a crying human baby.

100. Palmer, *Jack Rabbits of the United States*, 59.

101. Ibid., 51. While some rabbit carcasses from drives were discarded, they were occasionally used for pig feed or as fertilizer. At times a market existed for the fur, usually for the production of ornamental trimmings or felt to be used in hats. Only occasionally was the flesh used for human consumption; it was notorious for its unpleasant taste and texture.

102. Ibid., 66–67. Palmer dates the introduction of enclosed coursing to October 23, 1888.

103. Ibid. Palmer notes that the organization had accumulated $50,000 for its capital stock.

104. M. E. Allison, "Coursing," *American Field* 30 (November 24, 1888): 504.

105. Palmer, *Jack Rabbits of the United States*, 67.

106. Ibid.

107. Ibid., 68.

108. One county attorney from Kansas called the anti-coursing advocates "sentimental idiots." Correspondence to Governor Allen from William Glenn, March 28, 1916, Kansas Governor Henry J. Allen Records, 1919–1923, Correspondence file on coursing, Box 8, Folder 10, KSHS. Hereafter referenced as Allen Records.

109. Keith Thomas, *Man and the Natural World: A History of the Modern Sensibility* (New York: Pantheon, 1983). See also Norm Phelps, *The Longest Struggle: Animal Advocacy from Pythagoras to PETA* (New York: Lantern, 2007).

110. See Allen Records.

111. Allen Records, Correspondence to E. D. George, Secretary to the Governor, from Miss H. H. Jacobs, May 12, 1921.

112. Allen Records, Correspondence from John Ise and Editorial, "The Voice of the People," May 4, 1921. Ise highlights the inconsistency seen in the traditional argument that hares were a pest that needed to be controlled; in reality, the animals had already been caught.

113. Allen Records, Correspondence to Lilliam M. Mitchner from "pardon attorney," May 21, 1921.

114. F. B. Stutz, "As I See It," *Greyhound Racing Record*, October 17, 1947.

115. Paul Hartwell, e-mail message to author, August 19, 2008.

CHAPTER TWO: BOOM OR BUST

1. Gerald Leinwand, *1927: High Tide of the 1920s* (New York: Four Walls Eight Windows), 275.

2. John M. Findlay, *People of Chance: Gambling in American Society from Jamestown to Las Vegas* (Oxford: Oxford University Press, 1986), 7, 84.

3. Ibid., 84, 86, 89.

4. Don Hausler, "The Emeryville Dog Race Track," *Journal of the Emeryville Historical Society* 5, no. 4 (Winter/Spring 1995). The title of the issue is *Dog Racing in Emeryville, 1919–1921*. For more information on the Walker-Otis Bill, see Franklin Hichborn, *Story of the Session of the California Legislature of 1911* (San Francisco: James H. Barry, 1913).

5. Don Hausler of the Emeryville Historical Society provided the author with extensive information about the town's history.

6. There is some question about the 1906 date in Salt Lake City; other sources indicate that Smith may have showcased his new device in 1907 in Denver. Tim O'Brien, e-mail correspondence with author, August 4, 2012.

7. The track may have been open on Mondays and Thursdays as well. See "Blue Star Amusement Company," *Racing Greyhound Stud Book* (St. Louis: INGRA, 1928): 53–57, GHF.

8. Jack Bell, "Smith and Company Hit the Jackpot at Erlanger, Kentucky," *Miami News*, January 1939, reprinted in *Greyhound Racing Record*, January 16, 1965.

9. For one dogman's memories of this track, see Ralph Warner, "Emeryville Opened with a 'Roar' in 1919," *Greyhound Racing Record*, 1966, GHF.

10. Paul C. Hartwell, *The Road from Emeryville* (San Diego: California Research Publishing, 1980), 3.

11. Another key business partner of Smith's was Thomas A. Keen, known as the "Carpenter Cowboy." He helped build many of the early tracks and mechanical lures during his partnership with Smith. Later, he became the president of the International Totalizer Company. He died in 1952 under suspicious circumstances when his Cadillac exploded; a car bomb was found to be the cause of death. "Clues Meager in Blast Killing," *Prescott (Arizona) Evening Courier*, February 7, 1952.

12. "The Life of a Dog Racer," *St. Louis Post-Dispatch*, June 26, 1927, reprinted in *INGRA Stud Book*, GHF.

13. "St. Louis Dog Track Outdoes Baseball Parks," *Washington Post*, August 3, 1930. The article indicates that a recent derby at a dog track near St. Louis attracted 20,000 visitors, a larger crowd than the St. Louis Browns had drawn in that year for a baseball game. This same article notes, however, that the St. Louis Cardinals "also have drawn 20,000 spectators but few times this year."

14. Jesse Ollie Payne, interview by Rolland Kerns, tape recording, September 13, 1972, Oklahoma History Center, Oklahoma City, OK. The Capitol City Kennel Club/ Capitol Kennel Club operated in Charleston, West Virginia, in 1927 and 1929, and the Kanawha Kennel Club operated there in 1926 and 1928.

15. Joel Hooper, "Hooper Says No Verbal Trimming by the Barber," *Coursing News*, n.d., Joel Hooper Pioneer File, GHF. Hooper was born in 1899. Likewise, dogman Bill Ewalt stated, "In some towns you had to be faster than your dogs to get your kennel cages out of town ahead of the law. If you ran second, they had their own kind of cage for you." Robert Boyle, "Noisy Chase Discreetly Done," *Sports Illustrated* 26, no. 12 (March 20, 1967): 46.

16. The unpredictable cycle of greyhound tracks opening and closing as well as the sometimes marginal nature of track operations is evidenced by a district court case in Montana in 1938–1939, based on the Butte Greyhound Racing and Breeders Association's failure to pay bills to the Largey Lumber Company for the construction of the racetrack in 1931. See Largey Lumber Company v. Butte Greyhound Racing and Breeders Association, docket no. 36342, Largey Family Papers, MC 289, 82–85, Montana Historical Society, Helena, MT.

17. Robin Black, "Murray Kemp, Part 2," *Greyhound Review*, February 1983, 47–49. This essay is a first-person account narrated by Kemp but paraphrased and edited by Black. Kemp founded the Multnomah Kennel Club and served as president of the American Greyhound Track Operators Association (AGTOA) from 1966 to 1968.

18. Hartwell, *Road from Emeryville*, 11.

19. Ibid., 16.

20. The racing secretary is the track official responsible for selecting which greyhounds would be entered for each race. He (or she) must take into account a number of factors in order to match the dogs in the best manner possible.

21. AGTOA Encyclopedia Committee, *American Greyhound Racing Encyclopedia* (AGTOA, 1963), 9, GHF.

22. R. J. Allison, promoter of the Mid-Continent Park in Tulsa, commented on the dog track's resemblance to Churchill Downs; the author of the article observed that the dog track was a "gem for its size." Editorial, *Kansas City Star*, April 10, 1921, reprinted in *INGRA Stud Book*, 112, 114, GHF.

23. *St. Louis Star*, July 21, 1927.

24. Michael Kammen, *American Culture, American Tastes: Social Change and the Twentieth Century* (New York: Basic Books, 1999). In general, Kammen interprets popular culture as participatory and inclusive, and mass culture as commercialized, standardized, and far less participatory. Within this framework, greyhound racing presents somewhat of a paradox: while participatory in its gambling component, spectatorship of the races is essentially passive, although some forms of fan participation, such as collecting greyhound-related memorabilia, are active. Later, in the ultimate

move against passivity, some Americans became "active" in the culture of dog racing through the adoption of ex-racing greyhounds. For more on the "lure of the local," see Erika Lee Doss, *Twentieth-Century American Art* (New York: Oxford University Press, 2002).

25. David E. Kyvig, *Daily Life in the United States, 1920–1940: How Americans Lived through the "Roaring Twenties" and Great Depression* (Chicago: Ivan R. Dee, 2002), 157.

26. The accounts of the dogmen are supported by various contemporary newspaper articles. See "Fate of Dog Racing Lies in Courthouse," *Atlanta Constitution*, May 8, 1929.

27. *Washington Post*, "Florida Race Tracks to Have Oral Betting," July 13, 1927.

28. AGTOA Encyclopedia Committee, *American Greyhound Racing Encyclopedia*, 20.

29. Hartwell, *Road from Emeryville*, 63.

30. Ed Danforth, "Dog Race Case Rests in Hands of Judge," *Atlanta Constitution*, May 9, 1929.

31. A similar situation is described in "Fate of Dog Racing Lies in Courthouse." See also "6,000 Atlantans See Dog Racing Opening," *Atlanta Constitution*, May 2, 1929.

32. Hartwell, *Road from Emeryville*, 3.

33. Ibid., 5.

34. AGTOA Encyclopedia Committee, *American Greyhound Racing Encyclopedia*, 10–11.

35. Hartwell, *Road from Emeryville*, 63.

36. See appendix.

37. In his history of the Hialeah Park horse track, John Crittenden noted that dog racing began in Hialeah when James Harrison Bright and Glenn Curtiss, the aviation pioneer, established the dog track at Hialeah at the corner of 21st Street and Palm Avenue. He wrote that the *Miami Herald* reported crowds of 5,000 or more, but "attendance counts were often exaggerated in the 1920s." He also noted that some referred to Hialeah as "Dog Town" at the time. See John Crittenden, *Hialeah Park: A Racing Legend* (Miami: Pickering, 1989).

38. Paul Hartwell includes a photograph of Dempsey presenting a trophy to the owner of Mission Boy in 1924 at Hialeah, Florida (*Road from Emeryville*, 131). It is unclear whether such celebrities were paid for their appearance at the dog tracks. A 1926 article notes that Jack Dempsey "breezed through a workout" before a crowd of 2,500 at the Atlantic City, New Jersey, track but does not mention any remuneration. See "Jack Enjoys Day of Work with Boxers," *Atlanta Constitution*, August 26, 1926. Another article mentions Dempsey working out at the dog track during the afternoon before the races were held at night. See James P. Dawson, "Dempsey Arrives at His New Camp," *New York Times*, August 24, 1926.

39. Kyvig, *Daily Life*, 55.

40. Lynn Dumenil, *The Modern Temper: American Culture and Society in the 1920s* (New York: Hill & Wang, 1995), 85. See also Kyvig, *Daily Life*; Kammen, *American Culture*; Susan J. Matt, *Keeping up with the Joneses: Envy in American Consumer Society, 1890–1930* (Philadelphia: University of Pennsylvania Press, 2003); and Lawrence B. Glickman, *A Living Wage: American Workers and the Making of Consumer Society* (Ithaca, NY: Cornell University Press, 1999).

41. Kammen, *American Culture,* 73.

42. Ibid., 54.

43. Kyvig, *Daily Life,* 158.

44. Dumenil, *Modern Temper,* 80.

45. Kyvig, *Daily Life,* 27.

46. "Greyhound Racing in America and England Organized under One Large Association," *New York Times,* March 5, 1926.

47. But according to Hartwell, this did not take place until later, in a meeting held on October 11. At that point Sawyer became the new president and Hannah Smith became the new high commissioner. Former competitors of Smith, including Dr. A. L. Spindler and J. Homer Ellis, also opted to join hands with INGRA, creating a dynamic mix of personalities and, more than likely, conflicting ideas about the role of the association.

48. Tim O'Brien, O. P. Smith's grandson, disputes this, arguing that Hannah Smith never relinquished her position as commissioner. Tim O'Brien, telephone interview with author, October 1, 2010.

49. "Mrs. Hannah Smith, Widow of Late Dog-Racing Commissioner, Rears Family and Governs Sport," *St. Louis Star,* July 21, 1927. Even so, no proof has ever surfaced that the association was at any time under the sway of organized crime.

50. "Annual Meeting of the Executive Committee of the National Coursing Association," Concordia, KS, October 26, 1932, in *The National Coursing Association Greyhound Stud Book,* vol. 25 (Manhattan, KS: Chas. F. Horne, Keeper of the Stud Book, 1931–1932), 108.

51. The NCA was considering the creation of a racing division within the organization in order to protect the greyhound breeders and improve the track game. Greyhounds at the track were often owned by breeders who lived elsewhere, but the dogs were managed and trained by dogmen traveling from track to track. The dogmen leased the greyhounds from the breeders and were obligated to pay them a portion of the purses. During the early years the dogmen working at the tracks were not always paid by track management and were thus unable to pay the breeders. In other cases, dogmen simply did not pay up on their debts to the breeders. The traditional lease agreement was 65 percent for the lessee and 35 percent for the lessor, an arrangement, according to dogman F. B. "Happy" Stutz, that was adopted from sharecropping agreements in the Midwest. See F. B. "Happy" Stutz, "Needed—A New Look at Leases," GHF.

52. "Constitution and By-Laws," *INGRA Manual of Instructions and Stud Book* (St. Louis: INGRA, 1929), GHF.

53. *INGRA Stud Book,* 539, GHF.

54. This is a rather ambitious number given one article's estimate that 2,000 greyhounds were actively racing in 1928. See "Progress of Greyhound Racing" in *INGRA Stud Book,* GHF.

55. "Blue Star Amusement Company," in *INGRA Stud Book,* GHF.

56. Frank Anderson, the general manager of the Miami Beach Kennel Club during the 1930s, stated, "The green International [INGRA] pennant over the judge's stand is your assurance of the best in greyhound racing at all times." Tex Rickard Memorial Race Clippings, Miami Beach Kennel Club 1936 Scrapbook, MBKC scrapbooks, FIU.

57. "Constitution and By-Laws," *INGRA Manual of Instructions and Stud Book*, 33, GHF.

58. Paul Hartwell, e-mail message to author, August 25, 2008.

59. Ibid. Hartwell's father was allied with Smith's archrival, Heintz, so Hartwell's perspective might have been swayed by this association.

60. Hartwell, *Road from Emeryville*, 52.

61. See F. B. Stutz, "Two Pioneers Recall 106 Tracks of Yesterday," undated typed manuscript, GHF. This article was probably published in the 1960s in the *Greyhound Racing Record*.

62. *Coursing News*, n.d., Orville Barber Pioneer File, GHF.

63. Some of the greyhounds appeared to be improving, rather than becoming fatigued, the more consecutive races they ran. Track officials complained that the dogmen expected the racing secretaries to get their dogs into shape. See Bob Burtt, "The Racing Kennel: Part I: History," *Greyhound Racing Record*, January 25, 1952.

64. Boyd H. Rhodes Pioneer File, GHF.

65. Merrill Blair Pioneer File, GHF.

66. Hartwell, *Road from Emeryville*, 35.

67. Tim O'Brien disputes the problem was with the braking system and argues that the problem stemmed from the speed and gauge of the track. Tim O'Brien, telephone interview with author, October 1, 2010.

68. For a photograph of the first indoor dog track, taken on July 4, 1931, in Atlantic City, see "When They Raced Indoors," *Greyhound Racing Record*, February 6, 1948.

69. *NCA Stud Book*, vol. 25 (n. 50).

70. Smith v. American Electric Rabbit Racing Association, Inc., et al., 21 F. 2d 366 (1927). The case was brought to the Fifth Circuit Court of Appeals in 1928, but the rehearing was denied. The judge agreed with the conclusions of the District Court. See American Electric Rabbit Racing Association, Inc. v. Owen P. Smith, 26 F. 2d 1016 (1928). The legal disagreements over the lure were fueled by the two men's dislike for each other and persisted for a number of years. In 1927 the District Court of Louisiana addressed Smith's contention that Heintz had conspired to "make, use, sell, and lease unlawfully devices and apparatus [*sic*] embodying the inventions" covered by Smith's patents. Some parts of the litigation moved forward even after Smith's death. His widow, Hannah, carried on the battle over patent infringement, filing two cases that reached the U.S. Supreme Court in 1931. Hannah M. Smith v. Magic City Kennel Club, Inc., 282 U.S. 784 (1931) and Hannah M. Smith v. Springdale Amusement Park, 283 U. S. 121 (1931).

71. Hartwell, *Road from Emeryville*, 15, 25.

72. Ibid. J. Homer Ellis had opened the dog track in Tampa, the Six Mile Creek Kennel Club, in 1925. He also established tracks in Illinois, Ohio, Arkansas, Indiana, and West Virginia. See J. Homer Ellis Pioneer File, GHF.

73. This term is used in a letter, dated March 30, 1929, to Hannah Smith from promoter Frank Anderson. He says that if INGRA could be used as a household word, it would be "one of the wickedest blows that the out-laws could receive." Owen Patrick Smith Files, GHF.

74. Bob Burtt, "The Racing Kennel: Part II, The Booking System," *Greyhound Racing Record*, February 1, 1952, 5.

75. Greyhounds in smaller kennels probably received more individual care. The fate of ex-racing greyhounds after their racing careers were over is unclear, although dogs of limited talent were probably gassed. One article noted, "De Geers' [*sic*] policy is to keep cleaned out of dogs which don't make money." See "The Life of a Dog Racer," *St. Louis Post-Dispatch*, reprinted in *INGRA Stud Book*, 525, GHF. In contrast, an article printed in an INGRA publication indicated, "After racing days are over comes a well-merited award—retirement at the home kennel, where the hound settles down to the serious duty of raising a family." See "Progress of Greyhound Racing" in *INGRA Stud Book*, 518, GHF.

76. See "The Life of a Dog Racer," 523.

77. Breeding kennels, in contrast, could be much larger. By the late 1920s, world-class wrestler John Pesek kept 350 to 400 greyhounds at a time at his breeding ranch in Ravenna, Nebraska. Most facilities were probably not as large as Pesek's, however. See Geoff Pesek's forthcoming book on John Pesek. Geoff Pesek, e-mail message to author, January 17, 2012.

78. Bob Burtt, "The Racing Kennel, Part I: History," *Greyhound Racing Record*, January 25, 1952. Because the dogs required frequent care, some tracks provided housing for dogmen during the early years. A dog track in the Atlanta area was to include "a steel and concrete grandstand, kennels, training grounds, and cottages for the trainers." See "Dog Racing to Amuse Atlantans This Fall," *Atlanta Constitution*, September 18, 1927.

79. Kyvig, *Daily Life*, 48–51. Local and state governments had traditionally been responsible for road building. Construction quality varied dramatically from region to region. A boom in road building (beginning in 1921) resulted from a federal initiative to subsidize state highway construction. By the end of the decade the federal government was spending $2.5 billion per year on road development. Much still remained to be done, however, especially in the West and the South.

80. See letter from Rita Spencer Futrell, May 24, 1979, Forbe W. Spencer Pioneer File, GHF.

81. Kyvig, *Daily Life*, 41.

82. Hartwell, *Road from Emeryville*, 20.

83. Ibid., 21. See also letter to Carroll Blair from P. C. Hartwell, May 12, 1978, P. C. Hartwell Pioneer File, GHF.

84. One author notes that a "dog in his traveling box can be carried by express for only a fraction of what it costs to ship a horse." See "Progress of Greyhound Racing" in *INGRA Stud Book*, 521, GHF.

85. For a history of commercial dog food, see Katherine C. Grier, *Pets in America: A History* (Chapel Hill: University of North Carolina Press, 2006), 281–291.

86. Gene Randle Pioneer File, GHF.

87. http://okhistory.cuadra.com/starweb3/b.archives/servlet.starweb3 (accessed June 23, 2008). "Greyhounds Shipped by Plane," photograph by Waterhouse, Museum of the Ozarks History Collection, Oklahoma City, OK.

88. Hartwell states that wealthier people starting coming in the 1940s and 1950s. Paul Hartwell, e-mail message to author, August 18, 2008.

89. Paul Hartwell, e-mail message to author, August 24, 2008.

90. *INGRA Stud Book*, GHF.

91. Willie Hiblow Pioneer File, GHF.

92. "Ma Carroll, Pioneer," *Greyhound Racing Record*, November 17, 1950.

93. In an unpublished essay, "Sport of Queens: A Feminist View of Greyhound Racing Lore," written while she was a student at Arizona State University, Leslie Wootten has observed that women have remained "invisible and silent in this otherwise dynamic occupational folk group"; see Derby Lane Vertical Files, St. Petersburg, Florida. She also noted that women were not allowed to handle greyhounds at the tracks until the 1970s even though women owned, trained, and bred racing dogs. See also Leslie Wootten, "Five Minutes with TV Leanna Deanna," *Arizona Player*, February 15–March 14, 2008, 24.

94. Women frequently worked in the kennels in an unofficial capacity. Janet Strong, the wife of dogman Wayne Strong, shared an expression known in the greyhound business: "Don't have any more dogs than your wife can take care of." Janet Strong, personal interview with author, June 14, 2008. See also Leslie Wootten, "Sport of Queens."

95. "Sixty Minutes, Duane Randle," *Turnout*, August/September 1981, GHF. While Ray, Gene, and Duane worked at the tracks, Ned devoted his time to raising greyhounds on the family farm in Wichita and later in Ocala, Florida. Boyd Randle's grandson, Craig Randle, continued to work in the industry and has long served as a greyhound farm inspector for the National Greyhound Association (NGA; renamed from the NCA in 1973) and American Greyhound Council (AGC). Craig Randle, telephone interview with author, February 23, 2010. Many years later, when the property was sold to Francesca Field, she was told that it was unlikely that the family would have sold the property to a (female) outsider if greyhound racing were not already on the decline. The sale signified the end of a dynasty. Francesca Field, personal interview with author, April 23, 2009.

96. Robert M. Burtt, "Racing's Famous Father and Son Team," *Greyhound Racing Record*, March 20, 1953, 7, 11.

97. The cool-out boy was responsible for walking and bathing the greyhounds that had just finished racing. Greyhound handlers believed that this practice decreased the stiffness and soreness in the dogs.

98. It was not at all uncommon for a young man to work his way up from cool-out boy to racing secretary; in fact, this pattern continued for decades. Hartwell retired on July 1, 2009, after forty-seven years, three months, and three days in the greyhound racing business. He calculates that he served for a total of sixty-one years as a racing official. His brother, John Hartwell, also worked in the industry in various capacities throughout his life, including racing secretary, judge, and director of racing. Paul Hartwell, e-mail message to author, June 4, 2010.

99. Hartwell, *Road from Emeryville*, 20.

100. Ibid., 37.

101. John Kobler, *Capone: The Life and World of Al Capone* (New York: Da Capo, 1971), 112.

102. Hartwell, *Road from Emeryville*, 29–30. Capone may or may not have "owned" the track, but he could easily have used his influence to secure jobs for friends there. A *New York Times* article quotes a state investigator who charged that Hawthorne netted Capone $500,000 a year. See "Police Raid Dog Track," *New York Times*, July 26,

1929. Craig Randle stated that Gene Randle had shared a similar story with him about Capone changing the race results. Craig Randle, telephone interview with author, February 23, 2010. Murray Kemp also noted, "There was a story that he [Capone] was mingling in the crowd one night, and he didn't agree with the judges' decision about the outcome of a particular race. So he just walked into the infield and hung up the numbers the way he thought they should be, then walked back into the crowd. I wasn't present, but I was told nobody disturbed those numbers after he hung them up." See "Sixty Minutes, Murray Kemp," *Turnout*, August 1982, GHF.

103. Hartwell, *Road from Emeryville*, 32.

104. William Riley Burnett, *Dark Hazard* (New York: Harper and Brothers, 1933). See also *Dark Hazard*, directed by Alfred E. Green (1934), MP Motion Picture Collection, DVD transfer, UCLA Film and Television Archive.

105. The Franklin Kennel Club in Grove City, Ohio, operated briefly and sporadically during the late 1920s and early 1930s. Paul Grossman writes, "Financing for the plant was reputedly furnished by a then infamous Chicago gangster. . . . Pressure from local law enforcement officials caused the plant to cease operations in 1928." To this day, the school mascot for Grove City High School is a racing greyhound. See Paul W. Grossman, "Greyhound Memorabilia," August 15, 1988, GHF.

106. See Thomas Karsten File, GHF.

107. David G. Schwartz, *Roll the Bones: The History of Gambling* (New York: Gotham, 2006), 369.

108. This statement is based on an extensive survey of newspaper morgues with indexed files on dog racing. See the *Memphis Press-Scimitar* and the *Commercial Appeal*, University of Memphis, Special Collections Department, Memphis, TN; the *Boston Herald* at the Boston University Libraries, Special Collections; the *Oregonian* and the *Oregon Journal* at the Multnomah Public Library, Portland, OR; and the *Los Angeles Examiner* at the University of Southern California, Doheny Memorial Library, Special Collections, Los Angeles, CA.

109. "Canvass of Legislature Hints Dog Racing Repeal," *Boston Herald*, February 28, 1935.

110. www.akc.org (accessed June 13, 2012).

111. Susan Orlean, *Rin Tin Tin: The Life and the Legend* (New York: Simon & Schuster, 2011).

112. Susan Jones, *Valuing Animals: Veterinarians and Their Patients in Modern America* (Baltimore: Johns Hopkins University Press, 2003), 116.

113. "Dog Racing" in *The Blood-Horse* 25, no. 7 (February 15, 1936).

CHAPTER THREE: HORSES, HOUNDS, AND HUSTLERS

1. Sportswriter William Nack expressed a great passion for thoroughbred horse racing early in his writing career, a feeling that was shattered after Ruffian's breakdown and subsequent death in 1975. He later acknowledged that no horse had ever shown such "romantic possibilities" as she, and furthermore, Nack felt that Ruffian's death in the "Great Match Race" against Foolish Pleasure was, for him, the "unfinished symphony" of horse racing. William Nack, telephone interview with author, May 24, 2012. Nan Mooney also conveys this deep love of thoroughbred racing in her memoir, *My*

Racing Heart, although she, too, is troubled by abuses in the sport. See Nan Mooney, *My Racing Heart: The Passionate World of Thoroughbreds and the Track* (New York: Perennial, 2003).

2. Interview with greyhound track executive, 2010. The name of the interviewee has been withheld by mutual agreement for purposes of confidentiality.

3. "Canvass of Legislature Hints Dog Racing Repeal," *Boston Herald,* February 28, 1935. There were a few additional legislative efforts to legalize dog racing in Kentucky, but they failed and did not receive as much publicity.

4. Marjorie Mears, "Woof! Woof! They're Off!" *Washington Post,* August 31, 1930.

5. The Jockey Club maintained the (thoroughbred horse) *American Stud Book.*

6. Paul Hartwell, e-mail message to author, August 18, 2008.

7. Norman Baker, "Going to the Dogs—Hostility to Greyhound Racing in Britain: Puritanism, Socialism, and Pragmaticism," *Journal of Sport History* 23, no. 2 (Summer 1996): 97–119; Mike Huggins, "Going to the Dogs," *History Today* 56, no. 5 (May 2006); "Racing Greyhounds after the 'Tin Rabbit,'" *Literary Digest* (October 22, 1927): 54–60; "British Greyhounds and Gambling," *Literary Digest* (January 7, 1928): 18–19; Mike Huggins, "'Everybody's Going to the Dogs?' The Middle Classes and Greyhound Racing in Britain between the Wars," *Journal of Sport History* 34, no. 1 (Spring 2007): 401–444.

8. "Boston Is Big Betting Center with Worker Chief Victims," January 11, 1940, MBKC scrapbooks, FIU.

9. John Kieran, "Sports of the Times," *New York Times,* May 17, 1937.

10. Several individuals in American greyhound racing history who were unusually effective, although certainly not without controversy in some cases, included T. L. Weaver, Jerry Collins, Joe Linsey, Al Ross, Murray Kemp, Izzy and David Hecht, and David and Arthur Funk. In a 1982 interview, Kemp noted that "the image of greyhound racing is reflected by the track operators in many places. I'm not throwing any bouquets at myself, but I must have been doing something right to have them change the name of Multnomah Kennel Club to Murray Kemp Greyhound Park. I've always tried to conduct myself like a gentleman and in an honorable manner." "Sixty Minutes, Murray Kemp," *Turnout,* August 1982, GHF.

11. For a thorough study on how Kentucky became a powerful force in the horse-racing industry, see Maryjean Wall, *How Kentucky Became Southern: A Tale of Outlaws, Horse Thieves, Gamblers, and Breeders* (Lexington: University Press of Kentucky, 2012).

12. Voters would often sanction dog racing in a state or county, only to decry its presence in their own city. "Hanson Board Bars Dog Track," *Boston Herald,* February 7, 1939; "Racing Beaten at Plebiscite by 64 Votes," *Boston Herald,* February 8, 1939; "Marshfield Gives Dog Racing Cold Reception," *Boston Globe,* January 27, 1939.

13. Paul Hartwell, *Road from Emeryville* (San Diego: California Research Publishing, 1980), 69.

14. Eugene Martin Christiansen, telephone interview with author, December 2, 2009. He was referring in particular to Florida in the 1950s.

15. Owen P. Smith, George Sawyer, Martin J. Hyland, et al. v. Commonwealth of Kentucky, 275 U.S. 509 (1927).

16. "Dogs Lure Thousands," *Cincinnati Enquirer,* August 16, 1925. See also "Stake Race Planned," *Cincinnati Enquirer,* August 30, 1925.

17. "Dogs Lure Thousands."

18. Smith v. Kentucky, Court of Appeals case file no. 53151, Box 3238, Kentucky State Archives, Frankfurt, KY.

19. Ibid.

20. Ibid. See also "Kentucky Dog Racing Fate Now with Court," *Washington Post,* September 17, 1925.

21. Dogman F. B. "Happy" Stutz wrote, "Although thirty years or more have passed, the word 'injunction' still reminds the old-time racing man of perilous days ahead." See F. B. Stutz, "As I See It," *Greyhound Racing Record,* June 2, 1962.

22. Ibid.

23. Smith v. Kentucky, Court of Appeals case file. See also "Betting on Dog Races Illegal in Kentucky," *Washington Post,* February 27, 1926. This case was filed in January 1926.

24. Transcript of Record, Supreme Court of the United States, filed June 14, 1926.

25. Smith v. Kentucky, 275 U.S. 509 (1927). The court record is available in the Gale Group database, "U.S. Supreme Court Records and Briefs, 1832–1978: Making of Modern Law."

26. Earlier in the brief Stanley wrote that the dog track in Erlanger cost $50,000 to erect.

27. The Kentucky Court of Appeals was the highest court in Kentucky at the time.

28. Smith v. Kentucky, 275 U.S. 509 (1927).

29. "Horses in Court," *New York Times,* December 14, 1927.

30. Eugene Taylor Mack, "Patterns and Images of Greyhound Racing" (master's thesis, University of Kansas, 1991), 26–27.

31. "Horses in Court."

32. "Supreme Court of U.S. Hears Kentucky Argue How Dog and Horse Wagers Differ," *New York Times,* December 9, 1927.

33. "Horses in Court." See also "Supreme Court of U.S. Hears Kentucky Argue How Dog and Horse Wagers Differ." There was an attempt in the late 1940s to legalize dog racing in Kentucky, but it failed. Stutz discusses the lobbying efforts of the Greyhound Owners Benevolent Association (GOBA) in Kentucky in his regular column. See F. B. Stutz, "As I See It," *Greyhound Racing Record,* March 19, 1948.

34. "Racing Protest in Erlanger," *Kentucky Post,* May 10, 1926.

35. For a thorough review of the early history of horse racing in New York, see Steven A. Riess, *The Sport of Kings and the Kings of Crime: Horse Racing, Politics, and Organized Crime in New York, 1865–1913* (Syracuse, NY: Syracuse University Press, 2011).

36. This was the first race in New York to garner significant publicity (see "New York to Get Its First View of Greyhound Racing on July 27," *New York Times,* July 18, 1928), but other races took place prior to this date, including races in Rochester, New York, in 1927 (see "Dog Races Continue," *New York Times,* September 7, 1927). A dog track in Rochester (the Monroe Greyhound Association) also operated in 1928. See also Hartwell, *Road from Emeryville,* 146.

37. If one wagers to win, he gets a blue picture. To place, he gets a black picture, and to show, he gets a brown picture. After the race, the pictures are repurchased at the payoff window: blue are $10, black are $6, and brown are $4. Gambling

techniques used in New York at this time were also sometimes referred to as "option wagering." A 1913 loophole in the New York gambling law did state that "a Gentleman could bet with his friend." This line was interpreted in a number of ways. An article in the *New York Times* noted that New York governor Charles Evans Hughes wrote into the state constitution "a prohibition against bookmaking and pool selling. It has never been illegal to bet. The constitutional prohibition is against the operation, or machinery of betting." See "Dog Racing Issue Raised for State," *New York Times*, May 16, 1937.

38. "2,000 Fans Attend Opening Dog Races," *New York Times*, July 28, 1928. The court structure in New York is different from many other states: the supreme court in New York is the court of first resort. What is referred to in New York as the Court of Appeals is what is known as the state supreme court in many other states.

39. "Grand Jury Upholds Sale of Dog Photos," *New York Times*, August 31, 1928.

40. "Jury Calls Hounds in Gaming Inquiry," *New York Times*, July 25, 1931.

41. See "Dogs to Race Tonight in First Event Here," *New York Times*, July 27, 1928; "2,000 Fans Attend Opening Dog Races," *New York Times*, July 28, 1928; "5,000 See Dog Races at Dongan Hills," *New York Times*, August 1, 1928; "Defers Dog Race Ruling," *New York Times*, August 5, 1928; "Held as Dog Race Bettors," *New York Times*, August 18, 1928; "Dog Races Tomorrow Last on Regular Card," *New York Times*, September 21, 1928.

42. Some of the dog racing at the Mineola Fair Grounds may have featured whippets rather than greyhounds, although the two were often confused by reporters. See "Would End Dog Race Bets," *New York Times*, June 24, 1930. See also Hartwell, *Road from Emeryville*, 151.

43. "Commission Unanimously Opposed to the Legalization of Dog Racing," *New York Times*, February 17, 1936. See also "Oppose New York Dog Bill," *Daily Racing Form*, May 29, 1936.

44. "Dog Betting Bill Put Up," *New York Times*, January 9, 1936. See also Mack, "Patterns and Images of Greyhound Racing," 29.

45. "Commission Unanimously Opposed to the Legalization of Dog Racing."

46. Letters to the Sports Editor, "Condemns Dog Racing," *New York Times*, February 15, 1936.

47. "Urges Veto of Dog Bill," *New York Times*, May 29, 1936.

48. "Judge Assails Ban on Racing of Dogs," *New York Times*, June 11, 1936; "Dog Racing Upheld by Mineola Court," *New York Times*, June 17, 1936; Reed v. Littleton, 289 N.Y.S. 798, June 16, 1936.

49. "Lehman Is Urged to Veto Dog Bill," *New York Times*, June 2, 1936.

50. James J. Morris, Letters to the Sports Editor, "Defends Dog Racing," *New York Times*, February 22, 1936.

51. Reed v. Littleton, 289 N.Y.S. 798 (1936).

52. "Dog Racing Upheld by Mineola Court."

53. "Dog Race Measure Vetoed by Lehman," *New York Times*, May 22, 1937. Assemblyman Leonard W. Hall was one of the bill's supporters. For a full account of this battle, and a number of track raids that ensued, see Ryan H. Reed's three-part series in the *Greyhound Review:* "The Great New York War of '37, Part 1," July 2009, 33–35; "The

Great New York War of '37, Part 2," August 2009, 21–23; "The Great New York War of '37—Finale," September 2009, 37–39.

54. "Dog Racing Issue Raised for State," *New York Times*, May 16, 1937. The top of the cartoon reads, "As the Dog Racing Bill Is Debated."

55. Ibid. The author also lists some of the ways in which greyhounds can be abused so as to manipulate their racing ability. He notes,

> Ways of "stopping" a dog are dashing a few drops of oil of mustard on his eyes so that he cannot see the rabbit, putting a tack through one side of his muzzle so that when the leather is knocked against his jaw in the hurly-burly of the race the point will penetrate the skin, causing the dog to flinch, run wide, and lose ground; sandpapering the pads of his feet so he will be running on the "quick" and not try; placing a nettle between his toes or under his leg, and snapping a rubber band around his tail.

56. Ibid. His comments about greyhounds training on live rabbits and his description of the rabbit as a "victim" were more widely seen at the time, however.

57. Ibid.

58. John Kiernan, "Sports of the Times," *New York Times*, May 17, 1937.

59. Ibid.

60. "Sharp Clash Marks Dog Racing Hearing," *New York Times*, May 18, 1937. In a letter to the governor on November 26, 1939, Swope decries the "vicious Republican organization in Nassau" and specifically criticized District Attorney Littleton. He writes, "When he [Littleton] appeared before you to argue for approval for the law (which, incidentally, was full of chicanery), accompanied by Levy, Russ Sprague and others of the vicious Republican organization in Nassau, he was ostensibly opposing the same group in a criminal action. I think Littleton's conduct was shockingly unethical." Herbert Bayard Swope, letter, November 26, 1937, Herbert H. Lehman Papers, Special Correspondence Files, Rare book and Manuscript Library, Columbia University Library, http://lehman.cul.columbia.edu/ldpd_0883_0050 (accessed May 8, 2012).

61. "Dog Racing," *New York Times*, May 17, 1937.

62. "The Facts About Dog Racing," *Our Dumb Animals* 70, no. 8 (August 1937): 128.

63. Reed v. Littleton, 275 N.Y. 150 (1937). Before reaching the Court of Appeals, the case was heard at the Supreme Court Appellate Division in 1936. The court records (from 1936 and 1937) are available at the New York State Library.

64. See "Dog Track Loses Plea," *New York Times*, July 27, 1937. The plaintiff (Joseph Meyers and the Orangeburg Kennel Club) brought the case to federal court, but the judge determined that he had redress in state court. See also "Dog Races Raided at Orangeburg," *New York Times*, July 25, 1927, and Reed, "The Great New York War of '37—Finale."

65. Thoroughbred horse racing had already been legalized by the courts. Although gambling on greyhound racing was never legalized in New York, some constituencies still wanted to see the sport active in the state. Several articles in the *Greyhound Racing Record* from the 1950s showcased New York state breeders who raced their dogs at various "exhibition races," or in some cases, at county fairs (without gambling), but this genre of dog racing was only practiced on a limited scale. An internal FBI report from

the 1970s investigating dog track promoter and Greyhound Hall of Fame pioneer Murray Kemp (known for successfully managing Multnomah in Portland, Oregon) noted that he was "attempting to start greyhound racing in New York," and he had been making inquiries at "very high state and city levels." Despite these rumblings pari-mutuel greyhound racing officially remained illegal in the Empire State. See Federal Bureau of Investigation Internal Report, New York, Field Office File 92–8518, FOIA request no. 1116343-000. See also Marcia King, "Racing Greyhounds: Bred to Run or Born to Die?" *Dog Fancy*, September 1991 and October 1991, http://www.adopt-a-greyhound.org/about/body_king.html (accessed August 24, 2010). See also Sports Editor's Mailbox, D. Stark-Riemer, "Cruelty Called Mark of Greyhound Racing," *New York Times*, June 15, 1975, referencing Steve Cady, "Two Borough Presidents Back Greyhound Racing for City," *New York Times*, June 3, 1975.

66. Robin Black, "Murray Kemp, Part 2," *Greyhound Review*, February 1983, 47–49. This essay is a first-person account narrated by Kemp but paraphrased and edited by Black. At first glance, the fact that individual Hollywood stars frequented the tracks in Florida while the film industry as a whole rejected greyhound racing in California seems perplexing. It is likely, however, that studio executives feared competition for the entertainment dollar, whereas an individual movie star could apparently still effectively promote his or her own image at the dog tracks without adverse consequences.

67. Hartwell, *Road from Emeryville*, 76. F. B. "Happy" Stutz recalled dog tracks at Culver City, Beverly Fairfax, Emeryville, Compton, Baden, Sacramento, El Cerrito, Bayshore, San Jose, Belmont, San Bernardino, and Santa Cruz. See F. B. Stutz, "Two Pioneers Recall 106 Tracks of Yesterday," undated manuscript, GHF. For another report on early greyhound racing in California, see Paul Portelli, "Early Racing in California," *Greyhound Racing Record*, October 22, 1954. He notes that a special guest at the Bayshore Kennel Club was District Attorney Mathew Brady.

68. *Los Angeles Examiner* newspaper clippings files, Dog Racing, 1933–1947, Doheny Memorial Library, University of Southern California, Los Angeles, CA.

69. See "You Can Help," *Our Animals* 28, no. 11 (February 1935). The SF/SPCA advocated supporting SB 662, which would prohibit the use of live animals in training and racing dogs. See also Frank Piazzi, "The Cruelty of Dog Racing," *Our Animals* 26, no. 11 (February 1933); "Cruelty in Training Racing Dogs," *Our Animals* 27, no. 7 (October 1933); and Charles W. Friedrichs, "Racketeering under the Guise of Sport," *Our Animals* 31, no. 3 (June 1937).

70. Editorial, "A Vicious Proposition," *Los Angeles Examiner*, September 25, 1946. Another effort in the state legislature had tried to resurrect dog racing in 1946. See *Los Angeles Examiner* clippings files, Dog Racing, 1933–1947.

71. Earl Warren, interviews by Amelia R. Fry and members of the Regional Oral History Staff, 1971–1972, tape recording and transcript, 114, University of California, Bancroft Library, Berkeley, CA (hereafter Warren interviews).

72. C. M. Goethe to Earl Warren, letter, March 16, 1939, Gambling Subject File, Attorney General Office Files, Earl Warren Papers, California State Archives, Sacramento, CA.

73. State Humane Association of California to Earl Warren, letter, March 15, 1939, Earl Warren Papers.

74. El Cerrito was in the county adjoining that of Alameda. The district attorney of Alameda at the time was Earl Warren. According to Kemp, Warren was "so incensed at Blackjack Jerome operating right outside his jurisdiction that he vowed his first act, if elected Attorney General, would be to close Blackjack Jerome's operation." Black, "Murray Kemp, Part 2," 49. For more information on the El Cerrito Kennel Club, see Mervin Belfils, "El Cerrito Kennel Club," September 1975, www.elcerritowire.com/history/pages/elcerritokennelclub.htm (accessed August 14, 2010).

75. Earl Warren to John J. Jerome, letter, March 14, 1939. Earl Warren Papers.

76. "Warren Bans Dog Races," *San Francisco News*, March 14, 1939. The article noted that the El Cerrito track was the first to be affected by the new ruling. There were numerous attempts during the 1930s to legalize greyhound racing in California. In 1935 a dog-racing bill was vetoed, and in 1937 the governor threatened to veto a dog-racing bill again. Two of the bills under consideration in 1939 were Melvyn Cronin's A.B. 1750 and Pierovich's S.B. 878.

77. Warren interviews, 113–114. Dogman Clarence Connick, during a 1982 interview, had a different opinion about Jerome. He noted that "a fellow named Black Jack Jerome owned the track in El Cerrito. You talk about hanky-panky. Well, anything that could possibly go wrong went wrong at El Cerrito. There was a lot of fooling around with the races that had nothing to do with the dogmen. Plus, the state got none of the take, so there was no supervision. Jerome took what he wanted, plus he owned half the bookie joints in the Bay area." See "Sixty Minutes, Clarence Connick," *Turnout*, February 1982, GHF.

78. Warren interviews, 114.

79. Ibid., 115. He stated, "So that night they went on the loudspeaker and told the people that they had been informed by the attorney general that it was not legal to operate, that they were not going to fight with the law, and that Saturday night would be their last night. And they did close that Saturday night."

80. Ibid. This statement is not entirely true, however. County fairs occasionally featured dog racing at the time, although legalized pari-mutuel gambling was not a part of these races. See "Racing Revived in California," *Greyhound Racing Record*, October 30, 1953.

81. "California to Vote on Dog Races," *Greyhound Racing Record*, June 25, 1948. In 1946 pro-greyhound-racing forces supported Proposition No. 2, which would have legalized gambling on greyhound racing.

82. Arden Hartman, telephone interview with author, December 15, 2009.

83. Richard L. Neuberger was an Oregon state senator and journalist. The article was originally published in *The Nation* on September 8, 1951. See Herbert L. Marx, Jr., ed., *Gambling in America* (New York: H. W. Wilson, 1952), 104–108.

84. Robin Black, "Multnomah's 50th Anniversary," *Greyhound Review*, July/August 1982, 78–82.

85. The Massachusetts legislature passed the pari-mutuel bill for horse and dog racing in June 1934. After the governor signed the bill, voters were required to decide whether they wanted to introduce pari-mutuel wagering into their own counties.

86. Francis H. Rowley, "Dog Racing," editorial, *Our Dumb Animals* 72, no. 1 (January 1939): 14. He wrote that the greyhounds are

shunted back and forth across the country, from one race track to another, with no opportunity to lead a natural life. While they race and make money for their owners they are well cared for, as any other valuable piece of property would be, but their racing life is brief and they are then thrown into the discard and neglected. Greyhounds are bred by the thousands for just one purpose, and the men who breed them are not humanitarians or, for the most part, even dog lovers.

87. Rowley's concerns about the humane treatment of greyhounds resonated more widely in the 1990s and beyond when voters decided during the 2008 election to end live greyhound racing in Massachusetts by 2010. Indeed, Rowley's criticism that training methods were unsavory, and that racing greyhounds were "shunted back and forth across the country, from one race track to another, with no opportunity to lead a natural life" came about fifty years before the majority of New Englanders, and, indeed, many Americans, were ready and willing to hear this argument.

88. One of the code words used by the press to denote organized crime or otherwise unwanted proponents of greyhound racing was "outsider."

89. A 1939 article included in the MBKC scrapbooks noted,

When the horse men made a drive for legalization in 1934, they found, much to their disgust, that the old gang of bootlegging days, now in control of dog racing, had tied themselves up to the horse racing bill. By the expenditure of large sums the dog racing crowd maneuvered the situation so that they could issue an ultimatum to the horse men. There would either be both dog racing and horse racing in Massachusetts, or there would be neither. In other words, O'Hare and his gang had the votes in the House and Senate. The horse men, although despising the dog racing interests, were forced to go along with them in order to attain their own objective.

See "Racket-Ruled Dog Racing Born in Legislative Deal," December 30, 1939, MBKC scrapbooks, FIU.

90. Jack Beatty, *The Rascal King: The Life and Times of James Michael Curley (1874–1958)* (Cambridge, MA: Da Capo Press, 2000), 366. In 1923 wages had totaled $115 million, but in 1935 they were down to $25 million. Taunton's industrial wages fell from $8 million to $3 million during the same decade.

91. "Racket-Ruled Dog Racing"; "Dog Track Propaganda Offset Attempts to Clean Up Sport," January 22, 1940, MBKC scrapbooks, FIU.

92. Larry Fontes Pioneer File, GHF. Bill Veeck, in his tell-all memoir documenting his experiences as the owner of Suffolk Downs in Massachusetts, claimed that Wonderland's powerful lobbyist, Clarence King, wrote the legislation legalizing racing in Massachusetts. This is in stark contrast to other states, where horse racing appears to have had the upper hand in state legislatures during the 1930s. See Bill Veeck, with Ed Linn, *Thirty Tons a Day* (New York: Viking, 1972), 105.

93. Editorial Views, "State Lottery Schemes," *Springfield Republican*, March 18, 1934. See also "Ely Warns Party It Faces Disaster," *New York Times*, August 8, 1935.

94. "State Lottery Schemes." See also F. Lauriston Bullard, "Dog Racing Issue Upsets Bay State," *New York Times*, March 10, 1935.

95. "Ely Warns Party It Faces Disaster."

96. In his 1972 memoir Bill Veeck argues that in Massachusetts greyhound-racing interests wielded more political power than horse-racing proponents. He writes, "In describing Clarence King as the most influential lobbyist in the state I was probably doing him an injustice. He is, in all probability, the most powerful single figure in the legislature." See *Thirty Tons a Day*, 110–115. Sociologist Christopher Wetzel is currently examining the dynamics between greyhound- and horse-racing interests in Massachusetts. He is analyzing voting patterns (for and against dog racing) from 1935 to the present on a county-by-county basis. See http://sites.google.com/site/wetzelcd/research-projects and http://manyeyes/alphaworks.ibm.com/manyeyes/visualizations/voting-outcomes (accessed July 22, 2010). Looking at these data, he noted,

> Over the last eighty years there was always less support for greyhound racing than thoroughbred racing. As such, it becomes interesting to think about Bill Veeck's assertion . . . that greyhound racing was long the dominant force in the state legislature. . . . To the extent that there is support, it tends to be concentrated in a few areas—the south shore, the north shore, and along the Connecticut border. . . . The south and north shore areas were also hosts to the few tracks in Massachusetts that endured over the years. . . . Even in these areas, support for greyhound racing seems to have waned over the years but has persisted the most in the track host communities (Boston/Revere, Taunton).

Christopher Wetzel, e-mail correspondence with the author, September 30, 2010.

97. "Propose Straw Vote on Betting Program," *New York Times*, June 26, 1934.

98. "Betting Bill Passed in Mass.," *New York Times*, June 30, 1934.

99. This strategy prevented the circulation of initiative petitions to suspend operation of the law until a binding statewide referendum. In order to adopt the law each county in the state needed only to pass a referendum.

100. The declared "revival of racing" included both horse and dog racing. F. Lauriston Bullard, "Revival of Racing on in New England," *New York Times*, July 29, 1934.

101. F. Lauriston Bullard, "Gambling Outlook Upsets Bay State," *New York Times*, November 25, 1934. This is one of several articles that discuss voter regret over the introduction of legalized gambling. Bullard writes, "It might seem that the people, having legalized the gambling system, are now somewhat astonished over what they have done."

102. "Dog Race Foes Get Setback," *Boston Herald*, April 27, 1935.

103. "State House to Be Crowded Next Tuesday," *Boston Herald*, March 2, 1935.

104. Religious leaders also opposed a lottery bill that was in the legislature. See also "Cardinal Urges Lottery Defeat," *Boston Globe*, May 21, 1935.

105. Bullard, "Dog Racing Issue Upsets Bay State."

106. "Hanson Board Bars Dog Track," *Boston Herald*, February 7, 1939; "Racing Beaten at Plebiscite by 64 Votes," *Boston Herald*, February 8, 1939; "Marshfield Gives Dog Racing Cold Reception," *Boston Globe*, January 27, 1939; "Methuen Citizens Vote Disapproval of Permit Granted for Dog Racing," *Boston Herald*, March 25, 1937. All newspaper clippings are from the Boston University Mugar Memorial Library *Boston Herald* newspaper morgue.

107. "Dog-Race License Sought by Braves," *New York Times*, December 8, 1934.

108. "'Curleyism' Doomed, Republican Asserts," *New York Times*, August 25, 1935.

109. Curley was notorious for firing qualified people and hiring his own cronies. See Jack Beatty, *The Rascal King: The Life and Times of James Michael Curley* (Cambridge, MA: Da Capo, 2000), 357.

110. "'Curleyism' Doomed, Republican Asserts."

111. First Annual Report of the State Racing Commission, 1935, Boston Public Library, Boston, MA (hereafter BPL).

112. Massachusetts State Racing Commission letter and report to the governor, October 26, 1939, Leverett Saltonstall Papers, Massachusetts Historical Society, Boston, MA (hereafter MHS).

113. The Yankee Network was an American radio network.

114. Racing Commission, Letters from Saltonstall, ca. 1940, Saltonstall Papers, MHS. Some items in this collection give evidence of the state patronage system; for instance, the governor lists appointees in the state racing commission, their salaries, and, most important, the political connection that helped them obtain the position.

115. Revere Dog Racing Association, letter to governor from Leland C. Bickford, May 17, 1940, Saltonstall Papers, MHS.

116. Revere Dog Racing Association, letter to governor from Leland C. Bickford, April 1, 1941, Saltonstall Papers, MHS. See also "Dog Racing under New Direction—Merger Brings About Set Up Approved by Governor," *Boston Post*, March 24, 1940.

117. Revere Dog Racing Association, letter to governor from Leland C. Bickford, March 24, 1940, Saltonstall Papers, MHS.

118. Ibid., March 26, 1940.

119. U.S. Department of the Treasury, Internal Revenue Service, *75 Years of IRS Criminal Investigation History, 1919–1994* (Washington, DC, 1996). Hayes was found guilty of income tax evasion.

120. Letter to governor from "A Business Man," Boston, April 25, 1940, BPL.

121. "Sent Family Away after Getting Threats," *Fitchburg Sentinel*, February 25, 1937.

122. Dan Parker, "Massachusetts Goes to the Dogs," *Saturday Evening Post*, January 6, 1940, 16–17, 56–60.

123. Ibid.

124. "Racket-Ruled Dog Racing." This charge was repeated by Virgil Peterson during the Kefauver hearings for the U.S. Senate Special Committee to Investigate Organized Crime in Interstate Commerce in Washington, DC. Peterson was the operating director of the Chicago Crime Commission and also represented the American Municipal Association. He testified on July 6, 1950, that O'Hare was the manager of the Hawthorne Kennel Club and the "czar of dog racing for the Capone syndicate." http://onewal.com/kef/kefp.html (accessed April 23, 2012).

125. *Daily Record*, November 8, 1939, MBKC scrapbooks, FIU.

126. O'Hare's associates, including James J. Egan, a Boston promoter, helped establish dog racing in Massachusetts, which, aside from Florida, continued to be one of the most popular venues for dog racing in the country. Regarding the Madison Kennel Club, see John Kobler, *Capone: The Life and World of Al Capone* (New York: Putnam, 1971), 237; for the Lawndale Kennel Club, see Frank Spiering, *The Man Who Got Capone* (New York: Bobbs-Merrill, 1976), 82; for the Miami Beach Kennel Club, see Parker, "Massachusetts Goes to the Dogs," 16–17.

127. Kobler, *Capone*, 237–238.

128. Parker, "Massachusetts Goes to the Dogs," 56.

129. "All Dog Track Applications Are Rejected," *Christian Science Monitor*, February 12, 1940.

130. Parker, "Massachusetts Goes to the Dogs," 17.

131. "There Goes Swifty Cry Rings in Legislative Halls," January 3, 1940, MBKC scrapbooks, FIU.

132. See "Atlantic City Prepares Attractions for Greatest Influx of Visitors in History," *Washington Post*, June 17, 1934. In a later article, the *Washington Post* wrote that after ten weeks of dog racing, Convention Hall would be "transformed into the world's largest church, a football field, and then an ice rink for ice hockey." See "Huge Sanctuary Built on Stage for Convention," *Washington Post*, September 16, 1934.

133. The four tracks in operation usually handled about $70,000–$80,000 a night, combined; one facility in Pennsauken reached $80,000 on its own during one night of betting in 1934. See "New Jersey Finds Dog Races Illegal" and "Jersey Seeks Way to Revive Racing," *New York Times*, August 12, 1934.

134. "Dog Race Curbs Ordered," *New York Times*, August 8, 1934.

135. "Racing Board Assailed," *New York Times*, August 23, 1934.

136. Gimbel v. Peabody et al., 114 N.J.L. 574, 178 A. 62. See also "New Jersey Finds Dog Races Illegal," *New York Times*, September 30, 1934; "Dog Racing Banned in Jersey by Court," *New York Times*, April 9, 1935.

137. Dog Racing and Gambling Vertical Files, Hollywood Dog Racing Program, December 26, 1972, Lied Library, University of Nevada Las Vegas.

138. Mutt derbies were held for children and their pet dogs at the dog tracks. All dogs were allowed to race and no gambling took place. Proceeds from admission tickets were donated to charity. Lycan writes, "It is hard to imagine a better publicity gimmick than the Mutt Derby." The idea was to encourage children to become patrons of the dog track when they were old enough to gamble. Gilbert L. Lycan and Walter C. Grady, *Inside Racing: Sports and Politics* (New York: Pageant, 1961), 71. For a story about such an event at the Rocky Mountain Kennel Club in Colorado, see Lorraine Marshall Burgess, "It's Derby Day for Dogs," *American Home*, August 1954.

139. Lycan and Grady, *Inside Racing*, 70–76.

CHAPTER FOUR: HALCYON DAYS AND FLORIDA NIGHTS

1. "Dog Racing Is Newest Sport at Miami Resort," *Charleston Daily Mail*, April 6, 1922.

2. *Sports Slants #8*, narrated by Ted Husing, Warner Brothers Vitaphone (ca. 1932), DVD transfer, Wisconsin Historical Society, Madison, WI.

3. According to pari-mutuel statistics published by the Florida State Racing Commission, which, obviously, only documented legal transactions at the tracks, the handle for thoroughbred horse racing in Miami during the 1930s was consistently higher than it was for greyhound racing. For example, the 1934 report shows that the total attendance figures for the 1933–1934 dog-racing season was 1,026,397, whereas the total for horse racing was 564,627. Likewise, the 1940 report indicates that during the 1938–1939 season, total attendance figures were 1,408,141 for dog racing and 830,701 for

horse racing. It is important to note, however, that there are usually more dog-racing days than horse-racing days. See Annual Reports of Florida State Racing Commission, microfilm reels 6364 & 6365, State Archives of Florida, Tallahassee, FL (hereafter SAF).

4. "The Sports Parade," in *Tropical Sportland*, Warner Brothers Vitaphone, 1943.

5. *Sports Slants #8.*

6. The leisure industry and sporting scene first emerged during Reconstruction, when escalating numbers of sportsmen, tourists, and invalids seeking a healthier environment turned to Florida's salubrious climate. Larry Youngs, "The Sporting Set Winters in Florida: Fertile Ground for the Leisure Revolution, 1870–1930," *Florida Historical Quarterly* 84, no. 1 (2005): 59. See also Paul S. George, "Passage to the New Eden: Tourism in Miami from Flagler through Everest G. Sewell," *Florida Historical Quarterly* 59, no. 4 (April 1981). Americans benefiting from industrialization placed an increasing value on personal recreation. Outdoor sports such as swimming, tennis, and golf all gained popularity as did equestrian sports favored by the upper class. In his popular travel guide George Barbour asserted as early as 1882 that Florida was "rapidly becoming a northern colony" (quoted in George, "Passage to the New Eden," 441). The tourist industry aggressively marketed new ideas about how and where to spend the winter months: a 1905 issue of *Harper's Weekly Advertiser* declared that "outdoor recreation is becoming a necessary part of our modern life." See also "Where Shall I Spend the Winter?" *Harper's Weekly Advertiser* 49 (January 7, 1905): 28.

7. Flagler, who struck it rich at Standard Oil as John D. Rockefeller's business partner, first visited Florida in 1878 and devoted himself to railroad expansion in the state soon thereafter. By 1894 the Florida East Coast Railway reached as far as Palm Beach, and in 1896 the line extended to Biscayne Bay in Miami. Flagler focused much of his attention on the development of Miami Beach, located on an island only a short distance from Miami. But most critically, he established much of the infrastructure necessary to transform Miami into a growing resort for tourists. Flagler dredged a portion of the bay in Miami and built the dock that established the city as the primary terminal for his own FEC Steamship Company. Incorporated in 1896, with a population of only around 3,000, Miami was soon accessible by both railroad and steamboat. Miami Beach was still a peninsula in 1920, but it became part of an island in 1925 with the digging of the Haulover Cut. See Abraham D. Lavender, *Miami Beach in 1920: The Making of a Winter Resort* (Charleston, SC: Arcadia Publishing, 2002), 26.

8. Motor access to Miami continued to improve. In 1915 the Dixie Highway Association finally settled on an eastern and western route that would link the northern and southern portions of the United States. The northern terminus was Sault Sainte Marie, Michigan, but Chicago, Detroit, Indianapolis, and Cincinnati were other key northern cities included on the route. The road ended in Miami. For more information on the Dixie Highway and the development of southern highways, see Howard Lawrence Preston, *Dirt Roads to Dixie: Accessibility and Modernization in the South, 1885–1935* (Knoxville: University of Tennessee Press, 1991), and Nick Wynne, *Tin Can Tourists in Florida, 1900–1970* (Charleston, SC: Arcadia Press, 1999). Abraham D. Lavender notes that "after investing heavily in Miami Beach real estate, Fisher crafted a compromise so that the Dixie Highway was not a single route linking the north and south, but

rather a complicated network of roads that went through ten states. It would connect both the northeastern United States and the Great Lakes region to Miami Beach." See Lavender, *Miami Beach in 1920*, 18. The Dixie Highway was not completed until the late 1920s.

9. Miami Beach was well positioned for rapid expansion once the city was incorporated in 1917. Fisher is best known for his creation of the Indianapolis Motor Speedway. Arriving by way of the new Dixie Highway that he himself had helped promote, Fisher soon bought more than 200 acres of swampland in South Florida. Many observers believed this to be a foolish purchase, and it did in fact take his laborers a full ten years to dredge out the muck and clear the mangrove swamp. Access to Miami Beach across Biscayne Bay was yet another challenge. An incomplete wooden bridge to the island formerly derided as "John Collins' Folly" was, by 1913, expanded and rechristened Collins Bridge. Earlier, in 1896, Collins had inspected the area and by 1907 began to plant avocado groves. He, along with a business partner, established the Miami Beach Improvement Company in 1912. *Mr. Miami Beach*, written, produced, and directed by Mark J. Davis (Arlington, VA: PBS Home Video, 1998).

10. By 1920 new, stylish bathing suits for women were becoming increasingly popular. Beach clubs, casinos, and baths, including the Miami Beach Club, Hardie's Casino, and Smith's Casino, were attracting large crowds. See Lavender, *Miami Beach in 1920*, 116–119.

11. At the peak of the city's initial development in 1925, Miami Beach recorded more than $17,700,000 in new construction, with 7,500 real estate licenses issued. In the same year the city boasted fifty-six hotels, eight hundred private homes, eight bathing spots, three golf courses, and three polo fields.

12. Lots on Lincoln Road that had sold for $7,000 in June 1925 exploded in value, commanding a price of $35,000 a mere six weeks later. Nearby Miami grew in size from 13 to 43 square miles in 1925. Paul S. George, "Brokers, Binders, and Builders: Greater Miami's Boom of the Mid–1920s," *Florida Historical Quarterly* 65, no. 1 (July 1986): 41.

13. "Paradise Regained," *Fortune* 13, no. 1, January 1936.

14. Gregory W. Bush, "'Playground of the USA': Miami and the Promotion of Spectacle," *Pacific Historical Review* 68, no. 2 (May 1999): 153–172.

15. Ibid., 154–155.

16. Muriel Murrell, *Miami: A Backward Glance* (Sarasota, FL: Pineapple Press, 2003), 150.

17. Herbert L. Hiller, *Highway A1A: Florida at the Edge* (Gainesville: University Press of Florida, 2005), 252.

18. To support the growing tourism industry the local population grew from about 600 to about 15,000 within five years.

19. Joann Biondi, *Miami Beach Memories: A Nostalgic Chronicle of Days Gone By* (Guilford, CT: Insiders' Guide / Globe Pequot Press, 2007), 17.

20. Paul C. Hartwell, *The Road from Emeryville* (San Diego: California Research Publishing, 1980), 35.

21. Ann Armbruster, *Life and Times of Miami Beach* (New York: Knopf, 1995), 69. Steven Gaines makes a similar observation and points to the Miami Beach Kennel

Club. See Steven Gaines, *Fool's Paradise: Players, Poseurs, and the Culture of Excess in South Beach* (New York: Three Rivers, 2009), 42.

22. Ron Chepesiuk, *Gangsters of Miami: True Tales of Mobsters, Gamblers, Hitmen, Con Men and Gang Bangers from the Magic City* (Fort Lee, NJ: Barricade, 2010). See also http://www.americanmafia.com/Feature_Articles_447.html (accessed August 20, 2010).

23. In 1939 state senator Ernest R. Graham of Miami accused horse and dog track operators of bribing public officials, hiring gangsters, employing legislators, and influencing legislation. See James Hodges, "Senate Will Begin Investigation on Monday on Charges of Corruption in Florida Racing," *Miami Herald*, April 23, 1939. There were also accusations that racetracks were connected to the underworld via bookmakers. See James Hodges, "Dade County to Lose Racetrack Control Wedge, Bookies Hit," *Miami Herald*, April 27, 1939. All clippings from Miami Beach Kennel Club 1939 scrapbook #2, MBKC scrapbooks, FIU.

24. T. H. Weigall, *Boom in Paradise* (New York: Alfred H. King, 1932), quoted in Hiller, *Highway A1A*, 8.

25. Armbruster, *Life and Times of Miami Beach*, 121. Some forms of gambling were legalized in Florida in 1931.

26. For more on the effort to legalize pari-mutuel wagering in Florida, see Susan Hamburger, "The Controversy over Pari-Mutuel Betting in Florida, 1925–1931," available at http://www.la84foundation.org/SportsLibrary/NASSH_Proceedings/NP1994/NP1994g.pdf (accessed August 3, 2012). See also Susan Hamburger, "'And They're Off!': The Development of the Horse Racing Industry in Florida" (PhD diss., Florida State University, 1994).

27. First Annual Report of Florida State Racing Commission, 1932, microfilm reels 6364 & 6365, SAF.

28. Some permits may have been submitted even when applicants lacked funds to open a racing facility. In such cases, the purpose of filing for a license may have been to thwart operations of other tracks. Competition for the entertainment dollar fueled such actions. Minutes of the Florida State Racing Commission, July 11, 1932, Minute Book #1, Series 1271, Carton 1, File 1, 44, SAF.

29. The St. Petersburg Kennel Club (later known as Derby Lane) was the occasional exception. The 1932 report lists total attendance figures as follows: West Flagler Kennel Club, 213,222; Biscayne Kennel Club, 191,970; Miami Beach Kennel Club, 167,943; Clay County Kennel Club, 129,806; St. Petersburg Kennel Club, 94,866; Palm Beach Kennel Club, 72,585. The 1934 report lists total attendance figures as follows: Miami Beach Kennel Club, 209,283; West Flagler Amusement Company, 193,418; Biscayne Kennel Club, 187,028; St. Petersburg Kennel Club, 157,936; West Florida Racing and Athletic Association, 110,582; Clay County Kennel Club, 104,557; Palm Beach Kennel Club, 63,593. By 1939 the numbers had improved for the St. Petersburg Kennel Club. The 1939 report lists the following tracks with the highest attendance figures: West Flagler Kennel Club, 247,562; Miami Beach Kennel Club, 240,961; St. Petersburg Kennel Club, 199,352; Broward County Kennel Club, 142,346; Jacksonville Kennel Club, 133,262. See Annual Reports of Florida State Racing Commission, microfilm reels 6364 & 6365, SAF.

30. Fourth Annual Report of Florida State Racing Commission, 1935, 5, microfilm reels 6364 & 6365, SAF.

31. In 1935 West Flagler sued, charging that Miami Beach was benefiting from favoritism and receiving preferred racing dates. See "Florida Racing Group under High Court Fire," *Miami Herald,* December 2, 1935.

32. Minutes of the Florida State Racing Commission, Tallahassee, Florida, November 28, 1942, Minute Book #8, Series 1271, Carton 1, File 8, SAF.

33. See Richard Schickel, *Intimate Strangers: The Culture of Celebrity in America* (Garden City, NY: Doubleday, 1985).

34. Tex Rickard and Commodore G. R. K. Carter built the Miami Beach Kennel Club in 1927. When Rickard died unexpectedly, Carter turned the kennel club over to a holding company. Marty Hyland and Frank Anderson then assumed control over operations. Hyland had opened a number of dog tracks around the country. In 1928 Hyland sold his interests to Edward J. O'Hare, who became president. Anderson served as general manager. See Harry Sullivan, "Miami Beach Kennel Club," *Greyhound Racing Record,* January 31, 1947.

35. For an account of the Weaver family and the history of Derby Lane, see David Samuels, "Going to the Dogs," *Harper's Magazine* 298, no. 1785 (February 1999): 52–63.

36. Raymond Arsenault, *St. Petersburg and the Florida Dream* (Gainesville: University of Florida Press, 1996), 204. St. Petersburg was known as the "Sunshine City."

37. Vertical Files, Derby Lane Archives, St. Petersburg, FL.

38. Mary Margaret Winning, personal interview with author, February 21, 2009.

39. Night lighting was first used in Derby Lane in 1925 and in 1924 at the Miami Kennel Club in Hialeah, Florida.

40. Arsenault, *St. Petersburg,* 204. See also Stuart B. McIver, *Touched by the Sun,* vol. 3, *Florida Chronicles* (Sarasota, FL: Pineapple Press, 2001), 8.

41. For a complete list of baseball spring training venues in Florida, see appendix D in Kevin McCarthy, *Baseball in Florida* (Sarasota, FL: Pineapple Press, 1996).

42. Hearst Metrotone News Vol. 4, no. 240, "Canine Tracks Do Rushing Business," UCLA Film and Television Archive. Weekly returns from the dog track are not reported to the racing commission, but year-end data from 1932–1933 indicate that all eight Florida dog tracks' pari-mutuel sales were $8,568,869, while pari-mutuel sales from the Gables Racing Association and the Miami Jockey Club were $10,578,069.

43. Armbruster, *Life and Times of Miami Beach,* 92.

44. Advertisement, "Southern Fashions at Miami Beach," *Miami Herald,* February 23, 1936, Miami Beach Kennel Club 1936 Scrapbook, MBKC scrapbooks, FIU.

45. See, for example, "Philadelphians Join J. E. Widener at Races," *Miami Herald,* January 24, 1936, and "Pennsylvanians Attend Races at Hialeah Park," *Miami Herald,* February 12, 1936.

46. Jack Dempsey may have also been involved with the establishment of the track. Groundbreaking for the Miami Beach Kennel Club took place on October 20, 1928.

47. Advertisement, "More Than a Racetrack . . . A Florida Showplace!" January 9, 1937, Miami Beach Kennel Club 1937 Scrapbook, MBKC scrapbooks, FIU.

48. Miami Beach Kennel Club 1937 Scrapbook, MBKC scrapbooks, FIU.

49. Similar ads were used for other Miami attractions. For more on women and advertising, see Roland Marchand, *Advertising the American Dream: Making Way for Modernity, 1920–1940* (Berkeley: University of California Press, 1985), 181–185. Marchand notes that advertising in fashion featured elongated women's bodies, linking them with elite culture and high social status.

50. "The Year Rounder," February 15, 1936, Miami Beach Kennel Club 1936 Scrapbook, MBKC scrapbooks, FIU.

51. "Rusty's Glimpse of Fashion Road," *Miami Daily News,* February 16, 1936.

52. Gaines, *Fool's Paradise,* 11.

53. Ibid. See also "Paradise Regained"(n. 13).

54. "Hialeah," *Miami Herald,* January 29, 1936.

55. Derby Lane Vertical Files, Derby Lane Archives, St. Petersburg, Florida. Live music performed by a band was an important component of the races, but it was eventually replaced by recorded music.

56. "Canine Tracks Do Racing Business," Hearst Metronome News, vol. 4, no. 240, 1933, UCLA Film and Television Archive, and Script, "Never Catch the Rabbit," Sports with Bill Corum, no. 6, Production #64306, April 27, 1936, Library of Congress, Washington, DC.

57. "Dog Days Are Good for Greigs' 60-year-old Racing Business," *Orlando Sentinel,* March 29, 1987.

58. Craig Dulch, "Puppy Love," *Palm Beach Post,* August 1, 1993. He does not specify which humane society (local or national) objected to the practice.

59. "Monkey Jockeys Barred in New Jersey Dog Racing," *New York Times,* August 9, 1934. Monkey jockey races took place in a number of states in addition to Florida and New Jersey, including California, Ohio, Oklahoma, Kansas, and Texas. See http://newspaperarchive.com (accessed June 19, 2012).

60. Ibid. The New Jersey State Racing Commission ruled against the use of monkey jockeys on August 8, 1934.

61. Minutes of the Florida State Racing Commission, Tallahassee, Florida, February 16, 1937, Minute Book #5, Series 1271, Carton 1, File 5, SAF. The denial in 1933 can be found in minute book #2, from the February 27, 1933, meeting.

62. Footage from this film has not been located.

63. Newspaper clippings, Miami Beach Kennel Club 1937 Scrapbook, MBKC scrapbooks, FIU.

64. One example of a reported greyhound attack was cited by Joan Dillon in a magazine feature about greyhound adoption. She notes that a Revere, Massachusetts, newspaper in January 1983 reprinted an article from August 20, 1935, titled "Saugus Man Saves Girl Attacked by Six Greyhounds." An eighteen-year-old girl apparently fell "screaming" into a pack of unmuzzled greyhounds that were being walked by an eighteen-year-old boy. The person who extracted her from the melee was praised for his bravery; the reporter noted that "it took plenty of nerve and courage to battle the savage animals." The purpose of this 1983 article was to prevent "vicious dogs" from being boarded in Revere, the site of the Wonderland Greyhound Track. See Joan Dillon, "Early Adoption Pioneers," *Celebrating Greyhounds* (Spring 2000).

65. A film shot at the Miami Beach Kennel Club was also advertised. The footage

was described in newspaper promotions as motion picture scenes of "Florida's Finest Dog Track" as "photographed" by Floyd Traynham and "described" by Graham McNamee for Universal Newsreel. Footage from this film has not been located.

66. Some early footage shows greyhounds starting races in harnesses rather than in starting boxes.

67. Script, "Never Catch the Rabbit," Sports with Bill Corum.

68. Newspaper clippings, Miami Beach Kennel Club 1937 Scrapbook, MBKC scrapbooks, FIU.

69. Minutes of the Florida State Racing Commission, Tallahassee, Florida, October 3, 1936, Minute Book #5, Series 1271, Carton 1, File 5, 5, SAF.

70. "Miami Dog Tracks Steal Play from Rivals for Night Trade," *New York Press,* February 16, 1939, Miami Beach Kennel Club 1939 Scrapbook no. 2, MBKC scrapbooks, FIU.

71. July 11, 1932, meeting, Minute Book #1, Series 1271, Carton 1, File Folder 1, page 46, SAF.

72. "Greetings to Organized Labor of Miami," *Miami News,* August 29, 1935, Miami Beach Kennel Club 1936 Scrapbook, MBKC scrapbooks, FIU. The advertisement was printed again on September 3, 1936.

73. Advertisement, Miami Beach Kennel Club 1936 Scrapbook, MBKC scrapbooks, FIU.

74. Advertisement, *Miami Herald,* February 6, 1936.

75. "O. P. Smith, Founder of Greyhound Racing in America," January 18, 1939, Miami Beach Kennel Club 1939 Scrapbook no. 2, MBKC scrapbooks, FIU.

76. "Rusty's Glimpse of Fashion Road," *Miami Daily News,* February 16, 1936. The use of Rusty (or other rabbits) as a promotional mascot for greyhound tracks continued well into the 1970s.

77. Photograph of Jayne Mansfield, Robert T. Stevenson, Bennie Sorenson, and Ronnie Behrens at Miami Beach, GHF.

78. Hoye Perry, personal interview with author, February 20, 2009. The lead-outs march the racing dogs from the track's kennel area (specifically referred to as the lock-out kennel, or colloquially, the Jenny Pit, Jinny Pit, or Ginny Pit) to the starting boxes. Until 1929, greyhound owners were responsible for leading out their own dogs. Jack Fisher changed the standard and decided that tracks should hire local boys (usually athletes themselves) for this task. See Jack Fisher Pioneer File, GHF.

79. See Rosalind Gill, *Gender and the Media* (Malden, MA: Polity, 2007); Anthony Cortese, *Provocateur: Images of Women and Minorities in Advertising* (Lanham, MD: Rowman & Littlefield, 2008); Jib Fowles, *Advertising and Popular Culture* (Thousand Oaks, CA: Sage, 1996); Diane Barthel, *Putting on Appearances: Gender and Advertising* (Philadelphia: Temple University Press, 1988).

80. Greyhound racing consciously promoted this link. See the cover of *Greyhound Racing Record,* February 15, 1952.

81. M. J. Deegan, "Dog Jewelry," *Sociological Origins* 3, no. 1 (2003): 50.

82. The muzzle is cited as being used to protect greyhounds from fighting one another.

83. Don Hausler, "The Emeryville Dog Race Track," *Journal of the Emeryville Historical Society* 5, no. 4 (Winter/Spring 1995): 1. Reprinted from "Grayhounds [sic] Chew Up a Mechanical Rabbit at Races," *Oakland Tribune,* May 30, 1920.

84. "New Sport of Kings," January 10, 1943, Miami Beach Kennel Club 1943 Scrapbook, MBKC scrapbooks, FIU.

85. Twelfth Annual Report of Florida State Racing Commission, 1943, microfilm reels 6364 & 6365, SAF.

86. See Hartwell, *Road from Emeryville*, 136, for a photograph of racing fans in a horse-drawn vehicle en route to the Biscayne track.

87. Gary Mormino, *Land of Sunshine, State of Dreams: A Social History of Modern Florida* (Tallahassee: University Press of Florida, 2008), 95.

88. Ibid., 77.

89. Ibid., 93.

90. Biondi, *Miami Beach Memories*, 86.

91. T. J. English, *Havana Nocturne: How the Mob Owned Cuba . . . and Then Lost It to the Revolution* (New York: William Morrow, 2008).

92. Mormino, *Land of Sunshine*, 92. See also English, *Havana Nocturne*; Robert M. Burtt, "Racing in Cuba," *Greyhound Racing Record*, September 29, 1950; "The Cuba Inaugural Issue," *Greyhound Racing Record*, July 20, 1951; *Greyhound Racing Record*, May 18, 1951; and Bob Burtt, "The Sad Story of Cuba," *Greyhound Racing Record*, November 25, 1955.

93. Craig Randle, whose uncle Gene Randle raced his greyhounds in Cuba, believed that Meyer Lansky was "unofficially" the owner of the Havana track. He notes that in the early years, the mobsters were the only ones with enough money to build the dog tracks. Craig Randle, personal interview with author, November 22, 2011.

94. "New Regime at Daytona," *Greyhound Racing Record*, July 28, 1950. See also "Sixty Minutes, Jerry Collins," *Turnout*, May 1983, GHF.

95. Ed McLaughlin, "Governor Warren Visits Havana Track," *Greyhound Racing Record*, March 14, 1952; Robert Burtt, "Collins Buys Havana Track," *Greyhound Racing Record*, October 12, 1951; see also Jerry Collins Pioneer File, GHF.

96. 53rd Annual Report of the Division of Pari-Mutuel Wagering, 1984, State Library of Florida.

97. "Tampa Spends $75,000 in Improvements," *Greyhound Racing Record*, November 19, 1954.

98. Wes Singletary, personal interview with author, December 23, 2008.

99. Ibid. See also McCarthy, *Baseball in Florida*.

100. Michael Y. Sokolove, *Hustle: The Myth, Life, and Lies of Pete Rose* (New York: Simon & Schuster, 1990).

101. D. Parker, "Sumptuous New Dog Track Awaits Yanks," ca. 1950, MBKC scrapbooks, FIU. The name of the newspaper is not listed.

102. Tim Hollis, *Florida's Miracle Strip* (Jackson: University Press of Mississippi, 2004), 23. The critic that Hollis specifically references is Tom Fiedler, who discussed the area's development in 1993.

103. Ibid., 23. Hollis writes that "less sophisticated" southerners visited this area.

104. Terry McGrath, "Ebro's Nursery Makes Fans Happy," *Greyhound Racing Record*, September 27, 1957.

105. Andrew Hurley, *Diners, Bowling Alleys, and Trailer Parks: Chasing the Dream in Postwar Consumer Culture* (New York: Basic Books, 2002), 282.

106. Mormino, *Land of Sunshine*, 95.

107. Ibid., 96.

108. See Tim Hollis, *Dixie before Disney: 100 Years of Roadside Fun* (Jackson: University Press of Mississippi, 1999); Tim Hollis, *Glass Bottom Boats and Mermaid Tails: Florida's Tourist Springs* (Mechanicsburg, PA: Stackpole, 2006); Chester H. Liebs, *Mainstream to Miracle Mile: American Roadside Architecture* (Boston: Little, Brown, 1985); Peter Genovese, *Roadside Florida: The Definitive Guide to the Kingdom of Kitsch* (Mechanicsburg, PA: Stackpole, 2006); Larry Roberts, *Florida's Golden Age of Souvenirs, 1890–1930* (Tallahassee: University Press of Florida, 2001); Ken Breslauer, *Roadside Paradise: The Golden Age of Florida's Tourist Attractions, 1929–1971* (St. Petersburg: RetroFlorida, 2000); Margot Ammidown, "Edens, Underworlds, and Shrines: Florida's Small Tourist Attractions," *Journal of Decorative and Propaganda Arts* 23 (1998): 238–259.

109. Author's personal collection.

110. "There's Nothing Like a Night at the Greyhound Races!" *Greyhound Racing Record*, December 31, 1960.

111. Palm Beach Kennel Club Advertisement, *Greyhound Racing Record*, January 5, 1963.

112. "So Magnificent! Greyhound Racing," *Greyhound Racing Record*, November 5, 1960.

113. Greyhound Hall of Fame File 01-0327, GHF.

114. Newspaper clippings, MBKC scrapbooks, FIU.

115. Cover, *Greyhound Racing Record*, September 7, 1951; Cover, "Watch for Me at Cloverleaf," *Greyhound Racing Record*, September 24, 1960.

116. Photograph of Leontine M'Gregor, Miami Beach Kennel Club 1939 Scrapbook no. 2, MBKC scrapbooks, FIU.

117. Photograph of bunny waitresses from the Playboy Club, *Greyhound Racing Record*, December 8, 1962. For a photograph of Phoenix "bathing beauties" with muzzled racing greyhounds, see cover, "Phoenix' Phairest," *Greyhound Racing Record*, September 19, 1964.

118. See *Greyhound Racing Record*, December 3, 1960. The artist's name is Weakley.

119. As worded by Karal Ann Marling, in *Debutante: Rites and Regalia of America Debdom* (Lawrence: University Press of Kansas, 2004), 146.

120. "The Greyhounds Visit 'Miss New Hampshire,'" *Greyhound Racing Record*, April 22, 1955. The longtime master of ceremonies for the Miss America competition, Bert Parks, was even pictured at the Palm Beach Kennel Club in 1967. But the influence of Miss America on cultural customs was sometimes more diffused. The competition (and others like it) opened the door even wider for the use of increasingly bare female bodies in advertising, a technique seen in dog-racing promotions for decades.

121. "Prettiest Girl Anywhere," *Greyhound Racing Record*, March 14, 1959; "Two Photogenic Winners," *Greyhound Racing Record*, April 6, 1963.

122. J. M. Browne, "Miss U.S.A. Presents Trophy at Miami Beach Kennel Club," *Greyhound Racing Record*, April 6, 1963.

123. In addition to holding a special stakes race, Derby Lane sponsored a float for the Festival of States, which culminated in a parade (and ball) where a "Miss Sungoddess" was crowned.

124. Photograph Collections, GHF.

125. Ibid. See also Don Beninati, "Tucson Gaining National Renown," *Greyhound Racing Record*, April 10, 1953. He writes, "Visiting major league players and stars from motion picture units on location in Tucson have added to the glamour of the turnouts."

126. Biondi, *Miami Beach Memories*, 86.

127. Mormino, *Land of Sunshine*, 92.

128. Cover, *Greyhound Racing Record*, March 28, 1959.

129. Marshall Parsons, "A Studio by Day, a Dog Plant by Night," *Greyhound Racing Record*, November 22, 1958.

130. *Dark Hazard*, directed by Alfred E. Green (1934), DVD transfer at UCLA Film and Television Archive, and *Hole in the Head*, directed by Frank Capra (1959; Beverly Hills, CA: MGM Home Entertainment, 2001), DVD.

131. Gary Guccione, e-mail message to author, July 19, 2012. The cost of televised sports had already escalated considerably by the mid–1960s. For more detailed information on the history of televised sports (and the rise of popularity of television in general), see the website of the Museum of Broadcast Communications, http://www.museum.tv/ (accessed August 3, 2012).

132. Will Cummings, e-mail message to author, July 20, 2012.

133. Mormino, *Land of Sunshine*, 45.

134. This was one of the few notable exceptions where successful national exposure was achieved in greyhound racing. *Greyhound Racing Record* boasted that "millions" watched the race throughout the country. See *Greyhound Racing Record*, January 28, 1955.

135. "Greyhounds Seen by 45 Million Viewers on *Steve Allen Show*," *Greyhound Racing Record*, October 19, 1956.

136. Ibid.

137. Greyhound-racing promotions linking airlines, stewardesses, and dog racing were popular during the postwar period.

138. Lady Greyhound was bred in Clay Center, Kansas, by Roy Lee and registered with the National Coursing Association in Abilene.

139. The bus line was founded in 1914, but the Greyhound Corporation was incorporated in 1929. See Margaret Walsh, "Pedigree Marketing and Its Value," *History Today* 56, no. 5 (May 2006): 36–39.

140. Lady Greyhound Files, GHF. See also "There Is a Real 'Greyhound,'" *Kansas City Star*, June 17, 1962. All of the greyhound publications erroneously state that the award was from the "American Humane Society" but in all likelihood it was given by the American Humane Association.

141. The Kefauver Campaign (the Senate Special Committee to Investigate Crime in Interstate Commerce) conducted hearings in more than two dozen cities. See Pat Frank and Luther Voltz, "Florida's Struggle with the Hoodlums," *Collier's*, March 25, 1950.

142. Second Interim Report of the Special Committee to Investigate Organized Crime in Interstate Commerce, Senate, 82nd Cong., 1st sess., 1951, 2, 10. The S & G Syndicate headquartered in Miami Beach was long believed to be under the sway of Capone's operatives.

143. The tracks were in Miami, Tampa, and Jacksonville. Final Report of the Special Committee to Investigate Organized Crime in Interstate Commerce, Senate, 82nd Cong., 1st sess., 1951, 73–74. Long after the Kefauver hearings, Johnston continued to be closely watched by the FBI. In 1961 the Bureau interviewed Johnston and reported that "Johnston has been considered for many years to be close to several Chicago hoodlums. He operated as a close associate of Eddy O-Hare [sic] who later was murdered in gang land fashion in Chicago." The report also indicated that Eddie O'Hare operated dog tracks in Chicago and Florida, and "trusted Johnston and named him beneficiary of some of his business interests." However, Johnston maintained during the interview that "I am not and have never been connected in any way with the Capone mob or any other mob" and that O'Hare was also not associated with the "rackets." Federal Bureau of Investigation, Chicago Special Agent in Charge Report to FBI Director, July 13, 1961, FOIA request no. 1189785-000.

144. Robert M. Burtt, "The Sport of Queens Comes of Age," *Greyhound Racing Record*, August 28, 1953.

145. Ernest Havemann, "Lean, Swift and Big in Florida," *Sports Illustrated*, February 6, 1961.

146. Gaming analyst Will Cummings notes that the thoroughbred Triple Crown television ratings are not particularly high, with the Breeders' Cup held in the fall second in popularity. In previous years, ABC's *Wide World of Sports* carried a few horse-racing events, such as the Travers Stakes at Saratoga, but few others appeared on television. At present, two dedicated horse-racing networks (TVG and HRN) broadcast essentially paid programming in pursuit of the gambling dollar. Will Cummings, e-mail correspondence with author, August 4, 2012.

147. Eugene Martin Christiansen observed that thoroughbred horse racing could have been a mass spectator sport, but industry leaders failed to work with the broadcast networks after World War II when they became increasingly powerful. He states that the horse-racing industry "dropped the ball," and as a result, horse racing is generally "invisible" to the American public, and rarely on television. In contrast to greyhound racing, he believes that horse racing did, at one point, have a chance to popularize the sport through national television exposure. He argues that the dog-racing industry was never really a candidate for regular national publicity through the leading networks. Eugene Martin Christiansen, telephone interview with author, December 2, 2009.

148. Ibid.

149. Jai alai is a Basque sport that involves human athletes in a ball-based game played in an open-walled space called a fronton. The sport is similar to handball but the players (usually two to four) use a long, curved wicker basket that is strapped to the wrist to handle the ball.

150. "Dog Racing: Down the Straight at 40 m.p.h.," *Time*, January 22, 1965.

151. The periodical was initially published by GOBA and later taken over by AG-TOA. Concerning horse versus dog racing, see "Horsemen Behind Sinister Campaign," *Greyhound Racing Record*, April 22, 1955. See also Robert M. Burtt, "Defeat in New Hampshire," *Greyhound Racing Record*, May 13, 1955. Other headlines in the same publication reflected a cutthroat relationship between the two: "Multnomah [Oregon] Fights Enemies of Racing" from August 15, 1952, and "Racing Killed in Maryland,"

from May 29, 1953, are but two examples. "Horsemen behind Sinister Campaign" refers to problems in New Hampshire.

152. Federal Bureau of Investigation Internal Report, New York, Field Office File 92–8518, FOIA request no. 1116343-000.

153. Tom Butler, "They Come to Sit and Watch," April 2, 1964, MBKC scrapbooks, FIU.

154. Mormino, *Land of Sunshine*, 112.

155. Michael Kammen, *American Culture, American Tastes: Social Change and the Twentieth Century* (New York: Basic Books, 1999).

156. Journalists reported this as well. In 1960 there were 3.5 million fans visiting the dog tracks and 2 million going to the horse tracks. See Ernest Havemann, "Lean, Swift and Big in Florida."

CHAPTER FIVE: DOGGONE MAD

1. Wayne Strong, personal interview with author, April 24, 2009.

2. The term "utilitarian" in this context does not relate to "utilitarianism," the animal rights philosophy often associated with Peter Singer.

3. Larry Tye, "Ethics of Racing are Part of Larger Animal Question," *Boston Globe*, November 11, 1992.

4. Keith Thomas, *Man and the Natural World: A History of the Modern Sensibility* (New York: Pantheon, 1983), 129.

5. Matthew Scully, however, makes a convincing argument in that with dominion comes the obligation to act kindly and morally. See Matthew Scully, *Dominion: The Power of Man, the Suffering of Animals, and the Call to Mercy* (New York: St. Martin's, 2002).

6. Animal protectionists often argue that the ethos of compassion toward animals first emerged during the Axial Age, but the sentiment was not embraced as a social movement until the late nineteenth century. See Bernard Unti, "The Kindness to Animals Ethic in Human History," public lecture, HSUS Animal Care Expo, May 14, 2010, Nashville, TN.

7. For more on Victorian compassion for pets, see James Turner, *Reckoning with the Beast: Animals, Pain, and Humanity in the Victorian Mind* (Baltimore, MD: Johns Hopkins University Press, 1980). For an exploration of this new pattern in pet ownership, see Michael Schaffer, *One Nation under Dog: Adventures in the New World of Prozac-Popping Puppies, Dog-Park Politics, and Organic Pet Food* (New York: Henry Holt, 2009), and Joel Stein, "It's a Dog's Life," *Time* (May 19, 2003): 60–62.

8. Dr. Jill Hopfenbeck, telephone interview with author, October 21, 2011. She notes, "That was the start of a long road that led me to become an anti-racing activist. I really did not become an 'activist' until I joined in on the GREY2K ballot initiative in 1999. It was by no means an instantaneous event."

9. Louise Weaver, personal interview with author, February 20, 2009.

10. Susan Netboy, "Greyhound Advocacy and Adoption—A History," *Celebrating Greyhounds* 13, no. 1 (Spring 2008): 27. She writes, "For 70 years the dog racing industry had enjoyed a free ride completely beyond the scrutiny of the mainstream press." During an interview with the author in late 2011, Netboy acknowledged that she was

specifically thinking about the humane movement and could see how gambling and other issues may have been under scrutiny by the press.

11. "They Run for Their Lives," *Argosy* 346, no. 5 (May 1958): 27–29, 95. The industry countered the premise in this article that greyhounds were too vicious to be adopted. In all likelihood, an article printed in the *Greyhound Racing Record* on June 21, 1958, addressed this claim from *Argosy*, noting that "the recent 'sensational-type' story in a national magazine that greyhounds must be killed when unable to race because they are too vicious to become pets has drawn a flood of protest from followers of the sport." See "Demand Is Great for Greyhound Pets," *Greyhound Racing Record,* June 21, 1958.

12. "They Run for Their Lives," 27.

13. Minutes of the National Coursing Association in Abilene, KS, April 23, 1958, printed in the *Greyhound Stud Book,* vol. 51 (Abilene, KS: National Greyhound Association, 1958), 247, GHF. The damaging and "detrimental" article was discussed during the spring business meeting. President Leland Fisher stated that he was willing to put $1,000 down to prove that greyhounds did make good pets. He was willing to give this money to the *Argosy* editor's favorite charity if this were not the case.

14. See Louis Pegram, "It Seems to Me . . . ," *Greyhound Racing Record,* January 23, 1953. He uses the term "put away" to describe the dogs that are not usable. See also Louis Pegram, "Overproduction of Greyhounds?" *Greyhound Racing Record,* May 23, 1952; and Bob Burtt, "Pups Are No Good," *Greyhound Racing Record,* March 7, 1952.

15. See Louis Pegram, "It Seems to Me," 17. He notes, "For some five years now we have been producing far more greyhounds in this country than can be used to profitable advantage. It is hardly logical we should import dogs of still unproven ability when each year several thousand greyhounds must be put away."

16. Burtt, "Pups Are No Good."

17. Don Cuddy notes, "Farmers have chosen to breed quantitatively rather than qualitatively, and are less selective than they might be. The country is polluted with inferior greyhounds." See "Sixty Minutes, Don Cuddy," *Turnout,* January 1981. Tom Walsh states that by 1940, there was already an oversupply of greyhounds in the United States. See Tom Walsh, "The History of Greyhound Racing, Part III: The War Years," *Racing Greyhounds* 5, no. 6 (June 1992). See also Louis Pegram, "It Seems to Me."

18. See Donald Higbee, "Are Small Kennels Doomed?" Part I, *Greyhound Racing Record,* August 25, 1950, and Higbee, "Are Small Kennels Doomed?" Part II, *Greyhound Racing Record,* September 1, 1950. Paradoxically, in more recent years, it was sometimes the small-scale "backyard breeders" who put the industry's reputation in jeopardy.

19. Gary Guccione, e-mail message to author, August 21, 2009.

20. According to Craig Randle, Ned Randle oversaw a "state-of-the-art" greyhound farm in Wichita, Kansas. During the early 1950s he had almost 100 dogs at his farm. Then, beginning in the late 1950s or early 1960s, he moved to Ocala, Florida, and managed a farm with around 80 to 100 dogs until the late 1970s. Craig Randle, telephone interview with author, February 23, 2010.

21. Ibid.

22. "Sixty Minutes, Dick Andrews," *Turnout,* April 1981, GHF.

23. Gary Guccione, e-mail message to author, July 29, 2009.

24. "Sixty Minutes, Tom Sellman," *Turnout*, November 1980, GHF.

25. Connick and others formed the Greyhound Trainers Guild in 1967. He was elected as president and still held this office in 1983. See Clarence Connick Pioneer File, GHF.

26. "Sixty Minutes, Clarence Connick," *Turnout*, February 1982, GHF. Craig Randle, personal interview with author, November 22, 2011.

27. Breeder Campbell Strange stated, "I have no desire to raise 200–300 pups a year as some breeders do. I think it's a joke the way these people operate, employing two full-time workers plus a helper or two to raise that many pups. Not only do these pups have very little chance to succeed under such conditions, but such an operation has a very negative impact on the entire industry, in terms of too many pups being raised for so few openings at the track." See "Sixty Minutes, Campbell Strange," *Turnout*, April 1984, GHF.

28. One dogman, Jim Frey, referred to some kennel helpers as "doggy-sitters." See Jim Frey, interview by Gwynn Thayer, tape recording, July 2, 2011, Baylor University Institute for Oral History, Waco, TX.

29. Artificial insemination in racing greyhounds was improved by Richard and Sharyn Conole, who were inducted as pioneers into the Greyhound Hall of Fame in 2009. See Gary Guccione, Greyhound Hall of Fame 2009 Spring Program, April 23, 2009, Abilene, KS.

30. Ibid.

31. Gary Guccione, e-mail message to author, April 13, 2012.

32. Gary Guccione, telephone interview with author, June 4, 2008.

33. The conception rate grew from about 65 percent to 90 percent. Guccione, GHF Spring 2009 Program.

34. Craig Randle, telephone interview with author, February 23, 2010.

35. Previously, racing kennels were usually limited to around twenty-five dogs. For example, at the Loveland dog track in Colorado, for many years, the management mandated an "eighteen-dog active list" with six extra greyhounds available if necessary. The dogmen could not replace these twenty-four dogs and were not permitted to run dogs that were not on the list. As a result, greyhounds on the racing list were kept in training for longer periods and they "didn't have throwaway dogs." Craig Randle, telephone interview with author, February 23, 2010. See also Bob Burtt, "The Racing Kennel: Part V, Replacements," *Greyhound Racing Record*, February 22, 1952.

36. http://www.gra-america.org/the_sport/at_the_track/gradingsystem.html (accessed August 18, 2010).

37. William L. Drozd, director of racing at Tucson Park, quoted in "A Race for Their Life," *Tucson Citizen*, ca. 1992, Luce newspaper clippings from the HSUS greyhound racing files, HSUS, Gaithersburg, MD. "Grading off" is the terminology employed to describe this phenomenon.

38. For a discussion on pet overpopulation, see Bernard Unti, *Protecting All Animals: A Fifty-Year History of the Humane Society of the United States* (Washington, DC: Humane Society Press, 2004), 85–113; and Lawrence Finsen and Susan Finsen, *The Animal Rights Movement in America, from Compassion to Respect* (New York: Twayne, 1994), 149–152.

39. Unti, *Protecting All Animals,* 91.

40. James A. Grisanzio, "Going to the Dogs," *Animals* (March/April 1993): 21. Carter Luke provided specific data on the number of greyhounds taken to MSPCA shelters for disposal. In 1985, 2,500 were euthanized at a fee of $3 per dog. When the fee rose to $12, fewer dogs were taken in. In 1991, 427 were euthanized at MSPCA facilities.

41. Carter Luke, personal interview with author, September 17, 2008.

42. Larry Tye, "Greyhounds Pay the Price of Racing's Shadow World," *Boston Globe,* November 8, 1992.

43. Some critics have compared greyhound farms to puppy mills, a link that is somewhat misleading. Robert Baker, who has extensive experience investigating puppy mills, noted,

> While I have visited over 1,000 wholesale commercial breeders raising dogs for pet stores, I have only been to a few greyhound breeding farms. The most dramatic difference I noticed at the greyhound breeding farms, from the puppy mills, is the large exercise runs available for the greyhounds. At puppy mills, the dogs are confined in tiny cages, many inside barns, never seeing the light of day. In general, I believe that the greyhound breeding farms are much more humane than the puppy mills.

See Robert Baker, e-mail message to author, May 20, 2010.

44. See http://www.greyhounds.org/gpl/contents/proof.html (accessed August 18, 2010); David Wilkening, "End of the Track," *The Weekly* 3, no. 10 (December 9, 1992); Larry Tye, "A Wrenching Duty for Veterinarians," *Boston Globe,* November 11, 1992; "Greyhound Racing Exposé," *Inside Edition,* CBS, aired March 5, 1990, DVD.

45. See *Greyhounds: Running for Their Lives,* created by Eitan Weinreich, National Geographic Explorer, aired January 3, 1993, DVD, and Larry Tye, "Greyhounds Pay the Price of Racing's Shadow World," *Boston Globe,* November 8, 1992.

46. Ibid., 27.

47. Pusey does note that greyhounds raised from puppyhood make fine pets, but those that grew up racing do not. "They Run for Their Lives," 28.

48. "Promoters Step Up Efforts to Legalize Dog Racing," *News of the Humane Society of the United States,* Spring 1975.

49. "Society Cites Dog Racing Cruelties," *News of the Humane Society of the United States,* Summer 1973. Many dogmen, such as Bill Maloney, who was interviewed for *Inside Edition,* also state that they would rather have them euthanized than see them in an abusive home later on. Maloney stated, "I may be cruel in some people's eyes, but I would much rather the dog be put to sleep. I know he's not being abused. Not because the people are cruel, they kill them with kindness. They feed them everything on earth. They walk them around; they're all fifty pounds overweight." "Greyhound Racing Exposé," *Inside Edition.*

50. Leslie Wootten, *The Wootten Machine: A Greyhound Racing Memoir* (MFA thesis, Arizona State University, 2001), 12.

51. See Larry Tye, "Adoption a Better Option," *Boston Globe,* November 8, 1992. Craig Randle notes that some dogmen believe that the racing industry should "never have gotten in bed with the pet people." Randle, who works in Abilene, Kansas, as an

inspector for the greyhound industry, strongly disagrees with this point of view and believes that greyhound adoption was a positive change. Craig Randle, personal interview with author, November 22, 2011.

52. Joan Dillon dates the beginning of the adoption movement to 1982 in St. Petersburg, Florida, through the efforts of Ron Walsek and REGAP. See Joan Dillon, "Early Adoption Pioneers," *Celebrating Greyhounds* (Spring 2000): 10–12.

53. Susan Netboy, "Greyhound Advocacy and Adoption—A History," *Celebrating Greyhounds* 13, no. 1 (Spring 2008): 25–28.

54. www.agcouncil.com (accessed 4/13/2009). See also Larry G. Dee, "Racing Greyhound Adoption Programs," in *Canine Sports Medicine and Surgery,* edited by Mark S. Bloomberg, Jon F. Dee, Robert A. Taylor (Philadelphia: W. B. Saunders, 1998). The AGC was a joint effort of NGA and AGTOA.

55. The AGC partnered with the ASPCA (then under the leadership of Roger Caras) in 1992 and gave them grant money ($100,000) to help with ex-racing greyhound adoptions. This caused a great deal of controversy within animal protection circles.

56. Raymond Madden, "Imagining the Greyhound: 'Racing' and 'Rescue' Narratives in a Human and Dog Relationship," *Continuum: Journal of Media & Cultural Studies* 24, no. 4 (August 2010): 503–515.

57. Dan Geringer, "They Are Making a Killing," *Sports Illustrated,* August 11, 1975.

58. "Society Cites Dog Racing Cruelties," *News of the Humane Society of the United States,* Summer 1973.

59. Unti, *Protecting All Animals,* 21.

60. "Greyhound Racing Exposé with Geraldo Rivera," *20/20,* aired June 6, 1978, DVD.

61. F. B. "Happy" Stutz discussed the term "unnecessary cruelty" in an essay likely published in the *Greyhound Racing Record.* Citing the examples of fishing, hunting, and horse racing (specifically, when horses are subject to beatings in the home stretch of a race in order to make them run faster), he argues that "some form of cruelty is necessary if we are to continue our American way of life." See F. B. "Happy" Stutz File, GHF.

62. Advertisement, "For Sale Live Jackrabbits," *Greyhound Racing Record,* December 18, 1953, 14. The cost was $2.50 per jackrabbit. The rabbits were from Waco, Texas.

63. S.3180 (95th Cong., 2nd sess., June 7, 1978) proposed to prohibit the use of live lures in dog racing, training, and other purposes. The bill was an amendment to the AWA and was sponsored by Senator Birch Bayh (Indiana) along with three cosponsors. The bill was read twice and referred to the Senate Committee on Environment and Public Works. No further record of the bill exists. See also: http://www.thomas.gov (accessed September 29, 2010).

64. Wayne Strong, personal interview with author, April 24, 2009.

65. "Greyhound Racing Industry Wounded by HSUS Onslaught," *Humane Society News* 23, no. 4 (Fall 1978). See also "Footnotes," *Greyhound Review,* July 1978.

66. Tim Kidd, "Coursing: Sport or Mindless Slaughter," *Wichita Eagle-Beacon,* October 30, 1977. See also "Sixty Minutes, Murray Kemp," *Turnout,* August 1982, GHF.

67. Minutes of the National Coursing Association in Abilene, KS, October 1973, printed in the *Greyhound Stud Book,* vol. 73 (Abilene, KS: National Greyhound Association, 1973), 69, GHF.

68. Only 10 percent of the membership responded to the poll. See Minutes of the National Coursing Association, in Abilene, KS, October 1976, printed in the *Greyhound Stud Book*, vol. 76 (Abilene, KS: National Greyhound Association, 1976): 52–53, GHF. The *Wichita-Eagle Beacon* also cited a 1977 NGA poll in which 1,250 members responded: 55 percent were for continuing coursing and 45 percent opposed it. See Tim Kidd, "Coursing: Sport or Mindless Slaughter."

69. Minutes of the National Coursing Association, in Abilene, KS, October 1976, printed in the *Greyhound Stud Book*, vol. 76 (Abilene, KS: National Greyhound Association, 1976), 54–55.

70. Gail Eisnitz had been working for the HSUS since 1983, although not as an undercover agent. In retrospect, Eisnitz acknowledged that she liked the dogmen she met, but she made the beginner's error of becoming too close to the group that she was investigating. Gail Eisnitz, telephone interview with author, April 28, 2009.

71. F.S. 828.122, the Animal Fighting Act, forbids the baiting of animals. Violation of this act is a felony.

72. "Florida's Felony Greyhound Raid," *Humane Society News*, Spring 1989. Several years later, he was quoted in a *Life* magazine article, stating, "I'm not what you'd call a pet lover. . . . You don't see me kissing my dogs and making like a fool with 'em. I'm the master, and they're the servant." See Jack McClintock, "Run or Die," *Life*, June 1991.

73. After a decade of efforts led by the HSUS, in 1986 Florida made it a felony offense to use live lures for the baiting of animals. The punishment is up to five years in prison and/or a $5,000 fine. Those attending the "fighting or baiting of animals" are guilty of a misdemeanor and can face up to one year in prison and/or a $1,000 fine. In 1986 the Florida Game and Fresh Water Fish Commission adopted regulations prohibiting the importation of jackrabbits. The Florida Division of Pari-Mutuel Wagering (Florida's state racing commission) also does not permit the use of live lures. See "Florida's Felony Greyhound Raid," 28–30. In 1969 the Florida state legislature authorized changing the name of the Florida State Racing Commission to the Florida Divison of Pari-Mutuel Wagering as part of a reorganization of the executive branch of the state government. The new entity became part of the Division of the Department of Business Regulation.

74. "Men Acquitted of Using Live Rabbits to Train Greyhounds," *Ft. Pierce Tribune*, November 17, 1989. The men actively sought to have their licenses reinstated.

75. "Florida's Felony Greyhound Raid."

76. Grisanzio, "Going to the Dogs," 18–23.

77. Interview with anonymous veterinarian, 2011. The name of the interviewee has been withheld by mutual agreement for purposes of confidentiality.

78. See Colin Jerolmack, "Tracing the Profile of Animal Rights Supporters: A Preliminary Investigation," *Society and Animals Journal of Human-Animal Studies* 11, no. 3 (2003): 245–263. Jerolmack uses the term "affluent" (251). Rachel Einwohner argues that the movement is "overwhelmingly female and middle class." See Rachel Einwohner, "Gender, Class, and Social Movement Outcomes," *Gender and Society* 13, no. 1 (February 1999): 56. She further argues that "race, class, and gender structure protest activity and shape social movement outcomes" (73). Lyle Munro posits that women have

often enjoyed a high standing within animal advocacy circles and notes that "women's ideas are the prevailing ideas of the movement." See Lyle Munro, "Caring About Blood, Flesh, and Pain: Women's Standing in the Animal Protection Movement," *Society and Animals Journal of Human-Animal Studies* 9, no. 1 (2001): 43–61. Wesley Jamison and William Lunch argue that active followers of the animal rights movement tend to be urban, well-educated females. See Wesley Jamison and William Lunch, "Rights of Animals, Perceptions of Science, and Political Activism: Profile of American Animal Rights Activists," *Science, Technology, and Human Values* 17, no. 4 (Autumn 1992): 438–458. Corwin R. Kruse and Kenneth Shapiro both note the predominance of women in the movement as well. See Corwin R. Kruse, "Gender, Views of Nature, and Support for Animal Rights," *Society and Animals Journal of Human-Animal Studies* 7, no. 3 (1999): 179–198, and Kenneth Shapiro, "The Caring Sleuth: Portrait of an Animal Rights Activist," *Society and Animals Journal of Human-Animal Studies* 2, no. 2 (1994): 145–165.

79. Robert Dawson, personal interview with author, February 14, 2010.

80. Organizations such as PETA advocate for the discontinuation of all uses of animals for human benefit. Dog racing is not one of its major campaigns, although PETA does frequently speak out against horse racing. The ASPCA speaks out against both dog and horse racing, but again, the organization is involved in a wide array of animal protection initiatives and does not focus exclusively on anti-racing campaigns. Their website indicates, "The ASPCA is opposed to any and all cruel practices involved in the sport of racing dogs, horses or other animals, whether for speed, endurance or both, on tracks, trails or snow. The ASPCA deplores the use of drugs and other substances that either mask pain or enhance performance at the expense of health and well-being." See http://www.aspca.org/About-Us/policy-positions/racing (accessed August 3, 2012).

81. http://www.humanesociety.org/issues/greyhound_racing/ (accessed June 28, 2012). In a recent blog post HSUS president Wayne Pacelle wrote of the serious problems in the industry, stating that "it's now time for us to add the reform of horse racing to our positive agenda for horses, since the industry has failed to regulate itself after a series of high-profile incidents, such as breakdowns by Barbaro and Eight Belles." http://hsus.typepad.com/wayne/2012/03/horse-racing.html (accessed June 28, 2012). It appears, however, that in earlier years the HSUS embraced a more aggressive approach toward horse racing. See "Keeping Racing Out of Your State," *Humane Society News* (Fall 1983). The author details the "extensive cruelty" involved in both sports and proposes that both forms of racing come to an end. In contrast to this earlier stance, HSUS may now be attempting to find a more centrist approach, one that challenges society without pressing an agenda too rapidly.

82. William Nack, telephone interview with author, May 24, 2012. Nack recalled a discussion in which he aired his concerns about the welfare of thoroughbred horses: the individual in the horse-racing business with whom he spoke finally acknowledged to him, with some frustration, that thoroughbred horses were "livestock." Nack also noted that when he covered horse racing in the 1960s and 1970s, people seemed to have more affection for dogs than for horses. HSUS president Wayne Pacelle notes that unlike dogs, horses sometimes occupy a "gray area" between pets and livestock. While some horses serve as companion animals, many others are used as work animals or

even slaughtered for food. Wayne Pacelle, telephone interview with author, August 13, 2012.

83. Dr. Andrew Rowan of the HSUS has raised this point. Bernard Unti, e-mail correspondence with author, August 4, 2012.

84. Wayne Pacelle, telephone interview with author, August 13, 2012.

85. See Gary Guccione, "Horsin' Around," *Greyhound Review*, May 2010. The Jockey Club established the Equine Injury Database in 2008 and released a preliminary analysis for a one-year period (2008–2009) showing 2.04 fatal injuries in thoroughbreds per 1,000 starts. From 2008 to 2010, the rate was 2.00. See http://jockeyclub.com/initiatives.asp (accessed June 30, 2012). In contrast, a fourteen-year study (1993–2007) indicated a range of 1.0 to 2.66 injuries per 1,000 greyhound starts, with "almost all of these injuries being treatable," as quoted in Linda Blythe, James R. Gannon, A. Morrie Craig, and Desmond P. Fegan, *Care of the Racing and Retired Greyhound* (Abilene, KS: American Greyhound Council, 2007). See also Walt Bogdanich, Joe Drape, Dara L. Miles, and Griffin Palmer, "Mangled Horses, Mangled Jockeys," *New York Times*, March 25, 2012. Certain tracks, such as those in New Mexico, Arizona, and California, were shown by the *New York Times* to be especially dangerous for thoroughbred racers. See also "How the Times Analyzed Data on Horse Injuries," *New York Times*, March 24, 2012, http://www.nytimes.com/2012/03/25/us/how-the-times-analyzed-data-on -horse-injuries.html (accessed March 26, 2012).

86. Interview with Dr. Larry Bramlage in Ron Mitchell, ed., *Best of Talkin' Horses: Chat with Some of Thoroughbred Racing's Most Prominent Personalities* (Lexington, KY: Eclipse, 2008), 154.

87. Dr. Jon Dee, telephone interview with author, October 11, 2011. Flyball is a physically demanding, competitive sport for canines involving racing, hurdling, jumping, and ball catching. See http://www.flyball.org/index.html (accessed August 10, 2012). Rules are set by the North American Flyball Association (NAFA).

88. Mark Beech, "An Uncertain Environment," *Sports Illustrated*, August 11, 2003.

89. The photograph, taken by Jakob Schiller, was printed on March 25, 2012, in the *New York Times*.

90. Horse-racing leaders are in fact looking at the greyhound-racing industry as they seek to find solutions (such as adoption and retirement farms) for horses that can no longer race. See Tom LaMarra, "Dogs' Plight a Lesson for Horse Racing?" posted on BloodHorse.com on April 22, 2009, http://www.bloodhorse.com/horse-racing/articles/50339/dogs-plight-a-lesson-for-horse-racing (accessed April 27, 2009). See also Gary Guccione, "Horsin' Around," *Greyhound Review*, May 2010. A thoroughbred horse-racing consultant told Guccione that he advises the horsemen to "look no further than what the Greyhound people have done the last 20 years. We tell them that Greyhound racing has dealt with that issue [post-racing adoption] very effectively."

91. William Nack, telephone interview with author, May 24, 2012. Nack based much of his criticism about the use of corticosteroids on his discussion with veterinarian Dr. Gregory Ferraro. See also William Nack, *My Turf: Horses, Boxers, Blood Money, and the Sporting Life* (Cambridge, MA: Da Capo, 2003); William Nack, *Ruffian: A Race Track Romance* (New York: ESPN Books, 2007); William Nack, *Secretariat* (New York: Hyperion, 2010).

92. Hal Herzog, *Some We Love, Some We Hate, Some We Eat* (New York: Harper Perennial, 2010), 171.

93. In one case it can be shown that some cockfighters were also in fact greyhound racing fans. In a peculiar intersection of these two oft-maligned modes of entertainment, the United Gamefowl Breeders Association (UGBA) was encouraged in 1988 to patronize the Pensacola dog track during their annual meeting; they were given complimentary daily passes to the track. One feature race was even run in recognition of the UGBA group, with their organizational name printed in the program.

94. Michael Atkinson and Kevin Young, "Reservoir Dogs: Greyhound Racing, Mimesis, and Sports Related Violence," *International Review for the Sociology of Sport* 40, no. 3 (2005): 342–343.

95. Editorial cartoon, Steve Benson, "Arizona's Ultimate Blood Sport," *Arizona Republic,* March 17, 1992.

96. Evans has since resigned his position. See *Pedigree Dogs Exposed,* produced by Jemima Harrison, BBC One, August 19, 2008. See also Dr. Jon Dee, telephone interview with author, October 11, 2011.

97. See Phil Maggitti, "See How They Run: A Look at the Hidden Side of Greyhound Racing," *Animals' Agenda* (March 1992): 12–18.

98. "Sixty Minutes, Pat Dalton," *Turnout,* July 1982, GHF.

99. "Sixty Minutes, Herb Koerner," *Turnout,* January 1984, GHF.

100. Greg Farley quoted in Sylvia Phillips, "Running for Their Lives: The Ugly Underside of Greyhound Racing," *Animals' Agenda* (May 1986).

101. "Greyhound Racing Exposé," *Inside Edition.* According to an April 26, 1992, article in *Naples News,* Dan Rather, Joan Rivers, Peter Jennings, Barbara Walters, *20/20,* and *60 Minutes* have all covered greyhound racing in a negative fashion.

102. Peter Michelmore, "Hidden Shame of an American Sport," *Reader's Digest* 141, no. 844 (August 1992), and McClintock, "Run or Die" (n. 72). In 1991 *People* had also printed an article about the abuse.

103. The event was painstakingly followed by the local television news.

104. Joyce Valdez, "Carcasses of 7 More Dogs Found," *Arizona Republic,* January 6, 1992.

105. Editorial cartoon, Steve Benson, "Benson's View," *Arizona Republic,* January 12, 1992.

106. "Vote No to Dog Racing on August 27th," People Against Killing Dogs, Birmingham, Alabama, HSUS Greyhound Files, HSUS. See also Gary Karasik, "You Can Bet Their Life on It," *Miami Herald,* October 21, 1990.

107. Garrison Wells, "Colorado Canines Stride for Their Lives," *Denver Business Journal* 42, no. 40 (June 21, 1991). David Wolf, the director of the National Greyhound Adoption Program in Philadelphia, states in the article that 50,000 to 90,000 greyhounds are killed each year. Grisanzio, "Going to the Dogs," 20.

108. "A Dog's Life," in *Village Voice* "Jockbeat," Luce press clippings from March 10, 1992, HSUS Greyhound Racing Files, HSUS.

109. "Save a Life," in *Ladies' Home Journal* 109 (May 1992), 200; Fred Halliday, "A Race to the Death," *Penthouse* (September 1990): 112–113.

110. Guccione states, "Breeding statistics were published regularly in the old NCA

Coursing News as early as the mid–1960s, so they've never been much of a secret. Prior to that, every registered breeding was listed in the magazine for anyone that cared to count them. Litters were also listed in the publication." Additionally, greyhound litter sizes vary from one to fifteen but have long averaged about 6.5, according to Guccione. As for adoption figures, groups receiving AGC grants are required to turn in adoption data. Many other groups do not. According to Guccione, "a good number of them would have nothing to do with participating, so that made getting an absolute accurate number impossible." Gary Guccione, e-mail message to author, May 27, 2009. In 1993 AGTOA president George Johnson was asked if he knew how many greyhounds were euthanized each year. He responded, "No. It's of no interest to us. When a dog is through racing, he will go back to his owner, to an adoption program, or to some place away from the race track." In this same article Tim Horan, managing editor of the *Greyhound Review*, the official publication of the NGA, was asked for euthanasia data. He responded, "I don't have a clue. We don't keep those records." See Grisanzio, "Going to the Dogs."

111. Regarding these statistics, Guccione states, "The 50,000 figure was always a travesty. I mentioned that to ASPCA President [at the time] Roger Caras, who was known to repeat the number in presentations. He told me that it was 'just a number,' a symbolic number indicating that the total was large." Gary Guccione, e-mail message to author, May 27, 2009.

112. Gary Guccione, e-mail message to author, May 27, 2009. Some of the ambiguity, confusion, and debate may stem from the practice of "culling" litters, where pups that lack the natural physique necessary for racing are killed. (In recent years, with a higher demand for greyhound puppies regardless of their ability to race, it is unlikely that as many pups are killed; instead, they are adopted out at an early age.) Many of these dogs are not registered because culling often takes place well before the pups are tattooed at two months old.

113. "A Race for Their Life," *Tucson Citizen,* ca. 1992, Luce newspaper clippings from the HSUS greyhound racing files, HSUS.

114. GREY2K USA, Fact Sheets, "Commercial Dog Racing in the United States," http://www.grey2kusa.org (accessed August 14, 2010).

115. Greyhound Protection League, "Answers to Commonly Asked Questions," http://www.greyhounds.org (accessed August 14, 2010).

116. Gary Guccione, telephone interview with author, June 4, 2008.

117. Robert Baker, telephone interview with author, April 11, 2009.

118. The dog track was located on Stock Island in Key West, Florida. Its closure by the state in midseason was very unusual. Maggitti, "See How They Run."

119. "Man Says He Killed Thousands of Dogs for $10 Each," *USA Today,* May 22, 2002. See also "State-by-State News Update: Arizona," *Greyhound Network News* 2, no. 1 (Spring 1993). Otis McClellan's greyhound kennel was described by witnesses as a "canine concentration camp."

120. In 1991 Susan Netboy founded this anti-greyhound racing organization based in California. See Greyhound Protection League website, www.greyhounds.org (accessed August 1, 2010).

121. See Susan Lederer, "Political Animals: The Shaping of Biomedical Research

Literature in Twentieth-Century America," *Isis* 83, no. 1 (March 1991): 61–79; John Parascandola, "Physiology, Propaganda, and Pound Animals: Medical Research and Animal Welfare in Mid-Twentieth Century America," *Journal of the History of Medicine and Allied Sciences* 62, no. 3 (July 2007): 277–315; and Unti, *Protecting All Animals*, 63–84.

122. Memo to Dr. W. Ron DeHaven from Neil Williamson, December 4, 1989, Director's Files, AWI, Alexandria, VA.

123. Netboy stated that approximately 3 percent were deeply disturbed by the situation, 15 percent cooperated, and 20 percent were basically compliant. Susan Netboy, telephone interview with author, December 30, 2011.

124. Erik Ingram, "Army Discharges Greyhounds," *San Francisco Chronicle*, October 13, 1989.

125. Class B dealers are only permitted to obtain dogs from certain sources, including other dealers licensed by the USDA, municipal or contract pounds, and individuals who have bred or raised the animals themselves. But contrary to the rules, these dealers often obtain animals from unlicensed individuals known as "bunchers." See "The Case against Random Source Dog and Cat Dealers, Submitted to the House Subcommittee on Livestock, Dairy and Poultry as Testimony in Support of the Pet Safety and Protection Act of 1996," August 1, 1996, Director's Files, AWI, Alexandria, VA. See also letter to FBI Director William S. Sessions from Congresswoman Barbara Boxer, October 24, 1989, Director's Files, AWI, Alexandria, VA.

126. This time Ludlow's license was revoked for ten years and would not be reinstated until he demonstrated compliance with the Animal Welfare Act. See AWA Docket 95–24, USDA Consent Decision and Order, May 19, 1995, Director's Files, AWI, Alexandria, VA.

127. See Mike Winikoff, "Greyhounds Dying in Research Labs: The Real Finish Line" and *The Ark Trust* (Fall 1999): 2–3, http://www.aavs.org (accessed August 24, 2010). See also Patricia Gail Burnham, "Greyhounds in Medical Research," *Sighthound Review* (September/October 1989): 18.

128. Cathy Liss, personal interview with author, April 28, 2008.

129. See Winikoff, "Greyhounds Dying in Research Labs"; Burnham, "Greyhounds in Medical Research"; and "Off Track," produced by Ken Shiffman and Amy Kasarda, *CNN*, aired October 15, 2000.

130. Memorandum from Dr. Sallie B. Cosgrove, March 16, 1989, and memorandum from Dale L. Brooks, January 24, 1989, Director's Files, AWI, Alexandria, VA.

131. Denver, Colorado, television broadcast, KMGH-TV, November 3–5, 1993. Provided to the author by Susan Netboy of the Greyhound Protection League.

132. "Executive Committee Reduces Meet Budget," *Greyhound Review*, November 1989, 52–53.

133. Special Task Force on Horse and Dog Racing, Hearings, 93rd Tennessee General Assembly, 1st sess., December 14, 1983, tape recording, Tennessee State Library and Archives, Nashville, TN.

134. "Tracks Bar Lab Use of Racing Animals," *Arizona Republic*, August 20, 1993. Dan Luciano, manager of the American Greyhound Racing, Inc.'s forty kennel operators in Arizona, stated, "The American Greyhound Track Operators, a professional organization of track owners, opposes the sale or donation of these dogs for research. The

public perception of our industry is tied to greyhounds being treated humanely, and frankly, the public perception of the life of laboratory-research animals is not a good one." See "The Ultimate Finish Line: Greyhounds Sold into Biomedical Research," *Greyhound Network News* 2, no. 3 (Fall 1993).

135. The term 4-D is used in 21 U.S.C. § 644, which regulates "transactions, transportation, or importation of 4-D animals to prevent use as human food." Veterinarian Dr. Brad Fenwick notes that the 4-D meat classification can include cattle with broken legs, eye infections, or cancer. He further notes that the microorganisms that cause disease in cattle are rarely the same ones that cause disease in dogs. Fenwick also points out that raw meat is not fed to pups prior to going to race training. Raw meat is generally used for adult racing greyhounds. Dr. Brad Fenwick, e-mail correspondence with author, June 22, 2012.

136. This phrase was used by former Iowa track veterinarian Arthur Strohbehn. See Nancy Shulins, "Running for Their Lives," *St. Louis Post-Dispatch*, August 8, 1993.

137. One track veterinarian, who asked not to be identified, stated that he would not handle this meat without gloves and that he would prefer to see it irradiated before it was served raw to the racing greyhounds. Interview with track veterinarian, 2009. The name of the interviewee has been withheld by mutual agreement for purposes of confidentiality.

138. Christine Dorchak, e-mail correspondence with author, September 12, 2011.

139. *Ensuring the Welfare of the Racing Greyhound*, American Greyhound Council, National Greyhound Association, Abilene, KS (2003), VHS. In October 1991, however, Gary Guccione had indicated that the industry was funding (through the AGC) studies on the quality of meat and was also working with racing commissions to encourage the use of a higher quality of meat. See Marcia King, "Racing Greyhounds: Bred to Run or Born to Die?" *Dog Fancy* (October 1991): 44. The HSUS specifically rejects the claim that 4-D meat is used in commercial dog food.

140. "Greyhound Breeding, Raising, and Training as Viewed by 25 Prominent Breeders and Trainers," National Greyhound Association, reprinted from the *Greyhound Review*, 1979–1980, GHF. Don Cuddy notes that the "quality is getting worse as the prices escalate" (66). The feed market for racing greyhounds is now dominated by large companies that provide cheap 4-D meat such as Qual-Pet and Monfort. See "4-D Meat: A Deadly Meal," *Greyhound Network News* 2, no. 2 (Summer 1993): 5, and *St. Petersburg Times*, February 5, 1999.

141. Brad Fenwick, DVM, MS, PhD, is board certified in veterinary microbiology. As of 2012 he is a professor in the College of Veterinary Medicine, University of Tennessee. Fenwick has been working with greyhounds and the racing industry for fifteen years, specializing in the areas of general health, infectious diseases, and genetic-based determination of pedigree.

142. One Cornell University study found sulfa drugs, procaine, and salmonella in various samples. See King, "Racing Greyhounds," 45. Dr. Linda Blythe cites a number of studies conducted by Kansas State University that discuss the presence of salmonella in greyhound feces and/or 4-D meat. Linda Blythe, telephone interview with author, September 28, 2011.

143. John R. Kohnke, "Nutrition for the Racing Greyhound," in Bloomberg et al., *Canine Sports Medicine and Surgery*.

144. See Brian Luke, *Brutal: Manhood and the Exploitation of Animals* (Chicago: University of Illinois Press, 2007), and Gail Bederman, *Manliness and Civilization: A Cultural History of Gender and Race in the United States, 1880–1917* (Chicago: University of Chicago Press, 1996).

145. Keith Dillon, interview by Gwynn Thayer, April 22, 2009, tape recording, KSHS.

146. "Greyhound Breeding, Raising, and Training" (n. 140). Horse meat advertisements were frequently posted in industry publications during the 1950s and 1960s.

147. Dan Geringer, "They're Making a Killing," *Sports Illustrated*, August 11, 1975.

148. http://www.agcouncil.com/ (accessed August 18, 2010).

149. Typical violations include overcrowding, dirty yards, and a lack of fresh water. Gary Guccione, telephone interview with author, May 12, 2009.

150. The AGC has also addressed the problem of overbreeding. Gary Guccione, e-mail message to author, May 11, 2009.

151. Guccione said that at first they expelled about six to eight members per year, but it has been "gradually reduced" to about two to three per year. He attributes this to getting rid of the "bad apples" early on. Gary Guccione, telephone interview with author, May 12, 2009.

152. *Soundness Examination of the Racing Greyhound,* James R. Gannon, Sandown Veterinary Clinic, Blackburn, Australia (ca. 1990), VHS, National Greyhound Association, Abilene, KS.

153. *Greyhound Training: At the Farm,* American Greyhound Council and Tel-Air Interests, Inc. (1990), VHS, National Greyhound Association, NGA. See also Herb "Dutch" Koerner, "Raising, Training, and Conditioning the Racing Greyhound," in Bloomberg et al., *Canine Sports Medicine and Surgery.*

154. Kelly has worked with Issue Strategies Group, Inc., Kelly Strategic Counsel, Inc., and MSK Ventures, Inc.

155. The opening date of the Greyhound Hall of Fame in Abilene, KS, was April 21, 1963. See "Hall of Fame a Showcase for Sport," in "NGA, Abilene Celebrate Golden Anniversary," special newspaper edition, 1995, National Greyhound Association, Abilene, KS.

156. *Ensuring the Welfare of the Racing Greyhound.* The production does not address the issue of animal cruelty head on and instead paints the "animal rights" movement as a unified group of individuals who are against greyhound racing because they do not approve of any activity that uses animals for human benefit.

157. This device can be powered by a car battery and is easily built by hand with standard tools. An old coonskin cap, a coyote hide, or even an old bottle with a predator call placed inside is attached to a 300-yard string. With battery power and a handheld device the trainer urges the greyhound to chase after the fake lure, which moves rapidly in a straight line over the ground.

158. Keith Dillon, "Artificial Lures," in Bloomberg et al., *Canine Sports Medicine and Surgery.* Guccione notes that "all the breeders/trainers use basically the same process, starting with drag lures (whether a Jack-A-Lure or something similar) . . . then eventually graduate to the whirlygig, then on to the training track, then finally the official-size track. The main variation may be with the schedule—how soon they start, how long

they go with that particular procedure before graduating to the next." See Gary Guccione, e-mail message to author, July 26, 2010.

159. He made 440 of them and charged $135 a piece. See Larry Tye, "Live Lures Remain an Issue," November 8, 1992, *Boston Globe*, HSUS Greyhound Racing Files, HSUS. Dillon eventually sold the design for the device to the NGA. Keith Dillon, telephone interview with author, August 2, 2008.

160. *The Winning Alternative: Mechanical Lure Training*, produced by the American Greyhound Track Operators Association and the National Greyhound Association (ca. 1989), VHS, National Greyhound Association, Abilene, KS.

161. According to the HSUS, Keith Dillon stated in an NGA seminar held in October 1983 that he still used live lures on 10 percent of his greyhounds. This same article quotes an individual in the greyhound business as stating that about 8 percent of trainers use the Jack-A-Lure exclusively. See "Why We Oppose Greyhound Racing," *Humane Society News* (Winter 1985).

162. The sports medicine conference in Orlando has been taking place since 1988. Gary Guccione, telephone interview with author, May 12, 2009.

163. Blythe et al., *Racing and Retired Greyhound*.

164. Bloomberg et al., *Canine Sports Medicine and Surgery*. See also Keith Dillon, interview, April 22, 2009. In the early years of dog racing, veterinary care tended to be cost-prohibitive, so the dogmen often managed basic veterinary care (such as deworming) on their own. See also "Greyhound Breeding, Raising, and Training as Viewed by 25 Prominent Breeders and Trainers."

165. That being said, the number of greyhounds lost to disease in earlier years was significantly higher.

166. Specifically, the letter states that they had "decided to withdraw from competition for the opportunity to provide public relations services to the AGTOA."

167. Ronald R. Mueller, Senior Vice President/Director of Ketchum Public Relations, to George Johnson, Jr., September 16, 1988, personal papers of Robert Baker, provided to the author by Baker.

168. For instance, it was printed in Maggitti, "See How They Run," 16, and "Industry Admits Its Image Tainted by Live Lures," *Humane Society News*, Spring 1989, 29.

169. Janet Winikoff, "A Losing Bet: Greyhound Racing's Impact on Shelters," *Animal Sheltering*, March/April 2008, 21–29.

170. According to a representative of the Animal Welfare Information Center, the terms "horse and dog races" were excluded in the definition of exhibitor by a decision by the USDA, Animal and Plant Health Inspection Service (APHIS) Office of the General Counsel, based on the fact that racing is gaming or gambling and therefore not exhibiting.

171. Commercial kennels in Colorado and Kansas are subject to state regulations, but greyhounds have been specifically exempted. See Jordan Curnutt, *Animals and the Law: A Sourcebook* (Santa Barbara, CA: ABC-CLIO, 2001), 252.

172. http://www.humanesociety.org/issues/abuse_neglect/ (accessed February 4, 2012).

173. Humane Society of the United States, "Animal Cruelty Laws: Where Does Your State Stand?" http://www.hsus.org/legislation_laws/state_legislations/animal_cruelty _laws_where_does_your_state_stand.html (accessed August 14, 2010).

174. Alabama has county racing commissions rather than a single state racing commission.

175. Texas Administrative Codes, Chapter 319, Sec. 319.203.

176. Curnutt, *Animals and the Law,* 255. Curnutt cites 1991, but records at the State Library of Florida indicate that this new law was enacted on December 16, 1992.

177. See http://www.azracing.gov/statute.htm (accessed August 24, 2010).

178. Curnutt, *Animals and the Law,* 255.

179. Ibid., 257. The Wisconsin mandate is referenced on the state website at http://www.doa.state.wi.us (accessed September 29, 2010); New Hampshire references this on the state website at http://gencourt.state.nh.us/rules/state_agencies/pari800.html (accessed September 29, 2010).

180. "4-D Meat: A Deadly Meal" (n. 140).

181. Curnutt, *Animals and the Law,* 253. Curnutt cites Alabama, Arizona, Connecticut, Idaho, Iowa, Kansas, Massachusetts, New Hampshire, Oregon, Texas, and Wisconsin as states that banned the use of live lures beginning in the 1980s. Other states have general anticruelty laws that cover the use of live lures.

182. http://thomas.loc.gov/cgi-bin/thomas (accessed September 29, 2010). The earlier example refers to H.R. 4631, 96th Cong., when Representative Glenn Anderson of California and fifty-seven cosponsors wanted to amend the AWA by prohibiting the use of live lures and coursing. The bill was referred to the House Committee on Agriculture. See http://thomas.loc.gov (accessed September 29, 2010).

183. *Greyhound USA,* November 1986, 19.

184. Robert Baker, telephone interview with author, April 11, 2009.

185. Wayne Strong, personal interview with author, April 24, 2009.

186. Curnutt, *Animals and the Law,* 256.

187. Fenwick uses the word "bogus." Brad Fenwick, telephone interview with author, September 24, 2011.

188. Christine Dorchak, e-mail correspondence with author, September 12, 2011.

189. Gary Guccione, telephone interview with author, June 4, 2009; Robert Baker, telephone interview with author, April 11, 2009.

190. Christine Dorchak, e-mail correspondence with author, September 12, 2011.

191. The dogmen point out that their work demands caring for the dogs "24/7" and keeping a busy schedule 365 days of the year. One greyhound adoption pioneer with extensive knowledge of greyhound farms (and raising cattle) noted that "greyhound work is harder than being a rancher." Teddy Palmer, August 12, 2012, telephone interview with author.

192. Wayne Strong, personal interview with author, April 24, 2009.

193. It is likely that much of this language was put forth by AGC's PR firm, which was instructed to be proactive rather than reactive in fighting "animal rights" extremists. By labeling anti-racing advocates as part of the radical animal rights contingent, the industry attempted to delegitimize their position.

194. *Ensuring the Welfare of the Racing Greyhound.*

195. "A Losing Game," *Tucson Citizen,* February 27–28, 1992, HSUS Greyhound Racing Files, HSUS. This statement was made by Treva Slote, a Maricopa County Animal Control advisory board member.

196. Critics allege, for example, that GREY2K USA often uses footage from Spain (which uses racing galgos rather than greyhounds) to demonstrate the cruelty of dog racing. The Tijuana Hot Plate refers to a technique of electrocution. This story was reported on *Prime Sports—Press Box* in the early 1990s. Footage provided to the author by Susan Netboy.

197. King, "Racing Greyhounds."

198. www.grey2kusa.org/who/index.html (accessed June 16, 2012).

199. Dr. Gail Golab, director of the AVMA animal welfare division, e-mail correspondence with author, August 13, 2012. The AVMA's policy on animals used in entertainment, in shows, and for exhibition (approved by the AVMA executive board in June 2012) reads as follows:

> The AVMA supports the humane and ethical use of animals in spectator events, shows, exhibitions, motion pictures, and television in accord with existing federal, state, and local animal protection laws. Examples of such events include, but are not limited to, animal exhibitions, racing events, field trials, polo, rodeo, and the use of animals for any audiovisual media. The AVMA encourages all organizations involved with animals in such events to develop, implement, and abide by guidelines or standards that ensure humane treatment, respect for the animal, appropriate veterinary care, and veterinary oversight of the animals before, during, and after use. External third-party review and assurance of animal welfare standards is recommended. Animal welfare guidelines or standards must prohibit the intentional injury or death of animals as a part of training or for any entertainment purposes. Similarly, activities that substantially compromise animal welfare should be prohibited. Such activities include handling and contact by the general public of animals that are ill, of unknown health status, or that are of a vulnerable age such as neonatal to juvenile non-domestic *Carnivora* and non-human primates. Similarly, the AVMA condemns the fraudulent use of drugs and non-nutritive agents, as well as procedures intended to alter the performance, conformation, appearance, or other functions of animals in competition. The AVMA urges its members to report such activities to the appropriate authorities.

CHAPTER SIX: THE FALL

1. Stock car racing, which originated in North Carolina and appealed to working-class audiences from the Piedmont South, established a comfortable niche in Daytona Beach and later drew fans from around the country. See Daniel S. Pierce, *Real NASCAR: White Lightening, Red Clay, and Big Bill France* (Chapel Hill: University of North Carolina Press, 2010).

2. Gambling consultant Eugene Martin Christiansen of Christiansen Capital Advisers, LLC, has concluded that the eventual demise of greyhound racing in American culture is as inevitable as was the replacement of ocean liners by jet airplanes as the new standard means of international travel. Animal advocates would perhaps be surprised to hear this industry analyst only grudgingly acknowledge the impact of various anti-racing campaigns, noting that their efforts may have had a "limited effect." Eugene Martin Christiansen, telephone interview with author, December 2, 2009. During a

1986 AGTOA conference in Naples, Florida, Christiansen pointed out that from 1974 to 1984 greyhound racing's share of the U.S. gambling market decreased from 3.8 percent to 2.6 percent, even though the overall takeout had increased from $195.6 million to $479 million. He also noted that wagering on greyhounds had failed to keep up with growth in personal income during the same period, reporting instead a 20 percent decline in total dollars wagered. Christiansen concluded that despite the increase in number of racing days between 1974 and 1984 (from 3,842 to 8,661) and the corresponding growth of the aggregate greyhound racing handle, the sport had lost significant ground relative to the overall commercial gambling market. Eugene Martin Christiansen, "The U.S. Gambling Marketplace: Is Greyhound Racing Getting Its Share?" 36th AGTOA National Conference, 1986, Lied Library, University of Nevada, Las Vegas, NV.

3. According to the 2008 annual report issued by the Kansas Racing and Gaming Commission, the live handle at the Woodlands track peaked in 2003 and gradually declined; similarly, the live handle at the Wichita facility peaked in 2001 and steadily declined. See http://krgc.ks.gov/images/stories/pdf/Annual_reports/2008_annual_report_final.pdf (accessed June 30, 2012).

4. *Wisconsin Promotional Video on Greyhound Racing* (Discover Wisconsin Productions, Inc., 1988), VHS. See also Advertisement, "Cleaner than a Hound's Tooth!" *Turnout*, February 1984, GHF. Gary Guccione notes that this claim was first made by a *Sports Illustrated* reporter in the 1960s or 1970s. Gary Guccione, e-mail correspondence with author, January 14, 2013.

5. Will Cummings, e-mail message to author, December 2, 2009. Cummings noted that dog racing was doing better than horse racing during the 1980s. Eugene Martin Christiansen observed that the capital required to open a dog track was still significantly less than that required for a horse-racing facility, and individual entrepreneurs could still manage to open a greyhound track with relative ease. Eugene Martin Christiansen, telephone interview with author, December 2, 2009. Eugene Taylor Mack also noted that during the 1980s a number of experts declared that "where the dogs and horses have competed, the dogs have literally run the horses out of town." Eugene Taylor Mack, "Patterns and Images of Greyhound Racing in the United States" (MA thesis, University of Kansas, 1991), 34, quoting Greg Farley, "New Track in a Race for Public's Betting Dollar," in *Greyhound USA*, 1989. See also, in the same article, Missouri Thoroughbred Owners and Breeders Association president Lem Klemme, who stated, "The dogs kill the horse industry wherever they've been or are going." See J. E. Vader, "Paws: While the Horse Racing Industry Is Ailing, Greyhound Tracks across the U.S. Are Booming, with Bettors by the Thousands Eagerly Going to the Dogs," *Sports Illustrated*, June 26, 1989, 46–50.

6. The *Daily Racing Form* tracked these data until the 1980s. In 1970 the top six spectator sports (in descending order) were listed as thoroughbred horse racing, football, baseball, basketball, hockey, and greyhound racing. In 1981 the listings were thoroughbred horse racing, baseball, football, basketball, hockey, and greyhound racing. See "Survey on Sports Attendance" (Hightstown, NJ: Daily Racing Form, 1970, 1981), both located at the Keeneland Library in Lexington, Kentucky. Given these reports attesting to the popularity of dog racing, optimism was high in the greyhound-racing industry. In 1980 former AGTOA president Perrine Palmer had stated, somewhat

optimistically, "I think that greyhound racing will continue to grow and expand. If it ever hits one of the big metropolitan areas like New York, Chicago, Detroit, San Francisco, or Los Angeles, I think it will be overwhelmingly successful." "Sixty Minutes, Perrine Palmer," *Turnout*, April 1980, GHF.

7. In 1974, for instance, the highest attendance levels were reported in Florida, Massachusetts, Colorado, and Arizona, in descending order. *Pari-Mutuel Racing: A Statistical Summary Prepared by the National Association of State Racing Commissioners* (Lexington, KY: NASRC, 1974). According to the *Greyhound Racing Record*, dog racing was New England's top spectator sport in 1964, attracting 1,286,054 fans. See advertisement, *Greyhound Racing Record*, November 7, 1964, 5.

8. http://www.wonderlandgreyhound.com/history.html (accessed August 18, 2010). Wonderland boasted the most prestigious middle-distance stake in the United States and featured more All-American greyhounds than any other track. An All-American is a greyhound named to AGTOA's annual team. There are eight on the team each year, so it is reserved for the "supposed eight best." Gary Guccione, e-mail message to author, June 16, 2010.

9. *Jacksonville Business Journal* 5, no. 51 (September 21, 1990): 9.

10. Eleven states legalized greyhound racing between 1970 and 1990: Alabama (1973), New Hampshire (1973), Nevada (1973), Vermont (1976), Connecticut (1976), West Virginia (1976), Rhode Island (1977), Iowa (1985), Texas (1986), Wisconsin (1987), and Kansas (1989).

11. Steven Crist, telephone interview with author, March 26, 2012.

12. The AGC has employed Marsha Kelly as a public relations expert. NGA has no public relations affiliation. AGTOA contracted with Hill and Knowlton for public relations for many years and later worked solely with Peggy Mackinnon.

13. The *Greyhound Racing Record* was originally under the domain of the Florida dogmen.

14. AGTOA weakened internally after a period of relative strength during the 1970s and 1980s. The association was eventually forced to downsize its operations. For those who believed that AGTOA had failed to lead the industry aggressively during the 1980s, its even more compromised state throughout the 1990s did not bode well for greyhound racing.

15. "Sixty Minutes, Aubrey Wallis," *Turnout*, March 1981, GHF.

16. "Sixty Minutes, Arthur Watson," *Turnout*, May 1982, GHF. Several years before, in 1980, South Dakota track manager Ken Guenthner had proposed the appointment of a commissioner of greyhound racing, one similar to Pete Rozelle's position at the NFL at the time. See "Sixty Minutes, Ken Guenthner," *Turnout*, February 1980, GHF. This suggestion had actually been made much earlier in "High Commissioner Is Suggested," *Greyhound Racing Record*, March 26, 1948.

17. "Never Roll, the World's Greatest Greyhound, Finishes Biggest Season," *Life*, October 12, 1942; Dick Andrews's dog Marathon Hound received a great deal of national publicity, including appearances on the *Merv Griffin Show*, *Good Morning America*, and *Lifestyles of the Rich and Famous*; see Dick Andrews Hall of Fame File and Marathon Hound File, GHF.

18. Ryan H. Reed, "The Wild and Crazy 1970s," Part II, *Greyhound Review*, October 2008.

19. This depended on the contract. A star greyhound booked at one track was

occasionally unable to race at other tracks, at least during the current season, unless the owner was permitted to pull his dog out for a special event such as a stakes race. Gary Guccione, e-mail message to author, July 15, 2010. Guccione further explained that currently, tracks will let a greyhound under contract travel to stakes races under the condition that the dog return to the "home track" afterward. He notes that it may not have always been this way. When it was not, the tracks that did not allow for the greyhound to compete in the derby would have been subject to loud complaints, giving the appearance that the restriction was a common occurrence. He further states that before the 1980s tracks may have been stricter about allowing dogs to race at other venues. On a related note, when trying to move a dog to another track (not necessarily for a special stakes race), this could be much more difficult to maneuver. He explains, "The star dog was a big drawing card, and if the owner or kennel was simply wanting to move him or her from the home track to Track B, the home track would often, if not nearly always, have a problem with that. But whether that was spelled out in the contract, I'm not sure. [I] bet it was."

20. "Sixty Minutes, Aubrey Wallis," *Turnout*, March 1981, GHF.

21. The Greyhound Hall of Fame was a joint project of NGA and AGTOA. It was originally located next to the NGA building in Abilene, Kansas. The opening date was April 21, 1963.

22. Carl Timothy Hoffman, *This Is Greyhound Racing* (n.p.: 1972), 50.

23. See "Hall of Fame a Showcase for Sport," *NGA, Abilene Celebrates Golden Anniversary,* special newspaper edition, 1995, National Greyhound Association, Abilene, KS.

24. According to the Greyhound Hall of Fame, Rural Rube raced from 1938 to 1940 and won forty-one of eighty-three races, including the first Wonderland Futurity; Real Huntsman won $62,493.55 from June 1949 to September 1951; Traffic Officer won the National Coursing Futurity in 1926; Downing won the first Hollywood World Classic and numerous other major races; Flashy Sir was the World's Champion who ruled the dog tracks as "Mr. Greyhound" from 1944 to 1947; Miss Whirl held distance records at a number of tracks and won two Flagler International Classics; Marathon Hound was the World's All Time Leading Money Winner in dog racing as of 1984; and Keefer was a racing star in Florida, also featured in Leslie A. Wootten's book, *Keefer: The People's Choice* (Sedona, AZ: The Memory Works, 2007).

25. Ibid., 169.

26. Ibid., 121; Francine Schwadel, "Red-Hot Racing Dog Wins People's Hearts Even When He Fails," *Wall Street Journal*, April 16, 1986.

27. "Point Publicity Toward Home Track Operators Are Advised," *National Greyhound Update* 4, no. 4 (May 1989). Deford spoke at AGTOA's 39th national conference on March 13, 1989, at the Grand Hotel in Point Clear, Alabama. See Gary Guccione, e-mail message to author, July 29, 2009.

28. Ralph stated that he had received death threats over the issue: if his legislation supporting dog racing were approved, his life was in danger. See Jerry Gillam, "Dog-Racing Bill Turned Down by Assembly Panel," *Los Angeles Times*, April 16, 1975. See also Jerry Gillam, "Life of Greyhound Bill Sponsor Threatened," *Los Angeles Times*, March 18, 1975. Ralph, with Hardie, supported AB 455, which would have legalized greyhound racing in late 1974. See John Berthelsen, "Dog Racing's Frontrunner . . . Prop. 13 Author, Backer, Has Lot to Gain," *Sacramento Bee*, August 6, 1976.

29. http://library.uchastings.edu/ballot_pdf/1976g.pdf (accessed August 14, 2012).

30. Berthelsen, "Dog Racing's Frontrunner."

31. Promotional literature, ca. 1976, Proposition 13 Files, California Democratic Council Records, 1947–1988, Southern California Library, Los Angeles, CA.

32. Los Angeles, Orange, San Bernardino, Fresno, Santa Clara, Alameda, San Diego, and Sacramento.

33. William Farr and William Hazlett, "Greyhound Racing Plan Is 'Major Rip-Off,' DA Says," *Los Angeles Times,* August 26, 1976.

34. Rather than having all members of the state racing commission appointed by the governor, as was typical in other states, Hardie proposed that only one member would be appointed in this manner. Other members would be appointed by various politicians who would not be required to secure legislative confirmation. See Charles A. O'Brien, "An Analysis of Proposition 13," July 29, 1976. This document was distributed by O'Brien, the co-chairman of People Against Proposition 13, during a press conference in Los Angeles. Proposition 13 Files, California Democratic Council Records, Southern California Library, Los Angeles, CA.

35. Ibid.

36. Editorial, "Prop. 13: It's a Dog," *Los Angeles Times,* September 16, 1976.

37. Ibid. See also Editorial, "Dog Racing: No on 13," *Los Angeles Times,* November 1, 1976; Editorial, "A Bad Proposition," *Sacramento Bee,* August 11, 1976. See also promotional literature, ca. 1976, Southern California Library.

38. The horse-racing industry was not listed in People Against Proposition 13 literature, but individuals associated with horse racing may have belonged to the group. Likewise, organizations associated with the film industry were not officially involved, although a group called Actors and Others for Animals was listed as well as a number of individual actors.

39. Political spots from 1976, feature on Proposition 13, Greyhound Racing, Trailers Collection, #359, reel number 81, UCLA Film and Television Archive.

40. "Interim Hearing on Proposition 13," Greyhound Racing Initiative Statute, Senate Committee on Governmental Organization, October 15, 1976, San Francisco, CA, transcript, 3, California State Archives, Sacramento, CA.

41. Ibid., 10, 43, 45.

42. Ibid., 104.

43. Ibid., 38. Labor groups that opposed dog racing in California included the United Automobile Workers and the United Farm Workers of America.

44. A number of journalists have argued that greyhound tracks exploit the poor—especially African Americans—and are intentionally situated in impoverished areas. A 1989 article appearing in *Esquire* chastised Alabama dog track operator Paul William Bryant, Jr., son of the legendary football coach Paul "Bear" Bryant, for opening greyhound tracks in poor African American communities and preying on the most vulnerable members of society, including families on welfare. Whether the establishment of dog tracks in low-income areas is a quantifiable pattern remains to be seen. Dog-racing critics would doubtless call such locations vulnerable and easily exploited, but proponents would argue that these were precisely the communities that welcomed the sport of dog racing with open arms. William M. Adler, "The Bear Trap," *Esquire* (September

1989): 204–212. See also "Racetracks Thriving in Industrial Areas Because of—Not Despite—Unemployment," *Wall Street Journal*, July 16, 1980.

45. "Interim Hearing on Proposition 13," 65. See also Dan Geringer, "They're Making a Killing," *Sports Illustrated*, August 11, 1975. Danny Williams asserted in the *Sports Illustrated* article that the greyhounds were "killers" that would "kill anything that moves away from them except humans. They'll chase and kill horses, cows, dogs, cats, anything. Once they taste that live rabbit when they're pups, they're killers for life."

46. "Interim Hearing on Proposition 13," 64–66.

47. "Brown Opposes Greyhound Racing Plan," *Los Angeles Times*, September 30, 1976.

48. Robert Fairbanks, "Dog-Racing Loss Is Landslide," *Los Angeles Times*, November 4, 1976.

49. Jack Sherck, telephone interview with author, November 5, 2009.

50. F. B. "Happy" Stutz, "In California, Money Talked," GHF.

51. See "Sixty Minutes, Campbell Strange," *Turnout*, April 1984, GHF.

52. Gary Guccione, e-mail message to author, September 29, 2009.

53. Kansas Greyhound Breeders' Educational Association, Inc., "The Kansas Greyhound Industry," ca. 1954, Kansas State Historical Society, Topeka, KS (hereafter KSHS).

54. Al M. Bissing, to "Friend Louis," letter, November 24, 1980, Al Bissing Pioneer File, GHF.

55. "Bets on Dogs Legal in State," *Topeka Capital*, June 25, 1954, Ethics of Amusements Clippings, vol. 1, 1890–1976, KSHS.

56. "Fatzer Says Pari-mutuel Bets Illegal," *Topeka Capital*, July 4, 1954, Ethics of Amusements Clippings, vol. 1, 1890–1976, KSHS.

57. R. W. Reid, "Law's Loophole Interpreted as Unconstitutional," *Wichita Evening Eagle*, May 7, 1955.

58. Kansas Greyhound Breeders' Educational Association, Inc., "The Kansas Greyhound Industry," ca. 1954, KSHS.

59. Dick Snider, "Kansans Look at Greyhound Racing," *Greyhound Racing Record*, September 10, 1954.

60. Roger Verdon, "Abilene's Greyhound Industry Searches for Recognition in Home State," *Kansas Business News*, May 1981.

61. Gaming industry analyst Will Cummings describes the postwar expansion of legalized dog racing as beginning in the West and traveling to New England in the 1970s. This expansion moved to Alabama and thereafter continued into the Midwest and in Texas.

62. This assessment is based on the track's handle.

63. Will Cummings, e-mail message to author, December 2, 2009.

64. He pointed to the declining handles at tracks in Alabama, Arizona, Arkansas, Colorado, Connecticut, and Florida. Testimony of Dana Nelson, Executive Director, Kansas Racing Commission, Senate, Federal and State Affairs Committee, February 5, 1992, SB 516, RH MS 716, Box 28, Kansas Collection, University of Kansas Libraries, Lawrence, KS.

65. Gary Guccione, e-mail message to author, September 18, 2009. Guccione says

that the legislation was such that it was "impractical for the tracks to invest in a racino—the state was taking so much money and leaving so little to the developer/operator." See Gary Guccione, e-mail message to author, September 18, 2009. Racinos—casinos that also permit gambling on horse or dog races—are discussed in greater detail later in the chapter.

66. Alan Hoskins, "Goodbye Woodlands," *Greyhound Review*, October 2008, 25–27. The article notes that the Woodlands closed because "the Woodlands and the Kansas Lottery Commission could not agree on the percentage of revenues the track would have to pay."

67. Gary Guccione, e-mail message to author, November 6, 2009. Emprise, which later reemerged as Delaware North, was the first significant example of corporate ownership of greyhound facilities. The business had been established by two members of an immigrant family, the Jacobs brothers, who opened a popcorn and peanut vending business in Buffalo, New York, in 1915. Delaware North gradually evolved into a major corporate behemoth that managed sports concessions as well as a number of racetracks.

68. Ibid.

69. They completed their competitive southwestern circuit with the inclusion of summer racing in 1947 at the Agua Caliente Track in Tijuana, Mexico, since dog racing in California proper was illegal.

70. Leslie Wootten, "Growth: Part II of a Three-Part Series on the History of Greyhound Racing in Arizona," *Greyhound Review*, October 2004, 68. See also Robert Burtt, "The New and Beautiful Greyhound Park," *Greyhound Racing Record*, December 4, 1953.

71. In addition to the tracks that they already managed, during the 1960s the Funks established the Amado Greyhound Park (1963), Apache Junction Park (1965), Yuma Greyhound Park (1965), and Black Canyon Greyhound Park (1967).

72. One journalist wrote that by 1968, Emprise had a 51 percent interest in the Funks' tracks; Shawn McKinnon, "Dog Racing Could Return to Henderson by March," *Vegas Review Journal*, August 26, 1989.

73. Leslie Wootten, "Weathering the Storm: Part III, The History of Greyhound Racing in Arizona," *Greyhound Review*, November 2004, 41.

74. http://lesliewootten.net/Index_files/page0005.htm (accessed August 18, 2010). Leslie A. Wootten, "Feature Article 1b."

75. Amy Wang, "Phoenix Greyhound Racetrack to Shut Down," *Arizona Republic*, September 26, 2009. These changed circumstances as well as external market factors such as the establishment of a state lottery in 1981 and subsequently of Indian gaming rendered dog racing in Arizona unable to maintain the level of popularity that it had once enjoyed. Even a $17 million renovation at the Phoenix Greyhound Park in 1988 failed to spark additional interest. From 1998 to 2009, attendance at the track declined by 56 percent.

76. Bill Lee, telephone interview with author, February 18, 2008.

77. "Sixty Minutes, Arden Hartman," *Turnout*, June 1982, GHF.

78. Bill Lee, Arden Hartman, and Jim Larson, StoryCorps interview by Alex Kelly, July 21, 2008, American Folklife Center, Library of Congress, Washington, DC.

79. United Track Racing was a part of the May 1990 acquisition; they were partners with Wembley. At the time, Wembley owned six greyhound tracks in the United Kingdom as well as Wembley Stadium. See Peter Sleeth, "British Firm Buying Three Colorado Dog Tracks," *Denver Post,* December 22, 1989, and Lynn Howell, "Mile High Kennel Club Ushers in a New Era," *Denver Post,* June 4, 1990. Bill Lee notes that Linsey and Ross had 4,700 stockholders when they sold to Wembley. Wembley then purchased the majority of stocks and became a private company. Previously, stockholders (with 100 stocks or more) could obtain a free season pass to the dog track. Lee notes that individuals with these stock holdings had felt a sense of ownership at Mile High. Bill Lee, telephone interview with author, December 14, 2009.

80. Bill Lee, telephone interview with author, December 14, 2009.

81. Longtime animal advocate and lobbyist Gladys Sargent, who partnered with pro-horse racing interests and antigambling religious groups to defeat a dog-racing bill in California in 1969, speculated that the pro-racing forces behind legalization efforts were Florida-based organized crime syndicates. She stated that she had even received death threats for campaigning against the bill, although she never suffered harm. She continued to fight against dog racing when the possibility of legalization was resurrected several years later. Gladys W. Sargent, interview by Jacqueline S. Reinier, February 28 and March 9, 16, and 23, 1989, tape recording, California State Archives, Sacramento, CA.

82. Joseph M. Linsey Pioneer File, GHF.

83. Federal Bureau of Investigation Reports, June 21, 1968, and July 1, 1968, FOIA request #1116344-000.

84. Ibid. Linsey stated in the early 1980s that "we don't have any wise guys hanging around" at his Massachusetts tracks. He also declared, "Greyhound racing is the most honest pari-mutuel sport in existence. There is absolutely no hanky-panky of any kind and I dare anyone to tell me differently." See "Sixty Minutes, Joe Linsey," *Turnout,* n.d., GHF.

85. Federal Bureau of Investigation Reports, June/July 1968, FOIA request #1116344-000. Joe Linsey's connection to organized crime is mentioned specifically in Hank Messick, *Lansky* (New York: G. P. Putnam's Sons, 1971), 32, 69, 223, 276.

86. Vincent Teresa with Thomas C. Renner, *My Life in the Mafia* (Garden City, NY: Doubleday, 1973).

87. Jim Chaney, "Owner Says Dog Tracks 'Clean,'" *Raleigh News and Observer,* April 10, 1953.

88. Ibid. Morehead City was rumored to be under the control of the Costello syndicate, while Moyock was allegedly under the influence of gambling ringleaders from Cleveland, Ohio, including John G. Masoni and Samuel C. and Joseph C. Lombardo.

89. Editorial, "All or None," *Raleigh News and Observer,* September 16, 1952.

90. Charles Craven, "Seawell Speaks Out on Dog Racing Bill," *Raleigh News and Observer,* May 19, 1959.

91. "North Carolina Dog Racing Bill Worrying Virginians," *Raleigh News and Observer,* May 14, 1959.

92. David Cooper, "Dog Racing Measure Defeated in House Committee 28 to 17," *Raleigh News and Observer,* May 28, 1959.

93. Hartwell noted that with the closure of the North Carolina tracks in 1954, the "curtain rang down on the final act of racing as it had been in the early years." These were some of the last tracks to operate without official supervision and under a "shaky pari-mutuel law." Paul C. Hartwell, *The Road from Emeryville* (San Diego: California Research Publishing, 1980), 95.

94. According to newspaper reporter Larry Werner, the Funks frequently borrowed money from Emprise; see Werner, "Past Dealings Raise Questions About Funks," *Las Vegas Review-Journal*, ca. 1982, Dog Racing Subject Files, University of Nevada, Reno, Special Collections, Reno, NV. See also Ray Ruester, "Emprise Links with Organized Crime Claimed; Hearing Set," *Daytona Beach Morning Journal*, June 17, 1971.

95. "New Probe in Car Bombing Set," *Rocky Mountain News*, October 20, 1989.

96. The Funks later attempted to establish a track near Las Vegas in Henderson, Nevada. Dog racing was first legalized in Nevada in 1973. The project was plagued with controversies and difficulties from the start. Only nine months after opening in January 1981, Las Vegas Downs closed its doors permanently. Wayne Strong stated that the kennels at Las Vegas Downs were "terrible." See "Sixty Minutes, Wayne Strong," *Turnout*, n.d., GHF.

97. Wally Wood, "Honesty and Integrity or . . . Feudalism?" *Greyhound Racing Record*, June 4, 1948. Wood appears to have been a guest writer from the *Greyhound Digest*. For another reference to dogmen and feudalism, see "An Industry at Odds," *Fort Myers News-Press*, December 6, 1992. In this article Jack Cory, chief lobbyist for the FGA and NGA, states, "The 18 dog-track owners in Florida think they are barons in a feudal society. And the individuals that own the athletes that perform at the track are merely servants. . . . They've had that philosophy for 62 years, and they've been unchallenged. Unfortunately, as happens in dictatorial societies, they've destroyed the empire. The pari-mutuel industry is falling down around them."

98. Jonathan Rand, "Dogs Deserve a Bigger Bite," *Miami News*, ca. July 1975, GHF.

99. The dogmen countered that the track owners were "skimming" from regular purses to pay for big-name stakes races.

100. Jim Frey, telephone interview with author, May 10, 2010.

101. Since they did not view themselves as traditional laborers, they did not adequately consider unionizing as a means of strengthening their bargaining position. Historically, breeding and training dogs had never been a unionized trade; it more closely resembled farmwork and animal husbandry.

102. The *Coursing News* was printed from 1911 to 1971, at which point its name was changed to the *Greyhound Review*.

103. A number of organizations filed for a charter of incorporation with the Florida secretary of state, including the Greyhound Benevolent Association, Inc. (established 4/22/68, dissolved 10/21/74); Greyhound Breeders Association of Florida, Inc. (established 9/6/84, dissolved 10/11/91); Florida Greyhound Association, Inc. (established 11/26/73, dissolved 7/16/92); Greyhound Owners Association of Florida, Inc. (established 10/07/27, dissolved 11/23/36); Greyhound Owners Association, Inc. (established 2/24/75, dissolved 4/22/02). However, the group known as FGOBA is in all likelihood the Florida Greyhound Association, Inc., as the charter of incorporation was provided

to the author by Jim Frey, who was involved with the strikes. In Massachusetts the New England Greyhound Association, Inc., filed for a charter with the Massachusetts secretary of state on January 7, 1975, and dissolved on November 17, 1986.

104. It appears that, at this early stage, only greyhound owners and breeders were allowed to join GOBA; greyhound trainers were not included. Its creation may also have been a belated response to the establishment of the track operators' association, AGTOA, in 1946.

105. The exact date of GOBA's initial incorporation is unknown, despite numerous attempts to find its charter of incorporation at the State Archives of Florida. When the organization was reestablished in the 1970s, the group (FGOBA) received its charter from the Florida secretary of state on November 26, 1973.

106. The tracks responded by turning to the circuit courts in their respective regions, an effort that led to a flurry of injunctions that did not help the dogmen's efforts.

107. Despite their initial zeal, the dogmen were unable to maintain a united front. But far more important, the group sought official affiliation, that is, a charter, with the American Federation of Labor. It hoped that this national association would provide dogmen with a stronger bargaining position as they battled the track operators. GOBA's desire to join this organization was something of a surprise given the AFL's traditional commitment to and association with craft or trade unions (skilled labor such as carpentry) rather than individual contractors. Breeders, owners, and trainers of greyhounds did not seem to fit into the AFL's labor community. Some of the men, such as Stutz, had long since distanced themselves from the title of "laborer" and instead prided themselves as tradesmen of a different ilk, men who carried on a unique rural tradition with roots in agriculture. Moreover, association with organized labor was an inauspicious goal at the time given the recent passage of the Taft-Hartley Act of 1947, which severely reduced the potency of the AFL (and all labor unions). For instance, "closed shops" had been eliminated, rendering untenable the dogmen's former demand that tracks hire only GOBA members. The decision to seek association with the AFL was a direct consequence of meetings with J. L. Rhodes, the assistant southern director of the AFL, who had explained to GOBA leadership the advantages of national union affiliation. More than 400 dogmen signed AFL authorization cards in support of the proposal. During an August 1948 meeting of the AFL leadership at the Drake Hotel in Chicago, GOBA's charter application was considered. By all accounts, it appeared at first as if the request would be rejected. The AFL executive council moved that the "application for charter be denied because the subject matter of collective bargaining contemplated by the organization is to be how much money the owner is to receive for the dogs and this is inconsistent with the objectives of the American Federation of Labor." (See Minutes of the Meeting of the Executive Council of the American Federation of Labor, George Meany Memorial Archives Library, National Labor College, Silver Spring, MD.) Yet a subsequent and rather opaque and ambiguous note in the minutes countermands the motion, effectively approving GOBA's admission into the federation. *Greyhound Racing Record* announced that GOBA had received its charter and would now be joining the Building Service Employees International Union. Under the AFL umbrella, GOBA was now to be officially known as the Greyhound Operators and Employees Benevolent Association, Local 346, with offices in Miami, Florida.

Having achieved this milestone, GOBA reversed course and dissolved itself entirely several days later. After acceptance into the AFL, GOBA members resigned en masse, probably in fear of reprisals from track management.

108. According to data provided to the author by Jim Frey, who was involved with the strikes in Florida. Frey speculates that about 90 percent of NGA members living in Florida were members of the GOBA (he refers to it as FGA, however). He also notes that non-NGA members supported GOBA, leading him to conclude that the total number exceeded 315. Jim Frey, e-mail correspondence with author, April 30, 2012.

109. "A Report on the Need for a Minimum, Guaranteed Purse in Florida's Greyhound Racing Industry," prepared by FGOBA, April 2, 1974, in Interim Hearing on Proposition 13, Greyhound Racing Initiative Statute, California Senate Committee on Governmental Organization, October 15, 1976, San Francisco, CA, California State Archives, Sacramento, CA. To remedy this problem the association passed a resolution calling upon the Florida state legislature to increase purses to 4 percent of the pari-mutuel handle, up from an average of 2.3 percent at the Florida tracks.

110. While dog tracks earned about a 35.2 percent rate of return on operating assets (investments), the dogmen were realizing only 3.3 percent on theirs. They estimated that out of the approximately thirty kennels booked at each major track, only the top ten would enjoy any profits at all. See "Report on Minimum, Guaranteed Purse," 4. The dogmen complained that even when handles went up, their purse earnings did not necessarily increase to a corresponding level. Many Florida tracks were using a sliding scale for purses, in which the percentage for purse money declined when the handle exceeded a set figure. Jim Frey notes that this was part of the dogman's problem. Flagler said they paid more, for example, but the competition was tougher. It cost the dog owners more to run at the high-end tracks, because the dogmen had to go through more greyhounds, and the kennel cost at better tracks was higher. Earnings were shared according to a special leasing system long used in the industry. Gary Guccione explains, "Usually the trainer is paid a flat salary and a commission percentage on earnings for each pay period. The deal between the owner of the dog and the kennel operator is usually 65/35, but at some of the major tracks we're hearing of there being more 50/50 deals, especially on better dogs." Gary Guccione, e-mail correspondence with author, June 16, 2010.

111. "Sixty Minutes, Paul Discolo," *Turnout*, February 1984, GHF.

112. "Sixty Minutes, David Hecht," *Turnout*, n.d., GHF. Joe Linsey later made the point that the dogmen would strike every ten or fifteen years. See "Sixty Minutes, Joe Linsey," *Turnout*, n.d., GHF. Both of these issues were probably published in the early 1980s.

113. Tensions had risen at Flagler when some of the kennel owners' demands for more money were not met. In addition to a higher percentage of purses, they wanted a reduction of distance races (so-called marathons and super marathons) on the track because they felt the race was too hard on their dogs. "David Hecht Attempts to Stop Track Boycott," *Miami Herald*, June 19, 1975. Marathons were nearly a half mile and super marathons were $9/16$ of a mile. Standard track lengths varied but were usually $5/16$, $3/8$, or $7/16$ of a mile.

114. The precise term here would be "strikebreakers," but the use of the word "scab" is appropriate because many of the dogmen themselves used the term. Greyhound trainer Mary Creamer stated that when kennels left Pensacola to go to South Florida to break the strike, she "did arrange for some kids to paint S-C-A-B on their kennel buildings while I stood watch." She also indicated that she had some the kids paint "Scab Express" on one of the dogman's trucks. See "Sixty Minutes, Mary Creamer," *Turnout,* April 1983, GHF. Dogman Dick Jordan's truck also had "Don't Bet on Dogs From Scab Kennels" written on it. See Bill Braucher, "Biscayne Off, Racing without Any Violence," *Miami Herald,* September 6, 1975.

115. When Strong was asked by other prisoners why he was incarcerated, he told them, "I wouldn't run my dogs." After this comment, he noted that the other prisoners, somewhat bewildered, "started easing away from me." Wayne Strong, personal interview with author, April 24, 2009.

116. Gary Guccione, e-mail message to author, May 17, 2010.

117. Hartwell, *Road from Emeryville,* 117.

118. Wayne Strong, personal interview with author, April 24, 2009.

119. In New Hampshire, twenty-three greyhound owners struck the Hinsdale and Seabrook Greyhound Parks in 1975. The boycott was launched by the New England Greyhound Association in order to gain a bargaining position for the dogmen. See Ryan H. Reed, "The Wild and Crazy 1970s," Part 1, *Greyhound Review,* September 2008, 67.

120. The track spokesperson countered, "Killing these fine racing dogs is a brutal and grandstand play that will not benefit the boycotting owners, the track or the racing industry." On July 18, 1975, the AGBA stated that it had been a "publicity gimmick" to draw attention to their difficulties. See "Breeders Just After 'Publicity,'" *Tucson Daily Citizen,* July 18, 1975. Leslie Wootten also argued that it was a publicity stunt. See Leslie Wootten, "Bad Blood," *Greyhound Review,* March 2010, 57–60.

121. Editorial, "A Brutal Stunt," *Tucson Daily Citizen,* July 18, 1975; Bill Braucher, "Kennelmen Oppose New Flagler Plan," *Miami Herald,* July 16, 1975; "Dogs Die to Intensify Boycott," *Scottsdale Daily Progress,* July 15, 1975.

122. Jim Frey, telephone interview with author, May 10, 2010. See also Jim Frey, interview by Gwynn Thayer, tape recording, July 2, 2011, Baylor University Institute for Oral History, Waco, TX.

123. http://www.greyhoundmovie.com (accessed June 24, 2012).

124. The companion bills (H.R. 3429 and S.-1734) were sponsored by Senator John B. Breaux (Louisiana) and Representative Jim Slattery (Kansas) along with ten cosponsors. See http://thomas.loc.gov (accessed September 29, 2010).

125. House Committee on Energy and Commerce, Subcommittee on Commerce, Consumer Protection, and Competitiveness, Interstate Greyhound Racing Act: Hearings on H.R. 3429, 101st Cong., 2nd sess., August 1, 1990, 18, 19, 23, 28.

126. Once again the multitiered greyhound industry was deeply divided over an issue fundamental to the financial underpinnings of the business. Whereas the dogmen knew that they were losing money, the track operators were satisfied with the status quo. During her testimony before the committee, AGTOA president Kay Spitzer

stated the association's position that "the greyhound industry is thriving in its present environment. That environment blends both private negotiations and state regulations. Our industry does not need another level of federal intervention." Ibid., 45. Several other speakers continued the testimony on AGTOA's behalf. Arden Hartman, general manager of the Mile High Kennel Club, pointed out that tracks bore all of the expenses of simulcasting. Ibid., 47. Hartman also submitted that simulcasting was not a threat to live racing. William Bissett, representing the Geneva Lakes Kennel Club in Wisconsin, charged that the industry was healthy overall and that the legislation appeared to be a "private relief bill" for greyhound owners. Ibid., 49. AGTOA thus based its objections essentially on the premise that the bill threatened free enterprise, but its unstated motivations were undoubtedly to remove the unwelcome prospect of decreased profits.

127. Ibid., 39.

128. Gary Guccione, e-mail message to author, March 6, 2009.

129. *Pari-Mutuel Racing: A Statistical Summary Prepared by the Association of State Racing Commissioners International* (Lexington, KY: ASRCI, 1996). In current dollars, the decline began after 1991. In constant dollars, which are developed by using the gross domestic product implicit price deflator, the decline began earlier, after 1987.

130. See Bill Lee, telephone interview with author, February 18, 2008. See also Frederick Mensch, "If Only . . . ," *Racing Greyhounds* 6, no. 1 (January 1993): 32–35.

131. Jack Sherck, telephone interview with author, November 5, 2009.

132. One consumer benefit to Internet gambling is its privacy and convenience; rather than going to the tracks or to an OTB parlor, individuals can take advantage of an anonymous gambling forum at home.

133. Will Cummings maintains that the downward spiral in greyhound racing began in the 1990s with the onslaught of Indian gaming. Will Cummings, telephone interview with author, December 2, 2009. Eugene Martin Christiansen asserts that pari-mutuel betting on greyhound racing began to decline in the 1960s due to a shrinking consumer base. Eugene Martin Christiansen, telephone interview with author, December 2, 2009.

134. A series of public votes from 1964 to 1988 revealed that the majority of Americans in more than twenty-five states were in favor of state lotteries. The introduction of state lotteries began with New Hampshire in 1964. Charles T. Clotfelter and Philip J. Cook, *Selling Hope: State Lotteries in America* (Cambridge, MA: Harvard University Press, 1991), 146. See also David G. Schwartz, *Roll the Bones: The History of Gambling* (New York: Gotham Books, 2006), 388.

135. After New Hampshire took the lead in legalizing state lotteries, other states began to follow, including New York and New Jersey. Gaming historian David Schwartz credits New Jersey with exploiting the power of state lotteries fully, noting that the state "unlocked the key to lottery prosperity: cheap tickets and frequent games." At first most of the lotteries were introduced in states located in the Northeast and parts of the Midwest. But this regional growth spurt in the 1970s was only the beginning. Fifteen states had embraced the lottery by 1981, and by 1990 thirty-six states had opted for legalization. The trend had moved westward and finally even captured much of the American South, which, as the heart of the Bible Belt, had long resisted the allure of

gambling's easy profits. By 2006 only Alabama and Arkansas remained lottery-free in the southern region. Schwartz, *Roll the Bones*, 388.

136. The 59th, 60th, and 61st annual reports issued by the Florida Division of Pari-Mutuel Wagering (1989–1990, 1990–1991, 1991–1992, respectively) all reported declining handles in greyhound racing. The Division of Pari-Mutuel Wagering was previously known as the Florida State Racing Commission. Steven Crist of the *Daily Racing Form* observed that the Florida lottery disproportionately affected dog over horse racing (i.e., more dog-racing fans were drawn to the lottery than horse-racing fans). Steven Crist, telephone interview with author, March 26, 2012.

137. To handicap is to predict the outcome of a race by analyzing past performances. Diehard greyhound fans acknowledge that handicapping a dog race is a "cerebral" effort with a steep learning curve, but many bettors no longer care to learn how to decipher a racing program. Arden Hartman, telephone interview with author, December 15, 2009, and Eugene Martin Christiansen, telephone interview with author, December 2, 2009.

138. The federal government first approved gaming on tribal lands as early as 1924, but facilities were not intended for non-Indians. Schwartz, *Roll the Bones*, 433.

139. The act established three classes of gaming on Native American reservations, but more important it required tribes (in most cases) to sign compacts with state governments so that they were also required, in essence, to pay a sum to the state. This had the effect of counterbalancing a landmark 1987 Supreme Court case, California v. Cabazon Band of Mission Indians, in which the court ruled that there could be no interference from states, counties, or municipalities when Indian tribes chose to run a gambling operation. Gaming analyst Will Cummings notes that the passage of IGRA was the "proximate result" of the Supreme Court decision, codifying and putting some limits on "an explosion which was about to occur anyway." Will Cummings, e-mail correspondence with author, August 4, 2012. For further study on Indian gaming, see Steven Andrew Light and Kathryn R. L. Rand, *Indian Gaming and Tribal Sovereignty* (Lawrence: University Press of Kansas, 2005); W. Dale Mason, *Indian Gaming: Tribal Sovereignty and American Politics* (Oklahoma City: University of Oklahoma Press, 2000); Angela Mullis and David Kamper, eds., *Indian Gaming: Who Wins?* (Los Angeles: UCLA American Indian Studies Center, 2000).

140. One of the first greyhound tracks to close because of Indian gaming was in South Dakota. In this case dog racing ceased only a decade or so after the establishment of "limited" casinos at Deadwood and the video lottery (slot-like machines) throughout the state. Will Cummings, e-mail message to author, December 2, 2009. Indian gaming revenues did grow steadily after the passage of IGRA, reaching $26.7 billion in 2008, up 2.3 percent from the previous year. These numbers dwarfed the revenues that had been posted just ten years before, according to published data compiled by the National Indian Gaming Commission. Kim Masters Evans, *Gambling: What's at Stake* (Farmington Hills, MI: Thomson Gale/Information Plus, 2005), 62.

141. Gary Guccione, "Footnotes: The Indian Gaming Factor," *Greyhound Review*, July 2009, 3–5.

142. Ibid.

143. For the first several decades in which greyhound racing was legal, dog tracks

had not been forced to compete directly with nearby casinos. Indeed, beginning in 1931, Nevada was for many years the only state that offered casino gambling. Nevada dominated the casino market from 1931 until Atlantic City, New Jersey, emerged as a stalwart competitor in the 1980s. As the cultural stigma on gambling weakened, other states began to circumvent prohibitions against casinos through the creation of riverboat gambling. Iowa led the charge in 1989, followed by Illinois, Mississippi, Louisiana, Missouri, and Indiana. Most riverboat casinos were located in the Midwest and central South; some posed a threat to greyhound tracks in Alabama and Arkansas.

144. Some tribal leaders concurred and explored the possibility of collaboration. In an impromptu meeting held at HSUS national headquarters in the mid–1980s, Native American leaders, who had appeared there unexpectedly, wished to discuss the possibility of instituting greyhound racing on tribal lands. According to former HSUS employee Robert Baker, who was present at the meeting, tribal representatives had been told by U.S. Senator Pete Domenici (who was sympathetic to the HSUS) that they needed to address the pressing issue of animal cruelty if they were considering involvement in greyhound racing. Baker notes that during the meeting the Native American representatives emphasized the abject poverty endemic to many reservations, but they also stated their belief that the introduction of dog racing could be a turning point for their economic outlook, their "golden calf." See Robert Baker, telephone interview with author, November 21, 2009. When pro-racing interests present at the meeting observed that Baker and the HSUS were successfully convincing the Native Americans that there were problems inherent to the sport, Baker alleges that they became quite concerned by this turn of events. Although the meeting ended "inconclusively," Baker was surprised and encouraged by how receptive the tribal leaders were to the arguments put forth by HSUS.

145. The planned owner-operator of the track was veteran dogman Wayne Strong. He had consulted with experts and determined that a 5,000-seat facility situated twenty miles north of Albuquerque would attract a sizeable clientele of racing fans. House Committee on Interior and Insular Affairs, Indian Gambling Control Act: Hearings on H.R. 1920 and H.R. 2404, 99th Cong., 1st sess., June 25, 1985, and September 18, 1985, 659–691.

146. They argued that the creation of a new federal agency to oversee Native American pari-mutuel facilities would supposedly be "inefficient and duplicative" and in fact belonged only under the purview of state government. A year later, during a Senate hearing at which AGTOA continued to reject the possibility of Native American greyhound facilities, the organization maintained that the creation of a National Gaming Commission constituted "the nose of the Federal camel under the tent of State regulation." House Committee, Indian Gambling Control Act: Hearings on H.R. 1920 and H.R. 2404, 298. Select Committee on Indian Affairs, Hearing on S. 902, 99th Cong., 2nd sess., June 17, 1986, 61–62.

147. The first casino outside of Nevada opened in Atlantic City, New Jersey, in 1978.

148. Gary Guccione, e-mail message to author, September 21, 2009. Eugene Martin Christiansen, e-mail message to author, December 2, 2009.

149. Gary Guccione, e-mail message to author, September 21, 2009. In some cases,

it was impossible to even establish a partnership: Rhode Island and Kansas were both unable to strike a political compromise during attempts to combine slot machines with dog tracks. The greyhound tracks in these states closed, but the slot machines remained.

150. A. G. Sulzberger, "Greyhound Races Face Extinction at the Hands of Casinos They Fostered," *New York Times,* March 9, 2012.

151. The proposal would offer greyhound kennels a "soft landing" for Iowa dog breeders, providing them with $4 to $10 million to get out of the business. Mike Glover, "Harrah's Asks to End Subsidies to Greyhound Racing," *Bloomberg Business-week,* March 17, 2010. See http://businessweek.com/ap/financialnews/D9EGKGR00 .htm (accessed June 23, 2012).

152. http://infoweb.newsbank.com (accessed June 21, 2012). "Animal Advocates Gather at Florida Capitol to Lobby for Animal Protection Legislation," *Targeted News Service,* January 18, 2012. SB 382 (Sachs, D-Delray)/HB 641 (Young, R-Tampa) would decouple greyhound racing from other forms of gambling.

153. Wayne Pacelle, telephone interview with author, August 13, 2012.

154. Ibid.

155. http://www.grey2kusa.org/pdf/GREY2KUSANationalFactSheet.pdf (accessed August 2, 2012). The first accusation has long been refuted by the industry, which, according to one leading breeder, crates the dogs as a general practice because that is "their security. . . . They'd rather be in that crate than just out in a big space, a big wide area." See *Greyhound Racing: The History and Heart of the Sport,* Greyhound Hall of Fame and American Greyhound Council (2001), VHS. The industry standard is to let the greyhounds out several times a day to relieve themselves in addition to their regular exercise and training schedule.

156. The future of greyhound racing depends somewhat on the availability of account wagering as well as the future interpretation of the Unlawful Internet Gambling Enforcement Act (UIGEA) of 2006. Account wagering, which in the past operated as telephone account wagering (TAB) and then on the Internet, is the "wave of the future" in pari-mutuel gambling, according to gaming analyist Will Cummings. He notes that the legality of account wagering has been defined and enforced differently in various states. He also observes that the interpretation of UIGEA has been "much murkier for greyhound racing" than for horse racing. Will Cummings, e-mail correspondence with author, August 12, 2012.

157. Martin Cohan, "And Leave the Greyhounds to Us?" *The Odd Couple,* season 2, directed by Hal Cooper, aired December 31, 1971 (Hollywood, CA: CBS Paramount Network Television, 2007), DVD.

158. In the later part of the episode, Felix gives in to Oscar's wish to race—and then sell—Golden Earrings. However, Felix continues to insist that the racing greyhound be loved and cared for appropriately by his new owner.

APPENDIX.

1. The sources used to create this list include reports from state racing commissions; interviews and written accounts from industry leaders from the NGA, AGTOA, and Derby Lane Kennel Club; interviews and written accounts from greyhound breeders,

trainers, and owners; records provided by animal protection organizations; digitized newspaper databases; newspaper morgues; records at the Greyhound Hall of Fame in Abilene, Kansas; Paul Hartwell's listing of tracks up to 1980, *The Road from Emeryville* (San Diego: California Research Publishing, 1980), which until now has been the only published list available; and other resources listed in the bibliography.

BIBLIOGRAPHY

SECONDARY SOURCES

Abt, Vicki, James F. Smith, and Eugene Martin Christiansen. *The Business of Risk: Commercial Gambling in Mainstream America*. Lawrence: University Press of Kansas, 1985.

Adler, William M. "The Bear Trap." *Esquire*, September 1989, 204–213.

Almirall, Leon V. *Canines and Coyotes*. Caldwell, ID: Caxton, 1941.

Anderson, Jerry W. *Let's Go to the Greyhound Races*. Colorado Springs, CO: Gold Enterprises, 1980.

Arluke, Arnold. *Just a Dog: Understanding Animal Cruelty and Ourselves*. Philadelphia: Temple University Press, 2006.

Arluke, Arnold, and Clinton R. Sanders. *Regarding Animals*. Philadelphia: Temple University Press, 1996.

Armbruster, Ann. *Life and Times of Miami Beach*. New York: Knopf, 1995.

Arsenault, Raymond. *St. Petersburg and the Florida Dream*. Gainesville: University Press of Florida, 1996.

Atkinson, Michael, and Kevin Young. "Reservoir Dogs: Greyhound Racing, Mimesis and Sports Related Violence." *International Review for the Sociology of Sport* 40, no. 3 (2005): 335–356.

Baker, Norman. "Going to the Dogs—Hostility to Greyhound Racing in Britain: Puritanism, Socialism, and Pragmaticism." *Journal of Sport History* 23, no. 2 (Summer 1996): 97–119.

Barnes, Julia, ed. *The Complete Book of Greyhounds*. New York: Howell Book House, 1994.

Baur, John E. *Dogs on the Frontier*. San Antonio, TX: Naylor, 1964.

Bederman, Gail. *Manliness and Civilization: A Cultural History of Gender and Race in the United States, 1880–1917*. Chicago: University of Chicago Press, 1995.

Beers, Diane L. *For the Prevention of Cruelty: The History and Legacy of Animal Rights Activism in the United States*. Athens: Swallow Press / Ohio University Press, 2006.

Beisel, Jennifer. "The American Upper Class and the American Horse Industry from 1865 to 1929." DA diss., Middle Tennessee State University, 2005.

Berneking, Carolyn B. "The Welsh Settlers of Emporia: A Cultural History." *Kansas Historical Quarterly* 37, no. 3 (Autumn 1971): 269–282.

Betts, John Rickards. "The Technological Revolution and the Rise of Sport, 1850–1900." *Mississippi Valley Historical Review* 40, no. 2 (September 1953): 231–256.

Biondi, Joann. *Miami Beach Memories: A Nostalgic Chronicle of Days Gone By*. Guilford, CT: Insiders' Guide / Globe Pequot Press, 2007.

Blanning, Charles, and Sir Mark Prescott, Bt. *The Waterloo Cup: The First 150 Years*. Winchester, UK: Heath House Press, 1987.

Bloch, Herbert A. "The Sociology of Gambling." *American Journal of Sociology* 57, no. 3 (November 1951): 215–221.

Bloomberg, Mark S., Jon F. Dee, and Robert A. Taylor, eds. *Canine Sports Medicine and Survey.* Philadelphia: W. B. Saunders, 1998.

Blythe, Linda L., James R. Gannon, A. Morrie Craig, and Desmond P. Fegan. *Care of the Racing and Retired Greyhound.* Topeka, KS: American Greyhound Council, 2007.

Bonnifield, Mathew Paul. *The Dust Bowl.* Albuquerque: University of New Mexico Press, 1979.

Bradshaw, John. *Dog Sense: How the Science of Dog Behavior Can Make You a Better Friend to Your Pet.* New York: Basic Books, 2011.

Bramson, Seth. *Miami Beach.* Charleston, SC: Arcadia Publishing, 2005.

Branigan, Cynthia A. *Adopting the Racing Greyhound.* New York: Wiley, 2003.

————. *The Reign of the Greyhound.* Hoboken, NJ: Wiley, 2004.

Brestrup, Craig. *Disposable Animals: Ending the Tragedy of Throwaway Pets.* Leander, TX: Camino Bay Books, 1997.

Buchele, Walter J. *Greyhound Racing Guide: A Complete Explanation Information Book on Greyhound Racing, Betting, and Handicapping.* Bonita Springs, FL: Naples-Fort Myers Kennel Club, 1971.

Burnell, Roy. *How to Win with Greyhounds.* North Sydney, NSW, Australia: Pollard, 1973.

Burnham, John C. *Bad Habits: Drinking, Smoking, Taking Drugs, Gambling, Sexual Misbehavior, and Swearing in American History.* New York: New York University Press, 1993.

Bush, Gregory W. "Playground of the USA: Miami and the Promotion of Spectacle." *Pacific Historical Review* 68, no. 2 (May 1999): 153–172.

Carnell, Simon. *Hare.* London: Reaktion, 2010.

Carson, Gerald. *Men, Beasts, and Gods: A History of Cruelty and Kindness to Animals.* New York: Charles Scribner's Sons, 1972.

Clarke, H. Edwards. *The Waterloo Cup, 1922–1977.* Hindhead, UK: Spur, 1978.

Cohen, Lizabeth. *A Consumers' Republic: The Politics of Mass Consumption in Postwar America.* New York: Vintage, 2003.

Coleman, Jon T. *Vicious: Wolves and Men in America.* New Haven, CT: Yale University Press, 2004.

Coleman, Sydney H. *Humane Society Leaders in America.* New York: American Humane Association, 1924.

Curnutt, Jordan. *Animals and the Law: A Sourcebook.* Santa Barbara, CA: ABC-CLIO, 2001.

Dary, David. *Seeking Pleasure in the Old West.* New York: Knopf, 1995.

Davies, Andrew. "The Police and the People: Gambling in Salford, 1900–1939." *Historical Journal* 34, no. 1 (March 1991): 87–115.

Davis, Susan E., and Margo DeMello. *Stories Rabbits Tell: A Natural and Cultural History of a Misunderstood Creature.* Brooklyn, NY: Lantern Books, 2003.

Deford, Frank. *There She Is: The Life and Times of Miss America.* New York: The Viking Press, 1971.

Derr, Mark. *A Dog's History of America: How Our Best Friend Explored, Conquered, and Settled a Continent.* New York: North Point Press, 2004.

————. *How the Dog Became the Dog: From Wolves to Our Best Friends*. New York: Overlook Duckworth, 2011.

Dumenil, Lynn. *The Modern Temper: American Culture and Society in the 1920s*. New York: Hill & Wang, 1995.

Dykstra, Robert R. *The Cattle Towns: A Social History of the Kansas Cattle Trading Centers*. New York: Knopf, 1968.

Einwohner, Rachel L. "Gender, Class, and Social Movement Outcomes: Identity and Effectiveness in Two Animal Rights Campaigns." *Gender and Society* 13, no. 1 (February 1999): 56–76.

English, T. J. *Havana Nocturne: How the Mob Owned Cuba . . . and Then Lost It to the Revolution*. New York: William Morrow, 2008.

Ewen, Stuart. *Captains of Consciousness: Advertising and the Social Roots of the Consumer Culture*. New York: McGraw-Hill, 1976.

Fairbanks, David. "Religious Forces and 'Morality' Politics in the American States." *Western Political Quarterly* 30, no. 3 (September 1977): 411–417.

Favre, David, and Vivien Tsang. "The Development of Anti-Cruelty Laws during the 1800s." *Detroit College of Law Review* 1 (Spring 1993): 1–35.

Fender, Brenna. "Racing Greyhounds." Honors thesis, University of South Florida, 1993.

Findlay, John M. *People of Chance: Gambling in American Society from Jamestown to Las Vegas*. New York: Oxford University Press, 1986.

Finsen, Lawrence, and Susan Finsen. *The Animal Rights Movement in America: From Compassion to Respect*. New York: Twayne, 1994.

Fiske, John. *Understanding Popular Culture*. Boston: Unwin Hyman, 1989.

Fleharty, Eugene D. *Wild Animals and Settlers on the Great Plains*. Norman: University of Oklahoma Press, 1995.

Flynn, Clifton P. *Social Creatures: A Human and Animal Studies Reader*. New York: Lantern, 2008.

Forsythe, James L. "The English Colony at Victoria, Another View." *Kansas History* 12, no. 3 (Autumn 1989): 175–184.

Foster, Mark S. *Castles in the Sand: The Life and Times of Carl Graham Fisher*. Gainesville: University Press of Florida, 2000.

Fox, Richard Wightman, and T. J. Jackson Lears, eds. *The Culture of Consumption: Critical Essays in American History, 1880–1980*. New York: Pantheon, 1983.

Francione, Gary L. *Animals as Persons: Essays on the Abolition of Animal Exploitation*. New York: Columbia University Press, 2008.

————. *Rain without Thunder: The Ideology of the Animal Rights Movement*. Philadelphia: Temple University Press, 1996.

Freeman, Bob, and Barbara Freeman. *Wanta Bet? A Study of the Pari-Mutuels System in the United States*. With Jim McKinley. n.p.: Freeman Mutuels Management, 1982.

Fudge, Erica. *Animal*. London: Reaktion, 2002.

Genders, Roy. *The Encyclopedia of Greyhound Racing: A Complete History of the Sport*. London: Pelham, 1981.

————. *Greyhounds*. New York: Arco, 1975.

George, Paul S. "Brokers, Binders, and Builders: Greater Miami's Boom of the Mid–1920s." *Florida Historical Quarterly* 65, no. 1 (July 1986): 27–51.

———. "Passage to the New Eden: Tourism in Miami from Flagler through Everest G. Sewell." *Florida Historical Quarterly* 59, no. 4 (April 1981): 440–451.

Grandin, Temple. *Animals in Translation.* New York: Scribner, 2005.

Grier, Katherine C. "Buying Your Friends: The Pet Business and American Consumer Culture." In *Commodifying Everything: Relationships of the Market*, edited by Susan Strasser, 43–70. New York: Routledge, 2003.

———. *Pets in America: A History.* Chapel Hill: University of North Carolina Press, 2006.

Griffin, Emma. *Blood Sport: Hunting in Britain since 1066.* New Haven, CT: Yale University Press, 2007.

Guccione, Gary. *Great Names in Greyhound Pedigrees.* Vol. 2, *The Eighties.* Abilene, KS: Greyhound Breeding Publishers, 1991.

———. "Origin and History of the Racing Greyhound and Coursing Dogs." In Bloomberg et al., *Canine Sports Medicine and Surgery*, 1–4.

———. "State of the Racing Greyhound Industry." *Proceedings of the North American Veterinary Conference* 16 (2002): 756–757.

Guither, Harold D. *Animal Rights: History and Scope of a Radical Social Movement.* Carbondale: Southern Illinois University Press, 1998.

Haller, Mark. "The Changing Structure of American Gambling in the Twentieth Century." *Journal of Social Issues* 35, no. 3 (Summer 1979): 87–114.

Hamilton, Ross. *Greyhound Betting for Profit.* Las Vegas: BGC Press, 1981.

Harbolt, Tami. *Bridging the Bond: The Cultural Construction of the Shelter Pet.* West Lafayette, IN: Purdue University Press, 2002.

Hausler, Don. "The Emeryville Dog Race Track." *Journal of the Emeryville Historical Society* 5, no. 4 (Winter/Spring 1995): 1–8.

Hawley, Ellis. *The Great War and the Search for a Modern Order: A History of the American People and Their Institutions, 1917–1933.* New York: St. Martin's Press, 1979.

Henderson, Amy. "Media and the Rise of Celebrity Culture." *Magazine of History* 6, no. 4 (Spring 1992): 49–54.

Herzog, Hal. *Some We Love, Some We Hate, Some We Eat: Why It's So Hard to Think Straight about Animals.* New York: Harper Perennial, 2010.

Hiller, Herbert L. *Highway A1A: Florida at the Edge.* Tallahassee: University Press of Florida, 2005.

Hollis, Tim. *Florida's Miracle Strip: From Redneck Riviera to Emerald Coast.* Jackson: University Press of Mississippi, 2004.

———. *Selling the Sunshine State: A Celebration of Tourism Advertising.* Tallahassee: University Press of Florida, 2008.

Horne, John. *Sport in Consumer Culture.* New York: Palgrave Macmillan, 2006.

Horowitz, Alexandra. *Inside of a Dog: What Dogs See, Smell, and Know.* New York: Scribner, 2009.

Huggins, Mike. "'Everybody's Going to the Dogs?' The Middle Classes and Greyhound Racing in Britain between the Wars." *Journal of Sport History* 34, no. 1 (Spring 2007): 401–444.

————. "Going to the Dogs." *History Today* 56, no. 5 (May 2006): 31–36.

Hunt, Julia C. "Racing into Culture: A Digital Ethnographic Study of the Development of a Culture of People Who Own Retired Racing Greyhounds." PhD diss., Regent University, 2007.

Hurley, Andrew. *Diners, Bowling Alleys, and Trailer Parks: Chasing the Dream in Postwar Consumer Culture.* New York: Basic Books, 2002.

Jackson, Erin N. "Dead Dog Running: The Cruelty of Greyhound Racing and the Basis for Its Abolition in Massachusetts." *Animal Law* 7 (2001): 175–219.

Jamison, Wesley V., and William M. Lunch. "Rights of Animals, Perceptions of Science, and Political Activism: Profile of American Animal Rights Activists." *Science, Technology, and Human Values* 17, no. 4 (Autumn 1992): 438–458.

Jerolmack, Colin. "Tracing the Profile of Animal Rights Supporters: A Preliminary Investigation." *Society and Animals Journal of Human-Animal Studies* 11, no. 3 (2003): 245–263.

Jones, Susan D. *Valuing Animals: Veterinarians and Their Patients in Modern America.* Baltimore: Johns Hopkins University Press, 2002.

Kammen, Michael. *American Culture, American Tastes: Social Change and the Twentieth Century.* New York: Basic Books, 1999.

Kellert, Stephen, and Miriam Westervelt. "Historical Trends in American Animal Use and Perception." *International Journal for the Study of Animal Problems* 4 (1983): 133–146.

Kete, Kathleen. *The Beast in the Boudoir: Petkeeping in Nineteenth-Century Paris.* Los Angeles: University of California Press, 1994.

————. ed. *A Cultural History of Animals.* Vol. 5, *The Age of Empire (1800–1920).* Oxford: Berg Publishers, 2009.

Kobler, John. *Capone: The Life and World of Capone.* New York: Putnam, 1971.

Kowalczyk, Andra. "Horse Race: Class and Gender: American Cultural Identity Viewed through Horse Racing." MA thesis, Middle Tennessee State University, 2005.

Kruse, Corwin R. "Gender, Views of Nature, and Support for Animal Rights." *Society and Animals Journal of Human-Animal Studies* 7, no. 3 (1999): 179–198.

Kyvig, David E. *Daily Life in the United States, 1920–1940: How Americans Lived through the "Roaring Twenties" and the Great Depression.* Chicago: Ivan R. Dee, 2002.

Lavender, Abraham D. *Miami Beach in 1920: The Making of a Winter Resort.* Charleston, SC: Arcadia Publishing, 2002.

Lavender, David. *The Great West.* Boston: Houghton Mifflin, 1965.

Lawrence, Elizabeth Atwood. "Conflicting Ideologies: Views of Animal Rights Advocates and Their Opponents." *Society and Animals Journal of Human-Animal Studies* 2, no. 2 (1994): 175–189.

Leavitt, Emily Stewart, and Diane Halverson. "The Evolution of Anti-Cruelty Laws in the United States." In *Animals and Their Legal Rights: A Survey of American Laws from 1641 to 1978,* 4th ed., 1–47. Washington, DC: Animal Welfare Institute, 1978.

Leddick, David. *In the Spirit of Miami Beach.* New York: Assouline Publishing, 2006.

Lederer, Susan E. "Political Animals: The Shaping of Biomedical Research Literature in Twentieth-Century America." *Isis* 83, no. 1 (March 1992): 61–79.

Levine, Lawrence W. *Highbrow/Lowbrow: The Emergence of Cultural Hierarchy in America*. Cambridge, MA: Harvard University Press, 1988.

Linzey, Andrew, and Paul Barry Clarke, eds. *Animal Rights: A Historical Anthology*. New York: Columbia University Press, 2004.

Luke, Brian. *Brutal: Manhood and the Exploitation of Animals*. Chicago: University of Illinois Press, 2007.

Lycan, Gilbert L., and Walter C. Grady. *Inside Racing: Sports and Politics*. New York: Pageant Press, 1961.

Mack, Eugene Taylor. "Patterns and Images of Greyhound Racing in the United States." MA thesis, University of Kansas, 1991.

Martin, John. *Tales of the Dogs: A Celebration of the Irish and Their Greyhounds*. Belfast: Blackstaff Press, 2010.

Marx, Herbert L., ed. *Gambling in America*. New York: H. W. Wilson, 1952.

Mason, Jennifer. *Civilized Creatures: Urban Animals, Sentimental Culture, and American Literature: 1850–1900*. Baltimore: Johns Hopkins University Press, 2005.

Mason, Jim. *An Unnatural Order: Uncovering the Roots of Our Dominion of Nature and Each Other*. New York: Simon & Schuster, 1993.

McBride, William E. *The Gambling Times Guide to Greyhound Racing*. Secaucus, NJ: Carol, 1990.

McKibbin, Ross. "Working-Class Gambling in Britain 1880–1939." *Past & Present* 82 (February 1979): 147–178.

Meltzer, George. "Social Life and Entertainment on the Frontiers of Kansas, 1854–1890." MA thesis, University of Wichita, 1941.

Messick, Hank. *Lansky*. New York: G. P. Putnam's Sons, 1971.

Meyer, Kristine K. "An Investigation of the Time in between Greyhound Races at St. Croix Meadows." MA thesis, University of Wisconsin, 1994.

Midgley, Mary. *Animals and Why They Matter*. Athens: University of Georgia Press, 1983.

Molyneux, J. "Vets on Track: Working as a Greyhound Vet." *In Practice* 27, no. 5 (May 2005): 277–279.

Mooney, Michael J. "Heartbreak at 45 mph: Scenes from the Life of a Racing Greyhound." *New Times Broward-Palm Beach*, May 21, 2009.

Mooney, Nan. *My Racing Heart: The Passionate World of Thoroughbreds and the Track*. New York: HarperCollins, 2002.

Mormino, Gary. *Land of Sunshine, State of Dreams: A Social History of Modern Florida*. Tallahassee: University Press of Florida, 2008.

Mullis, Angela, and David Kamper, eds. *Indian Gaming: Who Wins?* Los Angeles: Duane Champagne and UCLA American Indian Studies Center, 2000.

Munro, Lyle. "Caring about Blood, Flesh, and Pain: Women's Standing in the Animal Protection Movement." *Society and Animals Journal of Human-Animal Studies* 9, no. 1 (2001): 43–61.

Murrell, Muriel. *Miami, A Backward Glance*. Sarasota, FL: Pineapple Press, 2003.

Myers, B. R. "If Pigs Could Swim." *Atlantic Monthly* (September 2005): 134–139.

Nelson, Michael, and John Lyman Mason. *How the South Joined the Gambling Nation:*

The Politics of State Policy Innovation. Baton Rouge: Louisiana State University Press, 2007.

Nibert, David. *Animal Rights/Human Rights: Entanglements of Oppression and Liberation*. New York: Rowman & Littlefield, 2002.

Niven, Charles. *History of the Humane Movement*. New York: Transatlantic, 1967.

Opie, John. *Nature's Nation: An Environmental History of the United States*. New York: Harcourt Brace College Publishers, 1998.

Orlean, Susan. *Rin Tin Tin: The Life and the Legend*. New York: Simon & Schuster, 2011.

Pacelle, Wayne. *The Bond: Our Kinship with Animals, Our Call to Defend Them*. New York: William Morrow/HarperCollins, 2011.

Parascandola, John. "Physiology, Propaganda, and Pound Animals: Medical Research and Animal Welfare in Mid-Twentieth Century America." *Journal of the History of Medicine and Allied Science* 62, no. 3 (July 2007): 277–315.

Parker, Dan. "Massachusetts Goes to the Dogs." *Saturday Evening Post,* January 6, 1940.

Passmore, John. "The Treatment of Animals." *Journal of the History of Ideas* 36, no. 2 (April–June 1975): 195–218.

Patterson, Charles. *Eternal Treblinka: Our Treatment of Animals and the Holocaust*. New York: Lantern, 2002.

Paxson, Frederic L. "The Rise of Sport." *Mississippi Valley Historical Review* 4, no. 2 (September 1917): 143–168.

Phelps, Norm. *The Longest Struggle: Animal Advocacy from Pythagoras to PETA*. New York: Lantern, 2007.

Pope, Edwin. *American Greyhound Racing Encyclopedia*. Miami: American Greyhound Track Operators Association, 1963.

Preece, Rod, and David Fraser. "The Status of Animals in Biblical and Christian Thought: A Study in Colliding Values." *Society and Animals Journal of Human-Animal Studies* 8, no. 3 (November 2000): 245–263.

Preston, Howard Lawrence. *Dirt Roads to Dixie: Accessibility and Modernization in the South, 1885–1935*. Knoxville: University of Tennessee Press, 1991.

Rawling, J. C. *To Own a Racing Greyhound*. Strasburg, CO: Prairie Publications, 1975.

Reed, Ryan H. *Born to Run: The Racing Greyhound from Competitor to Companion*. Lexington, KY: Thoroughbred Times, 2010.

Regan, Tom. *The Case for Animal Rights*. Los Angeles: University of California Press, 2004.

———. *Empty Cages: Facing the Challenges of Animal Rights*. New York: Rowman & Littlefield, 2004.

Rentz, Douglas J. "Winning Talk and Losing Stories: An Ethnographic Case Study of the Gaming Social World at Victoryland Greyhound Park." PhD diss., Auburn University, 2001.

Richmond, Robert W. *Kansas: A Land of Contrasts*. 4th ed. Wheeling, IL: Harlan Davidson, 1999.

Riess, Steven A. *The Sport of Kings and the Kings of Crime: Horse Racing, Politics, and Organized Crime in New York, 1865–1913* (Syracuse, NY: Syracuse University Press, 2011).

Riley, Glenda. *Women and Nature: Saving the Wild West*. Lincoln: University of Nebraska Press, 1999.

Ritvo, Harriet. *The Animal Estate: The English and Other Creatures in the Victorian Age*. Cambridge, MA: Harvard University Press, 1987.

Rogers, Katharine M. *First Friend: A History of Dogs and Humans*. New York: St. Martin's, 2005.

Rollin, Bernard E. *Animal Rights and Human Morality*. Buffalo, NY: Prometheus, 1992.

Rudy, Kathy. *Loving Animals: Towards a New Animal Advocacy*. Minneapolis: University of Minnesota Press, 2011.

Ryder, Richard D. *Animal Revolution: Changing Attitudes towards Speciesism*. New York: Berg, 2000.

Salmon, Dutch M. H. *Gazehounds and Coursing: The History, Art and Sport of Hunting with Sighthounds*. Silver City, NM: High-Lonesome Books, 1977.

Samuels, David. "Going to the Dogs." *Harper's Magazine* 298, no. 1785 (February 1999): 52–63.

Sapontzis, S. F. *Morals, Reason, and Animals*. Philadelphia: Temple University Press, 1987.

Schaffer, Michael. *One Nation under Dog: Adventures in the New World of Prozac-Popping Puppies, Dog-Park Politics, and Organic Pet Food*. New York: Henry Holt, 2009.

Schwartz, David G. *Cutting the Wire: Gaming Prohibition and the Internet*. Las Vegas: University of Nevada Press, 2005.

———. *Roll the Bones: The History of Gambling*. New York: Gotham, 2006.

Scully, Matthew. *Dominion: The Power of Man, the Suffering of Animals, and the Call to Mercy*. New York: St. Martin's, 2002.

Shapiro, Kenneth. "The Caring Sleuth: Portrait of an Animal Rights Activist." *Society and Animals Journal of Human-Animal Studies* 2, no. 2 (1994): 145–165.

Shell, Mark. "The Family Pet." *Representations* 15 (Summer 1986): 121–153.

Shevelow, Kathryn. *For the Love of Animals: The Rise of the Animal Protection Movement*. New York: Henry Holt, 2008.

Shortridge, James R. *Peopling the Plains: Who Settled Where in Frontier Kansas*. Lawrence: University Press of Kansas, 1995.

Shultz, William. *The Humane Movement in the United States, 1910–1922*. New York: AMS Press, 1968.

Singer, Peter. *Animal Liberation: A New Ethics for Our Treatment of Animals*. New York: Avon, 1975.

———. *Ethics into Action: Henry Spira and the Animal Rights Movement*. New York: Rowman & Littlefield, 1998.

Smith, James. *History of the American Greyhound Derby: The Kentucky Derby of Greyhound Racing*. Seattle: CreateSpace, 2012.

Spencer, Donald D. *History of Gambling in Florida*. Ormond Beach, FL: Camelot, 2007.

Spiering, Frank. *The Man Who Got Capone*. New York: Bobbs-Merrill, 1976.

Stable, Owen, and R. M. Stuttard. *A Review of Coursing*. 2nd ed. London: British Field Sports Society, 1973.

Stallwood, Kim W., ed. *A Primer on Animal Rights*. New York: Lantern, 2002.

Sullivan, Mark. *The Ultimate Greyhound*. New York: Howell Book House, 1999.

Swallow, William. *Quality of Mercy: History of the Humane Movement in the United States.* Boston: Mary Mitchell Humane Fund, 1963.

Sweeney, Matthew. *The Lottery Wars: Long Odds, Fast Money, and the Battle over an American Institution.* New York: Bloomsbury, 2009.

Tansey, E. M. "Protection against Dog Distemper and Dogs Protection Bills: The Medical Research Council and Anti-Vivisectionist Protest, 1911–1933." *Medical History* 38 (1994): 1–26.

Temple, Robert. *The History of Greyhound Racing in New England.* Bloomington, IN: Xlibris, 2011.

TenEick, Virginia Elliot. *History of Hollywood Florida.* Port Salerno, FL: Patricia M. Smith and Florida Classics Library, 1989.

Teresa, Vincent, and Thomas C. Renner. *My Life in the Mafia.* Garden City, NY: Doubleday, 1973.

Thomas, Keith. *Man and the Natural World: A History of the Modern Sensibility.* New York: Pantheon, 1983.

Thorne, Terry, and Charles Blanning. *A Coursing Year.* Brookland, UK: Huddlesford, 1987.

Thornton, T. D. *Not by a Long Shot: A Season at a Hard-Luck Horse Track.* New York: Public Affairs, 2007.

Thurston, Mary Elizabeth. *The Lost History of the Canine Race: Our 15,000-Year Love Affair with Dogs.* Kansas City, KS: Andrews & McMeel, 1996.

Torres, Bob. *Making a Killing: The Political Economy of Animal Rights.* Oakland, CA: AK Press, 2007.

Turner, James. *Reckoning with the Beast: Animals, Pain, and Humanity in the Victorian Mind.* Baltimore: Johns Hopkins University Press, 1980.

Unti, Bernard. *Protecting All Animals: A Fifty-Year History of the Humane Society of the United States.* Washington, DC: Humane Society Press, 2004.

———. "The Quality of Mercy: Organized Animal Protection in the United States, 1866–1930." PhD diss., American University, 2002.

Walker, Douglas M. "Sin and Growth: The Effects of Legalized Gambling on State Economic Development." PhD diss., Auburn University, 1998.

Wall, Maryjean. *How Kentucky Became Southern: A Tale of Outlaws, Horse Thieves, Gamblers, and Breeders.* Lexington: University Press of Kentucky, 2012.

Walsh, E. G. *Lurchers and Longdogs.* Saul, UK: Standfast, 1977.

Walsh, Thomas A. *Greyhound Racing for Fun and Profit.* Deerfield Beach, FL: Liberty, 1991.

Wiebe, Robert H. *The Search for Order, 1877–1920.* New York: Hill & Wang, 1967.

Williams, Erin E., and Margo DeMello. *Why Animals Matter: The Case for Animal Protection.* Amherst, NY: Prometheus, 2007.

Williams, Francis Emmett. *Lotteries, Laws and Morals.* New York: Vantage, 1958.

Williams, William A. *Americans in a Changing World: A History of the United States in the Twentieth Century.* New York: Harper & Row, 1978.

Winograd, Nathan J. *Redemption: The Myth of Pet Overpopulation and the No Kill Revolution in America.* Los Angeles: Almaden, 2007.

Wise, Steven M. *Rattling the Cage: Toward Legal Rights for Animals.* Cambridge, MA: Perseus, 2000.

Wootten, Leslie A. "The Wootten Machine: A Greyhound Racing Memoir." MFA thesis, Arizona State University, 2001.

Youngs, Larry. "The Sporting Set Winters in Florida: Fertile Ground for the Leisure Revolution, 1870–1930." *Florida Historical Quarterly* 84, no. 1 (2005): 57–78.

INTERNET SOURCES

http://support.mspca.org/site/PageServer?pagename=adv_greyhounds [Massachusetts Society for the Prevention of Cruelty to Animals]

http://www.adopt-a-greyhound.org/ [The Greyhound Project, Inc.]

http://www.agcouncil.com/ [American Greyhound Council]

http://www.agtoa.com/ [American Greyhound Track Operators Association]

http://www.arci.com/jurisdictions.html [Association of Racing Commissioners International]

http://www.awionline.org/ [Animal Welfare Institute]

http://www.derbylane.com/ [Derby Lane]

http://www.flagreyhound.com/ [Florida Greyhound Association]

http://www.gra-america.org/ [Greyhound Racing Association of America]

http://www.greyhoundhalloffame.com/ [Greyhound Hall of Fame]

http://www.greyhound-data.com/ [Greyhound Data]

http://www.greyhoundpets.org/ [Greyhound Pets of America]

http://www.greyhounds.org/gpl/contents/entry.html [Greyhound Protection League]

http://www.grey2kusa.org/ [GREY2K USA]

http://www.humanesociety.org/issues/greyhound_racing/facts/greyhound_racing_facts.html [Humane Society of the United States]

http://www.ngagreyhounds.com/ [National Greyhound Association]

http://www.owenpsmith.com/ [Tim O'Brien's website on O. P. Smith]

http://www.sfspca.org/ [San Francisco Society for the Prevention of Cruelty to Animals]

SERIAL PUBLICATIONS

American Field, The
Animals
Animals' Agenda, The
Blood-Horse, The
Celebrating Greyhounds
Collier's
Coursing News, The
Daily Racing Form
Forest and Stream
Gaming Today
Greyhound, The
Greyhound Network News
Greyhound Racing Record
Greyhound Review, The
HSUS News

Life
National Greyhound Update, The
New Sporting Magazine, The
Our Animals
Our Dumb Animals
Outing Magazine
Racing Greyhounds
Sports Illustrated
Turnout

PRIMARY SOURCES

Ainsty. "A History of Coursing." In *British Sports and Sportsmen, Racing and Coursing.* London: Hazell, Watson & Viney, 1908.

Berkeley, Grantley F. *The English Sportsman in the Western Prairies.* London: Hurst & Blackett, 1861.

Brace, Timothy. *Murder Goes to the Dogs: Anthony Adams's Third Mystery.* New York: E.P. Dutton, 1938.

Burnett, W. R. *Dark Hazard.* New York: Harper & Brothers, 1933.

Butler, Thomas A. *The State of Kansas and Irish Immigration.* Dublin: McGlashan & Gill, 1871.

Cardew, A. R. D. *All about Greyhound Racing.* London: Elkin Mathews & Marrot, 1928.

Clarke, H. Edwards. *The Greyhound.* 6th ed. London: Popular Dogs, 1978.

Cox, Harding. *Coursing and Falconry.* London: Longmans, Green, 1892.

Crawfurd, Oswald. *A Year of Sport and Natural History: Shooting, Hunting, Coursing, Falconry, and Fishing.* London: Chapman & Hall, 1895.

Crist, Steven. *Betting on Myself.* New York: DRF Press, 2003.

Dalziel, Hugh. *The Greyhound: Its History, Points, Breeding, Rearing, Training, and Running.* London: A. Bradley, London & County Printing Works, 1886. Reprinted in Warwickshire, UK: Vintage Dog Books, 2005.

Dighton, Adair. *My Sporting Life.* London: Richards, 1934.

Dodge, Richard Irving. *Hunting Grounds of the Great West: A Description of the Plains, Game, and Indians of the Great North American Desert.* London: Chatto & Windus, Piccadilly, 1878.

Egan, Pierce. *Sporting Anecdotes, Original and Selected.* Philadelphia: Carey & Lea, 1822.

Galgo. *Dog Racing and Betting.* London: P. Watts, 1946.

Goodlake, Thomas. *The Courser's Manual or Stud Book.* Liverpool: Harris, 1828.

Graham, Joseph A. *The Sporting Dog.* New York: Macmillan, 1904.

Hartwell, Paul C. *The Road from Emeryville: A History of Greyhound Racing.* San Diego: California Research Publishing, 1980.

Harwood, W. S. "Coursing on Western Prairies." *Sports Library Outing Magazine* 37, no. 1 (October 1899): 45–50.

Hevener, Ron. *High Stakes.* n.p.: Pennywood Press, 2005.

Hoffman, Carl Timothy. *Greyhound Racing—America's Fastest Growing Sport.* n.p., 1974.

———. *This is Greyhound Racing.* n.p., 1972.

Holder, Charles Frederick. *The Californian.* Vols. 1–4. San Francisco: Californian, 1891–1894.

Jennings, Rienzi W. *Legalized Racing with Pari-Mutuel Wagering—A Potential Tax Source for Tennessee.* Memphis, TN: Bureau of Business and Economic Research, 1972.

Lantz, David E. *Destroying Rodent Pests on the Farm.* Yearbook of the Department of Agriculture. Washington, DC: GPO, 1917.

———. *The Rabbit as a Farm and Orchard Pest.* Yearbook of the Department of Agriculture. Washington, DC: GPO, 1908.

Lloyd, Freeman. *The Whippet or Race-Dog.* London: The Bazaar, Exchange and Mart Office, 1904. Reprinted in Alcester, UK: Vintage Dog Books, 2006.

Markham, Gervase. *Country Contentments, or, The Husbandmans Recreations.* 4th ed. London: Thomas Harper, 1631.

Matheson, James. *The Greyhound: Breeding, Coursing, Racing, etc.* London: Hurst & Blackett, 1929. Reprinted in Warwickshire, UK: Vintage Dog Books, 2005.

Murphy, John Mortimer. *Sporting Adventures in the Far West.* London: Sampson Low, Marston, Searle & Rivington, 1879.

Palmer, T. S. *The Jack Rabbits of the United States.* U.S. Dept. of Agriculture, Division of Ornithology and Mammalogy, Bulletin no. 8. Washington, DC: GPO, 1896.

Phillips, A. A., and Malcolm M. Willcock, ed. and trans. *Xenophon & Arrian, On Hunting.* Warminster: Aris & Phillips, 1999.

Richardson, Charles. *The Hare: Natural History & Coursing.* London: Longmans, Green, 1896.

Salt, H. S. *Animals' Rights.* New York: Macmillan, 1894.

Smith, A. Croxton. *Greyhound Racing and Breeding.* London: Gay & Hancook, 1927. Reprinted in Warwickshire, UK: Vintage Dog Books, 2005.

Somerset, Henry [8th Duke of Beaufort], ed. *The Badminton Library of Sports and Pastimes.* London: Longmans, Green, 1892.

Sportsman [pseud.]. *A Treatise on Greyhounds; with Observations on the Treatment and Disorders of them.* 2nd ed. London: T. Gosden, Sportsman's Repository, 1825.

Stonehenge [John Henry Walsh]. *The Greyhound.* 1st ed. London: Longman, Brown, Green & Longmans, 1853.

———. *The Greyhound in 1864.* 2nd ed. London: Longman, Green, Roberts & Green, 1864.

Tennessee General Assembly. *Report of the Special Task Force on Horse and Dog Racing to the Senate of the 93rd General Assembly.* Nashville, January 1984.

Thacker, Thomas. *The Courser's Companion.* 2nd ed. London: Derby, 1834.

Thompson, Laura. *The Dogs: A Personal History of Greyhound Racing.* London: Chatto & Windus, 1994.

Thoroughbred Racing and Parimutuel Wagering in Tennessee: Potential Economic Impacts. Prepared by Kenneth J. Burns for the Bureau of Business and Economic Research at Memphis State University, January 1984.

Veeck, Bill. *Thirty Tons a Day.* With Ed Linn. New York: Viking, 1972.

Woods, Leigh. *Gipsy the Greyhound.* London: Chapman & Hall, 1931.

Wootten, Leslie A. *Keefer: The People's Choice.* Sedona, AZ: Memory Works, 2007.

ARCHIVES AND MANUSCRIPT COLLECTIONS

Animal Welfare Institute. Records. Alexandria, Virginia.

Argus Archives. Records. Tom Regan Animal Rights Collection. North Carolina State University Libraries, Raleigh.

Boston Area Newspaper Morgue. Boston University.

California Democratic Council Records. 1947–1988. Southern California Library, Los Angeles.

Court of Appeals case files. Kentucky State Archives, Frankfurt.

Derby Lane Kennel Club Archives, St. Petersburg, Florida.

Dzendzel, Raymond. Collection. Michigan State Archives, Lansing.

Florida State Racing Commission Reports. State Archives of Florida and State Library of Florida, Tallahassee.

Greyhound Hall of Fame Collections, Abilene, Kansas.

Humane Society of the United States. Records. Gaithersburg, Maryland.

Huntington Library Collections, San Marino, California.

Las Vegas Newspaper Clippings. Nevada State Museum, Las Vegas.

Las Vegas Newspaper Clippings. University of Nevada, Reno.

Legislative Hearings and Government Documents. Tennessee State Library and Archives, Nashville.

Library of Congress Photograph Collections, Washington, DC.

Manning, Reg. Collection. Arizona State University Library, Tempe.

Massachusetts Society for the Prevention of Cruelty to Animals Archives, Boston.

Massachusetts State Racing Commission Reports. Boston Public Library.

McGowen, Courtney Swain. Records. 1978–1990. University of Nevada, Reno.

Memphis Newspaper Morgue. University of Memphis Library.

Miami Beach Kennel Club Scrapbook Collection. The Wolfsonian-Florida International University, Miami Beach.

Miami Newspaper Clippings Files. Miami/Dade County Public Library.

Minutes of the Florida State Racing Commission. State Archives of Florida, Tallahassee.

National Agricultural Library. United States Department of Agriculture, Beltsville, Maryland.

National Sporting Library, Middleburg, Virginia.

Newspaper Clippings from the *Los Angeles Examiner*. University of Southern California, Los Angeles.

Ohio Attorney General Office Case Files. Ohio Historical Society, Columbus.

Oregon Racing Commission. Records. Oregon State Archives, Salem.

Photograph Collections. State Archives of Florida, Tallahassee.

Photograph Collections and Vertical Files. Kansas State Historical Society, Topeka.

Portland Newspaper Clippings. Multnomah County Public Library, Portland.

Proposition 13 Hearings File. California State Archives, Sacramento.

Raleigh News and Observer. Clippings. North Carolina State University Libraries, Raleigh.

Ralph, Leon D. Papers. California State Archives, Sacramento.

Reilly, Senator Edward F. Papers. University of Kansas Library, Lawrence.

Saltonstall, Leverett. Papers. Massachusetts Historical Society, Boston.

Texas Racing Commission. Records. Texas State Library and Archives, Austin.

University of California Los Angeles Film and Television Archive.
Vertical Files. University of Nevada, Las Vegas.
Warren, Earl. Papers. California State Archives, Sacramento.

RECORDED ORAL HISTORIES

Dillon, Keith. Interview by Gwynn Thayer. Tape recording. April 22, 2009. Kansas State Historical Society, Topeka.

Frey, Jim. Interview by Gwynn Thayer. Tape recording. July 2, 2011. Baylor University, Waco, Texas.

Hartwell, Paul C. Interview by Gwynn Thayer. Tape recording. April 17, 2010. Greyhound Hall of Fame, Abilene, KS.

Lee, Bill, Arden Hartman, and Jim Larson. StoryCorps interview by Alex Kelly. Tape recording. July 21, 2008. American Folklife Center. Library of Congress, Washington, DC.

Payne, Jesse Ollie. Interview by Rolland Kerns. Tape recording. September 13, 1972. Oklahoma History Center, Oklahoma City.

Sargent, Gladys W. Interview by Jacqueline S. Reinier. Tape recording. February 28, March 9, 16, and 23, 1989. California State Archives, Sacramento.

Warren, Earl. Interviews by Amelia R. Fry and members of the Regional Oral History Staff. Tape recording. 1971–1972. University of California, Bancroft Library, Berkeley.

PERSONAL INTERVIEWS

Arthur Agganis: 2/14/10 (Personal, phone, and e-mail contact).
Robert Baker: 4/11/09 (Phone and e-mail contact).
William R. Bell: 2/11/10 (Personal contact).
Dennis Bicsak: 2/9/10 (Personal and e-mail contact).
Dr. Linda Blythe: 9/28/11 (Phone and e-mail contact).
Eugene Martin Christiansen: 12/2/09 (Phone and e-mail contact).
Steven Crist: 3/26/12 (Phone contact).
Will Cummings: 12/15/09 (Phone and e-mail contact).
Robert Dawson: 2/14/10 (Personal contact).
Dr. Jon Dee: 10/11/11 (Phone contact).
Keith Dillon: 4/22/09 (Personal and phone contact).
Christine Dorchak: 9/12/11 (E-mail contact).
Dr. William W. Dugger: 2/14/10 (Personal, phone, and e-mail contact).
Joan Eidinger: 2/2/12 (Phone contact).
Gail Eisnitz: 4/28/09 (Phone and e-mail contact).
Dr. Brad Fenwick: 9/24/11 (Phone contact).
Francesca K. Field: 4/23/09 (Personal and e-mail contact).
Jim Frey: 5/10/10 (Phone and e-mail contact).
Gary Guccione: 12/3/08 (Personal, phone, and e-mail contact).
Arden (Henry) Hartman: 12/15/09 (Phone contact).
John S. Hartwell: 7/26/08 (Personal and phone contact).
Paul C. Hartwell: 4/17/10 (Personal, phone, and e-mail contact).

Dr. Jill Hopfenbeck: 10/21/11 (Phone and e-mail contact).

Karen Keelan: 2/14/10 (Personal and e-mail contact).

Dr. Kent Law: 11/25/11 (Personal contact).

William Lee: 12/14/09 (Phone contact).

Cathy Liss: 4/28/08 (Personal, phone, and e-mail contact).

Carter Luke: 9/17/08 (Personal contact).

William Nack: 5/24/12 (Phone contact).

Susan Netboy: 12/30/11 (Phone and e-mail contact).

Tim O'Brien: 9/29/10 (Phone and e-mail contact).

Wayne Pacelle: 8/13/12 (Phone contact).

Teddy Palmer: 8/12/12 (Phone contact).

Hoye Perry: 2/20/09 (Personal contact).

Jeff Prince: 2/20/09 (Personal and e-mail contact).

Craig Randle: 2/23/10 (Personal and phone contact).

Vera Rasnake: 2/10/09 (Personal and e-mail contact).

David Schwartz: 2/2/08 (Personal and e-mail contact).

Jack Sherck: 11/5/09 (Phone contact).

Jim Shofstahl: 6/10/12 (Phone contact).

Sam Simon: 9/21/11 (Phone contact).

Wes Singletary: 1/25/09 (Personal and e-mail contact).

Janet Strong: 6/14/08 (Personal contact).

Wayne Strong: 4/24/09 (Personal and phone contact).

Jesse E. Sullivan: 8/6/08 (Personal contact).

Myra Sullivan: 8/6/08 (Personal contact).

Robert Trow: 7/26/08 (Personal contact).

Bernard Unti: 3/20/10 (Personal, phone, and e-mail contact).

Louise Weaver: 2/20/09 (Personal, phone, and e-mail contact).

Christopher Wetzel: 9/30/10 (Phone and e-mail contact).

Mary Margaret Winning: 2/20/09 (Personal contact).

AUDIO/VIDEO:

Born to Run. Produced by Race for Adoption. VHS. ca. 2005.

Martin Cohan, "And Leave the Greyhounds to Us?" *The Odd Couple,* season 2, 1971. DVD. Directed by Hal Cooper. Hollywood, CA: CBS Paramount Network Television, 2007.

Dark Hazard. Directed by Alfred E. Green. DVD transfer. 1934.

A Day at the Dog Races. Created by Damon L. Meharg. DVD. Boston: Videocraft Productions, 1989.

Dog Man: Growing Up with Greyhounds. Created by Claudette Sutherland. VHS. n.d.

Ensuring the Welfare of the Racing Greyhound. American Greyhound Council. VHS. 2003.

"Greta, the Misfit Greyhound." Walt Disney's Wonderful World of Color 9, 3 February 1963, Number 18.

Greyhound Racing: The History and Heart of the Sport. Greyhound Hall of Fame and American Greyhound Council. VHS. 2001.

"Greyhound Racing Exposé." *Inside Edition*. DVD. 1990.

"Greyhound Racing Exposé with Geraldo Rivera." *20/20*. DVD transfer. 1978.

Greyhounds: Running for Their Lives. Created by Eitan Weinreich. National Geographic Explorer. DVD. 1992.

Greyhound Training: At the Farm. American Greyhound Council and Tel-Air Interests, Inc. VHS. 1990.

Hole in the Head. Directed by Frank Capra. DVD. 1959. Beverly Hills, CA: MGM Home Entertainment, 2001.

How to Handicap the Greyhounds. White Leopard Video. VHS. 1988.

Johnny Eager. Directed by Mervyn LeRoy. DVD. 1942. Burbank, CA: Warner Home Video, 2009.

Mr. Miami Beach. Written, produced, and directed by Mark J. Davis. PBS Home Video. VHS. 1998.

Nature: Dogs That Changed the World. Thirteen/WNET New York and Tigress Productions Limited, Educational Broadcasting Corporation. DVD. 2007.

Never Catch the Rabbit. RKO Radio Sports Shorts with Bill Corum. Transcript. 1936.

Soundness Examination of the Racing Greyhound. James R. Gannon, Sandown Veterinary Clinic, Blackburn, Australia. VHS. ca. 1990.

Sport Slants #8. Narrated by Ted Husing. Warner Brothers Vitaphone. DVD transfer. ca. 1932.

Sprint through History. Greyhound Hall of Fame. VHS. ca. 1990.

Tropical Sportland. Warner Brothers Vitaphone. DVD transfer. 1943.

The Winning Alternative: Mechanical Lure Training. Produced by the American Track Operators Association and the National Greyhound Association. VHS. ca. 1989.

Wisconsin Promotional Video on Greyhound Racing. Discover Wisconsin Productions, Inc. VHS. 1988.

INDEX

Hartwell, Paul C.
  on early greyhound racing, 49–51
  as historian of greyhound racing, 18
  on horse racing, 72–73
  on INGRA, 53, 56, 59
  on strikes, 181–182
Hartwell, Paul, Sr., 49, 65, 135–136
Hartwell family, 49, 64–65
Harwood, W. S., 25, 27–28
Hayes, Martin, 92–93
Hecht, David, 181
Hecht, Isadore, 181
Heintz, George W., 46, 58–59, 215
Hempstead Coursing Club, 32
Hiblow, Willie, 63–64
His Master's Voice (film), 106–107
Hole in the Head (film), 2, 122
Holmes, Oliver Wendell, 77
Hooper, Joel, 48
Hopfenbeck, Jill, 132
horse racing
  animal advocacy and, 12, 143–145
  class and, 12, 102–104, 124, 129,
    143–144, 146
  competition from, 8, 19, 51–52, 70–
    83, 86–89, 93, 95, 100, 127–128,
    170–173
  greyhound racing compared to, 3, 10,
    20, 74 (fig.), 96, 169–170
  illegal gambling and, 98–99
  media coverage and, 127
  simulcasting and, 183
  World War II and, 111
HSUS. *See* Humane Society of the
  United States
Humane Society of the United States
  (HSUS)
  Baker, Robert, and, 161
  euthanasia estimates and, 136, 148
  Florida greyhound tracks and, 188
  4-D meat and, 153
  greyhound adoption and, 137–138
  greyhound industry and, 150, 188
  greyhound racing and, 143–144, 148,
    150, 165

Grey2K USA and, 165, 188
  horse racing and, 143–144
  investigations and, 142–143, 161
  live lures and, 140, 142–143, 161, 244
  pet overpopulation and, 136
  raids and, 142–143
  See also Pacelle, Wayne
hunting, 4, 21–22, 24, 27, 35–39, 145

IGRA. *See* Indian Gaming Regulatory
  Act
IHRA. *See* Interstate Horse Racing Act
Indian Gaming Regulatory Act (IGRA),
  186–187, 268
INGRA. *See* International Greyhound
  Racing Association
International Greyhound Racing
  Association (INGRA)
  banner and, 56, 57 (fig.), 85 (fig.)
  breeding and, 56
  Capone and, 53, 92
  constitution and by-laws, 54
  creation of, 7, 53–59
  dogmen and, 56, 58
  Hartwell's perceptions of, 56, 59
  Kentucky and, 76, 78
  O'Hare, Edward Joseph and, 53, 56,
    66, 92
  organized crime and, 92
  rules and, 74
  Smith, Hannah, 53, 214
  stud book and, 63
  training licenses and, 54
Interstate Greyhound Racing Act, 183–
  185. *See also* simulcasting
Interstate Horse Racing Act, 183 (IHRA).
  See also simulcasting
Ise, John, 42–43

Jack-A-Lure, 156
jackrabbits, 5, 21, 31–34, 37–42, 140–142,
  154. *See also* coursing; hares; rabbit
  drives; rabbits
Jerome, John J. "Blackjack," 84, 224
Jockey Club (United Kingdom), 24

Jockey Club, The (United States), 72, 79, 246

Johnny Eager, 2, 92

Johnston, William H., 125, 238

Kansas
    coursing in, 5, 28–30, 33–34, 40–42, 140–141
    greyhound breeding in, 48, 59, 63, 134, 155
    Greyhound Hall of Fame in, 169
    greyhound racing in, 11, 34–35, 47–48, 166, 174–175
    hunts in, 38
    jackrabbits in, 142
    legalization effort in, 174–175
    live lures and, 143
    military officers in, 36
    settlement in, 34
Kansas Greyhound Breeders' Association, 175
Kansas Racing Commission, 175
Karsten, Thomas, 67
Kefauver, Estes, 125
Ketchum Public Relations, 157
Kemp, Murray
    Butte, Montana, and, 48
    California dog racing and, 83, 224
    Capone and, 218
    dogmen and, 44
    Oregon dog racing and, 86–87, 219
    year-round racing and, 185
King, Clarence, 88–89, 226

Lady Greyhound, 124–126, 126 (fig.)
Lansky, Meyer, 98, 113, 235
Lawrence Coursing Club, 42
Lee, Bill, 176–177
Lehman, Herbert H., Governor, 79–80
Life (magazine), 13, 148, 169
Lingle, Ross, 184–185
Linsey, Joe, 177–178
Liss, Cathy, 151. *See also* Animal Welfare Institute
Ludlow, Greg T., 151

Luke, Carter, 136. *See also* Massachusetts Society for the Prevention of Cruelty to Animals

Martin, Dean, 121–122
Massachusetts Society for the Prevention of Cruelty to Animals (MSPCA), 82, 87, 136–137, 242
Massachusetts State Racing Commission, 91
McCarty, W. C., Col., 37
mechanical lure
    creation of, 6, 7 (fig.), 45, 51
    inside versus outside, 59
    Jack-A-Lure training and, 156
    live quarry versus, 6, 68
    nickname of, 104
    Smith, Owen Patrick and, 5–7, 21, 44–45
    See also Smith, Owen Patrick
Miami, 10, 95–96, 98–100, 108–109, 111–113, 127, 181–182
Miami Beach, 95–100, 102–104, 106, 108–112, 117, 119, 122, 128
Mineola Fair Grounds, 79–80, 82
Mission Boy, 69 (fig.), 169
Moran, George "Bugs," 66
MSPCA. *See* Massachusetts Society for the Prevention of Cruelty to Animals
Murphy, John Mortimer, 36–37
"Mutt Derbies," 94, 228

NASCAR, 166, 189
National Coursing Association (NCA), 17, 40, 54, 180. *See also* National Greyhound Association
National Coursing Club (England), 24–25
National Greyhound Association (NGA)
    AGC and, 154–155
    artificial insemination and, 135
    coursing and, 142
    greyhound registration and, 17
    HSUS and, 150
    Indian gaming and, 187

simulcasting, 183–185, 266. *See also* gambling; Interstate Greyhound Racing Act; Interstate Horse Racing Act
Sinatra, Frank, 2, 122, 123 (fig.)
slipper, definition of, 5, 30–31, 31 (fig.)
Smith, Hannah M., 53, 214–215
Smith, Owen Patrick
  bookmakers and, 50–51
  creation of lure and, 5–6, 7 (fig.), 21, 44, 70
  as founder of greyhound racing, 33, 44–48, 51
  gambling and, 46, 50–51
  Heintz and, 58–59
  INGRA and, 7, 53, 56, 92
  Kentucky and, 74–78
  lawsuits and, 75–78, 215
  rabbits and, 41, 70
Souza, Ed, 154
Spencer, Forbe, 60–62
Sports Illustrated (magazine), 127, 140, 169–170, 173
state racing commissions, role of, 54, 159–161, 183, 186
Sterling, Charles R., 59
Steve Allen Show (television show), 3, 124
St. Louis Coursing Association, 41
St. Petersburg Kennel Club. *See* greyhound tracks
Stonehenge (John Henry Walsh), 24–25
Strange, Campbell, 174, 241
strikes. *See* dogmen
Strohbehn, Arthur, 160
Strong, Wayne, 130, 181–182
Stutz, F. B. "Happy"
  California greyhound racing and, 173
  on cruelty, 243

early tracks and, 58
on rabbits, 21
reputation of greyhound racing and, 71
strikes and, 179

television shows, greyhounds and, 1–4, 124–127, 169, 189
Temple, Shirley, 106
thoroughbred horse racing. *See* horse racing
tourism, Florida and, 10–11, 95–98, 108, 112, 115, 128–129
track bookings. *See* booking system

Valley Hunt Club, 37–38
Veeck, Bill, 88, 225–226

Walker-Otis anti-racetrack gambling law, 45
Walsek, Ron, 138
Warren, Earl, 84, 86
Waterloo Cup (American), 29
Waterloo Cup (Great Britain), 24
Wayne, John, 121
WCTU. *See* Women's Christian Temperance Union
Weaver, T. L., 100
Wembley, USA, 177
William the Conqueror, forest laws and, 22, 24
Withers, Jane, 106
Wohlauf, Otto R., 56
Women's Christian Temperance Union (WCTU), 42
Wootten, Leslie, 18, 138, 170, 176, 217

Xenophon, on hunting, 22